Praise for *Why Read?*

"*Why Read?* makes passionate arguments for literature's soul-making potential." **—Raleigh News & Observer**

"Edmundson's many-faceted argument is forthright, rigorous, and inspiring as he convincingly links literature with hope, and humanism with democracy." **—Booklist**

"Provocative." **—Los Angeles Times**

"A focused appeal to students and teachers at the college level to use literature as a springboard into discussions about what matters deeply in life: questions of love, honor, heroism, work and spirituality." **—Cleveland Plain Dealer**

"A passionate argument . . . Edmundson is dead on target." **—The Washington Post Book World**

"Heavy stuff that makes you envy Edmundson's students . . . Edmundson's incisive mind analyzes what's gone wrong with education . . . He also goes a long way toward analyzing what's gone wrong with the country." **—Palm Beach Post**

"Stylish, erudite." **—Publishers Weekly**

"An eloquent advocate . . . Edmundson feels that students deserve, and need, more." **—Booklist**

"Engaging and controversial." **—Library Journal**

"A passionate, lucid defense of the life-changing potential of an education in the humanities . . . An engaging blend of social criticism, self-improvement wisdom, and appeal to fellow humanities professors. *Why Read?* is also beautifully articulated; Edmundson writes with a rare combination of force and humility." **—Willamette Week**

Praise for *Why Write?*

"[An] in-depth analysis of the positivity of literary pursuits . . . This informative and entertaining read will delight those interested in the writing process." —*Library Journal*

"[*Why Write?*] is filled with anecdotes about canonical writers, along with personal stories from the author's writing and teaching career. Edmundson is adept at finding quotes and telling tales from the English romantic poets, Greek philosophers, and American transcendentalists." —*Publishers Weekly*

"The 29 chapters of *Why Write?* sparkle along like a brook in springtime . . . It's deeply personal and broadly philosophical, filled with the distilled reflections of a lifetime asking sharp questions, listening to thoughtful answers, and then asking more questions." —*National Review Online*

"[Edmundson's] especially good on the importance of a writer finding his/ her voice and he offers plenty of encouragement. This book is very much a pep talk. The author is an optimistic, enthusiastic cheerleader on the sideline, encouraging us to sit down and try." —*Kirkus Reviews*

"*Why Write?* ponders why so many people try their hand at something that can be so time consuming and contain so many pitfalls, and Edmundson offers satisfying answers for readers and writers alike." —*Shelf Awareness*

"The latest in Edmundson's continuing noble effort to defend intellectual seriousness against triviality." —**Gerald Graff, professor of English and education, University of Illinois at Chicago, former president, Modern Language Association**

"So much more than a how-to book, *Why Write?* is Professor Edmundson's lifelong meditation on the meaning of writing and existence." —**David Clemens, founder and coordinator, Monterey Peninsula College Great Books Program**

"A high stakes venture, in which getting it right on the page is a way of bringing yourself back to life." —**Laura Kipnis, author of *Against Love***

"Edmundson is a genial and inspiring guide to the mysteries and very real practicalities of writing. The tone and fluency of this book are an education." **—Adam Phillips, author of *Missing Out***

"A warm, generous book about how to live—and even, in its wise last chapters, about how to grow old."
—Michael Gorra, author of *Portrait of a Novel*

"Full of wit, sage advice, and a well-honed passion for the art of writing, which in Edmundson's view looks much like the art of living well. Just the right companion for readers and writers."
—David Mikics, author of *Slow Reading in a Hurried Age*

Praise for *Why Teach?*

"If I meet any students heading to the University of Virginia, I will tell them to seek out Mark Edmundson . . . Mr. Edmundson reminds us of the power strong teachers have to make students rethink who they are and who they might become." **—Michael S. Roth, *The New York Times***

"A spirited and cheering read . . . Accurate and insightful, even inspiring."
—*Chicago Tribune*

"[A] deeply felt collection of explorations and reflections on an education in the liberal arts." **—*Kirkus Reviews***

"Edmundson's accessible prose will motivate both students and teachers. Highly recommended for all involved in higher education; an enjoyable and inspiring read." **—*Library Journal***

"A heartfelt, beautifully written, profound, and often hilarious appeal to rage against the machinery of modern education."
—*Booklist* (starred review)

"Addressing teachers, students, and parents, Edmundson defends the intellectual and spiritual value, even the usefulness, of the 'scholarly enclave.'"
—*Publishers Weekly*

"[A] provocative tome." **—*New York Journal of Books***

"A heartfelt and provocative book that will interest anyone who wonders what happened to the idea that college should be a life-altering, mind-expanding experience. With wry humor and hard-won wisdom, Mark Edmundson offers an inspiring vision of the liberal arts as a vehicle for personal transformation."   —**Tom Perrotta, author of *The Leftovers***

"In prose so fresh and personal it leaps off the page, Mark Edmundson launches a stinging critique of higher education today. Everywhere he sees teachers flattering students, confirming their prejudices, and training them for the success game rather than opening their minds to new ways of looking at the world. His teaching ideal, developed here in exemplary detail, is at once utopian and absolutely essential. This book deserves to be widely read."   —**Morris Dickstein, author of *Dancing in the Dark***

"Mark Edmundson's lively account of the way we educate now offers enjoyment and enlightenment."   —**Harold Bloom**

"Some of the best essays around about the meaning of a college education. Wise, passionate, frank, funny, and always intimately in touch with the texture of the classroom experience, this is a gift to all of us who care about the future of higher education."
     —**William Deresiewicz, author of *Excellent Sheep***

"You may not like everything Mark Edmundson has to say in this shimmering series of essays, but you will never again need to ask his question, 'Why Teach?' Read his answers and make your own revolution."
     —**Megan Marshall, author of *Margaret Fuller:
A New American Life***

"Mark Edmundson manages to be old-fashioned and radical at the same time, skeptical of every latest thing and yet deeply comprehending of students' hyperlinked and hyperactive lives. Edmundson is a school of one, a voice of calm and reflection with lessons worth teaching."
     —**Edward Ayers, president emeritus,
University of Richmond**

"A wonderful book. Indispensable reading for all those concerned with what higher education in America and in the world should be."
     —**J. Hillis Miller, Distinguished Research Professor,
University of California, Irvine**

The Heart of the Humanities

The Heart of the Humanities

Reading, Writing, Teaching

MARK EDMUNDSON

BLOOMSBURY

NEW YORK · LONDON · OXFORD · NEW DELHI · SYDNEY

Bloomsbury USA
An imprint of Bloomsbury Publishing Plc

1385 Broadway	50 Bedford Square
New York	London
NY 10018	WC1B 3DP
USA	UK

www.bloomsbury.com

BLOOMSBURY and the Diana logo are trademarks of Bloomsbury Publishing Plc

Why Read? first published 2004
Why Teach? first published 2013
Why Write? first published 2016
This collection published 2018

© Mark Edmundson, 2004, 2013, 2016, 2018

ISBN: TPB: 978-1-63286-308-9
       ePub: 978-1-63286-309-6

Library of Congress Cataloging-in-Publication Data is available.

2 4 6 8 10 9 7 5 3 1

Typeset by Westchester Publishing Services
Printed and bound in the U.S.A. by Berryville Graphics Inc., Berryville, Virginia

To find out more about our authors and books visit www.bloomsbury.com. Here you will find extracts, author interviews, details of forthcoming events and the option to sign up for our newsletters.

Bloomsbury books may be purchased for business or promotional use. For information on bulk purchases please contact Macmillan Corporate and Premium Sales Department at specialmarkets@macmillan.com.

For Harold Bloom, Richard Poirier, and Richard Rorty: Great Teachers.

Contents

Books are the best of things, well used; abused, among the worst. What is the right use? What is the one end, which all means go to effect? They are for nothing but to inspire.

—RALPH WALDO EMERSON, "THE AMERICAN SCHOLAR"

Introduction

Reading, writing, teaching: they form a triad. They are at the heart of the humanities.

We know all too well that these are not the most lavishly rewarded of pursuits. No one grows rich from reading and teaching. And though fame and fortune may arise from writing, they are anything but certain. So why would anyone want to spend a life in reading, writing, and teaching? Why would one want to be, in the broadest sense of the term, a humanist?

The world often seems to believe that reading, writing, and teaching are passive pursuits. The reader sits quietly, book in hand, not moving, making an occasional note: the image of passivity. And the writer? The writer is off on the sideline, not immersed in the worldly fray. The writer tries to make the record, standing apart from the pulling and hauling, and watching and wondering at it all. Statesmen and generals and business moguls write books, yes. But not until their *real* lives are over, not until they have done what they have come into the world to do. Then it is time for appraisal, and (often) self-sanctification.

And as to teachers, who are they? Aren't they people who have not quite grown up? They never gathered the strength to leave school and make their mark on the world, or fail trying. They stand in the bleachers cheering their students, on. But do they have the wherewithal to enter the game themselves and see what they can do? The teacher, to some, stands in suspended animation between youth and true maturity, unwilling to leave the cloisters and engage with the life of the world. Maybe he knows that having passed and failed so many he would be destined for failure in the larger sphere. He chooses to be a demigod, lording it over the tiny kingdom of his classroom, satisfied with small honors and grudging deference. In the darker, more determining provinces of his heart lies a certain muted anxiety: he is, he fears, frightened of life.

Reading, writing, teaching: at best they are not life, but preparations for life. At worst, they are evasions of life: activities the worldly ones hold in mild approbation when the lights are up, but sneer subtly at when they move off together into paneled rooms, amber glasses in hand, away from the ears of children.

But "do not think so, you shall not find it so," as Shakespeare's prince says: at least if you ponder the question. Reading and writing and teaching are potentially magic: they turn one object into another, though not with a flash of the hand and a stirring of the wand, but through work, hard and (why not say it?) noble work.

Reading, to start with. If it's not common knowledge, it should be: you can read your way out of your life. You can read your way from one state of mind toward another. For all writing that matters testifies to a fundamental truth: there are multiple ways of seeing the world. There are many angles; complex adjustments; visions and revisions.

My way isn't the only way, the beginning reader learns. And then the corollary: there may be better ways out there. Or at the very least I should experiment with the possibility that there are. We are all socialized one time. We grow up immersed in the manners and morals and the rituals of our tribe. We are told by our parents, our first teachers and coaches, and our religious leaders what life is: what to value and what to shun. All honor to them: all respect to parents and teachers and clergy. They give us terms for comprehending experience: they instill their preferred vocabularies. They help turn us from bawling, scrapping creatures into boys and girls and then young men and young women.

But most of these figures of authority know only one way and too often they feel it to be the sole right way. They do not know they speak one language and that in truth there are many. They believe that because they have the first words in a young person's life, those words must be the last. They often do not know that life is multiple, rich, and strange and forever coming to be.

But the great writers do know that. They know that they themselves could not quite find peace with the language of their tribe and have had to strike out and find a new idiom. John Keats valued life in a way that none of his contemporaries and none of his precursors ever quite did. He knew something about love, something about enchantment, and something about failure and pain that they did not understand. Keats loved Shakespeare as much as anyone ever has, but beyond Shakespeare there were surely other worlds: Keats was determined to find them. He began his quest by reading: he was inspired by Chapman's translation of Homer; the myth of Eros and Psyche; the tales of the god Hyperion. "Let us have the old poets and Robin Hood!" Keats says. Keats brought the riches of the past into the present and caused them to live on into the future.

You can read your way out of your own life and then in time you can enter a new one—though to do that, you will probably need to learn *writing*. But by reading, you can begin to make a move. Think of Malcolm X in jail in Norfolk, Massachusetts. At the time of his incarceration he was a petty thief and drug dealer. In time he would become a leader of the Nation of Islam, and then, breaking with the Nation, an independent warrior for racial justice.

The Malcolm Little who went off to prison had a lively mind: he had ideas, no one thought more or harder than he did. But when he stepped into debates in the prison yard, he was easily bested. He had no facts to buttress his arguments; didn't know what was new and what old. He'd done no real reading.

So he ordered books from the prison library, loaded his cell, and set to work reading. He was determined to read the best works: the great philosophers, the economists, the analysts of society as it is and ought to be. But he could make nothing of the books: his vocabulary was too small. But there were dictionaries. So Malcolm Little got one and went to work, looking up every word that puzzled him. But he spent so long in the dictionary that by the time he returned to the bottom of the page of his book, he forgot what the substance of the top had been. He was weak where he needed to be strong.

But the mind is a muscle. You can expand it and make it more powerful, adroit, and graceful, much as you can your body. You can build up your mind, if you have the grit and courage and the time. (Malcolm Little was not short on any of these.) So the prisoner set to work.

He did so by copying out the dictionary starting at aardvark and going to "z." He copied the words and he copied the definitions. That's slow work, even if you have an abridged dictionary on your hands. Malcolm copied out the dictionary all the way through and as he did, he learned the words, really learned them. You could say that he taught himself to read. And when he finally could read, the world opened up. Malcolm changed himself and he did it as prelude to changing the world. He reinvented himself with his reading: he transformed his mind the way a dedicated athlete changes his body: through hard work—demanding labor, that is also infinitely pleasurable. Some people don't like the life they've been given, some people don't like the words they've inherited: so they throw them back in and then try to acquire new ones. As Kanye West says, "I ain't played the hand I was dealt, I changed my cards."

Suddenly Malcolm Little made contact with all that he had been missing: he learned history and geography, and political thought. He learned some sociology and he read some philosophy books: Kant, Nietzsche, Schopenhauer, and Spinoza. The world cracked and opened up.

He writes, "I suppose it was inevitable as my word base broadened, I could pick up a book and read and now begin to understand what the book was saying. Anyone who has read a great deal can imagine the new world that opened. Let me tell you something: from then until I left that prison, in every free moment I had, if I was not reading in the library, I was reading on my bunk. You couldn't have gotten me out of books with a wedge."

Malcolm Little was interested in the fate of black people and what white people had done to them over the years. He was interested in other matters, too. He wanted to learn everything, or everything he could. Years later when he thought back over his life, he said that if all had been fair in the world and in America, he would have gladly spent his life as a scholar, reading and writing and learning. But there was other work to be done. It all came down to the humanistic triad: he read and he wrote and he taught, and he did so on a national and then on an international stage. One might not always concur with Malcolm X's vision, but there is no doubting his force and provocative power. Emerson talked about the American Scholar as someone who used solitude, books, and the contemplation of his past experience to remake himself. He probably did not imagine that anyone like Malcolm Little would step forward to fill the role. But that's exactly what happened.

The American Scholar, as Emerson envisions him, begins as a reader. She wants to know everything; she wants to meet up with the best that has been thought and said. The American Scholar isn't a passive reader.

She guards against over-influence; she knows that there is, as Emerson famously says, a creative reading as well as a creative writing. The Scholar reads. The past is a treasure trove, and the Scholar wants to encounter all of the riches she can—for she will make that treasure her own in time. But in the beginning the young scholar reads for the pure joy of reading. She sees more, knows more, perceives more and in more intricate detail: in Stevens's words, in what may be his most affirmative poem, "Chocorua to Its Neighbor," the scholar's "green mind bulges with complicated hues."

There are those who never stop reading and never stop taking their identity from being readers. They explore words for as long as the world allows them to do so. Such people have a becoming sense of modesty. There are so many marvelous books, so many splendid writers, why shouldn't they spend eternity, or whatever fraction of eternity is given them, consorting with the great? Why turn away from the heavenly chorus, for though ever changing, it never goes out of tune and there is never a false note?

Says Virginia Woolf, whose work has broken down doors for numberless women writers and artists: "I have sometimes dreamt . . . that when the Day of Judgment dawns and the great conquerors and lawyers and statesmen come to receive their rewards—their crowns, their laurels, their names carved indelibly upon imperishable marble—the Almighty will turn to Peter and will say, not without a certain envy when He sees us coming with our books under our arms, 'Look, these need no reward. We have nothing to give them here. They have loved reading.'" For Woolf, the best books have the power to perform an "operation on the senses. One sees more intensely afterwards; the world seems bared of its coverings and given an intenser life."

But, says a certain sort of reader, wonderful as the music of the great writers may be, it's not mine. I've got to make the record in my own fashion: I've got to tell the story as I see it, even if my story limps and stumbles, when other stories travel smoothly on the road. I'm not going to despise my life simply because it's mine. For an incessant reader, Emerson can be radically uncomfortable with reading. He's afraid he'll become addicted to the thoughts of others. He's afraid they'll mute his originality. He starts his greatest essay "Self-Reliance" by affirming that when we hear the best ideas of others we recognize them as having been our own: our thoughts come back to us with "a certain alienated majesty."

Emerson wanted to be original. He spent much of his writing trying to rev himself up to the point where he could write something without precedent. He bullied and inspired himself; he wheedled and cajoled and prayed. And if it did not quite work with him—he never became the poet he aspired to be—it did work for others. Emerson seeded the ground with inspirations for those to come—those who wrote against him and (often without saying as much) in his name. He is the great seed sower of American literature.

You almost cannot read him without wanting to write—for as much as Emerson loves reading, he insists that writing is its fulfillment. Writing is where reading leads, logically and naturally, because no one can whistle your ditty or compose your symphony, but yourself.

Emerson would have relished Walter Benjamin's story about the village schoolmaster who lived on a pittance but was committed to high intellectual ideals. When the book catalogs came to him from Berlin, the schoolmaster couldn't help but moon over all the enticing titles that he wanted to buy and read but could no more afford than a down payment on the near side of the moon. The solution? This was an Emersonian and enterprising schoolmaster. He sat down and wrote the books himself. Writers, Benjamin says, write books because the ones on hand are not the ones that they want to read. They want to conduct their own music: they want to put together their own band and play a number or two, and if anyone rises to dance, well and good. But making the music is the thing.

Why write? Writing gives you the chance to make up your own mind, not only in the primary sense of figuring out what you think, but in the larger sense: creating a mind that more or less hangs together, a mind in which the ideas don't jostle too much with one another or cancel each other out. I mean not having a mind that's devoted to pacifism but also delights in fantasias of war. I mean a mind at peace with itself, or at least aware of its warring factions, its proclivities for mental fight, its ongoing arguments with itself (those inner arguments that Yeats says are the source of poetry). Writing makes up your mind. Writing makes the intellect strong and the imagination, too. For the imagination grows dim in the day to day. The imagination grows weary.

Now what precisely do we mean by imagination? What is this faculty that has been so much celebrated and so feared? The imagination is often defined and frequently dissected. But to put it all most simply, one might only say that the imagination is the faculty that envisions life as it is and life as it might be. Surely it tells us where we are; it tells the imaginer where he or she is in the world. But it does more than function as a map. The imagination also creates, directly or implicitly, a version of the world as it might be. It is, in other words, a utopian faculty—sometimes indirectly, sometimes overtly. What the great Northrop Frye says is true: human beings live in two worlds. One is the world of their actual experience; the other is the world that they dream of living in, either with their fellows or (hush this thought in the current oversocialized world) all alone.

Writing unleashes the imagination. One never knows what one wants until the moment one asks what it might be. Writing, real writing, says that none of the books on the shelf will do because (again we must proceed sotto voce) the writer feels that there never has been a being quite like herself. As the sage says, "few and mean as my gifts may be, I actually *am*." She wants to find the truth, her truth, and if that happens to be truth for others, then let the celebrations begin and the bestowal of awards commence. If not, she will be satisfied that she has expanded her own consciousness, made up her own mind.

You can read your way out of your own life. But your chances of coming into a new one increase vastly if you are willing to learn how to write. Writing is always autobiography: it's making the record after your own fashion. It's going back to the start and beginning the process of socialization one more time, except this time you are the guide as well as the pupil. Your readers may jeer or smile: it hardly matters: you've made yourself again, made yourself of words: the most evanescent and enduring material that humans possess. Words are nothing but air, or the scratching of a pen or tapping of a set of keys. Shakespeare writes of how: "Not marble, nor the gilded monuments / Of princes shall outlive this powerful rhyme." In his case, he is surely right. Sports commentators have a line about the fate of aging athletes approaching the ends of their careers. Father time, they say, is undefeated. Perhaps so. But if humanity has any chance against Father Time it is in the realm of words. People write to keep on living after they are gone. People write because when they do, they join all the others who have written well and said their piece. A paradox: all writers are different and make themselves so, otherwise they would not be worth reading. But. But all writers are of a movement, a guild. Keats called it the "immortal freemasonry of intellect." A little grand? Maybe. But for me it does well enough.

The third pole of the humanities, the one that makes it a tent, a dwelling, no matter how vulnerable, is teaching. And though it is the most frequently practiced art of the humanities, it is also the most mysterious. Reading gives pleasure, immediate pleasure, when you've found the right books. And writing, though a difficult pleasure, is pleasure nonetheless. But teaching is often hard labor. Teaching can be a grind. It is one of what Freud called the impossible professions, along with governing and (of course) psychoanalysis. However well it goes, it never seems to go well enough, and sometimes it goes very badly.

Teaching, one might say, is often the way the writer prepares to write. As a teacher, she reads the books she needs to read. And she talks about those books with students. She does so over and over again and in time that talk becomes the rough draft for the books and essays—or the journal entries and letters—that she will write. In front of a group of students, or at the head of a table, the teacher gets to practice again and again what she will, in time, commit to paper. She reads as a teacher and she rehearses for the primary satisfaction, the satisfaction of writing.

But why teach? Assuming that you don't need the money, or you could do something else and get by. Assuming that there are other ways to get some reading done and other ways to create first drafts. Not all students want to learn, not all schools are congenial, not on all days does one want to step up in front of the class and try to do something that is so hard: get people to enlarge the sphere of their thoughts.

It is, finally, a mystery why we teach, when there are so many other more immediately prestigious and materially rewarding ways to live in the world. But I wonder: maybe we teach out of a certain sort of kindness and a certain sort of gratitude. We teach because we are grateful to those who came into our lives and helped us, often against considerable odds, to change our lives by changing, in the largest sense possible, our minds.

We've been done a favor—we've been given a break. To see a young person leap forward into mental freedom in the way that we once did is to be reminded of the best moments of our lives. We break out of the cocoon one more time; we feel what might really be wings begin to emerge; we rise with them, our charges, and have a look at the world from the air, as though for the first time. It looks different from there; it looks both less pressing and more significant. Do we understand? For a moment, we do not so much under-stand as over-look, and that is something to be grateful for.

There is a social aspiration in teaching too. Every student who has broken through and begun to think will one day be part of a citizenry less susceptible to lies and evasions than it might have been without him.

The individual who joins the group and stays a just man or woman, who will speak her peace, as Milton so wanted to do, affirming always the powers of "one just man" or woman, can remake that group, bringing it at least a step toward sanity. Men and women in groups can careen quickly toward madness: you don't need Freud and Nietzsche and Canetti to show you that, though they will. The educated man or woman is in the group but not fully of it: the soul who thinks individually is the braking mechanism on a vehicle that will, all too often, merrily drive itself over the cliff, or into the oncoming.

Milton loved the stalwart angel Abdiel; loved the prophet Ezekiel, even half loved Satan because they stood up for what they believed in in the midst of what they saw as tyranny. The majority is a tyrant—almost always a tyrant. The educated individual raises the group level, but struggles against the whole idea of groups with their binding magic.

To turn away from teaching is to turn away from collective human hopes and though one is often tempted to make such a turn, the fact remains that democracy is a grand experiment and not to be denigrated, even though (whisper this) the great virtue in the government by the collective is that it somehow and half-miraculously gives more room for the individual to govern or even to misgovern himself.

Reading and writing and teaching: they compose the triad that creates that grand and vulnerable structure of hope that we call the humanities. Is this life of contemplation and expression and teaching and learning the very best of lives? It can be lonely, it can be frustrating (for who listens?), it can be tedious as one makes one's way through the necessities. (Says Frye: What is old to the teacher is new to the student.) But is there any other life in which one can be so free? Is there any other life in which you can help others to liberate themselves so well? The humanist is the liberator of his own soul. In promise, the humanist is the liberator of mankind.

PART 1: *WHY READ?*

For Matthew, Beloved Son

Literary Life

Reading through a volume of modern poetry not long ago, I came upon some lines that seemed to me to concentrate a strong and true sense of what there is to gain from great writing. The lines were by William Carlos Williams and they ran this way: "Look at / what passes for the new," Williams wrote. "You will not find it there but in / despised poems. / It is difficult / to get the news from poems / yet men die miserably every day / for lack / of what is found there." Williams asserts that though all of us are surrounded all the time with claims on our attention—film, TV, journalism, popular music, advertising, and the many other forms that pass for the new—there may be no medium that can help us learn to live our lives as well as poetry, and literature overall, can.

People die miserably every day for lack of what is found in despised poems—in literary artwork, in other words, that society at large denigrates. My own life and the lives of many others I've known offer testimony for what Williams has to say. Reading woke me up. It took me from a world of harsh limits into expanded possibility. Without poetry, without literature and art, I (and I believe many others, too) could well have died miserably. It was this belief in great writing that, thirty years ago, made me become a teacher.

Yet most of the people who do what I do now—who teach literature at colleges and universities—are far from believing Williams. Nearly all of them would find his lines overstated and idealizing. Many now see all of literature—or at least the kind of literature that's commonly termed canonical—as an outmoded form. It's been surpassed by theory, or rendered obsolete with the passage of time. To quote Williams on the value of poetry, without suitable condescension, at the next meeting of the Modern Language Association would be to invite no end of ridicule.

Does everyone who teaches literature hold this dismissive attitude? Not quite. But those who are better disposed to literary art tend to an extreme timidity. They find it embarrassing to talk about poetry as something that can redeem a life, or make it worth living. (Though they may feel these things to be true.) Those few professors who still hold literature in high regard often treat it aesthetically. Following Kant, they're prone to remove literary art from the push and toss of day-to-day life. They want to see poems and novels as autonomous artifacts that have earned the right to be disconnected from common experience. One admires great literary works as aesthetic achievements. But on actual experience, they should have no real bearing at all.

Other professors who still call themselves humanists are often so vague in their articulated sense of what great writing offers—it cultivates sensitivity; it augments imagination; it teaches tolerance—that their views are easily swept aside by the rigorous-sounding debunkers. Yet Williams is anything but vague. The most consequential poems offer something that is new—or, one might say "truth"—that makes significant life possible. Without such truth, one is in danger of miserable death, the kind of death that can come from living without meaning, without intensity, focus, or design.

The moral of this book is that Williams has it right. Poetry—literature in general—is *the* major cultural source of vital options for those who find that their lives fall short of their highest hopes. Literature is, I believe, our best goad toward new beginnings, our best chance for what we might call secular rebirth. However much society at large despises imaginative writing, however much those supposedly committed to preserve and spread literary art may demean it, the fact remains that in literature there abide major hopes for human renovation. This book is addressed to teachers. We teachers of literature, and of the humanities overall, now often stand between our students and their best aspirations, preventing them from getting what literary art has to offer. With all the resources at hand to help our students change their lives for the better, and despite real energy and dedication, most of us still fail in our most consequential task. Purportedly guides to greater regions of experience, we have become guards on the parapets, keeping others out.

This book is also written to students and potential students of literature—to all those who might dream of changing their current state through encounters with potent imaginations. You are invited to read over the shoulders of your teachers. You are invited, if need be, to supplant them: For much of what teachers can offer, you can provide for yourself. It is often simply a matter of knowing where to start. It's a matter of knowing what you might ask for and get from a literary education.

In Marcel Proust's *In Search of Lost Time*, there is a passage that gets close to the core of what a literary education should be about. The passage offers a deep sense of what we can ask from a consequential book. Proust speaks with the kind of clarity that is peculiarly his about what he hopes his work will achieve. In particular, he reflects on the relation he wants to strike with his readers. "It seemed to me," he observes, "that they would not be 'my' readers but readers of their own selves, my book being merely a sort of magnifying glass like those which the optician at Combray used to offer his customers—it would be my book but with it I would furnish them the means of reading what lay inside themselves. So that I would not ask them to praise me or to censure me, but simply to tell me whether 'it really is like that.' I should ask whether the words that they read within themselves are the same as those which I have written."

What Proust is describing is an act of self-discovery on the part of his reader. Immersing herself in Proust, the reader may encounter aspects of herself that, while they have perhaps been in existence for a long time, have remained unnamed, undescribed, and therefore in a certain sense unknown. One might say that the reader learns the language of herself; or that she is humanly enhanced, enlarging the previously constricting circle that made up the border of what she's been. One might also say, using another idiom, one that has largely passed out of circulation, that her consciousness has been expanded.

Proust's professed hope for his readers isn't unrelated to the aims that Emerson, a writer Proust admired, attributes to the ideal student he describes in "The American Scholar": "One must be an inventor to read well. As the proverb says, 'He that would bring home the wealth of the Indies, must carry out the wealth of the Indies.' There is then creative reading as well as creative writing. When the mind is braced by labor and invention, the page of whatever book we read becomes luminous with manifold allusion. Every sentence is doubly significant, and the sense of our author is as broad as the world."

For Emerson, the reader can do more than discover the language of herself in great writing. Emerson's reader uses a book as an imaginative goad. He can begin compounding visions of experience that pass beyond what's manifest in the book at hand. This, presumably, is what happened when Shakespeare read Holinshed's *Chronicles* or even Plutarch's *Lives*. These are major sources for the plays, yes, but in reading them Shakespeare made their sentences doubly significant, and the sense of their authors as broad as the world.

Proust and Emerson touch on two related activities that are central to a true education in the humanities. The first is the activity of discovering oneself as one is in great writing. The second, and perhaps more important, is to see glimpses of a self—and too, perhaps, of a world—that might be, a self and world that you can begin working to create. "Reading," Proust says in a circumspect mood, "is on the threshold of the spiritual life; it can introduce us to it; it does not constitute it."

Proust and Emerson point toward a span of questions that matter especially for the young, though they count for us all, too. They are questions that should lie at the core of a liberal arts education. Who am I? What might I become? What is this world in which I find myself? How might it be changed for the better?

We ought to value great writing preeminently because it enjoins us to ask and helps us to answer these questions, and others like them. It helps us to create and re-create ourselves, often against harsh odds. So I will be talking here about the crafting of souls, in something of the spirit that Socrates did. "This discussion," Socrates said, referring to one of his philosophical exchanges, "is not about any chance question, but about the way one should live."

I think that the purpose of a liberal arts education is to give people an enhanced opportunity to decide how they should live their lives. So I will be talking about the uses of the liberal arts for the conduct of life. I will be describing the humanities as a source of truth. I will be asking teachers to think back to the days when reading and thinking about books first swept them in and changed them, and asking them to help their students have that kind of transforming experience.

A reader removed from the debates about the liberal arts that have been going on over the past few decades would, on hearing the aims for this book, perhaps smile at how superfluous and unoriginal they seem.

Of course, universities should present humanities students with what Matthew Arnold called "the best that is known and thought" and give them the chance to reaffirm or remake themselves based on what they find.

To the charge of lacking originality, I plead guilty. I have already cited Proust and Emerson; this book will be filled with the wisdom of many others, often similarly well-known. But as to my argument being super-fluous: I can assure you that is not the case. Universities now are far from offering the kind of experience that Allan Bloom, a writer with whose work I have something like a love-hate relationship, is describing when he observes that "true liberal education requires that the student's whole life be radically changed by it, that what he learns may affect his action, his tastes, his choices, that no previous attachment be immune to exami-nation and hence re-evaluation. Liberal education puts everything at risk and requires students who are able to risk everything."

By this definition, true liberal education barely exists in America now. It is almost nowhere to be found. We teachers have become timid and apologetic. We are not willing to ask the questions that matter. Into the void that we have created largely by our fear, other forces have moved. Universities have become sites not for human transformation, but for training and for entertaining. Unconfronted by major issues, students use the humanities as they can. They use them to prepare for lucrative careers. They acquire marketable skills. Or, they find in their classes sources of easy pleasure. They read to enjoy, but not to become other than they are. "You must change your life," says Rilke's sculpture of Apollo to the beholder. So says every major work of intellect and imagination, but in the university now—as in the culture at large—almost no one hears.

Total Entertainment All the Time

I can date my sense that something was going badly wrong in my own teaching to a particular event. It took place on evaluation day in a class I was giving on the works of Sigmund Freud. The class met twice a week, late in the afternoon, and the students, about fifty undergraduates, tended to drag in and slump, looking slightly disconsolate, waiting for a jump start. To get the discussion moving, I often provided a joke, an anecdote, an amusing query. When you were a child, I had asked a few weeks before, were your Halloween costumes id costumes, superego costumes, or ego costumes? Were you monsters—creatures from the black lagoon, vampires, and werewolves? Were you Wonder Women and Supermen? Or were you something in between? It often took this sort of thing to raise them from the habitual torpor.

But today, evaluation day, they were full of life. As I passed out the assessment forms, a buzz rose up in the room. Today they were writing their course evaluations; their evaluations of Freud, their evaluations of me. They were pitched into high gear. As I hurried from the room, I looked over my shoulder to see them scribbling away like the devil's auditors. They were writing furiously, even the ones who struggled to squeeze out their papers and journal entries word by word.

But why was I distressed, bolting out the door of my classroom, where I usually held easy sway? Chances were that the evaluations would be much like what they had been in the past: they'd be just fine. And in fact, they were. I was commended for being "interesting," and complimented for my relaxed and tolerant ways; my sense of humor and capacity to connect the material we were studying with contemporary culture came in for praise.

In many ways, I was grateful for the evaluations, as I always had been, just as I'm grateful for the chance to teach in an excellent university surrounded everywhere with very bright people. But as I ran from that classroom, full of anxious intimations, and then later as I sat to read the reports, I began to feel that there was something wrong. There was an undercurrent to the whole process I didn't like. I was disturbed by the evaluation forms themselves with their number ratings ("What is your ranking of the instructor?—1, 2, 3, 4, or 5"), which called to mind the sheets they circulate after a TV pilot plays to the test audience in Burbank. Nor did I like the image of myself that emerged—a figure of learned but humorous detachment, laid-back, easygoing, cool. But most of all, I was disturbed by the attitude of calm consumer expertise that pervaded the responses. I was put off by the serenely implicit belief that the function of Freud—or, as I'd seen it expressed on other forms, in other classes, the function of Shakespeare, of Wordsworth or of Blake—was diversion and entertainment. "Edmundson has done a fantastic job," said one reviewer, "of presenting this difficult, important & controversial material in an enjoyable and approachable way."

Enjoyable: I enjoyed the teacher. I enjoyed the reading. Enjoyed the course. It was pleasurable, diverting, part of the culture of readily accessible, manufactured bliss: the culture of Total Entertainment All the Time.

As I read the reviews, I thought of a story I'd heard about a Columbia University instructor who issued a two-part question at the end of his literature course. Part one: What book in the course did you most dislike? Part two: What flaws of intellect or character does that dislike point up in you? The hand that framed those questions may have been slightly heavy. But at least they compelled the students to see intellectual work as a confrontation between two people, reader and author, where the stakes mattered. The Columbia students were asked to relate the quality of an encounter, not rate the action as though it had unfolded across the big screen. A form of media connoisseurship was what my students took as their natural right.

But why exactly were they describing the Oedipus complex and the death drive as interesting and enjoyable to contemplate? Why were they staring into the abyss, as Lionel Trilling once described his own students as having done, and commending it for being a singularly dark and fascinatingly contoured abyss, one sure to survive as an object of edifying contemplation for years to come? Why is the great confrontation—the rugged battle of fate where strength is born, to recall Emerson—so conspicuously missing? Why hadn't anyone been changed by my course?

To that question, I began to compound an answer. We Americans live in a consumer culture, and it does not stop short at the university's walls. University culture, like American culture at large, is ever more devoted to consumption and entertainment, to the using and using up of goods and images. We Americans are six percent of the world's population: we use a quarter of its oil; we gorge while others go hungry; we consume everything with a vengeance and then we produce movies and TV shows and ads to celebrate the whole consumer loop. We make it—or we appropriate it—we "enjoy" it and we burn it up, pretty much whatever "it" is. Someone coming of age in America now, I thought, has few available alternatives to the consumer worldview. Students didn't ask for it, much less create it, but they brought a consumer Weltanschauung to school, where it exerted a potent influence.

The students who enter my classes on day one are generally devotees of spectatorship and of consumer-cool. Whether they're sorority-fraternity denizens, piercer-tattooers, gay or straight, black or white, they are, nearly across the board, very, very self-contained. On good days, there's a light, appealing glow; on bad days, shuffling disgruntlement. But there is little fire, little force of spirit or mind in evidence.

More and more, we Americans like to watch (and not to do). In fact watching is our ultimate addiction. My students were the progeny of two hundred available cable channels and omnipresent Blockbuster outlets. They grew up with their noses pressed against the window of that second spectral world that spins parallel to our own, the World Wide Web. There they met life at second or third hand, peering eagerly, taking in the passing show, but staying remote, apparently untouched by it. So conditioned, they found it almost natural to come at the rest of life with a sense of aristocratic expectation: "What have you to show me that I haven't yet seen?"

But with this remove comes timidity, a fear of being directly confronted. There's an anxiety at having to face life firsthand. (The way the word "like" punctuates students' speech—"I was like really late for like class"— indicates a discomfort with immediate experience and a wish to maintain distance, to live in a simulation.) These students were, I thought, inclined to be both lordly and afraid.

The classroom atmosphere they most treasured was relaxed, laid-back, cool. The teacher should never get exercised about anything, on pain of being written off as a buffoon. Nor should she create an atmosphere of vital contention, where students lost their composure, spoke out, became passionate, expressed their deeper thoughts and fears, or did anything that might cause embarrassment. Embarrassment was the worst thing that could befall one; it must be avoided at whatever cost.

Early on, I had been a reader of Marshall McLuhan, and I was reminded of his hypothesis that the media on which we as a culture have become dependent are themselves cool. TV, which seemed on the point of demise, so absurd had it become to the culture of the late sixties, rules again. To disdain TV now is bad form; it signifies that you take yourself far too seriously. TV is a tranquilizing medium, a soporific, inducing in its devotees a light narcosis. It reduces anxiety, steadies and quiets the nerves. But it also deadens. Like every narcotic, it will, consumed in certain doses, produce something like a hangover, the habitual watchers' irritable languor that persists after the TV is off. It's been said that the illusion of knowing and control that heroin engenders isn't entirely unlike the TV consumer's habitual smug-torpor, and that seems about right.

Those who appeal most on TV over the long haul are low-key and nonassertive. Enthusiasm quickly looks absurd. The form of character that's most ingratiating on the tube, that's most in tune with the medium itself, is laid-back, tranquil, self-contained, and self-assured. The news anchor, the talk-show host, the announcer, the late-night favorite—all are prone to display a sure sense of human nature, avoidance of illusion, reliance on timing and strategy rather than on aggressiveness or inspiration. With such figures, the viewer is invited to identify. On what's called reality TV, on game shows, quiz shows, inane contests, we see people behaving absurdly, outraging the cool medium with their firework personalities. Against such excess the audience defines itself as worldly, laid-back, and wise.

Is there also a financial side to the culture of cool? I believed that I saw as much. A cool youth culture is a marketing bonanza for producers of the right products, who do all they can to enlarge that culture and keep it humming. The Internet, TV, and magazines teem with what I came to think of as persona ads, ads for Nikes and Reeboks and Jeeps and Blazers that don't so much endorse the powers of the product per se as show you what sort of person you'll inevitably become once you've acquired it. The Jeep ad that featured hip outdoorsy kids flinging a Frisbee from mountaintop to mountaintop wasn't so much about what Jeeps can do as it was about the kind of people who own them: vast, beautiful creatures, with godlike prowess and childlike tastes. Buy a Jeep and be one with them. The ad by itself is of little consequence, but expand its message exponentially and you have the central thrust of postmillennial consumer culture: buy in order to be. Watch (coolly) so as to learn how to be worthy of being watched (while being cool).

To the young, I thought, immersion in consumer culture, immersion in cool, is simply felt as natural. They have never known a world other than the one that accosts them from every side with images of mass-marketed perfection. Ads are everywhere: on TV, on the Internet, on billboards, in magazines, sometimes plastered on the side of the school bus. The forces that could challenge the consumer style are banished to the peripheries of culture. Rare is the student who arrives at college knowing something about the legacy of Marx or Marcuse, Gandhi or Thoreau. And by the time she does encounter them, they're presented as diverting, interesting, entertaining—or perhaps as objects for rigorously dismissive analysis—surely not as guides to another kind of life.

As I saw it, the specter of the uncool was creating a subtle tyranny for my students. It's apparently an easy standard to subscribe to, the standard of cool, but once committed to it, you discover that matters are different. You're inhibited, except on ordained occasions, from showing feeling, stifled from trying to achieve anything original. Apparent expressions of exuberance now seem to occur with dimming quotation marks around them. Kids celebrating at a football game ironically play the roles of kids celebrating at a football game, as it's been scripted on multiple TV shows and ads. There's always self-observation, no real letting-go. Students apparently feel that even the slightest departure from the reigning code can get you genially ostracized. This is a culture tensely committed to a laid-back norm.

In the current university environment, I saw, there was only one form of knowledge that was generally acceptable. And that was knowledge that allowed you to keep your cool. It was fine to major in economics or polit-ical science or commerce, for there you could acquire ways of knowing that didn't compel you to reveal and risk yourself. There you could stay detached. And—what was at least as important—you could acquire skills that would stand you in good financial stead later in life. You could use your education to make yourself rich. All of the disciplines that did not traduce the canons of cool were thriving. It sometimes seemed that every one of my first-year advisees wanted to major in economics, even when they had no independent interest in the subject. They'd never read an economics book, had no attraction to the business pages of the *Times*. They wanted economics because word had it that econ was the major that made you look best to Wall Street and the investment banks. "We like economics majors," an investment banking recruiter reportedly said, "because they're people who're willing to sacrifice their educations to the interest of their careers."

The subjects that might threaten consumer cool, literary study in particular, had to adapt. They could offer diversion—it seems that's what I (and Freud) had been doing—or they could make themselves over to look more like the so-called hard, empirically based disciplines.

Here computers come in. Now that computers are everywhere, each area of enquiry in the humanities is more and more defined by the computer's resources. Computers are splendid research tools. Good. The curriculum turns in the direction of research. Professors don't ask students to try to write as Dickens would, experiment with thinking as he might, were he alive today. Rather, they research Dickens. They delve into his historical context; they learn what the newspapers were gossiping about on the day that the first installment of *Bleak House* hit the stands. We shape our tools, McLuhan said, and thereafter our tools shape us.

Many educated people in America seem persuaded that the computer is the most significant invention in human history. Those who do not master its intricacies are destined for a life of shame, poverty, and neglect. Thus more humanities courses are becoming computer-oriented, which keeps them safely in the realm of cool, financially negotiable endeavors. A professor teaching Blake's "The Chimney Sweeper," which depicts the exploitation of young boys whose lot is not altogether unlike the lot of many children living now in American inner cities, is likely to charge his students with using the computer to compile as much information about the poem as possible. They can find articles about chimney sweepers from 1790s newspapers; contemporary pictures and engravings that depict these unfortunate little creatures; critical articles that interpret the poem in a seemingly endless variety of ways; biographical information on Blake, with hints about events in his own boyhood that would have made chimney sweepers a special interest; portraits of the author at various stages of his life; maps of Blake's London. Together the class might create a Blake–Chimney Sweeper website: *www.blakesweeper.edu.*

Instead of spending class time wondering what the poem means, and what application it has to present-day experience, students compile information about it. They set the poem in its historical and critical context, showing first how the poem is the product and the property of the past—and, implicitly, how it really has nothing to do with the present except as an artful curiosity—and second how, given the number of ideas about it already available, adding more thoughts would be superfluous.

By putting a world of facts at the end of a key-stroke, computers have made facts, their command, their manipulation, their ordering, central to what now can qualify as humanistic education. The result is to suspend reflection about the differences among wisdom, knowledge, and information. Everything that can be accessed online can seem equal to everything else, no datum more important or more profound than any other. Thus the possibility presents itself that there really is no more wisdom; there is no more knowledge; there is only information. No thought is a challenge or an affront to what one currently believes.

Am I wrong to think that the kind of education on offer in the humanities now is in some measure an education for empire? The people who administer an empire need certain very precise capacities. They need to be adept technocrats. They need the kind of training that will allow them to take up an abstract and unfelt relation to the world and its peoples—a cool relation, as it were. Otherwise, they won't be able to squeeze forth the world's wealth without suffering debilitating pains of conscience. And the denizen of the empire needs to be able to consume the kinds of pleasures that will augment his feeling of rightful rulership. Those pleasures must be self-inflating and not challenging; they need to confirm the current empowered state of the self and not challenge it. The easy pleasures of this nascent American empire, akin to the pleasures to be had in first-century Rome, reaffirm the right to mastery—and, correspondingly, the existence of a world teeming with potential vassals and exploitable wealth.

Immersed in preprofessionalism, swimming in entertainment, my students have been sealed off from the chance to call everything they've valued into question, to look at new ways of life, and to risk everything. For them, education is knowing and lordly spectatorship, never the Socratic dialogue about how one ought to live one's life.

These thoughts of mine didn't come with any anger at my students. For who was to blame them? They didn't create the consumer biosphere whose air was now their purest oxygen. They weren't the ones who should have pulled the plug on the TV or disabled the game port when they were kids. They hadn't invited the ad flaks and money changers into their public schools. What I felt was an ongoing sense of sorrow about their foreclosed possibilities. They seemed to lack chances that I, born far poorer than most of them, but into a different world, had abundantly enjoyed.

As I read those evaluation forms and thought them over, I recalled a story. In Vienna, there was once a superb teacher of music, very old. He accepted few students. There came to him once a young man whom all of Berlin was celebrating. Only fourteen, yet he played exquisitely. The young man arrived in Austria hoping to study with the master. At the audition, he played to perfection; everyone surrounding the old teacher attested to the fact. When it came time to make his decision, the old man didn't hesitate. "I don't want him," he said. "But, master, why not?" asked a protégé. "He's the most gifted young violinist we've ever heard." "Maybe," said the old man. "But he lacks something, and without this thing real development is not possible. What that young man lacks is inexperience." It's a precious possession, inexperience; my students have had it stolen from them.

Cool School

But what about the universities themselves? Do they do all they can to fight the reign of consumer cool?

From the start, the university's approach to students now has a solicitous, maybe even a servile tone. As soon as they enter their junior year in high school, and especially if they live in a prosperous zip code, the information materials, which is to say the advertising, come rolling in. Pictures, testimonials, videocassettes, and CD-ROMs (some bidden, some not) arrive at the door from colleges across the country, all trying to capture the students and their tuition dollars.

The freshman-to-be sees photographs of well-appointed dorm rooms; of elaborate phys-ed facilities; of expertly maintained sports fields; of orchestras and drama troupes; of students working joyously, off by themselves. It's a retirement spread for the young. "Colleges don't have admissions offices anymore, they have marketing departments," a school financial officer said to me once. Is it surprising that someone who has been approached with photos and tapes, bells and whistles, might come to college thinking that the Shakespeare and Freud courses were also going to be agreeable treats?

How did we reach this point? In part, the answer is a matter of demographics and also of money. Aided by the GI Bill, the college-going population increased dramatically after the Second World War. Then came the baby boomers, and to accommodate them colleges continued to grow. Universities expand readily enough, but with tenure locking in faculty for lifetime jobs, and with the general reluctance of administrators to eliminate their own slots, it's not easy for a university to contract. So after the baby boomers had passed through—like a tasty lump sliding the length of a boa constrictor—the colleges turned to promotional strategies—to advertising—to fill the empty chairs. Suddenly college, except for the few highly selective establishments, became a buyers' market. What students and their parents wanted had to be taken potently into account. That often meant creating more comfortable, less challenging environments, places where almost no one failed, everything was enjoyable, and everyone was nice.

Just as universities must compete with one another for students, so must individual departments. At a time of rank economic anxiety (and what time is not in America?), the English department and the history department have to contend for students against the more success-ensuring branches, such as the science departments and the commerce school. In 1968, more than 21 percent of all the bachelor's degrees conferred in America were humanities degrees; by 1993 that total had fallen to about 13 percent, and it continues to sink. The humanities now must struggle to attract students, many of whose parents devoutly wish that they would go elsewhere.

One of the ways we've tried to be attractive is by loosening up. We grade much more genially than our colleagues in the sciences. In English and history, we don't give many D's, or C's, either. (The rigors of Chem 101 may create almost as many humanities majors per year as the splendors of Shakespeare.) A professor at Stanford explained that grades were getting better because the students were getting smarter every year. Anything, I suppose, is possible.

Along with easing up on grades, many humanities departments have relaxed major requirements. There are some good reasons for introducing more choice into the curricula and requiring fewer standard courses. But the move jibes with a tendency to serve the students instead of challenging them. Students can float in and out of classes during the first two weeks of the term without making any commitment. The common name for this span—shopping period—attests to the mentality that's in play.

One result of the university's widening elective leeway is to give students more power over teachers. Those who don't like you can simply avoid you. If the students dislike you en masse, you can be left with an empty classroom. I've seen other professors, especially older ones, often those with the most to teach, suffer real grief at not having enough students sign up for their courses: their grading was too tough; they demanded too much; their beliefs were too far out of line with the existing dispensation. It takes only a few such incidents to draw other professors into line.

Before students arrive, universities ply them with luscious ads, guaranteeing them a cross between summer camp and lotusland. When they get to campus, flattery, entertainment, and preprofessional training are theirs, if that's what they want. The world we present them is not a world elsewhere, an ivory tower world, but one that's fully continuous with the American entertainment and consumer culture they've been living in. They hardly know they've left home. Is it a surprise, then, that this generation of students—steeped in consumer culture before they go off to school; treated as potent customers by the university well before they arrive, then pandered to from day one—are inclined to see the books they read as a string of entertainments to be enjoyed without effort or languidly cast aside?

So I had my answer. The university had merged almost seamlessly with the consumer culture that exists beyond its gates. Universities were running like businesses, and very effective businesses at that. Now I knew why my students were greeting great works of mind and heart as consumer goods. They came looking for what they'd had in the past, Total Entertainment All the Time, and the university at large did all it could to maintain the flow. (Though where this allegiance to the Entertainment-Consumer Complex itself came from—that is a much larger question. It would take us into politics and economics, becoming, in time, a treatise in itself.)

But what about me? Now I had to look at my own place in the culture of training and entertainment. Those course evaluations made it clear enough. I was providing diversion. To some students I was offering an intellectualized midday variant of Letterman and Leno. They got good times from my classes, and maybe a few negotiable skills, because that's what I was offering. But what was I going to do about it? I had diagnosed the problem, all right, but as yet I had nothing approaching a plan for action.

I'd like to say that I arrived at something like a breakthrough simply by delving into my own past. In my life I've had a string of marvelous teachers, and thinking back on them was surely a help. But some minds—mine, at times, I confess—tend to function best in opposition. So it was looking not just to the great and good whom I've known, but to something like an arch-antagonist, that got me thinking in fresh ways about how to teach and why.

The World According to Falwell

I teach at the University of Virginia, and not far from me, down Route 29 in Lynchburg—whence the practice of lynching, some claim, gets its name—is the church of Jerry Falwell. Falwell teaches "the word of God," the literal, unarguable truth as it's revealed to him in the Bible and as it must be understood by all heaven-bound Christians.

For some time, I thought that we at the University of Virginia had nothing consequential to do with the Reverend Falwell. Occasionally, I'd get a book through interlibrary loan from Falwell's Liberty University; sometimes the inside cover contained a warning to the pious suggesting that though this volume might be the property of the Liberty University library, its contents, insofar as they contradict the Bible (which means the Bible according to Falwell) were of no particular value.

It's said that when a certain caliph was on the verge of burning the great library at Alexandria, scholars fell on their knees in front of him and begged him to relent. "There are two kinds of books here," the caliph purportedly said. "There are those that contradict the Koran—they are blasphemous. There are those that corroborate the Koran—they are superfluous." So: "Burn the library." Given the possibilities for fundamentalist literary criticism that the caliph opened up, it's a good thing that Liberty has a library at all.

Thomas Jefferson, the University of Virginia's founder, was a deist, maybe something more scandalous than that, the orthodox of Virginia used to whisper. The architecture of my university's central grounds, all designed by Jefferson, is emphatically secular, based on Greek and Roman models. In fact, the Rotunda, once the university's library, is designed in homage to the Roman Pantheon, a temple to the twelve chief pagan gods. Where the statues of those gods stand in the Pantheon, there, in the Rotunda library, were books. Books were Jefferson's deities, invested with powers of transport and transformation equal to anything the ancient gods possessed. As soon as they saw the new university, local divines went apoplectic. Where was the church? Unlike Princeton and Harvard, the state university didn't have a Christian house of worship at its center. From pulpits all over Virginia, ministers threatened the pagan enclave with ruin from above. In 1829, the Episcopal bishop William Meade predicted the university's ruin, because, as he put it, the "Almighty is angry" about the Rotunda. (It's probably only fair to report that in 1895 the Rotunda did burn down.)

Jefferson—deist (maybe worse), scientist, cosmopolitan—seems to have believed that the best way to deal with religion was to banish it, formally, from the university, and instead to teach the useful arts of medicine, commerce, law, and the rest. The design of my university declares victory over what the radicals of the Enlightenment would have called superstition, and what most Americans currently call faith or spirituality. And we honor Jefferson now by, in effect, rendering unto Falwell that which is Falwell's.

In fact, we—and I don't mean only at the University of Virginia; I mean humanists in general—have entered into an implied bargain with Falwell and other American promulgators of faith, most of whom have much more to recommend them than the Prophet of Lynchburg. They do the soul-crafting. They administer the spiritual education. They address the hearts of our students, and in some measure of the nation at large. We preside over the minds. We shape intelligences; we train the faculties (and throw in more than a little entertainment on the side).

In other words, we teachers strike an unspoken agreement with religion and its dispensers. They do their work, we do ours.

But isn't that the way it should be? Isn't religion private? Spirituality, after all, is everyone's personal affair; it shouldn't be the substance of college education; it should be passed over in silence. What professor would have the bad taste to puncture the walls of his students' privacy, to invade their inner lives, by asking them uncomfortable questions about ultimate values?

Well, it turned out, me. I decided that I was, in a certain sense, going to take my cue from religion. After all, I got into teaching for the same reason, I suspect, that many people did: because I thought it was a high-stakes affair, a pursuit in which souls are won and lost.

"How do you imagine God?" If you are going to indulge in embarrassing behavior, if you're going to make your students "uncomfortable," why not go all the way? This question has moved to the center of many of my classes—not classes in religion, but classes in Shakespeare, in Romantic poetry, in major nineteenth-century novels. That is, the embarrassing question begins courses with which, according to Jefferson, according to Falwell and other, more tempered advocates of faith, and according to the great majority of my colleagues in the humanities, it has absolutely nothing to do.

What kind of answers do I get? Often marvelous ones. After the students who are disposed to walk out have, sometimes leaving an editorial sigh hanging in the air, and after there's been a weekend for reflection, answers come forth.

Some of the accounts are on the fluffy side. I've learned that God is love and only love; I've heard that God is Nature; that God is light; that God is all the goodness in the universe. I hear tales about God's interventions into the lives of my students, interventions that save them from accidents, deliver them from sickness while others fall by the wayside. There's a whole set of accounts that are on the all-benevolent side—smiling, kindly, but also underramified, insufficiently thought-out. If God is all things, or abides in all things, then what is the source of evil? (By now, it's clear to the students that bad taste is my game; already I'm getting a little by way of indulgence.) A pause, then an answer, sometimes not a bad one. The most memorable exponent of smiling faith was a woman named Catherine, who called her blend of creamy benevolence—what else?—Catherinism.

But I respected Catherine for speaking as she did, for unfolding herself bravely. In general, humanities classes, where questions of ultimate belief should be asked and answered all the time, have nothing to do with those questions. It takes courage to make this first step, and to speak candidly about yourself.

Some of the responses are anything but underelaborated. These tend to come from my orthodoxly religious students, many of whom are well trained, maybe overtrained, in the finer points of doctrine. I get some hardcore believers. But in general it wouldn't be fair to call them Falwell's children, because they're often among the most thoughtful students in the class. They, unlike the proponents of the idea that God is light and that's all you need to know in life, are interested in delving into major questions. They care about understanding the source of evil. They want to know what it means to live a good life. And though they're rammed with doctrine, they're not always addicted to dogma. There's often more than a little room for doubt. Even if their views are sometimes rock solid, they don't mind seeing them besieged. Because given their interests, they're glad that "this discussion is not about any chance question, but about the way one should live."

Final Narratives

Religion is the right place to start a humanities course, for a number of reasons, even if what we're going on to do is to read the novels of Henry James. One of them is that religion is likely to be a major element in my students' Final Narratives, a term I adapt from Richard Rorty. A Final Narrative (Rorty actually says Final Vocabulary; I modify him slightly) involves the ultimate set of terms that we use to confer value on experience. It's where our principles are manifest. When someone talks feelingly about the Ten Commandments, or the Buddha's Four Noble Truths, or the innate goodness of human beings, or about all human history being the history of class conflict, then, in all likelihood, she has revealed something close to the core of her being. She's touched on her ultimate terms of commitment, the point beyond which argument and analysis are unlikely to go, at least very quickly. Rorty puts it this way: "All human beings carry about a set of words which they employ to justify their actions, their beliefs, and their lives. These are the words in which we formulate praise of our friends and contempt for our enemies, our long-term projects, our deepest self-doubts and our highest hopes. They are the words in which we tell, sometimes prospectively and sometimes retrospectively, the story of our lives."

Rorty's word "final" is ironic, or potentially so. His sense is that a "final" language ought to be anything but final. He believes that we ought to be constantly challenging, testing, refining, and if need be overthrowing our ultimate terms and stories, replacing them with others that serve us better. Certain people, says Rorty, are "always aware that the terms in which they describe themselves are subject to change, always aware of the contingency and fragility of their final vocabularies, and thus of their selves." But Rorty believes that most people never stray far from their initial narratives, the values that they're imprinted with while they're growing up. Most of us stay at home.

Rorty calls people capable of adopting new languages "ironists," because they inflect even their most fervent commitments with doubt. It's possible, they know, that what today they hold most intimately true will be replaced tomorrow by other, better ways of seeing and saying things. They comprehend what Rorty likes to call the contingency of their own current state.

Appreciating this contingency is very close to appreciating one's own mortality. That is, Rorty's ironists are people who know that they exist in time because it is time and the changes it brings that can make their former terminologies and their former selves obsolete. Terms that serve your purposes one day will not necessarily do so the next. The ironists' willingness to change narratives, expand their circles of self, is something of a brave act, in part because all awareness of existence in time is awareness of death. To follow the ironists' path is to admit to mortality.

In trying to make contact with my students' Final Narratives, I ask about more than religion. I ask about how they imagine the good life. I ask, sometimes, how they picture their lives in ten years if all turns out for the best. I want to know what they hope to achieve in politics, in their professions, in family life, in love. Occasionally, I ask how they conceive of Utopia, the best of all possible worlds, or of Dystopia, the worst. But usually, for me, the matter of religion is present, a central part of the question.

There is nothing new about beginning a humanistic inquiry in this way. At the start of *The Republic*, Socrates asks his friends what they think justice is. And for Socrates, justice is the public and private state conducive to the good life. The just state and the just soul are mirror images of each other, comparably balanced. Socrates is quickly answered. Thrasymachus, aggressively, sometimes boorishly, insists that justice is the interest of the stronger. Socrates isn't put off by Thrasymachus, not at all.

For Socrates recognizes that getting his students to reveal themselves as they are, or appear to themselves to be, is the first step in giving them the chance to change.

Posing the question of religion and the good life allows students to become articulate about who and what they are. They often react not with embarrassment or anxiety, but with surprise and pleasure, as if no one has ever thought to ask them such a question and they've never posed it to themselves.

But beginning here, with religion, also implies a value judgment on my part—the judgment that the most consequential questions for an individual life (even if one is, as I am, a longtime agnostic) are related to questions of faith. I also believe, for reasons I will get to later, that at this historical juncture, the matter of belief is crucial to our common future.

Most professors of the humanities have little interest in religion as a field of live options. Most of us have had our crises of faith early, if we've had them at all, and have adopted, almost as second nature, a secular vision of life. Others keep their religious commitments separate from their pedagogy, and have for so long that they're hardly aware of it. But what is old to the teacher is new to the student. This question of belief matters greatly to the young, or at least it does in my experience. Asking it can break through the ideologies of training and entertaining. Beneath that veneer of cool, students are full of potent questions; they want to know how to navigate life, what to be, what to do. Matters of faith and worldliness are of great import to our students and by turning away from them, by continuing our treaty with the dispensers of faith where we tutor the mind and they take the heart and spirit, we do our students injustice.

We secular professors often forget that America is a religion-drenched nation. Ninety percent of us believe that God knows and loves us personally, as individuals. More than the citizens of any other post-industrial nation, we Americans attend church—and synagogue, and mosque. We affirm faith. We elect devout, or ostensibly devout, believers to the White House; recent presidents have been born-again Christians. Probably one cannot be elected president of the United States—cannot be our Representative Man—without professing strong religious faith. The struggle over whether America's future will be sacred or secular, or a mix of the two, is critical to our common future.

Some may well disagree with me about the centrality of religious matters, matters of ultimate belief, in shaping a true literary education. I teach in the South, one of the more religiously engaged parts of the nation, after all. Fine. But I think the point stands nonetheless. Get to your students' Final Narratives, and your own; seek out the defining beliefs. Uncover central convictions about politics, love, money, the good life. It's there that, as Socrates knew, real thinking starts.

Circles

Rorty is a pragmatic philosopher, and like his pragmatic forebears Dewey and James, his preeminent task is to translate the work of Ralph Waldo Emerson into the present. Behind Rorty's reflections on Final Vocabularies, there lies one of the most profound passages that Emerson wrote. The passage is from the essay "Circles," and it stands at the core of the kind of literary education that I endorse.

In it Emerson brings forward a marvelous image for the way growth takes place in human beings, and perhaps, too, in society. The image he summons is that of the circle, the circle understood as an image of both expansion *and* confinement. "The life of man," he writes, "is a self-evolving circle, which, from a ring imperceptibly small, rushes on all sides outwards to new and larger circles, and that without end."

So far Emerson has made the process of human expansion seem almost automatic, as though it were a matter of natural evolutionary force. But, as is his habit, Emerson goes on to revise himself, expand himself through refinement. "The extent to which this generation of circles, wheel without wheel, will go, depends on the force or truth of the individual soul. For it is the inert effort of each thought, having formed itself into a circular wave of circumstance,—as, for instance, an empire, rules of an art, a local usage, a religious rite,—to heap itself on that ridge, and to solidify and hem in the life."

Emerson's insight is dialectical. Whatever gains we make in our knowledge of the self and the world, however liberating and energizing our advances may be, they will eventually become standardized and dull. What once was the key to life will become deadening ritual, common practice, a tired and tiresome Final Narrative. The critic Kenneth Burke is thinking of something similar when he talks about "the bureaucratizing of the imaginative"; Robert Frost touches on the point when he observes that a truth ceases to be entirely true when it's uttered even for the second time.

Emerson understands education as a process of enlargement, in which we move from the center of our being, off into progressively more expansive ways of life. We can see this sort of thing happening on the largest scale when the author of *Julius Caesar* becomes capable of creating the vast work that is *Hamlet*. Yet *Hamlet* is an outgrowth of *Caesar*; the character of Brutus expands—another circle on the great deep, if you like—into the revealing mystery that is Hamlet. But such rippling outward happens every day, too, as when a child leaves her family and goes out into the painful, promising world of school. Then the child's circle of knowing has to expand to meet the new circumstances, or she'll suffer for it.

The aim of a literary education is, in Emerson's terms, the expansion of circles. One's current circle will eventually "solidify and hem in the life." "But," Emerson immediately continues, "if the soul is quick and strong, it bursts over the boundary on all sides, and expands another orbit on the great deep, which also runs up into a high wave, with attempt again to stop and to bind. But the heart refuses to be imprisoned; in its first and narrowest pulses, it already tends outward with a vast force, and to intense and innumerable expansions."

This passage, eloquent as it is, breeds many questions. How shall we understand the substance of these expanding rings? What is their human content? How does one know that this or that new circle is conducive to better things than the old? Where does the impetus for enlargement come from? Is it always time to move outward, or is there a time in life when it makes sense to fall back, or to stand pat? What role do books have in this process? And what part does a teacher play? How does the student put herself in the way of the kind of expansion that Emerson describes? How does she know that it's coming to pass? Is it painful, pleasurable, both? Are such changes always for the better? Might they not also be changes for the worse?

For the purposes of literary education, I want to see these Emersonian circles as being composed of words. But the circles will also be alive with feeling. They will be rife with the emotions—the attractions and powers and taboos—that infuse the words that mean the most to us. Words like "mother" and "father" and "God" and "love" and "America" are not just blank counters in a game designed to fill up a stray hour. They are words with a history, personal and collective, words differently valued, differently felt, by each of us. We define them in ways partially our own, based on our experiences. And of course, the words also define us. So we might think of Emerson's circles as Rorty's Final Narratives. And we might think of the question about religion as a way to tap into one's ultimate terms, to make contact with one's outer-lying circles, and in so doing to initiate the process of growth.

It's time, no doubt, for a provisional thesis statement: the function of a liberal arts education is to use major works of art and intellect to influence one's Final Narrative, one's outermost circle of commitments. A liberal education uses books to rejuvenate, reaffirm, replenish, revise, overwhelm, replace, in some cases (alas) even help begin to generate the web of words that we're defined by. But this narrative isn't a thing of *mere* words. The narrative brings with it commitments and hopes. A language, Wittgenstein thought, is a way of life. A new language, whether we learn it from a historian, a poet, a painter, or a composer of music, is potentially a new way to live.

Grateful as I am for Rorty's translation and Emerson's luminous passage, there is one place where I must part company with them both (and with Allan Bloom as well). For my hopes, I think, are larger than theirs. I believe that almost anyone who has the opportunity to enjoy a liberal education—and such educations are not only to be had in schools; the world is full of farmers, tradesmen and tradeswomen, mechanics, lawyers, and, up to some crucial moment, layabouts, who've used books to turn their lives around—almost anyone is likely to be able to cultivate the power to look skeptically at his own life and values and consider adopting new ones. This ability—to expand one's orbits—is central to the health of democracy. The most inspired and inspiring Americans have always done so: others can and will join them. But the process is not an easy one. Allan Bloom is quite right: liberal education does put everything at risk and requires students who are willing to risk everything. Otherwise it can only touch what is uncommitted in the essentially committed student.

But Bloom, much, much more than Emerson and Rorty, believes that such risk and such change are only for the very few. Bloom sees Socrates' path as exclusively for an elite. It is not so.

For Ignorance

"What that young man lacks is inexperience": so said the maestro of the young prodigy. Part of what I hope to do by asking students to brood publicly about God and ultimate commitments is to let them recapture their inexperience. They need a chance to own what may be the most precious knowledge one can have at the start of an education, knowledge of one's own ignorance.

Plato and Aristotle both say that philosophy begins in wonder. But Ludwig Wittgenstein, perhaps closer to the point, thought that people came to philosophy, to serious thinking about their lives, out of confusion. The prelude to philosophy was a simple admission: "I have lost my way." The same can be true for serious literary study. At its best, it often begins with a sense of dislocation; it begins with a sense that one has lost one's way.

The best beginning reader is often the one with the wherewithal to admit that, living in the midst of what appears to be a confident, energetic culture, he among all the rest is lost. This is a particularly difficult thing to do. For our culture at large prizes knowingness. On television, in movies, in politics, at school, in the press, the student encounters authoritative figures, speaking in self-assured, worldly tones. Their knowingness is intimidating. They seem to be in full command of themselves. They appear to have answered all the questions that matter in life and now to be left musing on the finer points. They demonstrate their preternatural poise by withholding their esteem. Not to admire anything, Horace said, is the only way to feel consistently good about yourself. Most of the cultural authorities now in place, in art, in the media, and in academia, are figures who programmatically hoard their esteem and apparently feel quite good about themselves in the process.

Should one believe in God? What is truth? How does one lead a good life? All these questions the cultural authorities appear to have resolved. Only the smaller matters remain.

But the true student has often not settled these matters at all. Often she has not even come up with provisional answers that satisfy her. And finally, after years of observation and thought, she may be willing to wager that the so-called authorities probably haven't resolved them either. They're performing a charade, dispensing an unearned and ultimately feeble comfort. The true student demands more. And to find it, she is willing, against the backdrop of all this knowingness, to take a brave step. She is willing to affirm her own ignorance.

Beneath acculturation to cool, beneath the commitment to training and skills, there often exists this sense of confusion. And where it is, the student should be able to affirm it, and the teacher to endorse the affirmation.

"You must become an ignorant man again," says Wallace Stevens to his ephebe, or beginning poet. The same holds true for the beginning student of literature, and often for the teacher as well. The student must

be willing to become as articulate as possible about what he has believed—
or what he has been asked to believe—up until this point. He must be
willing to tell himself who he is and has been, and, possibly, why that will
no longer quite do. This exercise in self-reflection, deriving often from the
sense of displacement, of having lost one's way, can start a literary education. And once a student has touched his ignorance, he has acquired a
great resource, for in such ignorance there is the beginning of potential
change—of new and confident, if provisional, commitment. As Thoreau
puts it, "How can he remember well his ignorance—which his growth
requires—who has so often to use his knowledge?"

Again and again, the true student of literature will return to this ignorance, for it's possible that no truth she learns in the humanities will be
permanently true. At the very least, everything acquired by immersion
in literature will have to be tested and retested along the way. It's for this
reason that the teacher often enters a course with a sense of possibility
akin to the students'.

One of the most important jobs a teacher has is to allow students to
make contact with their ignorance. We need to provide a scene where
not-knowing is, at least at the outset, valued more than full, worldly
confidence. Thoreau heading to Walden Pond almost empty-handed, or
Emily Dickinson going up to her room in Amherst to engage in a soli-
tary dialogue with God, are grand versions of the kind of open and daring
endeavor that we can all engage in for ourselves. Emerson says that power
abides in transition, in "the shooting of the gulf, in the darting to an aim."
We're most alive when we're moving from one set of engagements to
the next. We're in motion then, but not fully sure where we're going,
feeling both our present ignorance and the prospect of new, vitalizing
knowledge.

Down the Hall

While I'm asking my questions about God and what makes a good life,
and affirming, when need be, a certain sort of ignorance, what's going on
in the classrooms of my colleagues down the hall, and for that matter, in
humanities classrooms across the country? A number of things, all well
worth remarking upon. There is training, there is entertaining, no doubt.
But many professors go at least some distance in resisting the ethos of the
corporate university and of American culture overall. What they do can
pass well beyond the university's ad brochures, where the students bask

on the grass in all-approving sunlight, or hover around a piece of machinery that's high-tech, high-priced, and virtually unidentifiable.

Many professors of humanities—professors of literature and history and philosophy and religious studies—have something of consequence in common. Centrally, they attempt to teach one thing, and often do so with real success. That one thing is reading. They cultivate attentiveness to written words, careful consideration, thoughtful balancing, coaxing forth of disparate meanings, responsiveness to the complexities of sense. They try to help students become more like what Henry James said every writer ought to be, someone on whom nothing is lost. Attentiveness to words, to literary patterns and their meaning-making power: that remains a frequent objective of liberal arts education.

It was the New Critics who brought the phrase "close reading" to the fore in American education. Robert Penn Warren, Cleanth Brooks, William K. Wimsatt, and a number of other influential scholars pioneered an approach to reading that continues on, in various forms, into the present. The well-wrought students of Brooks and Warren were ever on the lookout for irony, tension, ambiguity, and paradox. To find these things, they had to scrutinize the page in front of them with exacting care. All to the good.

But what happens in most New Critical readings is that the master terms themselves—call them, if you like, elements in the New Critics' Final Narrative—take precedence over the actual poem. So rather than measuring the particular vision of John Donne, with all his manifold religious commitments and resistances, his sexual complexities, his personal kinks and quirks, the New Critic reworks Donne into a collection of anointed terms. Donne's "maturity"—to put matters in a compressed way—becomes a function of his capacity to cultivate paradox and irony.

Some writers are more responsive to New Critical values than others, and surely Donne is one of them. His work *is* replete with irony and ambiguity. Yet with the imposition of the rhetorical terms—terms that have no significant place in Donne's own Final Narrative—the poet becomes a function of New Critical values rather than a promulgator of his own.

The New Critical student, by encountering the right poems in the right way, undergoes a shaping, a form of what the Greeks called *paideia*. For the qualities that he learns to value in poems can also be cultivated in persons. So the ideal student (and the ideal professor) of New Criticism is drawn to the ability to maintain an ironic distance on life, the capacity to live with ambiguities, the power to achieve an inner tension than never breaks. The ideal New Critical student, like the ideal New Critical poem, is prone to be sophisticated, stoical, calm, intent, conventionally masculine, and rather worldly. What such a student is not likely to be is emotional, mercurial, rhapsodic, or inspired. The New Critical ethos—what we might call, after Keats, an ethos of negative capability, the capacity to be "in uncertainties, Mysteries, doubts, without any irritable reaching after fact & reason"—surely has its value. But it is one ethos among many. To reduce literature to that one ethos, when it contains a nearly infinite number, robs great writing of its diversity, and life of its richness.

The Harvard University scholar Walter Jackson Bate purportedly used a Marx Brothers style routine to capture what he thought of as New Critical close reading. "Close reading," he'd mutter, and push the book up near his nose. "Closer reading": with a laugh, digging his face down into the book. Then finally, "Very close reading," where nose and book kissed and not a word of print was legible. Bate's routine suggests that with a certain kind of exclusive attention to the page, life disappears. The connection between word and world goes dark (or becomes somewhat deviously implicit). The reader is left adrift, uncompassed, in a sea of sentences.

Foucault, Industrial Strength

There was this much to be said for the New Critics: they were prone to specialize in reading and teaching works with which they were spiritually aligned. Donne and the New Critics genuinely do have something in common, though they also part company at important points. The violence of applying the anointed terms to Donne or Marvell or Keats's odes, or Shakespeare's sonnets is real, though hardly overwhelming. But down the hall in the humanities building now—and on the shelves of the library devoted to recent literary and cultural study—one finds work that is best described as out-and-out rewriting of the authors at hand. In fact, we might call these efforts not so much criticism as transformation.

Terry Eagleton, a Marxist critic drawing on the work of Pierre Macherey, describes a good deal of current criticism as quite simply an exercise in rewriting. One approaches the work at hand, and recasts it in the terms of Foucault, or Marx, or feminism, or Derrida, or Queer Theory, or what have you.

So a current reading of, say, Dickens's *Bleak House* is not so much an interpretation as it a reworking and a revision of the novel. Dickens is depicted as testifying, albeit unwittingly, to Foucault's major truths. In *Bleak House,* we are supposed to find social discipline rampant, constant surveillance, the hegemony of the police, a carceral society. Whatever elements of the novel do not cohere with this vision are discredited, or pushed to the margin of the discussion. (In a Foucaultian reading of Shakespeare's *Henry IV,* Stephen Greenblatt, often a fine critic, manages to leave Falstaff virtually unmentioned.) Thus the critic rewrites Dickens in the terms of Foucault. One effectively reads not a text by Dickens, but one by another author. Dickens's truth is replaced by the truth according to Michel Foucault—or Fredric Jameson or Hélène Cixous—and there the process generally ends.

It may be that the truths unfolded by Foucault and the rest are of consummate value. It may be that those authors are indispensable guides to life, or at least to the lives of some. If so, all to the good.

If so, they, the critics, ought to be the objects of study in themselves. Let us look at Foucault, for instance, and see how one might lead a life under his guidance. What would you do? What would you do, in particular, as a denizen of an institution that produces precisely the kind of discipline that Foucault so detests? For a university, in Foucaultian thinking, is a production center, a knowledge-producing matrix which creates discourses that aid in normalizing people and thus in making them more susceptible to control. In fact, if you are a university citizen, you live in the belly of the beast. How, given what you've learned from Foucault, will you work your way out?

But these questions are virtually never asked. What usually happens is that professors apply the terminology to the work at hand, to Dickens or Emerson or Eliot, then leave it at that. The professor never measures the values and the shortcomings of the ruling critical idiom itself. For what authors who create comprehensive views of life offer is what Frost thought of as grand metaphors. "Great is he who imposes the metaphor," the poet said. But then it is the task of the reader, on encountering such metaphors, to see how far one can ride them out. At what point do they stop putting us in an illuminating relation to life? Where do they break down? Darwin's thinking about natural selection may help us to understand the animal kingdom. But should we use it to justify a society where all-out competition reigns? Perhaps this is a point where the grand Darwinian metaphor fractures.

Foucault would teach us that all disciplines discipline. That is, that every area of intellectual inquiry—psychology, sociology, history, literary criticism—tends toward providing reductive norms for human creations and for human behavior, thus delimiting possibility. Is this true? If so, what is there to do about it? What is there to do, in particular, if you are someone who, while using Foucault as the creator of your master narrative, at the same time is working in an institution, giving grades, collecting data, compiling reports, that effectively assault all that Foucault would seem to stand for?

This is not an unanswerable question. But surely it is the sort of question one must ask of one's own Final Narrative. In my experience, teachers of the humanities rarely do so. They rarely put the class's master terms on display, rarely make them the object of scrutiny and criticism.

If Foucault is your patron saint of wisdom (suggestive as I sometimes find him, he is not mine—to me he is a builder of dungeons in the air), then by all means bring him to the fore. Teach him directly. Let us see what language he has to unfold, what his Final Narrative entails. And if a language is also a way of life, we want to know what kind of life Foucault enjoins. A language, once taken on as an ultimate narrative, is not a set of markers, not merely a map, but a set of commitments, however contingent those commitments might be. It's necessary to test the author at hand, that is, as the source for a way of life.

When you apply Foucault to Dickens and don't turn in the direction of Foucault and interrogate his reach and value—his application to life— you lose what benefit Foucault may bring. When you translate Dickens into Foucault, you lose what benefit Dickens might have had to deliver. You leave with precious little, when there was so much that you might have had.

There is another disadvantage in applying theory to literature. To adapt a distinction made by Richard Poirier: literature tends to be dense; theory tends to be difficult. I can take my children, ages twelve and fourteen, to a production of *Hamlet*: no doubt they'll sleep through some of it, daydream through some more. But they'll also wake up at times—be shocked, puzzled, tickled, and occasionally illuminated. The best literature tends to be a layered experience. Even a beginning reader can get something from it. Then there's further to go, into legitimate complexity, true density and depth. Theory, on the other hand, tends to be an all-or-nothing affair. You get it or you don't. Face young people with a page of Derrida, whose reflections on the defining limits of Western thought are anything but valueless, and they're likely to depart with no benefit at all. Nothing is available for them. They don't get it, period. Then, once you've surmounted the difficulty, Derrida, like most theorists, tends to be a bit too available—theorists tend to have an astounding capacity to say the same thing over and over again.

If you set theory between readers and literature—if you make theory a prerequisite to discussing a piece of writing—you effectively deny the student a chance to encounter the first level of literary density, the level he's ready to negotiate. Theory is used, then, to banish aspiring readers from literary experience that by rights belongs to them.

The hasty reader might mistake my view for the "antitheory" position. For there are any number of professors of humanities who simply detest any and all far-reaching analytical work. I've written a book about contemporary theorists that's not at all unadmiring, and on occasion I teach their work. But experience has shown me that there are more viable and more varied options for students in literature itself, and that contemporary theory, though not without its appeals, tends to be implausibly extreme in its vision of experience and, accordingly, untenable as a guide to life. Can you live it? Alas, it's generally the case that no one can live out the latest version of theoretical apostasy and that, just as depressing, no one, even the theory's most devoted advocates, is even mildly inclined to try.

Interpretation

Interpretation is the name of the game, says Stanley Fish, and all humanities professors must play. Fish is probably the best-known American literary critic at work today. His books on literary theory and on Milton are much consulted in the academy. To Fish, interpretation is a test of ingenuity. It's a way to demonstrate intellectual prowess. Often interpretation is a chance to push your reader's and student's credulity as far as possible, then a step further. Fish has observed that his aim as an interpreter is not to find truth but to be as interesting as he can be. Emphatically, the objective is not to make past wisdom available to the uses of the present, however badly such wisdom may be needed. For Fish, what literary critics do is inevitably without consequences: it changes nothing in academia or in the public world. Interpretation, for Fish, is a self-delighting and self-promoting game. He cites with full approval the view that "literary interpretation . . . has no purpose external to the arena of its practice; it is the 'constant unfolding' to ourselves 'of who we are' as practitioners; its audience is made up of those who already thrill to its challenges and resonate to its performances."

I suspect that Fish finds the seriousness with which he's regarded to be supremely amusing. I suspect that as a brilliant satirist unfolding one piece of performance art after another, he takes delight in pushing his academic readers as far into the ridiculous as possible. I've no doubt that Fish will be greatly relieved when people stop taking him literally, begin regarding him as the stern moralist that he actually is, and understand that he has always hoped we would do the opposite of what he recommended. In reading Fish on interpretation, one should become disturbed by one's own practice—by the practice of interpreting for the sake of interpreting, as something to do, because one is good at it, as a way to advance one's career—and try something better. By pretending to endorse things as they are, in their current near-absurdity, Fish is no doubt trying to stir professorial rebellion. But to Fish's probable surprise, professors have not seen that he is the closest thing the academy has to a Jonathan Swift.

But isn't it a good thing, this exercise of mind that students undergo when they interpret texts with ingenious rigor? Doesn't it strengthen the intellect, improve the powers of discernment, enhance capacities for what's called critical thinking?

Critical thinking is now much revered in humanities departments. We pride ourselves on dispensing it. But what exactly is critical thinking? Often it is no more than the power to debunk various human visions. It is, purportedly, the power to see their limits and faults. But what good is this power of critical thought if you do not yourself believe something and are not open to having these beliefs modified? What's called critical thought generally takes place from no set position at all. There is no committed vantage, however transient. Rather, one attacks from any spot that one likes, so everything is susceptible to denunciation. "One is clever and knows everything that has ever happened," as Nietzsche puts it in his passage on the Last Man, "so there is no end of derision." For the critical thinker there is no end of derision. When one thinks critically in behalf of creating a Final Narrative, that is something else again. Then you are sifting visions for their applications to life. A great deal is at stake. But most of what now passes as critical thinking takes place in a void.

In general, critical thinking is the art of using terms one does not believe in (Foucault's, Marx's) to debunk worldviews that one does not wish to be challenged by.

What happens when you teach critical thinking unattached to some form of ethics, or some process of character creation? What you help inculcate, I believe, is the capacity to use the intellect in ever more adroit ways. This kind of education does make the student smarter, in some abstract sense. It makes him more adept at the use of what the Frankfurt School thinkers liked to call instrumental reason. This sort of reason conceives the world in terms of problems and solutions. It is prone to abstraction, to the release of the intellect from the emotions, to extreme forms of detachment. The development of instrumental reason is good preparation for doing work in a corporation in which you look only at means and not at ends. You see processes, but not the ultimate performance. Then you go off, the better to enjoy Saturday night.

It may seem radical to be studying Foucault and Adorno. But students now do not study these figures, if by "study" we mean deciding after careful interpretation and long questioning whether the figures at hand have it right, whether the students ought to try to live with these writers as guides to life. On the contrary, students learn to apply the terms of analysis, like painters applying pigment to a house, or like systems analysts applying their standards to a particular disposition of persons and tasks. The values involved mean virtually nothing. You can be a close observer, you can write well, you can be brilliantly ingenious in making your terms appear to square with the poem at hand, you can even be someone on whom little or nothing is lost, and you can still be the sort of person who does what he is told without thinking much about it. You can still be someone who lives to follow orders.

What interpretation as currently taught encourages is a highly skilled, highly negotiable form of expertise that will often be prized by future employers in that it comes without inconvenient ethical baggage. Despite the rhetoric of subversion that surrounds it, current humanities education does not teach subversive skepticism (I wish that it did); rather, it teaches the dissociation of intellect from feeling—something that can be a prelude to personal and collective anomie. True education, as Friedrich Schiller rightly saw it, ought to fuse mind and heart. Current education in the liberal arts does precisely the opposite. At the end of this road lies a human type bitterly and memorably described in Weber: "Specialists without spirit, sensualists without heart; this nullity imagines that it has attained a level of civilization never before achieved."

"I'll die before I give you power over me," Narcissus liked to say to his many wooers, before he offended the goddess Hera and was forced to fall in love with his own image in a pool. The analysis of great works now often takes place beneath the auspices of Narcissus. The student is taught not to be open to the influence of great works, but rather to perform facile and empty acts of usurpation, in which he assumes unearned power over the text. Foucault applied at industrial strength is an automatic debunking agent. But the process leaves the student untouched, with no actual growth, just a reflexively skeptical stance that touches the borders of nihilism. Such activity, prolonged over the course of an education, is likely to contribute to the creation of what the philosopher James C. Edwards calls "normal nihilists." Normal nihilists are people who believe in nothing (except the achievement of their own advantage), and we may be creating them in significant numbers by not counting the ethical costs of our pedagogy. "It's easy to be brilliant," Goethe said, "when you do not believe in anything." And it's easy, too, to be brilliantly successful.

The sense of superiority that current liberal arts education often instills rhymes with some of the least creditable trends in our culture. It rhymes with a superior and exploitative relation to the natural world, with condescension to the poor, with a sense that nothing in the world matters unless it matters to Me. Analytic pedagogy, the pedagogy of instrumental reason, does not create these trends; far from it. But such pedagogy contributes to wrongs that it should be contending against.

What's missing from the current dispensation is a sense of hope when we confront major works, the hope that they will tell us something we do not know about the world or give us an entirely fresh way to apprehend experience. We need to learn not simply to read books, but to allow ourselves to be read by them.

And this process can take time. Describing his initiation into modern literature, into Kafka, Joyce, Proust, and their contemporaries, Lionel Trilling writes: "Some of these books at first rejected me; I bored them. But as I grew older and they knew me better, they came to have more sympathy with me and to understand my hidden meanings. Their nature is such that our relationship has been very intimate." "I bored them," says Trilling. Given the form of literary education now broadly available, it is almost impossible that a student would say of a group of books, "I bored them." No, in the current consumer-driven academy another word, differently intoned, would be on the tip of the tongue: "Boooooooring." We professors have given our students the language of smug dismissal, and their profit of it is that they know how to curse with it and to curse those things that we ourselves have most loved and, somewhere in our hearts, probably love still.

Good at School

Translation has been the order of the day for some time in the humanities, beginning with the relatively benign translations of the New Critics and moving on to the more and more strained recastings now current. The objective of humanistic study seems more and more to be the transformation of the best that has been known and thought into other, homogenizing languages, the languages of criticism, which we rarely take the time to interrogate or consider putting to use day to day.

When I entered graduate school in 1979 the reigning terms of translation were philosophical or, more accurately, antiphilosophical. These were the terms of deconstruction. When I was beginning at Yale, Paul de Man was working to propound a theory of antimeaning that he believed would have application to all of literature. From his point of view, writing that mattered culminated at points of undecidability. These are moments where two meanings come into play and it is impossible to make a determination as to which one supersedes the other. Undecidability is different from paradox, which is ultimately resolvable, and different too from oxymoron, in which the coupling of the terms reveals itself as an absurdity.

The end of Yeats's poem "Among School Children" asks us how we can know the dancer from the dance. The last four lines run this way:

> O chestnut-tree, great-rooted blossomer,
> Are you the leaf, the blossom or the bole?
> O body swayed to music, O brightening glance,
> How can we know the dancer from the dance?

To de Man, the final question is not resolvable. The poem at first seems to suggest that there is nothing so glorious as the moment when the dancer and the dance, form and experience, creator and creation merge. Thus the final line can be read as a celebration of full being outside of time. It's an affirmation of artistic transcendence. Yet, read somewhat differently, the poem also suggests that this moment may be illusory. Maybe we ought to take the last line literally rather than figuratively and try to figure out how we might actually achieve a skeptical detachment.

Please instruct me: how *can* I separate the dancer from the dance? Perhaps the feeling of timelessness and interfusion is a delusory one that needs combating; perhaps it is conducive to feelings of omnipotence, to godlike illusions. It is desirable to know the dancer from the dance, for such knowledge might free us from mystification. Yet study the poem as one might, it does not affirm one reading at the expense of the other. So we are suspended between assurances, committed neither to one side nor the other.

De Man's larger argument is that literature perpetually yields these moments of unreadability. And herein lies the clinching point: this is what makes literature a particularly distinguished and enlightening form of discourse. Writes de Man, "A literary text simultaneously asserts and denies the authority of its own rhetorical mode." That capacity simultaneously to affirm and to deny is, according to de Man, really all that literature yields that is of consequence. People, human beings who in other regards were not noticeably brain befuddled, took this notion seriously.

It is reasonable to be attuned to such moments, to be sure (and I think Yeats does offer one here and that de Man explicates it shrewdly); and it can be illuminating to ponder them. This de Manian moment is not unrelated to Buddhist accounts of self-annulment, the achievement of egolessness through meditation. But Buddhists reflect constantly on the reasons for such a quest and on what might be achieved by a human being once the ego is annulled. In de Man, there is no such reflection on ends. His findings, such as they stand, are never put to existential work.

De Manian suspension between alternatives may be a good place to begin, or to rebegin, serious literary inquiry. But to imagine that such doubt is all that literature yields, or the best that literature yields, that all those marvelous books, marvelous vision, can be reduced to a moment that balances on the head of a pin, well, as Huck Finn put it, that's too many for me.

But de Man need not be singled out here. Rather, virtually every critic or school of criticism that matters has worked to reduce literary experience, vast and varied as it is, into a set of simple terms. They've turned contingent literature into delimiting philosophy (or, one might say, "metaphysics"), which says that there is one mode of happiness, one kind of good, one form of ideal life for everyone.

Salient in the process of transforming literary variety into philosophical uniformity has been psychoanalysis. For psychoanalysis lets the critic become a temporary therapist, diving into the inner life of the work, finding its hidden chambers, telling a story about the work and the author that the author could not herself tell. Now the power of the critic grows exponentially, as he configures himself as the wise analyst and the author as the patient, on the scene for needful therapy. Whatever the benefits of psychoanalysis to living patients who elect to become part of the process—and I think that they can be real—there is nevertheless little indication that psycho-literary analysis does anything for the patient. It does, however, enrich the analyst with no little power.

Why did these approaches, these forms of translation, catch on? For many reasons, not insignificant among them the teacher's will to power over the texts that she teaches. But these translating approaches work in part because they're good at school. They give the teacher something coherent to teach. They give the students a portable knowledge, something to take away from the scene. And they give them an illusion of potency over works far more potent than they. Current literary analysis allows students to take up the stance of cool complacency that they, and all of us, have become accustomed to from living in a spectatorial culture. The knowing literary-critical stance may be more difficult to achieve than the TV watcher's accustomed disdain, but the two positions are not unrelated. In both, one assumes an unearned and potentially debilitating superiority. We will not have real humanistic education in America until professors, and their students, can give up the narcissistic illusion that through something called theory, or criticism, they can stand above Milton, Shakespeare, and Dante.

If the latter-day Dionysus is the god of humanities entertainment, the new Apollo is the god of humanities analysis, the one who confers power and skills on his devotees. When you hear a literary critic repeating terms over and over, whether they be "ideology" and "class struggle," or "repression" and "neurosis," or "patriarchy" and "oppression," you know that you are in the hands of a writer who is devoted to the soft institutional usurpation of literary power, the better to create other, less varied kinds of writing—and fewer vital options.

Practitioners of all disciplines must promise something, implicitly or overtly. They tell their students that eventually they will possess a certain sort of knowledge. To thrive in a university, a department must promise some kind of desirable prowess, whether it be understanding of the physical world, knowledge of history's laws, or, in this case, a capacity to analyze and describe works of art as though they were species of fauna. We have made literary study fit in, be good at school. But true humanistic study is not geared to generalized, portable truths; it is geared to human transformation. And that is something that catalogues cannot describe and to which the writing of detached literary critical essays is more or less irrelevant.

Works that matter work differently. Such works, in history, philosophy, psychology, religious studies, and literature, can do many things, but preeminent among them is their capacity to offer truth. So far we've left the quest of truth to Falwell and to faith. We, the supposed heirs of Socrates, have fled from our authentic vocations. Perhaps it is time again to confront the Sphinx, who now, as always, poses the riddle of life: What use will you make of the world? (And what use might it make of you?) How do you intend to live? It is time, perhaps, to help our students look into the Sphinx's eye (and to look there ourselves); time to see what we see.

Truth

Literature and truth? The humanities and truth? Come now. What could be more ridiculous? What could be more superannuated than that?

We read literature now for other reasons. We read to assert ourselves, to sharpen our analytical faculties. We read to debunk the myths. We read to know the other. We read, sometimes, for diversion. But read for truth? Absurd. The whole notion of truth was dispatched long ago, tossed on the junk heap of history along with God and destiny and right and all the rest. Read for truth? Why do that?

For the simple reason that for many people, the truth—the circle, the vision of experience—that they've encountered through socialization is inadequate. It doesn't put them into a satisfying relation to experience. That truth does not give them what they want. It does not help them make a contribution to their society. It does not, to advance another step, even allow for a clear sense of the tensions between themselves and the existing social norms, the prevailing doxa. The gay boy can't accept the idea that his every third thought is a sin. The visionary-in-the-making isn't at home with her practical, earth-bound, and ambitious parents. Such people, and I believe most people who go to literature and the liberal arts out of more than mere curiosity are in this group, demand other, better ways to apprehend the world—that is, ways that are better *for them*. And the best repository for those other ways are the works of the poets, as Williams said, and of the painters and composers and novelists and historians. Here one may hope for a second chance, a way to begin the game again, getting it closer to right this time around.

But how do we find this truth? How do we begin to extract it from literature? Well, to begin with, we must read and interpret the work.

Here arises a problem. We all know that there is no such thing as a perfect interpretation. In fact, some of the more sophisticated among us have come to believe that interpretation is by necessity interminable. It's a mark of shallowness to believe that we can get to the core of the poem. Do I dare? Do I dare? So says the Prufrock of contemporary academia.

What I take to be worthwhile interpretation is centered on the author. I do not join my colleague E. D. Hirsch in affirming that the author's intention ought to be the measure of the reading at hand. We can never discover as much. There are simply too many levels of the mind that contribute to creation, not all of them responsive to analysis.

No, the art of interpretation is to me the art of arriving at a version of the work that the author—as we imagine him, as we imagine her—would approve and be gratified by. The idea is not perfectly to reproduce the intention; that can never be done. Rather, the objective is to bring the past into the present and to do so in a way that will make the writer's ghost nod in something like approval. That means operating with the author's terms, thinking, insofar as it is possible, the writer's thoughts, reclaiming his world through his language. In preparing to write *Fearful Symmetry*, Northrop Frye did all he could to merge with William Blake, to relive and in so doing to re-create his vision. And he did it with grand success.

The teacher's act of inspired ventriloquism need not be perfect. All that he needs to do is to supply a vision, based on the work at hand, that is as ramified as possible and that offers a fertile alternative to what the students in class are likely to believe, or are likely to believe that they believe.

But that's impossible, one might say. You can never satisfyingly reproduce an author's vision, or even come close. On the contrary, we do this sort of thing all the time. We describe books and films to each other. We use all the resources we can gather in order to explain one friend to another. We recount situations of almost unbearable complexity—the details of a long illness, the dynamics of a divorce—in hopes of using our accounts to move forward, to make the best of life, or what of life remains. Our powers of description, which need not stop at paraphrase, are often put to the test. They are among the most humanly necessary powers we possess. Who should be in a better position to deploy such powers than the professor who has been preparing for virtually all her life to do just that?

If this process of inspired re-rendering is impossible, why then do we freely apply various theories to texts? Shouldn't the impossibility of adequately apprehending *them* also offend our sense of just complexity? If we can theorize about reading, we can also evoke the experience of reading per se. All of the punctilious rhetoric about the impossibility of rendering literature, of making contact with it and adding another voice to the author's voice, illuminating what may be dark, making explicit what is implicit, all of this resistance may be nothing more than the timidity that stops us from turning a liberal arts education from a field for mind-sharpening exercises, into what Keats called a "vale of Soul-making."

The punctilious want perfect interpretation. They want to score 100, as they have on all tests all of their lives. But what presses us is too important to wait for perfection. What faces us is the prospect of a world where religious meaning withdraws and people are left in the midst of soul-destroying emptiness, hopping and blinking and taking their little poison for the day and their little poison for the night.

A comparison with truth as it is apprehended in religion can be illuminating. As the scholar Karen Armstrong observes, "Modern New Testament scholarship has shown that we know far less about the historical Jesus than we thought we did. 'Gospel truth' is not as watertight as we assumed. But this has not prevented millions of people from modeling their lives on Jesus and seeing his path of compassion and suffering as leading to a new kind of life. Jesus certainly existed, but his story has been presented in the Gospels as a paradigm."

The Gospels do not capture Jesus perfectly; the readers of the Gospels presumably do not capture their essence to perfection, should such perfection exist. But that has not stopped many people from having their lives changed—and to their perception, changed for the better—through encounter with Jesus and his much-mediated word.

The test of an interpretation is not whether it is right or perfect, but whether it leads us to a worldview that is potentially better than what we currently hold. The gold standard is not epistemological perfection. The gold standard is the standard of use.

Wordsworth's Truth

What does it mean to ask of a poem if it is true? What are we taking a poem—or any work of human intellect and imagination—to be, if it is potentially a source of truth? Why don't we follow Kant, and all the ideal-ists before and after him, in seeing art as purely disinterested? Why are we unable to concur with Sir Philip Sidney in his oft-cited view that the poet "nothing affirms and therefore never lieth"? Why not artistic purity? Why not art as purposiveness without any specific purpose?

What I am asking when I ask of a major work (for only major works will sustain this question) whether it is true is quite simply this: Can you live it? Can you put it into action? Can you speak—or adapt—the language of this work, use it to talk to both yourself and others so as to live better? Is this work desirable as a source of belief? Or at the very least, can it influence your existing beliefs in consequential ways? Can it make a difference?

Let us say that the work at hand is Wordsworth's "Lines Composed a Few Miles Above Tintern Abbey On Revisiting the Banks of the Wye During a Tour. July 13, 1798." The poem—it is anything but accidental—takes place not far away from a ruined abbey. In the midst of the ruins of religion—or the ruins of *conventional* religious prospects for him—Wordsworth finds himself forced to compound a new faith. This faith will not be based on preexisting scripture; it will not be a faith received from others. Wordsworth, spurred on by his return to a scene that was at the center of his childhood, will gather to himself those memories that give him the power to go on living and go on writing.

The world as Wordsworth has lately experienced it is stale, flat, and profitless. He lives in a din-filled city, among unfeeling people—and, worse yet, he senses that he is becoming one of them. He thinks of himself as abiding "In darkness and amid the many shapes / Of joyless daylight." Time upon time, he says, "the fretful stir / Unprofitable, and the fever of the world, / Have hung upon the beatings of my heart." There is a dull ache settling into his spirit, one that the eighteenth century would have called melancholy and we would now call depression. But rather than relying on religious consolation, as Dr. Johnson tried to do when he battled his own terrible despondency, or on drugs, as Wordsworth's dear friend Samuel Taylor Coleridge did, Wordsworth relies on himself. Laudanum, predecessor of today's antidepressant drugs, the serotonin reuptake inhibitors, and Coleridge's preferred source of solace, is not what's wanted. The poet will find consolation in himself or not at all.

And why should he not be disconsolate? For how can one bear life in its manifold sorrows, with all of its horrible sufferings, the sufferings of children and the innocent preeminent among them (think of the horrors unfolding in the world as you read this page, as I write it) and not go mad? Virtually all of us are bound to suffer as well—"pain of heart, distress, and poverty," if not of one sort then of another, to use Wordsworth's phrasing from "Resolution and Independence." But what seems to trouble Wordsworth most is that amidst this commonality of suffering, we still treat one another with rank callousness, with "greetings where no kindness is," "rash judgments," "sneers." Without the figure of a loving (or at least a just) God presiding over the world, ready at some point to dispense rewards to the worthy, and punishment or correction to the erring, it is no easy matter to find a reason not to despair. Where is Wordsworth, who seems devoid of religious faith (pious Coleridge always feared for Wordsworth's soul) to find any reason to continue on?

Wordsworth's answer is that there is a part of himself that is free from the fallen society in which he's immersed. It is a part that lives on deep in him, although covered over by custom, convention, and fear. And in this region of half-remembered being he finds hope, or, as he puts it, "life and food / for future years."

He remembers himself as a child free in nature, with a spirit that belongs to nothing but the gorgeous, frightening natural world and has not been colonized by the city and its dispiriting ways. He thinks of the time "when first / I came among these hills; when like a roe / I bounded o'er the mountains, by the sides / Of the deep rivers, and the lonely streams, / Wherever nature led." In memories of that free self, Wordsworth finds an authentic pleasure, a vision of life lived without the anxieties that attend on awareness of death. The child in Wordsworth is free of that mortal fear; he senses that he will return painlessly to the natural world that brought him forth and gave him his vital, unambiguous force.

There is something in the poet that was there before civilization left its imprint. That something is free and it makes Wordsworth freer, however temporarily. In the last phase of the poem, he worries, edging again toward gloom, about whether in time the freedom will be foreclosed. He is becoming aware, in other words, of the merely transitory power that Emerson associated with even the most impressive human expansions. In time, they can "solidify and hem in the life." Maybe this contact with nature existing inside of him won't serve Wordsworth as an antidote all his life through.

Some critics like to look at this poem as a major moment in "the Romantic invention of childhood." But that is too ironic and distancing a notion. For the poem asks us to look into our own childhoods and into the lives of the children around us, and to see if they might not have something to teach us. May they show us how to live in a less guarded, more joyous and exuberant way? Could they teach us how, for a while, to stanch our fears of the future, and live in the present moment in nature? ("We are blessed always if we live in the present," says the American Wordsworthian, Thoreau.)

And what about this nature? The poem asks us to look around at nature as it exists in our moment, and to consider what sort of restoration is to be found there. It suggests that in nature is the perpetuation of human vitality, that between civilization and nature there is a dialectic, and that letting one element in the tension grow too mighty, as Wordsworth's eighteenth-century forebears seem to the poet to have done, can be killing. This poem has legitimate connections to the best current ecology movements. The work can add to—or create—the conviction that in the love of wilderness and its preservation, there lies hope for humanity.

In "Tintern Abbey," one also encounters the bracing hypothesis that depression or melancholia or what-have-you is a great force, to be sure, but that it is a force we may combat through individual resourcefulness and faith. Maybe the answer to one's despondency does not lie in nature or memory or childhood per se, but Wordsworth's poem enjoins us to feel that it lies somewhere within our own reach. The site of our sufferings, what J. H. Van den Berg called the overfilled inner self, may also be the source of our cure. We are creatures who have the capacity to make ourselves sick, collectively and individually, but we often have the power to heal ourselves as well.

All these things, and many more besides, readers may draw from "Tintern Abbey." They may say, "Yes, of course, I've always thought so, but never quite had the words to say as much." Or "All right, I'll try Wordsworth's cure, or something like it. It could very well work." Others will be put off by this particular vision. Perhaps they'll find it too self-absorbed. Where are the others? What is Wordsworth to give to the poor? What is Wordsworth's role in the larger human hope for liberation or freedom from want? These are valuable questions. And if the answers—and there are answers—do not satisfy the individual reader, then he will legitimately look for another place to put his allegiances, another circle to expand into. Or perhaps he will stay with some enhanced confidence in his own.

But asking critical questions should not devolve into a mere parlor game. That is, we should not teach our students that the aim of every reading is to bring up the questions that might debunk the wisdom at hand, then leave it at that. We must ask the question of belief. Is this poem true? Can *you* use this poem? Or are you living in a way that's better than the poem suggests you might live? To these queries, we should expect only heartfelt answers.

By refusing to ask such questions once we have coaxed the work's vision forward, we are leaving our students where we found them. And if we leave them in the grasp of current social dogma, we are probably leaving them in the world of the normal nihilist; we are leaving them to the ideology of the consumer university, center of training and enter-taining, in its worst manifestations. We may turn "Tintern Abbey" into a species of diversion, or we may turn it into an occasion for acquiring analytical techniques, but in doing so we are mistaken. For there is a deep force in the poem that we can put to saving uses in the present.

We ask often what we think of great works. What, we might also ask, would the creators of those works think of us? What would the Word-sworth of "Tintern Abbey," replete with drawbacks though that poem may seem to some, think of our posturing analytics?

But, one might say, all I have produced here is a reading, itself a trans-lation of Wordsworth, no different from the application of, say, Foucault's terms to Wordsworth's poem. Isn't that right?

I don't think so.

Granted, my account of Wordsworth would not match the poet's own, word for word. Granted, there are points at which, brought to life to listen, the poet might part company with the description at hand (or with the more expansive account of the work that I would offer in a classroom). But I have tried to be true to the poem. I have attempted, acting something like its advocate before the court of readers' opinion, to make the best possible case for its application to life. And as a teacher I have done so, in fact I must do so, as though I believed in the poet's every word.

The fact is that I do not. I may want, in time, to register my quarrels with this vision of experience, and I may want to offer the criticisms of others. But before those criticisms arrive, the poem needs to have its moment of maximum advocacy; it requires, and by its power it has earned, a display of full faith. And the testament to that faith takes place in a language integrally related to the language of Wordsworth. The teacher speaks of nature and childhood and memory. And that is a much different thing from speaking of discipline and norms and discourses, as Foucault might do in the face of this work. There is a difference between evocative description and what Eagleton and Macherey call rewriting. Both reimagine the work. Both bring the past into the present. But the difference in approach is so great as to constitute not a difference in degree, but a difference in kind. One is re-presentation, one translation.

The activity I have in mind is in some regards anticipated by Nietzsche's precursor in philosophy, Arthur Schopenhauer. "What is life?" That, to Schopenhauer, is the question at the core of all consequential art works. Schopenhauer believes that "every genuine and successful work of art answers this question in its own way with perfect correctness." The reader's task is to bring the works' wisdom to the fore: "The works of the poets, sculptors, and representative artists in general contain an unacknowledged treasure of profound wisdom . . . Everyone who reads the poem or looks at the picture must certainly contribute out of his own means to bring that wisdom to light; accordingly he comprehends only so much of it as his capacity and culture admit of; as in the deep sea each sailor only lets down the lead as far as the length of the line will allow." For Schopenhauer, however, the artists reveal one major truth and one only, that of the Life Will in its sublime potency. To us now, literature, and the arts in general, reveal truths that are multiple. Every artist that matters gives us a world of words that we may translate into a world of acts. Poets, to modify Shelley a little, are the too often unacknowledged legislators of the word.

Professional literary critics shy away from the process I have been describing, in part because they fear they can never get the poem exactly right, never render it into the present in a way that would satisfy some abstract standard of perfection. But perfection is not at issue here. What we really need to do is to use Wordsworth as the basis for constructing and conveying a Final Narrative, a way of seeing and saying things, which is potentially better than what our students or readers possess. Your visions being true to every moment in the poem is less important than that you offer live options to those around you. The chances are that as a teacher, you will need a Wordsworth to offer such vital options—you will need a visionary's help. You and I will not be able to do so on our own. And so the vision will be much more Wordsworth's than ours. But the key is to offer our students something potentially better than what they have, and to see if it resonates with their own best aspirations.

Identification

The questions I pose about "Tintern Abbey" and about virtually every other work of art are inseparable from the matter of identification. That is, I ask students to perform a thought experiment. I ask them to use their powers of empathy and imagination to unite with another being. In the case of "Tintern Abbey," the being is the poet, but I have no qualms about asking readers to identify themselves with characters in novels, with Pip in *Great Expectations*, with Isabel Archer in *The Portrait of a Lady*, with Rastignac in *Old Goriot*, with Emma in Jane Austen's novel. I often ask them to find themselves, or to discover what is unknown in themselves, among the great characters in literature as well as within the imaginations that bring those characters to life.

Discussing James's *Portrait of a Lady*, I begin with a simple question. Does James love Isabel Archer?

Almost all of my students do. They find her vital, benevolent, charming, a full embodiment of what is best about America. They're drawn to her verve and her courage, particularly at the start of the book when she is young and on her own and, with an American insouciance, refusing offers of marriage from one Old World potentate after the next. They love Isabel, often, because in her they see their own best selves. They identify with all that is freshest and most promising in her.

Almost as a reflex my students tend to take the next step: James must love his heroine, too. They all love Isabel, after all, and in loving Isabel love some part of themselves. Surely James concurs.

But then we begin to read the novel—that is, to interpret it—and some surprising things happen. James's disdain for his heroine, which is not unalloyed with considerable affection, is there on the page nearly from the start. In lengthy, authoritative, and summary accounts he attacks her with the greatest force. It's clear that he detests what he takes to be her shallowness, her glib self-confidence, her habit of thinking far too highly of herself. James writes that Isabel "had no talent for expression and too little of the consciousness of genius; she only had a general idea that people were right when they treated her as if she were rather superior." And later in the same passage: "Her thoughts were a tangle of vague outlines . . . In matters of opinion she had had her own way, and it had led her into a thousand ridiculous zigzags. At moments she discovered she was grotesquely wrong, and then she treated herself to a week of passionate humility. After this she held her head higher than ever again; for it was of no use, she had an unquenchable desire to think well of herself." James can admire Isabel, too; he is far too fine a novelist to give us a simple portrait. But his dislike for her American egotism at many points reaches contempt.

In a sense, Isabel's horrid fate, marriage to the disgusting, fortune-seeking Gilbert Osmond, is James's punishment for her. In terms of novelistic probability, the marriage seems rather forced. What we see of the courtship falls far short of persuading us that Isabel would actually give in and marry Osmond. But a purgative marriage—a punishment— is what Isabel needs, so the master of realistic fiction bends plausibility and brings it to pass. Isabel's small-time hubris, the vanity of provincial America, summons Gilbert Osmond and the almost equally appalling Madame Merle to deliver to Isabel the chastening that, as I believe James sees it, she so deserves. Brash Isabel early in the book announces that she might rather go without clothes than be defined by them. By the end, James has her dressed in so many layers of drapery that the four-piece suit Woolf said T. S. Eliot favored looks liberating by contrast. And then James is content, for Isabel has been chastened. She has learned to submit. She has learned to surrender her American wildness in the interest of something else, something more European and refined and more modestly fitted to an awareness of human limits. Then James does admire her—her submission to fate is rather awful and rather touching. One recalls the sufferings that the Marquis de Sade visits on the unworldly, Rousseauian Justine, whose naive sense of human nature the Divine Marquis despises. It may not be going too far to say that in *Portrait* James is our Marquis, and Isabel is the one whose virtue finds its reward. What James detests in this novel and chastens with purgatorial zeal is the American wildness to be found in Emerson, in Whitman (whom James notoriously poked fun at), and in Emily Dickinson. That the spark should be alive in a woman is probably all the more frightening to James.

The first time I discussed this book in class I was surprised by the result. Most of the students were outraged that, on reasonably close examination, it was clear that James's sentiments about the young Isabel were, to put it kindly, critical. What made this perception particularly difficult is that those harsh Jamesian sentiments had now to be seen as in some measure about them, about their own possible naïveté, about their own unthinking self-love—that is, about the aspect of themselves that they had discovered in Isabel. Many declared themselves anti-Jamesian. "Henry James must be one of the cruelest authors ever to write," one essay began. They saw James, I believe accurately, as the enemy of a certain kind of American spirit—though by no means an unambivalent enemy.

But a few of the students felt differently. What they came to believe was that Isabel needed to be chastened. She deserved it. She had found her apt fate as surely as a protagonist in a Greek tragedy finds his. Osmond was exactly what she needed and exactly what she deserved so as to "suffer into truth," to use a Sophoclean formulation. Two of the students were candid enough, and brave enough, to say that, in fact, they felt that the harsh discipline that James was applying to Isabel ought well to be applied to them. They were like Isabel Archer in her earliest manifestation, and like her needed submission to purgatorial cleansing. As the book burned away what was most noxiously self-assertive in Isabel, so they hoped that it might do the same for them. Or at least it might begin the process. Such puritanical resolve on the part of early twenty-first-century American students struck me as both a little frightening and quite moving.

As someone who far prefers Emerson to James, indeed who prefers the young Isabel to James, as a temperament, I was temporarily saddened that people so young could be drawn to puritanical self-dislike. But I soon saw that my response was neither here nor there. It didn't much matter. I had done my job, which was to put students in a position to read and then to be read by the work at hand. Everyone who sat through that class was in a position to know himself better by virtue of the exchange. In this discussion, the process of "identification," of seeing oneself in a literary character, was essential.

Few activities associated with literary study are in worse repute than identification. Teachers in middle school—grades six to eight—by now caution against it, seeing it as a block to serious study. Surely it has no place in a college classroom. Surely no professor should endorse it publicly.

Sometimes what worries teachers about identification is the belief that it's inseparable from wish-fulfillment. You become one with a heroic figure and leave your small, timid self behind. What you have then is a mere daydream. I find both wish-fulfilling fantasies, as literature provides them, and daydreaming to be precious human activities, for reasons that I'll later explain. But the process of identification that went on with Isabel—by young men and by women both—was not a matter of wish-fulfillment. On the contrary, in the identification process any simple narcissism underwent serious challenge by James. This is so because in studying James, as in studying any consequential writer, the step that follows identification is analysis of a firm but generous sort.

Still there's something about the process that can make the professional critic squirm. Perhaps it's the release of emotion that's involved, the fact that when we work with identification we don't sound like scientists who command a rigorous discipline. Perhaps we don't sound official or academic enough. Maybe we're worried about our authority. But as inspired religious teachers and artists of every stripe demonstrate all the time, the process of human growth—when it entails growth of the heart as well as of the mind—is never particularly clean or abstract. To grow it is necessary that all of our human qualities come into play, and if some of those qualities are not pretty, then so be it. But to keep them to the side so as to preserve our professional dignity—that is too much of a sacrifice. (Men and women die every day, perish in the inner life . . . for lack of what we have to offer.)

In general, academic literary study over the past two decades has become ever colder and more abstract. But there is one area of exception. Many feminist teachers have been willing to deal with emotion and the facts of daily life in their classrooms. Against prevailing orthodoxies, these professors have insisted on speaking personally, and have made sure that their students have had a chance to do so. Some feminists, it's true, have surrendered to pressure for high-toned theoretical respectability, but many have stuck to their guns and talked intimately and immediately about experience. It's in classrooms of this sort that students can at times connect the books they read to their own lives. Something similar can be true in classes on race, at least when students can talk candidly. (For a variety of complex reasons, though, they almost never can be direct and honest on this subject, even with the best-intentioned professors presiding.) But such classrooms are, alas, just about the only places where bringing together word and world is still the objective.

Milan Kundera speaks about novels as being populated by "experimental selves." These selves are persons whom we might be or become, or who signify aspects of the self. The novelist—with our assistance—sends them forth into the world, to see what the world will make of them, and they of it. They are the fictive human embodiments of what Nietzsche would call thought experiments. These selves are not after a long-lasting truth. Rather, they engage in an inquiry; they try, in good Emersonian fashion, to expand their particular orbits on the deep, sometimes successfully, sometimes not. Dickens's Pip needs to surrender his great expectations and expand into a life of humane, well-measured decency; Austen's Emma needs to see that the world has more living and feeling beings in it than herself and those few she holds in high regard. But part of what those characters learn is that no way of seeing things is final. They don't look, and cannot look, for a final resting place sanctioned by a larger authority than themselves. As Kundera puts it, "The world of one single Truth and the relative, ambiguous world of the novel are molded of entirely different substances. Totalitarian Truth excludes relativity, doubt, questioning; it can never accommodate what I would call the *spirit of the novel*."

The rise of the novel coincides with a realization expressed, or perhaps created, by the development of democracy. That realization is of the great span of individuals to be found in the world, of the sheer proliferation of divergent beings. The commonplace that we each have a novel within us actually touches a consequential truth. It suggests that there are as many mysteries, as many ways of being, as there are lives. Whitman asserts this idea by being a deeply inward lyric poet who also recognizes the divergence of human lives around him—the balance he strikes between the intensity of the personal lyric and the breadth of the novel is part of what makes him a major figure, and one who speaks to the movement of his times. I think that a humanistic education begins in literature because, unlike philosophy, literature does not assume that one or two or five paths are enough to offer human beings. There are too many of us, and we are all too different; we all have our open-ended truths to pursue.

Gender and Identification

As I mentioned, some of the students who identified themselves with Isabel Archer were male. They did not read as men. Rather they read as human beings, finding in Isabel some of their own griefs and hopes. More and more I see this happening.

I frequently teach the *Iliad*, generally derided as the most outmoded of books, something to be tossed onto the junk heap of history. When

I was teaching as a graduate student at Yale, the book was chiefly considered as an opportunity to reflect on the way that women were regarded in the Homeric period, and then to reflect on how much had changed or was changing.

Is the *Iliad* a book replete with vital possibilities, or is it a mere historical curiosity? Is it locked in the past, or a potent guide to the present and the future? A number of my students—men and women both—initially thought that it was a period piece and nothing more. The way the poem treated women disgusted them. In the *Iliad*, they said, a woman has the status of a few bullocks or a bronze tripod or two. True. Some, like Helen, are beautiful, and that beauty is a sort of power, but it is a limited, debased power compared to what the men wield. This is all well worth saying, well worth pointing out.

What the men have is the heroic life, with all its possibilities for glory. As C. M. Bowra describes it: "The essence of the heroic outlook is the pursuit of honour through action. The great man is he who, being endowed with superior qualities of body and mind, uses them to the utmost and wins the applause of his fellows because he spares no effort and shirks no risk in his desire to make the most of his gifts and to surpass other men in his exercise of them. His honour is the centre of his being, and any affront to it calls for immediate amends. He courts danger gladly because it gives him the best opportunity of showing of what stuff he is made. Such a conviction and its system of behaviour are built on a man's conception of himself and of what he owes to it, and if it has any further sanctions, they are to be found in what other men like himself think of him. By prowess and renown he gains an enlarged sense of personality and well-being; through them he has a second existence on the lips of men, which assures him that he has not failed in what matters most. Fame is the reward of honour, and the hero seeks it before everything else."

The class was about ready to concur that such a worldview was a thing of the past, or should best be, when one of the women students, usually quiet, spoke up. She said that the poem mattered to her because she could see things from Achilles' point of view. The moment that caught her attention first was the one in which Achilles' father tells him that he must be the best in every undertaking. He can simply never accept the second place. "I'm an athlete," she said, "and that's how I was raised by my parents and my coaches. I was told that I had to win at everything. I had to come in first all the time. After a while, though, I had to stop living like that. It's too much."

"Have you ever wanted to go back to it?" someone asked.

"Yes," she said, "all the time. It makes life incredibly intense." By which she meant, I suppose, that such a life provides ongoing energy; it allows for full, unambivalent human exertion, in the midst of a culture that often encourages self-dividing responses. If Wordsworth's meditative return to childhood is one viable answer to melancholia, then surely unbridled competitiveness is another. Competition can be a way to give what's vital in you more life. You could see that what had once been closed off and left behind for this student began to open again. The life of competition, the *agon*, is not for everyone, and it will not be approved by all. But if it is your highest aspiration, the thing you most want, then, whether you take the path or not, it is worth knowing about your attraction to it. Homer's heroic life is the life of *thymos*, the thirst for glory, and if you are, at whatever depths, an individual driven by *thymos*, by the desire for glory and praise, despite the moral censors you've thrown up against that drive, you need to deal with the fact in one way or another. I know no better way to begin doing so than through Homer.

Another classroom scene can help to illustrate the kind of teaching I want to endorse. A student in the same class, a young African-American woman, professes in her opening essay on the good life to be an ardent Christian. She believes in doing unto others as you would have them do unto you, in turning the other cheek. She believes Jesus to be the most perfect of mortals. But she reads the *Iliad* and, after a period of indifference, she's galvanized by it. What sweeps her in is a life where triumph matters above all else. She is fascinated by the fact that the warriors in the poem always seek victory. Envy is not a vice to them; it goads them to glories. The young woman, who, it comes out, wants to be a well-to-do corporate lawyer, has no trouble seeing some of herself in the unapologetic ambitions of Homer's heroes.

But then, too, she wants to be a Christian? Jesus' originality lies partly in his attempt to supersede admiration for the ambition and self-vaunting of Homer's heroes—an admiration very much alive in the Roman empire Jesus is born into. Which will it be, my student needs to ask herself, Jesus or Achilles?

Of course, what she really needs is a live synthesis of the two. And it is her task to arrive at it. But without the encounter with Homer, and without our raising the simple and supposedly elementary question of identification—Is there anything in you that is Achillean?—she might not have had access to her own divided state. With such self-knowledge achieved, she is in a position for productive change. This was an instance not only of reading and interpreting a book—we spent a long time coming to understand the heroic code and considering Homer's highly equivocal attitude toward it—but of allowing the book to interpret and read the reader.

Some teachers say that we must teach books like the *Iliad* because they show us a world so different from our own that it presses the values of this, our world, into sharp contrast. On the contrary, I teach the *Iliad* because in many significant ways, Homer's world is ours, though we are not always able to see as much immediately. In a passing remark about Homer, Nietzsche observes that part of what makes his world hard to assimilate for moderns is that to Homer's heroes, jealousy is not a negative emotion, not a feeling to be suppressed. Rather, one's desire for the first place is proudly announced. One revels in the hunger for dominance. In a culture where pagan values contend with Christian values—that is to say, in our culture—often the Christian aspirations to modesty and grace serve to cover over lust for glory and other kindred drives. Reading Homer can peel the cover back and allow us to see ourselves as we are. This great book—among the greatest and the most disturbing in the Western tradition—is anything but a period piece. Rather, it is a book that lives very much in the present. It is news that stays news, to cite Ezra Pound's still valuable, still newsworthy description of what makes literature literature.

Yet exactly how far is one to go in expanding literary meanings to make them apt for the present and future? It's unlikely that Homer ever imagined a pervasive cult of the warrior, however sublimated, that would be comprehensively open to women. By what right do I, or my students, enlarge his sense to fit our needs? I think that, having established the author's vision, insofar as it's possible, and having been as true to him as, say, Bowra seems to me to be true to an aspect of Homer, we are free to enlarge the work, always being aware of what it is we do. The test of the reading that leaves the provinces of the author's vision is use. What can we do with this work? What aspects of our lives does it illuminate? What action does it enjoin? We test the work, then, against the template of experience, as my students did. They wondered what would happen to them if they brought Homer's vision to life here and now. The ultimate test of a book, or of an interpretation, is the difference it would make in the conduct of life.

But Shakespeare?

Does the work contain live options? Does it offer paths one might take, modes of seeing and saying and doing that we can put into action in the world? How, in other words, does the vision at hand, the author's vision, intersect with—or combat—your own vision of experience, your own Final Narrative?

Do you want to second Wordsworth's natural religion? It's not a far-fetched question at a moment when many consider ecological issues to be the ultimate issues on the world's horizon. Is it true, what Wordsworth suggests in "Tintern Abbey" about the healing powers of Nature and memory? Can they fight off depression? Not an empty question in an age when antidepressant drugs have become unbearably common. Is Milton's Satan the shape that evil now most often takes—flamboyant, grand, and self-regarding? Or is Blake's Satan—a supreme administrator, mild, bureaucratic, efficient, and congenial, an early exemplar of Hannah Arendt's "banality of evil"—a better emblem? Or, to strike to the center of the tensions that often exist between secular and religious writing, who is the better guide to life: the Jesus of the Gospels, or the Prometheus of Percy Bysshe Shelley, who learned so much from Christ, but rejected so much as well—in particular Jesus' life of celibacy?

All right, one might say, but those are Romantic writers, polemicists, authors with a program. Even Henry James might be considered part of this tradition, albeit as an ambivalent anti-Romantic. What about other writers? What about, for instance, the famous poet of negative capability, who seems to affirm nothing, William Shakespeare? The most accomplished academic scholars of Shakespeare generally concur: they cannot tell what Shakespeare believed about *any* consequential issue. How can you employ Shakespeare in a way of teaching that seeks to answer Schopenhauer's question "What is life?" And if you can make nothing of Shakespeare, greatest of writers, then what value could this approach to literature, this democratic humanism as we might call it, possibly have?

If Sigmund Freud drew on any author for his vision of human nature—right or wrong as that vision may be—it was Shakespeare. The Oedipus complex, to cite just one instance of Freud's Shakespearean extractions, might just as well be called the Hamlet complex, as Harold Bloom has remarked. From Shakespeare, Freud might also have gathered or confirmed his theories of sibling rivalry; of the tragic antipathy between civilization and the drives; of bisexuality; of patriarchal presumption; of male jealousy; of all love as inevitably being the love of authority; of humor as an assault on the superego; and a dozen more psychoanalytical hypotheses. Shakespeare may not have affirmed these ideas out and out—he is not, it's true, a polemicist in the way that Blake is. But the question remains: Does Shakespeare/Freud work? Does their collaboration, if it is fair to call it that, illuminate experience, put one in a profitable relation to life, help you live rightly and enjoy your being in the world?

Readers of Freud's *Group Psychology and the Analysis of the Ego* will recall the daunting image of the leader Freud develops there. The leader, from Freud's point of view, is a primal father. In him the crowd places absolute trust, the trust of the child as it was aimed at his own father early on in life. Here is how Freud describes the primal and primary figure: "The members of the group were subject to ties just as we see them today, but the father of the primal horde was free. His intellectual acts were strong and independent even in isolation, and his will needed no reinforcement from others . . . He loved no one but himself, or other people only in so far as they served his needs. To objects his ego gave away no more than was barely necessary . . . Even to-day the members of a group stand in need of the illusion that they are equally and justly loved by their leader; but the leader himself need love no one else, he may be of a masterful nature, absolutely narcissistic, self-confident and independent."

In Shakespeare, whose work he read intensely from early on in life to the end, Freud could have seen precisely such a dynamic of leadership unfold. When we first encounter Prince Hal, later to become the mighty Henry V, he seems to be something rather different from the leader that Freud describes. He is mischievous, witty, and dissolute, and bosom friends with the prince of dissipation, Sir John Falstaff. In the three plays in which Hal appears, developing into King Henry V, we see a metamorphosis. However free-form he may be in the beginning, by the time he invades France in the last play of the trilogy, Hal has become as cold and self-contained as the figure Freud describes. Hal banishes Falstaff, who has taught him so much, and he hangs his old drinking buddy, Bardolph. By the end of the play, Hal, a little like Michael Corleone at the end of Francis Ford Coppola's masterpiece, *The Godfather Part II*, truly loves no one but himself. Despite some subdued ironies directed against the king in *Henry V*, the play suggests that, as humanly off-putting as the self-loving Hal may be, he is nonetheless a superbly effective monarch. For the people need such rulers. With kings who can also jest, who can take themselves lightly, if only at times, they can have nothing serious to do. Such figures do not command allegiance. Falstaffian figures cannot activate the fantasies of omnipotence that we all, Freud argues, attached to our fathers when we were children, and that we still nurse in the unconscious. Northrop Frye observes that men will die for a brutal autocrat, but not for a joking backslapper. Freud, and Shakespeare as well, can offer reasons why this might be so.

Freud believed that in reading the book of Shakespeare, he read the book of nature. Even if he did not draw his theory of the leader directly from Shakespeare's pages, he could at least have found it corroborated here. In fact, Freud's vision of the leader and Shakespeare's are barely distinguishable, except that Freud is rather disgusted by the human weakness the vision reveals, and Shakespeare seems to see Hal's sort of kingship as simply necessary.

From *Hamlet*, Freud draws much of the material he needed to formulate the Oedipus complex. He does so directly. But all through Freud there are instances of convergence with Shakespeare. What these instances indicate, at least to me, is that Freud effectively acts as a literary critic of Shakespeare. He takes the work at hand and draws a theory of human nature and of human social life from it. Freud has seen that Shakespeare poses the question "What is life?" and he has done his best to construe his answer.

And this, in fact, is what literary criticism ought to do. A valuable literary critic is not someone who debunks canonical figures, or who puts writers into their historical contexts, or, in general, one who propounds new and brilliant theories of interpretation. A valuable critic, rather, is one who brings forth the philosophy of life latent in major works of art and imagination. He makes the author's implicit wisdom explicit, and he offers that wisdom to the judgment of the world.

When he encounters works that are not wise but foolish, what he does, in general, is to leave them alone—he doesn't teach them, or write about them, or give them any more notice than they already have. The world is aflood with bad ideas and flawed visions: the true critic seeks and finds live options; he heralds forgotten news that is still new. He discovers the discoveries of art.

The truest example of literary criticism I know of is this one: one July day in 1855, Ralph Waldo Emerson, by far the preeminent man of letters in America, received by post a volume of poetry from an absolutely unknown carpenter living in Brooklyn, New York. The volume had been privately printed, since no commercial publisher would touch it. Its author sold it door to door; he also reviewed it himself, anonymously: "An American bard at last," one of the reviews began. Emerson, who in himself concentrated the prestige of all of our current literary Nobel Prize winners rolled into one, did not do what one might expect. He did not take the volume and toss it into the trash.

He took it into his home, read it, and immediately, with a shock of recognition, felt its genius. He called it the greatest piece of wit and wisdom that America had yet produced. He overwhelmed the unknown author with praise. He endorsed the book to everyone he knew.

Emerson himself had always hoped to matter preeminently as a poet. In his essay on the uses of poets and poetry, he described the kind of writer he thought America most needed and that he himself aspired to be, someone responsive to the variety, energy, and promise of the new nation: "Our logrolling, our stumps and their politics, our fisheries, our Negroes, and Indians, our boasts, and our repudiations, the wrath of rogues, and the pusillanimity of honest men, the northern trade, the southern planting, the western clearing, Oregon, and Texas, are yet unsung. Yet America is a poem in our eyes; its ample geography dazzles the imagination, and it will not wait long for metres." It was clear to Emerson that much as he wanted to fill that role, he never would. He was a poet of the inner self, not of teeming democracy. But when he saw someone else rise to the task, he didn't turn away with resentment, or offer measured, feline praise. When Walt Whitman sent Emerson the first volume of *Leaves of Grass*, Emerson forgot himself and embraced a new hero.

Hamlet

Poetry, Horace said, ought to give pleasure and instruct. And one need not look only to Freud to find instruction in the work of Shakespeare. There are other ways to go.

The Romantics took Hamlet as the representative contemporary individual, and their instinct was in many ways just. Hamlet stands between the Homeric figure that Bowra describes and the Christian ethos. He feels impelled by his father's ghost to take revenge and murder King Claudius. Hamlet the Elder is a figure steeped in the old heroic code. He would have looked to Achilles as an exemplar. When someone kills a member of your clan, you don't turn the other cheek, or even call on God to deliver just punishment. You strike, in as quick and deadly a way as you can.

Hamlet is responsive to this warrior code. Yet at the same time, he feels constrained by a Christian sense of right and wrong. *Thou shalt not kill. Thou shalt not take revenge.* Hamlet is a thinker, a deeply inward man with a Christian conscience. But along with that conscience he possesses the residue of a Homeric drive for ascendancy. He wants preeminence.

The tension between these two ways of life, Christian and Homeric, informs the language of the play, the language that Hamlet himself speaks. No interpretation of the play is complete without a careful study of the protagonist's idiom. But such responsiveness is only part of a full reaction to the play. At the beginning of his first solioquy, Hamlet makes his Christian commitment clear, calling out "God, God," and wishing that "the Everlasting had not fix'd / His canon 'gainst self-slaughter." Suicide can, of course, be a noble end in the classical world. In Christianity it is entirely forbidden.

Not much later, Hamlet moves from the idiom of Christianity to the idiom of classical antiquity. His dead father is "Hyperion," his usurping uncle a "satyr." Then his mother is weeping Niobe. He cries out against Gertrude for marrying his uncle—"my father's brother, but no more like my father / Than I to Hercules." In part, Hamlet wishes he could be Hercules, the better to rise to his father's revenge. But to his Christian conscience, Hercules is a throwback, a barbarian ideal.

Paul Cantor, the source of this Nietzschean reading of *Hamlet,* summarizes the situation: "In some ways, the figure of the ghost encapsulates the polarities Hamlet faces. As the ghost of his *father,* dressed in military garb and crying for revenge, it conjures up the world of epic warfare and heroic combat. But as the *ghost* of his father, rising out of what appears to be purgatory, it shatters the narrow bounds of the pagan imagination and opens a window on the eternal vistas of Christianity. In short, the ghost is at one and the same time a pagan and a Christian figure, and as such points to the heart of Hamlet's tragic dilemma as a modern Christian charged with the ancient pagan task of revenge."

Hamlet is caught between two worldviews, two circles or narratives— a state that may be the essential condition of tragedy. He is looking toward both Jesus and Achilles, two dutiful sons whose piety is in dramatic opposition, to see which way he needs to go.

The result is delay, irresolution. But, we must ask—and our students with us—is Hamlet's lot not sometimes ours, too? Many of the crises that give us the greatest pain and that are, in their effects on our day-to-day lives, potentially tragic, involve the collision of these two sets of values, Christian and pagan. Are we for or against capital punishment? Shall we follow the old classical code of honor or the modern code of mercy when a fellow citizen has been wronged? And abortion? Shall we do as the classical world did and, without excessive qualms, snuff out the newborn or unborn for our own advantage, or even our own convenience? Or shall we go the way of the Gospels and be, like Jesus, shepherds of souls? (Not some souls, but all of them.) Contemplating suicide, some of our contemporaries will also inevitably hear voices contending in a way that evokes Hamlet. To the classical world, as Shakespeare accurately dramatizes it in *Julius Caesar,* suicide can be an honorable end. It offers a dignified exit from a life that would otherwise end in shame. To the Christian mind, suicide is associated with acedia, or despair, the crime against the Holy Spirit, and the one unforgivable sin.

When these two worldviews, Christian and classical, enter conflict, it is unlikely that we will be able to find a satisfying compromise. Hegel believed that tragedy began when two highly desirable and mutually exclusive courses of action collided with each other. For Hegel, tragedy is two rights making a wrong. Two rights make a wrong for Hamlet, and often, I suspect, for us as well, as we confront prospects for action—revenge, suicide, abortion—that dramatically divide our spirits. Encounters of this sort will not offer satisfying resolutions. There is not likely to be any plan of action that can leave us fully at peace. And frequently, the result will be grief of tragic proportions.

Not every interpretation geared to discovering usable truths leads us to happiness. Not every such reading answers questions. Tragic awareness, which Shakespeare often bequeaths, can only reveal to us that certain griefs are not fully negotiable, cannot be readily converted into happiness or tranquillity. (Robert Frost thought that a central element of a literary education was learning to distinguish grief from grievances. Grievances may be remediable; griefs are to be suffered.) But perhaps in the foreknowledge of such sorrows there is some consolation; at least one will not be taken entirely by surprise.

Good Medicine?

Is the kind of literary education that I'm endorsing here a form of therapy? Yes and no. Yes, in that this kind of teaching, like Socrates', like Freud's, offers possibilities for change that are not only intellectual but also emotional. When we're talking about Final Narratives, we're talking about ultimate values, and strong feelings inevitably come out; tensions similar to the ones that proliferate in Freudian analysis can arise. (I sometimes preside over a raucous classroom.) But there is also a crucial difference. Patients come to psychoanalysis because they suffer from the past. Their obsessions, in some measure unconscious, with past events prevent their living with reasonable fullness in the present. The form of teaching that I espouse assumes a certain ability to live now (that is to say, a certain sanity) and so aims itself not primarily at unearthing the past, but at shaping the future. What will you be? What will you do?

There is a story about a psychoanalyst who, after the first day's intake interview, asked his patients an unexpected question. "If you were cured right now, if you were well, what would you do?" There would usually come forth a list. "I'd get married; I'd travel; I'd go back to school and study law." To which the therapist, trusting his instincts, sometimes replied, "Then why don't you go off and do those things?" Assuming that he posed that question at the right moment, to the right patient, then what the analyst had observed was that the analysand was not caught in the past, but was actually alive enough to the promise of futurity (healthy enough) to expand out of his existing sphere.

In a marvelous passage in his book on Freud, the philosopher Paul Ricoeur describes the moment when the Oedipus complex stops being a regressive trap for the individual and begins to be a sign of future promise, a provocation to do some fresh work in the world. This is the moment when the father is no longer the mystical foe, but an ambivalent ally whose own contributions to the world one can, however subtly, however strongly, revise. The person who stands on the edge, between regression and progress, past and future, is the one who has made herself ripe for literary education.

So the approach to teaching the humanities I am describing is not therapeutic per se. Nor, as I hope the discussion of Hamlet shows, is it to be written off as a way of dispensing elevating platitudes. It's not an exercise in cheering yourself up. Teachers should feel free to introduce the most appalling visions to their students. To read the Marquis de Sade, with his insistence that sexualized cruelty is the deepest desire of all men and women, is to encounter a way of apprehending life that can qualify as a vital option, if only to some. The objective of this kind of teaching is not to pretend that the Marquis does not exist, or that the disgustingly anti-Semitic Celine is not a writer worth serious study, or that Pound's fascism puts him out of bounds. Rather, it is to encounter such works and put them to the test of imagined experience. What would it be like to go Sade's way? What is to be gained and what lost in the life of the libertine?

It is not the professor's business to eradicate every form of what he takes to be retrograde and disgusting behavior. All student perspectives are welcome in class; whether they are racist, or homophobic, or whatever, they must be heard, considered, and responded to without panic. The classroom I am describing is a free space, one where people can speak their innermost thoughts and bring what is dark to light. They may expect to be challenged, but not to be shouted down, written off, or ostracized. Bitter, brutal thoughts can grow prolifically in the mind's unlighted cellars. But when we bring them into the world and examine them dispassionately, they often lose their force.

A few sessions into studying Orwell's *Nineteen Eighty-Four*, I asked a question that touched on the students' sense of self. "If you woke up tomorrow in Orwell's world, what path would you take? Would you try to blend in, as most people do? Or would you resist, in Winston Smith's way, defending truth as you perceived it, against all the surrounding lies? Or would you go Julia's route and live for pleasure in the midst of an insanely puritanical world?" (Julia, it's said, is a "rebel from the waist down.") The first answer I got shocked me. "I'd be O'Brien," a young woman said. O'Brien may be the most memorable character in the book: he's a gifted intellectual and high functionary of the inner party, who has become a horrible sadist. He takes a nearly sexual delight in reducing Smith from a resister to a cringing lump. "I'd try to put myself on the top, just like I try to now," Elizabeth went on. "And I think a lot of people here would do the same thing." As soon as Elizabeth said as much, we weren't having an ordinary conversation anymore, but a dialogue about the way we ought to live our lives.

A good classroom is a free-speech zone, where everything can be expressed, and where, at times, one will read authors who are not, in the teacher's opinion, conducive to a form of the good life, but are prophets of cruelty and hatred. We will explore their visions. We will bring to the fore the experimental selves they provide, and ask ourselves: what would it mean to live like that?

Most of the books we teach, especially to the young, will contain, implicitly or overtly, versions of the good life that we can endorse. But not all. We will, I hope, have faith that, given fair hearing, those imaginative voices that lead to health, generosity, energy, humor, and compassion will win out over the other sort. But we will also know that such a victory is not foreordained.

Not long ago I met a very likable and generous professor of humanities. He was mild-mannered, but no pushover. What he had to say about his own way of teaching fascinated me.

"It seems to me," he said, "that every generation of humanities teachers has worked, subtly and quietly, to make students into more progressive people. We've encouraged them to be skeptical about religious belief. We've helped them to be more open-minded in their response to others, particularly when they're different. And we've particularly worked to persuade the guys that their masculinity won't be lost if they become more sensitive than they were before. We've tried to suggest that a no-holds-barred capitalism isn't the best thing for everyone and we've tried to push in the direction of more and more social and economic equality. We've tried to change the way people get pleasure out of life. We've shown them that there's more than TV; they can enjoy poetry and opera and philosophy. You can probably say that we've tried to make them more civilized."

I found this well put and plausible. Maybe America would be a better place if this professor's educational goals came to fruition. It would be a more humane country if we all became more sensitive, more community minded, less materialistic, more civilized.

"So," I said, "it's as though what you're trying to do is make them into honorary Europeans, postmodern, postreligious citizens of Paris or Brussels?"

He agreed. That was exactly what he was shooting for. But thinking further on the matter, it strikes me that it's a very bad idea for us teachers to have a preexisting image of how we want our students to turn out, even as potentially attractive an idea as this teacher was offering. No, I think that what we need is for people to understand who and what they are now, then to be open to changing into their own highest mode of being. And that highest mode is something that they must identify by themselves, through encounters with the best that has been known and thought. We all have promise in us; it is up to education to reveal that promise, and to help it unfold. The power that is in you, says Emerson, is new in nature. And the best way to release that power is to let students confront viable versions of experience and take their choices.

It will come as little surprise when I say that what I have been endorsing here is a form of humanism. Humanism has a long and complex history, but for the purposes of this book, I want to describe humanistic education in a relatively condensed way. To me, humanism is the belief that it is possible for some of us, and maybe more than some, to use secular writing as the preeminent means for shaping our lives. That means that we might construct ourselves from novels, poems, and plays, as well as from works of history and philosophy, in the way that our ancestors constructed themselves (and were constructed) by the Bible and other sacred texts.

To me, the drawback of significant past versions of humanism is that they have all come with latent and overt ideas about the person they wanted to see emerge from the process of reading and thinking. Like my friend the kindly professor, humanists have known from the start what sort of person they hoped to create. The New Critics, with their emphasis on those qualities—a capacity for irony and ambiguity, the power to maintain inner tension—that they saw as conducive to maturity, did precisely this, encouraging their devotees to be responsive to a preexisting model. Matthew Arnold, who usefully announced to the world that in the time to come poetry might have to replace religion as the source of spiritual sustenance, was himself narrowly committed. Arnold gave us the touchstones, passages at the heart of true literature, passages that all of us needed to grapple to our souls so as to become genuinely educated. But Arnold's stoical resignation, the discourse of tempered middle age, will not do for everyone.

Later on, Jacques Derrida undermined Jean-Paul Sartre's humanism by pointing out the metaphysical, which is to say the subtly coercive, base on which it rests. Asked to provide a standard that could guide the individual in his choice of actions—with action understood to be at the core of the existentialist's philosophy of life—Sartre makes the mistake of responding in a generalizing and delimiting way: Act always in such a manner that you are working to create a self that could serve as a model for others. We are back with Kant, back under the shadow of the categorical imperative, and back to a coercive form of pedagogy that is not at all consistent with hopes for self-reliant freedom. Even Heidegger, who in the "Letter on Humanism" tries to distance himself from Sartre, is accurately criticized by Derrida for propounding a kind of philosophical monotheism. Derrida sees that Heidegger himself has a preordained ideal to which all human development should aspire. Heidegger celebrates something called Being and, more precisely, the individual's apprehension of and identification with a pure state of existence. For Heidegger, the highest human destiny is to be the "shepherd of Being." Yet Derrida himself, as shrewdly as he may write in "The Ends of Man," has nothing of a positive nature to offer. He has no vision of possible human development. Derrida limits himself to the work of clearing away superannuated and delimiting modes of humanistic thinking, and then can do no more.

T. S. Eliot, in the great essay "Tradition and the Individual Talent," tried to found a humanism by positing the existence of literary monuments that could be modified by the intervention of this or that newly canonical writer. Encountering Eliot on the canon, I think of Kierkegaard, who said of Hegel that the *Phenomenology* would rank as one of the greatest of all works if only its author had the sense to finish by saying that it was merely a thought experiment, only one idiosyncratic version of the way that it all is. One might say something similar of Eliot. If only the monuments were explicitly and joyously *his* monuments, his and no one else's. If only he told us all to go out and make, from the profusion of magnificent works that surround us, something on the order of a quotidian liturgy, a secular scripture, as Frye liked to call it, of our own. "I must Create a System," as Blake, Frye's great teacher, put it, "or be enslav'd by another Mans." Eliot, the potential liberator, becomes a creator of what Blake, hyperbolist that he sometimes was, called "mind-forg'd manacles." Even Frye, author of the greatest book of visionary literary criticism yet written—for it takes visionary powers to make a past writer's vision live in the present—eventually throws his wonderful energy and intelligence into forming a system. The master system of *Anatomy of Criticism* reveals all of literature's meanings; in it all readers should believe. But such systems pass quickly away. They will always be replaced by other coercive and exclusionary intellectual organizations that offer the comforts of collective, institutional religion—at least, until we can discover what Blake knew: that all deities ultimately reside in the individual human breast.

Disciples

It is sometimes hard for us critics to see that we are disciples. Or that we ought to be. The fact does not sort well with our dignity. But in fact the true T. S. Eliot scholar is not a grubber after Eliot-related facts, or the creator of ingeniously baroque readings of Eliot. He is not the source of minutiae for the Eliot newsletter or any other such thing. No, he is far more important than that, and also far less.

He is, or ought to be, Eliot's disciple. He is responsible for so immersing himself in Eliot that only he and very few others can plausibly bring Eliot's vision alive in the current world, which, as the critic deeply believes (or why would he have become a deep student of Eliot to begin with?), has sore need of it. He is the one who will know instinctively—as Frye knew of Blake, as Bate knew of Keats and Johnson, as Orwell knew of Dickens—precisely how his author would feel in response to virtually any event that comes to pass around us.

We fancy we are saying something merely rhetorical when we talk about how authors who matter live on forever. But it is not figurative speech at all, if a literary culture is unfolding as it should. No, the scholar by dint of hard work and imagination can, at will, merge himself with the authors who matter to him. By the exercise of his own heart's intelligence, he manages to keep them alive in the present. By sacrificing some of his individuality to the thoughts and feelings of another, by giving up himself, he becomes a light of knowledge to all around him. And when the scholar does not do so, our common culture suffers.

When I was in graduate school, I became a student of Freud. It seemed necessary then to learn absolutely everything I could about him. I read his works numberless times; I read everything about him that I could get. And his vision fully infiltrated my mind. On any given subject, then and now, I can offer a plausible Freudian response, though by this time I believe at best a significant fraction of what Freud did. This kind of study involves a certain self-annulling, not unrelated to the annulment of self that Eliot describes in "Tradition and the Individual Talent." There, Eliot speaks of the poet's surrender of personality in order to make way for the influence of past poets. "What happens is a continual surrender of himself as he is at the moment to something which is more valuable." Such learning—and I don't mean to single myself out here; many people have it—is part of what a scholar's education is about. My job as a Romanticist is not primarily to say unprecedented things about the Romantics, or to go to conferences and impress my fellow scholars, most of whom actively dislike the authors they teach, anyway. My job is to continue the lives of the poets on in the present, to make them available to those living now who might need them.

It's not necessary to be a lifelong scholar of this or that writer to make his work available to the uses of the present and future. Learning surely helps a great deal, but energy, imagination, and a little judiciousness go a long way, too. What's most important, I think, is to find the writer at the peak of his potential for life. You can dwell on Dostoyevsky as the writer who conveys an astounding and just portrait of a certain sort of murderer in *Crime and Punishment*. But ultimately, one probably does more for students by helping them to understand Dostoyevsky's vision of life as an insane, ever-blackening turbulence that we can only navigate humanely by recourse to religious faith.

A given age is likely to be infused to the core with standard prevailing opinion, which is the product of the moment. The day is generally suffused with—recall William Carlos Williams's lines—"what passes for the new." One way to break through that prevailing opinion is to have recourse to the best that has been known and thought in the past. Offering past wealth to the present is what a scholar is supposed to do.

Sometimes someone steps from our ranks whose own vision of matters is worthy of consideration in its own right. But most of us cannot lay fair claim to that power. Rather, we are the powers that keep Chaucer and Spenser and Milton from fading into oblivion. This is a noble task. And rightly universities give people security, relative calm, and a solid sustenance to let it unfold.

Are you so original? Such an adept translator or rewriter of texts? Come out from behind the pretense. Write us your own novel or poem or essay, take up matters where there is more pressure on the individual to compound his way of apprehending things, and let us see what you have on offer. Then we may judge whether you might not have been better off with the genuinely noble, if also more modest, process of discipleship. And if you stay with true discipleship, who knows? Does Plato not go at least as far as Socrates? Does Frye at his best not do more than complete Blake? Such achievement must come naturally, through a process that begins in some measure of self-annulment. Yet it is a self-annulment that can be amply rewarded. As Camille Paglia puts it, "Great teachers live their subject. The subject teaches itself through them. It uses them and, in return, charges them with elemental energy."

Exemplars

The kind of teaching I endorse entails impersonation. The teacher tempo-rarily becomes the author, valuing what the author values, thinking as the author would. George Orwell does this for Dickens in his wonderful essay on the novelist. Marilyn Butler does it for Jane Austen; Harold Bloom for Wallace Stevens; Geoffrey Hartman and Walter Jackson Bate for Keats. Helen Vendler has done it for many contemporary poets in her review-essays. With unparalleled brilliance, Northrop Frye does it in his book on William Blake, *Fearful Symmetry.* These critics merge with their authors and by doing so become more than who they are.

Such critics are not only valuable in themselves, but valuable in dialogue with one another. Consider what is to be gained by juxtaposing Butler and Frye on the subject of the Romantics. For years, Frye immersed himself in Blake's work; he thought and probably even dreamed as Blake would. And the result is a remarkable transfiguration. Frye becomes Blake, or at least a highly plausible version of Blake. It is a Blake who is alive to the needs of Frye's present, an available, cogent Blake who speaks to Frye's society and, I believe, to our own.

Listen to Frye, in one of many memorable passages, matching the eloquence of Blake to bring him to us. "Inspiration," writes Blake-Frye, "is the artist's empirical proof of the divinity of his imagination; and all inspi-ration is divine in origin, whether used, perverted, hidden or frittered away in reverie. All imaginative and creative acts, being eternal, go to build up a permanent structure, which Blake calls Golgonooza, above time, and, when this structure is finished, nature, its scaffolding, will be knocked away and man will live in it. Golgonooza will then be the city of God, the new Jerusalem which is the total form of all human culture and civilization. Nothing that the heroes, martyrs, prophets and poets of the past have done for it has been wasted; no anonymous and unrecog-nized contribution to it has been overlooked. In it is conserved all the good man has done, and in it is completed all that he hoped and intended to do. And the artist who uses the same energy and genius that Homer and Isaiah had will find that he not only lives in the same palace of art as Homer and Isaiah, but lives in it at the same time."

This is Frye's version of Eliot's "Tradition and the Individual Talent." For Eliot, most of us must live outside the world of great works, looking on in awe. But Frye's imaginative world is a world for you and for me, a democratic world of art and creation that we can enter by making an honest attempt to write with visionary integrity. We need to render what we see as truly as we can. In so doing we can come into the world of genius—feeling, perhaps, the shock of recognition that Melville said united all who deployed the energies of creation, whether they succeeded in worldly terms or failed. (Melville put his own relation to worldly success memorably: "So far as I am individually concerned, & independent of my pocket, it is my earnest desire to write those sort of books which are said to 'fail.'")

What Frye offers, through reliance on the self, is entry into Keats's immortal freemasonry of intellect. The aim of a liberal arts education, from this perspective, is to show us that, as Walter Jackson Bate puts it, "we need not be the passive victims of what we deterministically call 'circumstances' (social, cultural, or reductively psychological-personal), but that by linking ourselves through what Keats calls an 'immortal freemasonry' with the great we can become freer—freer to be ourselves, to be what we most want and value."

Frye imagines opening the world of artistic freedom to ever growing numbers of people; he is self-consciously democratizing where Eliot is exclusionary. But the energies of art do not belong to everyone simply by virtue of being born. One has to strive to enter into the world of Homer and Isaiah and to draw on their powers. The most admirable individuals, for Frye and Blake, will be the ones who throw themselves into the life of creation; those who refuse the opportunity have turned away from what matters most in life. "The worship of God," wrote Blake, "is Honouring his gifts in other men each according to his genius and loving the greatest men best."

As arresting as this affirmation of genius may be, it probably should not go without challenge in a classroom. For perhaps there are other paths, and before the student is swept in by the attractions of Blake and Frye, and Keats and Bate, it's necessary to look critically at them.

Taking a deep initial delight in a book or an author is a little like falling in love. There is a nearly rapturous acceptance of all the author brings. The truth unfolds as if from above. But to adapt that vision to one's own uses, to bring it wisely into the world, more than love is necessary. One also has to apply a critical scrutiny to the work—consider its connotations, examine its antecedents, asking always: What would it mean to live this vision? The initial feeling of being swept off your feet by a book has got to be followed by more thoughtful commitment, as marriage follows love. When you say yes to an author's vision, you're entering into a marriage of minds. And such marriage ought not to take place without critical scrutiny.

In *Romantics, Rebels and Reactionaries,* Marilyn Butler is generally about as detached from her subject as Frye is immersed in his. But at one point, she steps forward and affirms her identification with Jane Austen, using Austen to contend against the self-generated visions that the Romantics and their proponents worship. Here is Butler: "In all Jane Austen's novels, characters are judged by their manners. But one is not born with manners, nor can one easily pick them up; one is taught them as a child by parents who had them. The issue of manners is raised more explicitly in German literature of Jane Austen's period than in English. In that country of legalized class distinctions, burger writers could not rise socially; they had to use their inner resources, and make a self-justifying system out of solipsism—Romanticism is such a system—because their manners, or lack of them, would always exclude them from the charmed circle of the hereditary aristocracy. For Jane Austen, the writer who expresses the ethos of the landed gentry, manners are indeed the passport. But true to her function at its highest, she idealizes manners and endows them with all their theoretical value . . . They proclaim that the old style of social responsibility is accepted, *duty* (the idealized reading of upper-class motivation) put before the new individualism."

Blake and Frye are avatars of Romantic individualism, and they are, to Butler, an error that must be attacked, both in the past and present; to her, they make a system out of an aggressive, resentful solipsism. For Butler, Romanticism is a plague, something that tears society apart, encouraging us to live only for ourselves. It must be shown up for what it is. Greatly preferring Blake-Frye as I do, full of gratitude to Frye for performing the task Schopenhauer sets out and making Blake's work unfold as a contemporary answer to the question "What is life?", I find little to agree with in Butler. But in teaching Austen alongside Blake, as I often do, Butler seems to me key in helping students to see the differences between the two and to begin to make some choices, choices that will matter not just in class but for future life.

Of course Blake does want us *all* to live in Golgonooza, the city of ongoing creation, but you get there by being an inspired artist, by trusting yourself and by being yourself with the greatest possible gusto. And this is not something that everyone is prone to do. As Oscar Wilde put it, "Most people are other people."

What matters about these critics is that they are writing accurately about their authors (at least insofar as I can see) and doing so with *the conduct of life* as their concern. They are asking what it means to live the authors at hand. They are mining them for vital options, questing for truth.

Orwell's Dickens

George Orwell's essay on Charles Dickens is not an academic investigation, a fresh interpretation from the standpoint of Marx or Freud or whomever else you might care to apply for the purposes of translation. Rather, the piece is an internal argument—it's Orwell contending with himself. He is pitting what I take to be his own early infatuation with Dickens against what he has learned later in life through his immersion in politics (and war) as well as through his study of Marx and other social thinkers. Orwell seems to be writing this essay because he needs to. He needs—while describing Dickens with all the accuracy he can muster— to find out whether he, and by extension his readers, ought to take to heart the truth in Dickens's work.

Dickens, as Orwell has come in time to see, has no social doctrine. Perhaps he is unmatched at dramatizing injustice but, to Orwell, Dickens has no conception of how various social arrangements conspire to create it. When Dickens wants to indict evil, or inhumanity, he indicts this or that inhumane person or inhumane act. His scope is entirely limited to what he can see in front of him. Dickens has no capacity to step back and to envision things in their larger, more general workings. "He has no constructive suggestions," Orwell says, "not even a clear grasp of the nature of the society he is attacking, only an emotional perception that something is wrong."

A case in point, for Orwell, is Dickens's view of education: "He attacks the current educational system with perfect justice, and yet, after all, he has no remedy to offer except kindlier schoolmasters. Why did he not indicate what a school *might* have been? Why did he not have his own sons educated according to some plan of his own, instead of sending them to public school to be stuffed with Greek? Because he lacked that kind of imagination."

"He lacked that kind of imagination": by which Orwell means that he lacked a political imagination. Theories of education, as Plato demonstrates in *The Republic*, are always political theories, blueprints for future societies. Dickens had no political theory. He was unable to conceive of an alternative to the slash-and-burn capitalism that was developing everywhere around him. He could protest against institutions, but he could not imagine their replacement with better ones. Rather, the man behind the functionary's desk must become a better man. Orwell, it's soon clear, is arguing with himself, for and against socialism, the doctrine that Dickens could have adopted and never did, and the doctrine that is tempting Orwell himself. When Orwell chides Dickens, early on in the essay, for not having a social imagination, what he means is that he has no imagination for socialism.

Orwell's argument with himself, and with his own prior love for Dickens, is so honest, nondogmatic, and uncommitted to preordained conclusions, that by the close of the essay he has, it seems, discovered something. The process of writing the essay appears to have remade his mind. Yeats said that when you have an argument with the world, you write an essay. When the argument is with yourself, it issues in a poem. This is an argument with the self that results in an essay replete with the passion that comes in the best poems.

Here is Orwell on the limits of the kind of socialist thought that he has been measuring Dickens against. "All [Dickens] can finally say is 'Behave decently,' which . . . is not necessarily so shallow as it sounds. Most revolutionaries are potential Tories, because they imagine that everything can be put right by altering the *shape* of society; once that change is effected, as it sometimes is, they see no need for any other. Dickens has not this kind of mental coarseness. The vagueness of his discontent is the mark of its permanence. What he is out against is not this or that institution, but, as Chesterton put it, 'an expression on the human face.'" In fact, Orwell now sees, Dickens's permanent radicalism may well be more attractive than the temporary discontent, aimed at the overthrow of an existing system, that so-called revolutionaries maintain. The revolutionaries want to replace the current system with another that will last for all time—the dictatorship of the proletariat, maybe—and that will almost inevitably solidify and hem in life.

Orwell in his youth seems to have fallen in love with Dickens. And the first phase in being influenced by a writer—influenced in the best sense—is precisely such love. But the process must go further than that. To actually adopt a writer's vision, the reader has to engage in critical examination. The writer needs to answer the hardest questions one can put to him, because, in effect, these are our questions, our perplexities about how to live and what to do. Just so, when we are on the verge of marriage, we need to know that love is at the core of it all. But we also need to think hard about our choice. What kind of mother or father will the person make? Will she bear with me in bad times as well as good, sickness as well as health, poverty and wealth alike? Posing such questions of an author's vision—can it sustain me in the hard hours as well as the sweet?—is central to the act of criticism that precedes consequential belief.

Some students will go even further. So far, we have been talking about two sorts of people: those who are reasonably comfortable with the values they've been socialized to accept, and those who feel an uneasiness with them, however latent. This second group is ripe for literary study. They need a second chance to come of age. But some of them will not be satisfied with what they find in books, however much it may draw them. They'll see that Shelley or Austen goes only so far, and they'll feel the need to complete and correct the writers they love by writing novels and poems and essays of their own. Writers become writers for many reasons, but one is that the books on the shelf are never quite the right books. They don't render the world in exactly the way that it is. So there is reason to write more. Walter Benjamin tells the story of a village schoolmaster who was too poor to buy books; when he saw a title in a catalog that intrigued him, he sat down and composed the volume himself. "Writers," Benjamin observes, "are really people who write books not because they are poor, but because they are dissatisfied with the books which they could buy but do not like."

Influence

When some teachers think about this approach to education, they find the issue of influence particularly troubling. They are concerned that they might become propagandists, rather than what they hope to be, critical thinkers who enjoin critical thought. They don't want to implant ways of seeing things in their students, using their authority and the powers of their grades. Rather, they want to echo the advice that Johnson gave Boswell, turn to their students and demand that they rid their minds of cant. What is to be put in the place of this cant—or doxa, or ideology, or, if you like, bullshit—the critical thinkers rarely say.

To me, there are few pleasures greater than being influenced: learning something I need to know from another. Longinus describes this feeling of connection with a great author in a splendid sentence when he says that when we encounter sublime wisdom, we feel that we have created what in fact we've only heard. The utterance so much echoes our latent wisdom that we take the author's words as our own. Emerson, greatly fearing influence, especially early in his career, speaks of the indignity of being "forced to take with shame our own opinion from another." But Emerson addresses us here as an aspiring original. To the true reader, every form of usable truth is welcome many times over. Later in life, Emerson is more circumspect: "Shall I tell you the secret of the true scholar? It is this: Every man I meet is my master in some point, and in that I learn of him."

Many of our students have grown up being suffused with TV, movies, video games. Is what is to be found in Blake and Dickens so much worse than what Paramount and Disney have to deliver? Should we suffer endless qualms lest the world according to Spielberg be displaced by the world according to Wallace Stevens? Yet there is something real about these concerns; teaching in the way that I describe does have its dangers.

To me, part of the risk of true teaching lies in the willingness to see students make choices, sometimes bad choices. We must not be afraid of submitting our students to influence. We face people who are on the verge of major decisions. Should I marry? Should I have children? Should I go into law? Should I stay in my parents' church? Such questions matter to young people, and they matter now. If thinking about these questions in a classroom can be dangerous, it can be much more dangerous not to think about them. The result of never brooding over major issues is likely to be that one follows the crowd. One takes common convention as a guide. Rich in use as convention can be, for some it is stifling, begetting lives of quiet desperation. We spend our days pursuing ends that outrage our natures, making ourselves sick, as Thoreau said, so that we can lay something up against our coming illness. A fundamental qualification for teaching literature should be the view that great books are worth studying, and because of the salutary effects that they can have on life. Why would a student wish to study with anyone who didn't think as much? Doing so would be like hiring a lawyer who had lost all of his faith in the law and didn't want to sully himself through contact with the corrupt legal system.

The professors who become most uneasy about asking their students real questions are often those with the most doubts about the capacities of everyday people to make their own decisions and to direct their own lives. These professors, whatever they may say, are fundamentally afraid of living in a democracy, where people think for themselves, rather than letting experts do their thinking for them. This fear is a scandal at the center of the current day academy. Though many professors claim to be on the left, the fact is that they do not trust, or sometimes even much like, everyday, relatively unschooled people. In fact, they tend to despise the people in whose behalf they claim to be working.

As disconcerting to me as the fears of those who think that students will be too easily swayed are the doubts of those who feel that human beings can be changed little, if at all, for the better. Eminent among these is Sigmund Freud. What Freud calls the transference is purportedly an inescapable part of life, perhaps even an element of every significant encounter. The theory of the transference suggests that we live eternally in the past, never in the present and future. To Freud, we perpetually approach figures of authority and figures of erotic interest not as the people they are in themselves, but rather as though they were figures from our past. The boss's injunctions are inflected with the mother's commands. The lover's carpings are the father's as well. We are lost in a world where, as J. H. van den Berg puts it, "everything is past and there is nothing new." We find ourselves amidst facsimiles of replicas of reproductions.

One of the reasons that Freud hated America as much as he did is that the nation seemed organized on the premise that the present could have a liberated relation to the past. We believed that it was possible to draw on the past, not be swallowed by it against our wills. Democracy, which depends on the enfranchisement of greater and greater numbers of people, on the widening of their possibilities, is inseparable from faith in the present and future.

To have gone into teaching is to have placed one's wager on the hopeful side of the question. By choosing to teach, we have declared a hope that the powers of nurture may be a little stronger than nature's. We've affirmed the hope that the present can be more alive than the constricting past. What is our proof beyond that hope? Do we have any evidence, besides our temperamental wish to think well of the world? I think so. As teachers we see proof all the time. We see proof, first of all, in the nearly miraculous works that we often teach. If a human being can write as Shakespeare or Blake did, coming from humble beginnings, with no advantages other than those they created themselves, then what is not to be hoped for from an individual man or woman? "A human being did that!" one says, reading their work. "And what might I, too, no less human, be able to achieve?"

Freud and all the other purveyors of the Gothic imagination may be right. It's possible that the present is bound so tightly to the past that it rarely breaks free. Edgar Allan Poe, the ultimate Gothic writer, delighted in depicting people who are fated from the start to be devoured by past sins, whether they committed them or not. Is there any doubt, once you see the enormous crack running through the House of Usher, what will happen to it and its residents by the tale's end? Poe, who sought his own doom ruthlessly enough, seemed to believe that all of us would eventually be sacrificed on the altar of long-ago transgressions.

Education is a gamble. Socrates was gambling when he asked his young friends to put their beliefs into play. Jesus was gambling when he told streetcorner denizens, in whose eyes he saw something unsatisfied, to get up and follow him, put aside the begging bowl or the tax collectors' book. The Buddha gambled when he told people that they could free themselves from the wheel of incarnation through meditation and awareness of the noble truths. This is what teachers, great and small, do: they wager that they can help people become one with their highest promise. Freud once said that the aim of therapy was to turn misery into common everyday unhappiness—and one admires the tough-mindedness in his remark. But Thoreau, himself an estimable figure, talked about bringing the past into the thousand-eyed light of the present, and living forever in a new day. And from what I can tell from *Walden*'s best pages, sometimes he did.

Thoreau and Emerson do not wish to throw out the past. Emerson, for his part, wrote a book on representative individuals, historical figures from whom we might learn. And Whitman said, in his preface to *Leaves of Grass*, that America does not repudiate what is done and gone. Rather, we draw on it for fresh life, ingest it and make it new, as the body does its food. If you've become a teacher, you've already entered the game on the Emersonian side; you're there to change people, help them live better. The scholar Andrew Delbanco quotes Emerson to exactly this effect: "The whole secret of the teacher's force lies in the conviction that men are convertible. And they are. They want awakening."

My first real teaching job was at a place called the Woodstock Country School, a tiny boarding school in Vermont. The headmaster, Robin Leaver, who was an educational genius after his fashion, worked chiefly from one premise. "Every kid who enters this school," he'd often say, "has something that he can do at least half-well and probably a lot better; it's something he can take joy in; and it's something that he can use to make the world better. Your job as a teacher is to help each kid find that thing." We had marvelous students at Woodstock; some of them seemed to have a dozen or so gifts ready to unfold. But the ones who got the most tireless and affectionate attention from the teachers were the ones who seemed to have little or maybe nothing going for them. These were the kids that the world outside liked to call losers. In fact, their parents sometimes told us precisely that: "My kid's a loser. Good luck with her." Leaver, who had an affection for, and understanding of, sixteen-year-olds that I've never seen surpassed, would have to work hard to stop himself from detonating when he heard this sort of talk; usually he succeeded.

Every week, we got together in a faculty meeting and discussed each student. There were as many as seventy-five, so the meetings would sometimes go for three hours or more. The kids in the most trouble got the most time. I can still see Robin leaning over at us, vast smile, blond hair, movie-star good looks, nearly absurd for someone headmastering a school in outer nowhere, saying somewhat ironically (somewhat): "You call yourselves teachers and you can't find *anything* in the world that Michael Long is interested in? Nothing? Nothing?" Someone might observe that he'd seen Michael following Bruce around. Bruce was the farmer who grew crops on the school grounds and kept up the land. "Then what are we waiting for?" Leaver would say, "Let's put him to work with Bruce. He can study English and math next term."

Sometimes these shots in the dark worked, sometimes not. But what did have an effect was the students' developing awareness that the people who taught at the school would do anything, anything, to deliver them from wasted lives. Given that affirmation, the students were often inspired to start searching on their own.

Twenty-five years after Woodstock closed, at a reunion on what had been the school property, Robin and I talked about why the place had finally run aground. I said it was because to make ends meet we had to take too many kids who had too many problems. They were impossible. No, said Robin. Those kids would have come along. But some of them needed years and years at the school; we just didn't have enough time. In some empirical, practical sense, what I said may have been true. A few of the kids we were accepting at the end were borderline dangerous. But the one who spoke then in the true spirit of democratic education was surely not me.

Proust

Perhaps the last century's most persuasive theorist of positive influence is Marcel Proust. In luminous passages, he tells us how he developed as a reader, and then how, having himself become a writer, he hoped that he might affect others.

Proust observes: "The mediocre usually imagine that to let ourselves be guided by the books we admire robs our faculty of judgment of part of its independence. 'What can it matter to you what Ruskin feels: feel for yourself.' Such a view rests on a psychological error which will be discounted by all those who have accepted a spiritual discipline and feel thereby that their power of understanding and of feeling is infinitely enhanced, and their critical sense never paralyzed . . . There is no better way of coming to be aware of what one feels oneself than by trying to recreate in oneself what a master has felt. In this profound effort it is our own thought itself that we bring out into the light, together with his."

In a society that loves technique and training, but is wary of emotion not routinized by the newspaper or the sitcom, one must be willing to learn how to feel, then frequently to be reminded. This was the gift that Wordsworth gave to John Stuart Mill, who was, when he encountered the poet, dead in his life of feeling; a perpetual inner frost seemed to have taken hold. From this condition Wordsworth delivered him. Eliot tells us that one of the main functions of poetry is to give names, however complexly metaphorical the names might be, to emotions that have abided for a long time unspoken in the heart. To name feelings with poetic sensitivity, Eliot suggests, is to make them live yet more strongly. So, learning to feel with Ruskin, Proust learned to feel as himself.

The contemporary novelist Robert Stone describes his goal as a writer this way: "I want my reader to recognize what I've made and say, 'That's it. That's the way it is.'" No one describes this process of recognition, this benign literary influence, more gracefully than Proust, in the passages I cited in part at the beginning of this book: "But to return to my own case," Proust writes, "I thought more modestly of my book, and it would be inaccurate even to say that I thought of those who would read it as 'my' readers. For it seemed to me that they would not be 'my' readers but readers of their own selves, my book being merely a sort of magnifying glass like those which the optician at Combray used to offer his customers—it would be my book but with it I would furnish them with the means of reading what lay inside themselves. So that I would not ask them to praise me or to censure me, but simply to tell me whether 'it really is like that.' I should ask whether the words that they read within themselves are the same as those which I have written (though a discrepancy in this respect need not always be the consequence of an error on my part, since the explanation could also be that the reader had eyes for which my book was not a suitable instrument)."

Here Proust is remarkably sanguine about the possibility of the reader recognizing himself precisely in the mirror of the book's words. But often there is more to it than that. Recall Emerson: he that would bring home the wealth of the Indies must carry out the wealth of the Indies. Or, more dramatically, Kierkegaard: he who would give birth to himself must know how to work. And so the visions of even the poets often need to be brought into line with our own aspirations and with the tempers of our times. Timeless in their uses as they may be, it can take skill to make them work here and now. As Proust in a more skeptical mood puts matters: "Reading is on the threshold of the spiritual life; it can introduce us to it: it does not constitute it."

Form and Feeling

Wordsworth said that he sought knowledge, but knowledge not purchased through the loss of power. Part of what makes literary education so important is that it offers something more than abstract knowing. It gives us wisdom that is replete with emotional force. The emphasis on form is what preserves art from the programmatic detachment that often informs more intellectualized ways of rendering experience.

There are many ways of thinking about form, from Kenneth Burke's Aristotelian view that form is the setting up and satisfying of expectations in the reader, to Kant's idea that form lifts the art object out of the push and toss of daily life and makes it a source for disinterested contemplation. But to me, form is best understood as the primary way that writers infuse their words with feeling. It provides the music of the work. Form is the sequence of notes that a sentence plays out, thus giving an emotional content to what could otherwise be a merely cognitive experience. And form is also the grander, symphonic structure of the work that lets us know in larger-scale terms what it would be like to live this vision— not moment to moment, as sentences do, but month to month, year to year. Where are the highs, where the despondencies?

The astounding comic buoyancy of a Dickens novel, its unflag-ging episodic invention, sprawling variety, and high-hearted tone, all contribute to a sense of what liberalism of Dickens's kind can be. For Dickens, liberalism isn't condescending, nor is it ever grudging; rather, it confers a vitality on the believer that makes him affirm life and hunger for more. And this is a function of the rambunctious form—sometimes it's an antiform, I suppose—of Dickens's major novels. Preeminently, form creates and reveals emotion.

The archetypal literary plot, the one adumbrated by Aristotle in *The Poetics*, can itself summon strong feelings. Many of us see ourselves in the protagonist who enters the world with strong desires, meets opposi-tion and reversal, changes through struggle, and emerges richer—if in nothing else than in breadth of consciousness. For many, this pattern illuminates life. As Robert McKee, a thoughtful analyst of film, says, "Most human beings believe that life brings closed experiences of abso-lute, irreversible change; that their greatest sources of conflict are external to themselves; that they are the single and active protagonists of their own existence[s]; that their existence[s] operate through continuous time within a consistent, causally interconnected reality; and that inside this reality, events happen for explainable and meaningful reasons." An adroit deployment of conventional (or one might call it "archetypal") plot brings these convictions about life home to the reader with considerable impact—though the work need not articulate them overtly. Balzac's sense of what life is about—struggle, rivalry, triumph, bitter failure—is almost perfectly in tune with the values implicit in traditional novelistic plotting, and that is one of the reasons that his books read as satisfyingly as they do. In his best novels (I think of *White Noise* in particular) Don DeLillo departs from most of the assumptions that McKee lays out, not only in the way he renders character but also by shaping his books without readily apparent beginning, middle, and end. His cogent rebellion against novelistic form is, at least to me, as fruitful as Balzac's affirmation. It remains for the reader to say what form or antiform might put him into the best relation to his own experience. What is gained and what lost when you map your life according to the archetypal plot—or when, in DeLillo's fashion, you refuse that mapping?

It's quite possible that attempting to shape one's life, or interpret it, in conformity with traditional plot will lead to nothing but frustration. All of the relevant assumptions about character and cause and effect might lead to self-idealization and the failure that often attends it. But such a shaping could also offer intensity and focus. The individual who shares DeLillo's sense of the relatively haphazard way of the world may be better tuned to withstand life's vagaries, though for him, the dangers of fading toward entropy abide.

Literary beauty, to my mind, is the effective interfusion of feeling and thought. At the point of interfusion, though, there is no sentiment and there is no form—they have disappeared into each other, in the way that Apollo and Dionysus disappear into one another in Sophoclean drama, as Nietzsche understood it.

Form tells us how it feels to live the author's truth. "Know then thyself, presume not God to scan; / The proper study of mankind is Man." Pope's opening lines from the Second Epistle of "An Essay on Man," with their vigor, point, and strong but contained energy, make modesty—"presume not God to scan"—into a source of extreme self-assurance. Awareness of human limitation can quicken the spirit more, the lines suggest, than commitment to impious daring. In the music of the lines, in the form, is an entire attitude, a bearing. Form conveys to us how someone who spoke these lines feelingly might comport herself, how she'd move and talk and sit. Wordsworth's phrase "hearing oftentimes / The still, sad music of humanity" exudes a tentative melancholy evocative of the loneliness that suffuses a poem from which God has departed. The poem's view of the world is as much in its sonorous vowels as in its overt sense. Both Pope's lines and Wordsworth's are studies in perfect interfusion, both studies in literary beauty. "That's how it is. That's true." A reader could say as much of either of them.

Disciplines

The kind of reading that I have been describing here—the individual quest for what truth a work reveals—is fit for virtually all significant forms of creation. We can seek vital options in any number of places. They may be found for this or that individual in painting, in music, in sculpture, in the arts of furniture making or gardening. Thoreau felt he could derive a substantial wisdom by tending his bean field. He aspired to "know beans." He hoed for sustenance, as he tells us, but he also hoed in search of tropes, comparisons between what happened in the garden and what happened elsewhere in the world. In his bean field,

Thoreau sought ways to turn language—and life—away from old stabilities.

Consider Proust, at the beginning of his career, writing to an editor to inquire if he might care for a piece of art criticism, one that would unfold the world view of the artist in something of the way, presumably, that Orwell unfolded Charles Dickens's: "I have just written a little study in the philosophy of art, if I may use that slightly pretentious phrase, in which I have tried to show how the great painters initiate us into a knowledge and love of the external world, how they are the ones 'by whom our eyes are opened,' opened that is, on the world. In this study, I use the work of Chardin as an example, and I try to show its influence on our life, the charm and wisdom with which it coats our most modest moments by initiating us into the life of still life. Do you think this sort of study would interest the readers of the *Revue Hebdomadaire*?"

The editor of the *Revue Hebdomadaire* thought not. But it would have interested me. For I think that in the works of all the consequential painters there is an answer to Schopenhauer's question "What is life?" That answer is difficult to coax forward, and few art critics have been able to do so. (Arnold Hauser comes most immediately to mind.) Such visions are easier to derive from words, from writings, in part because for most of us the prevailing medium, moment to moment, is verbal. We talk to ourselves. We talk to others. The circles that expand on the deep, or don't, are probably, for most of us, composed of words. Thus a critical part of making the nonverbal arts into the stuff of human expansion is verbal description. Criticism, acting in Proust's spirit, can turn the visions of the painters and composers into words, and so give us the chance to make better use of them. In humanistic criticism, there are few more difficult tasks than simply re-presenting a sculpture or a piece of music—describing the work and making it live.

I have chosen literature as a central source of vital words for a number of reasons. Since the Romantic period, literature has offered us a latent hypothesis. This is the view that there are simply too many sorts of human beings, too many idiosyncratic constitutions, for any one map of human nature, or any single guide to the good life, to be adaptable for us all. Such a realization, which coincides with the foundations of widespread democracy, as well as with the flourishing of novels, holds that there are multiple ways of apprehending experience, and multiple modes of internal organization, or disorder. Accordingly, there are many, many different ways to lead a satisfying, socially valuable life. This, as I've suggested, is what Milan Kundera is getting at when he calls the characters—and, by implication, the narrating voices—rendered in fiction "experimental selves." There are multiple ways to go, and confining theories of self, even those as penetrating as, say, Plato's and Kant's, cannot encompass the range of human difference.

The teacher begins the secular dialogue with faith by offering the hypothesis that there is no one human truth about the good life, but that there are many human truths, many viable paths. To set his students on them, he offers them multiple examples of what Arnold called the best that has been known and thought. This multiplying of possibilities— a condition enhanced by the rapid diffusion of culture around the globe—makes literature, which is inevitably the effusion of an individual mind, the most likely starting place, I would even say the center of human- istic education. As literary works are multiple, so are the number of potentially usable human visions of experience.

Beginning with this hypothesis, the teacher's task is often one of inspired impersonation. Against her students' Final Narratives, against their various faiths, she, with a combination of disinterest and passion, hurls alternatives. Impersonation: the teacher's objective is to offer an inspiring version of what is most vital in the author. She merges with the author, becomes the creator, and in doing so makes the past available to the uses of the present. The teacher listens to criticisms, perhaps engen- ders a few herself—but, always, ultimately, is the author's advocate, his attorney for explication and defense.

In this process it's important for the teacher to respect the possibility that however marvelous the books she puts before her students, some will in the end decide to stay as they are. They will wish, in Dr. Johnson's phrase, to repose upon the stability of truth—their own prior truth. Like Dr. Johnson, his contemporary Edmund Burke held certain conventional ways of thinking in the highest regard. Both men considered a nation's fund of common sense to be something like a slowly evolving epic poem, in which generation after generation deposited the wisdom it won through trial, success, error, and ensuing consideration.

In *Reflections on the Revolution in France*, Burke writes an homage to common wisdom, which he refers to under the name of prejudice, a word here devoid of its current racialist connotations. Teachers too eager to effect conversion should probably read Dr. Johnson and Edmund Burke regularly on the matter of conventional thinking at its best. Here is Burke addressing a sympathizer with revolutionary France: "We [in England] are generally men of untaught feelings; . . . instead of casting away all our old prejudices, we cherish them to a very considerable degree, and, to take more shame to ourselves, we cherish them because they are prejudices; and the longer they have lasted, and the more generally they have prevailed, the more we cherish them. We are afraid to put men to live and trade each on his own private stock of reason; because we suspect that this stock in each man is small, and that the individuals would do better to avail themselves of the general bank and capital of nations, and of ages. Many of our men of speculation, instead of exploding general prejudices, employ their sagacity to discover the latent wisdom which prevails in them. If they find what they seek, and they seldom fail, they think it more wise to continue the prejudice, with the reason involved, than to cast away the coat of prejudice, and to leave nothing but the naked reason; because prejudice, with its reason, has a motive to give action to that reason, and an affection which will give it permanence. Prejudice is of ready application in the emergency; it previously engages the mind in a steady course of wisdom and virtue, and does not leave the man hesitating in the moment of decision, skeptical, puzzled, and unresolved. Prejudice renders a man's virtue his habit; and not a series of unconnected acts. Through just prejudice, his duty becomes a part of his nature."

One might part company with Burke on the subject of how much power the individual mind can hope to possess—and I do—yet still listen respectfully to what he has to say about the "latent wisdom" that can inform conventional thinking. We need to be open to the possibility that our current students, who are less rebellious than any group I have encountered, may well know things that we do not.

History Now

The method of teaching I affirm begins with the self and its own sense of who it is and what its destiny might be. But it is important not to end there. Humanistic education has to go beyond individual being. Emerson remarked once that there is no history, only biography. Admire Emerson as I do, here I think that he is trapped in outrageous error.

History has many uses for life. It begins as a branch of literature: Herodotus is determined to tell us about the great deeds of the Greeks who fought against the Persians, so that those deeds will not fade from human memory. He sets up his major figures, as Plutarch does his noble

Greeks and Romans, as people worthy of emulation. In this respect, his work is in line with Homer and the epic poet's desire to preserve great deeds and great words for posterity. Herodotus offers the kind of exempla that literature, too, can give. From Plutarch to the present, Pericles to Rosa Parks, history is full of individuals who offer true inspiration.

But history doesn't only provide ideals. Its virtues are multiple. History too, one might say, is the noblest form of blackmail. Every leader of consequence knows that the eyes of the future will eventually fasten on him, and that he will pay with his reputation for even the best-hidden crimes. When Richard Nixon breaks through his manifold limits and opens up a dialogue with China, he's being responsive to history's noble blackmail.

In history, we also encounter large-scale narratives where we can find a place. Having made a commitment to, say, the teachings of the Savior, the future of socialism, or the progress of democracy, "an average unending procession," as Whitman described it, we want to locate the movement's origins. We want to see how the movement was born and what form its infancy and early growth took. And we want to join in the collective trajectory. By studying history we can attach ourselves to human efforts and human energies larger than ourselves and bring our personal force into the great wave of unfolding, collective hopes.

Literature, Aristotle tells us, is more philosophical than history; or, as Frye glosses him, philosophy presumes to tell us what must happen, history what has happened, and poetry what happens. There is the purportedly essential (philosophy), the contingent (history), and something in between (literature). But I would prefer to see in literature not so much a diagnosis of what happens but a prophecy of what can happen— a prophecy of how we can touch our version of that immortal freemasonry Keats describes. We are still trying to become the contemporaries of the great authors. Literature does many things. It puts us in contact with earthly hell, as we can best render it. But it also shows us the world we wish to live in, the place Blake and Frye think of when they use the word Golgonooza.

The cities that history unfolds are usually far different places. There what is most refractory about human experience reveals itself. Rome is built on slavery. Even exalted Athens burns with strife. Hegel refers to the slaughter bench of history; Marx talks about class struggle, but he might also have said class war, in which the descending classes are food for the upstarts. History, despite its glorious moments—despite the civil rights movement in America, despite the revolution that Jefferson and Washington led—is often a chronicle of misery. It shows where the best-laid plans tend to go.

History is frequently a cautionary antithesis to the hopes that literature ignites. For if *Lear* depicts horrors, one leaves the play nonetheless knowing that a human being wrote the play, a human being did *that*—and such achievement is a basis for hope. There is no such shaping force discernible behind history, despite the efforts of Hegelians of all stripes to reveal one. If literature and the arts can superbly render human freedom, history gives us the world of fate. And the student needs to measure every hope he has for self-creation, engendered by the poets and artists, against the realities of the recorded past. Not to be willing to engage this dialectic of power and limitation early on in life often condemns one to be the idealist in youth who becomes the disillusioned reactionary in old age. Without history to teach how hard it is, how ferociously fate can conspire against freedom, one is likely to be content with mere literary half-truths. Though the rise of democracy has injected a heretofore unimaginable hope into humanity's story, it still pays to consult history for a sense of how far we can fall and how fast.

In a liberal arts education, history is the necessary and profound rejoinder to the liberating arts—which is not to say that it cannot itself be a liberating art. But the literary comes first. Students need to be offered what hope they can accept, and to take it into a perilous future. Without a literary education, they may never find that hope. Fate, on the other hand, does not need to be sought and found. Fate will find you. History will find you. You can learn history from books, or life will teach it to you more intimately.

Always Historicize?

Historicizing is now the most influential intellectual fashion in the liberal arts. To qualify as a respectable scholar, one needs to put the work at hand into its historical context. That is, one must relegate it to the past. One must identify its analogues, its context, its conditions of engendering, the "social energies" that made it what it is. By no means should the real scholar see what the work can do in the present. That might open him up to criticism; it might make him look silly to actually profess something, rather than merely to affirm doubt and call it knowledge.

This is not to say that historical scholarship is without value. One needs to know the political context of Whitman's "Lilacs" elegy for President Lincoln; one needs to understand something of the Bible and something of Restoration politics to read Dryden's *Absalom and Achitophel.* But current scholars have gone far beyond that. To them, works of art are to be quarantined in the past, because living now we can't possibly understand them on their own terms. Good. We will understand them on what terms we can.

Scholars who historicize comprehensively, who deny the bearing of past greatness on the present, are persecuting the prophets, imprisoning their spirits. They are the descendants of Dostoyevsky's Inquisitor, who would protect the people from the dangerous word of the Savior by locking him away. I value few things as much as historical interpretations that allow us to read a past text in more nuanced ways. All honor to the bibliographers and the annotators. But to those who would clap the past away from the present—to paraphrase Blake at the close of *Milton,* they murder the Savior time on time.

True teachers of literature become teachers because their lives have been changed by reading. They want to offer others the same chance to be transformed. "What we have loved, / Others will love," says Wordsworth in *The Prelude,* "and we will teach them how." Literally the great poet is talking to his friend Coleridge, to whom the poem is written. But figuratively he speaks to all of us who have been changed by art and want to pay it forward, pass it along.

Why do teachers, especially at universities, turn against this hope, and teach that great writing is something we need to hold at arm's length? Why do they tell students to put the writing that matters at a historical distance, when students need to bring it closer to them, perhaps merge with it? To be entirely honest, I do not know. It may be that the weight of learning scholars must carry to be qualified to teach so stifles the imagination—so weighs it down—that it loses the power of sympathetic flight. This was what Nietzsche believed deep historical learning could do, and why he believed it was a danger as well as a potential virtue. There's a scene in Spenser where a questing knight is pinned down by the weight of his own armor, stuck to the ground and unable to fight. And that, perhaps, is the situation of our historicizers, pinned down by the bulk of their learning. As Nietzsche puts it, "The historical training of our critics prevents their having an influence in the true sense—an influence on life and action."

Or maybe institutional pressure for the conversion of imaginative power into academic knowledge is so strong that it forces the study of art to meet some high pseudo-scientific standards. Maybe we professors need to differentiate ourselves from grade school teachers (too feminine?) and show the investment bankers that we too are grown-ups, we too are mature? Does the need to be respected and respectable—the need to be beyond mockery—so infect university teachers that for it they sacrifice everything? Or are professors unwitting participants in the culture of cool, devoted to looking out at great art with the bemused, condescending detachment of the TV junkie? Have they taken up something not unlike the junkie's position, gazing down like slightly woozy gods on the passing show? Under the influence of dope (and its cultural equivalents), Ann Marlowe says, you can stem your anxieties. You can cultivate the illusion of having stopped time. But nothing Amazing will ever happen to you. (The changes that literature can bring on people are often just that, Amazing.)

Canons

Once you know what purpose you want literature to fulfill—the purpose that all things that matter go to fulfill, as Emerson suggested: to inspire—then a span of questions that now bedevils the humanities becomes easier to answer. You can think much more clearly and to better effect about canon formation, about multiculturalism, about cultural studies, about academic research.

The question of canon formation, despite all its fancy baggage, is really a question about what to teach. What books shall we get young people to read? Right now this is a terribly vexed issue for a number of reasons. Traditionalists like to go around snorting about how the new cultural studies types want to replace Brontë novels with bodice rippers off the supermarket racks. But when you ask the traditionalists exactly what makes a Brontë novel more worth reading than a bodice ripper, they often can't come up with much. They talk about subtlety and sophistication and depth, and they take up a condescending pose, the pose smug upper-middle-class types have greeted the unwashed with for hundreds of years. And of course, the cultural studies gang loves this kind of reaction. They're fulfilling their historical function of shocking hell out of the bourgeoisie.

What the defenders of consequential writing need to do is to stand up and say that a Brontë novel can help you live better—can, to use the idiom of this book, better enhance your expanding circle of self than the bodice ripper can. Until the so-called humanists take this step, they're going to be easy prey to the prophets of ersatz novelty.

For myself, I would largely leave the question of what to teach up to individual teachers, who could offer those books that they think can change their students' lives for the better. Let them select the books that are full of vital options. Let them choose the works that they themselves have been transformed by and that they think, now, can have the greatest effect on students. Some of the best classes I had as a student came when the professor went back to a book he'd read when young and became that young man again, fired by Woolf, or Joyce, or Mann.

I think that canonical works, the ones you read as part of a major—the books of which there may be many or few, depending on the teachers' views at a given time—ought to be the testing and transforming books that have influenced people in exciting ways over a long period. Teachers must not be guided by what they find "interesting," or by what they sense might become the subject of a bracing essay for *PMLA,* but on what could inspire their students to change, or to solidify their own commitments. We all get socialized once by our parents and teachers, ministers and priests. Studying the humanities is about getting a second chance. It's not about being born again, but about growing up a second time, this time around as your own educator and guide, Virgil to yourself.

Scholarly discourse should be more and more about the educational, or self-developing, properties of great writing. An essay on Shakespeare and love ought not to unfold the "ideology" of Shakespearean love, but let us know what, if anything, the author thinks that Shakespeare has to teach us about Eros. Scholarly knowledge will still be at a premium, but its objective will be to bring forward the author's vision, to make explicit what is implicit, to show the way to successful teaching.

So absurdly removed from day-to-day life is professional literary study that there is no major journal, on the order of *Raritan, Representations,* or *Critical Inquiry,* where teachers write to each other about ways they've found to teach this or that book. One has to look long and hard simply to find accounts of pedagogy. There are very, very few prominent scholars who have spent time writing about the actual dynamics of class exchange. In the waves of prose about the humanities that come out every year, students go virtually unmentioned. They are not quoted. They are not described. Anyone attending an academic conference or reading a professional journal for the first time would be forgiven for not knowing that what most of us spend most of our energies doing is teaching.

There is a sense among humanities professors that the field is drying up. All the major work has been done. Who wants to read yet another book on Alexander Pope? Well, I do, and students and common readers may as well, so long as the critic is willing to show what actual bearing Pope might have on the world we hold in common and on our individual lives. What human difference does he make? A brilliant book about Pope and the conduct of life could be of the highest value, and surely it is yet to be written. If what I am saying here is so, and literary criticism is not only a matter of interpretation, but a matter of reflecting on value, then the field is just opening up. The great bulk of meaningful work remains undone. And that, at least, might give some comfort to young people entering a field that must look utterly strip-mined.

I can't stress enough how despondent graduate students in the humanities often are at this point. They're some of the most admirable people to be found in their generation. With their prestigious undergraduate degrees, their splendid grades and board scores, they could go on to big-money careers in business and law. But they refuse. They want to study something that they're passionate about. Yet over time, almost all of them see that to thrive in the profession, they must make themselves marketable, and that often means betraying themselves. It means picking a subject that fits into the current conformity. It means spending years writing things that, on some deep level, they do not believe to be true. The exertion involved in having to get up every day, repair to one's word processor, and set to work defying one's nature in the interest of future employment, is not conducive to the psyche's health, or to the body's, either. These impressively gifted young men and women deserve better.

Their profession enjoins them to seek not what is true and humanly transforming but what is "interesting." That is, they seek out areas for research that are untouched, often untouched for very good reason. So the assistant professor begins a deep study of now unread and barely readable nineteenth-century domestic novels or boys' adventure books. Then he begins to teach those books, the better to get the monograph done, and in doing so becomes a waster of students' most valuable time and accordingly of students' lives. If a professor truly believes that nineteenth-century domestic fiction can expand the reader, make him more than he was, that is wonderful. I respect the daring. The independence of mind is to be admired. But to teach without the conviction that the book at hand might become someone's secular Bible is to betray the heart of the humanities.

To some, it may seem that literary study is at its end. But I believe we may be at the inception. We can begin to come to terms with Arnold's view that in the absence of faith in transcendental religion, poetry may have to do. We can begin learning to talk about poetry in order to render it as the secular scripture that it needs to be.

Do students, in order to be changed, need to read books that touch on their own experience, and in particular their own identity? Sometimes. If you are to adapt the world of a book to your own, to be influenced by it, it's probably helpful for the book to intersect with your past experience. So occasionally it will only be sensible for the young black man to start with Malcolm X, for the young black woman to pick up Zora Neale Hurston.

But identification also moves across the boundaries of race, class, and gender. I, growing up in the white working class, found no book more fascinating when I was seventeen than *The Autobiography of Malcolm X*. From Malcolm I learned a good deal about race relations in America; I learned about the forms of racism endemic to the South, but also, more shockingly, to the North, where I was growing up. (We were virtuous, we white northerners, especially compared with the mad Confederates we saw on TV hurling rocks in Selma—or so I imagined before I read Malcolm X.) But I acquired other things from that book as well. Malcolm X learned to read and write well in prison, relatively late in life. In page after rhapsodic page, he describes the joys of reading, the pleasures of expression, the lure of knowledge. Malcolm was persuaded, and persuaded me, that you could use the powers you acquired from books to live better yourself and to do something for the people around you. In terms of literal identity, Malcolm X and I had virtually nothing in common, but reading his book shaped me in ways that continue to matter thirty-five years after the first encounter.

So by all means, give the young black student who's barely heard of Malcolm a copy of the *Autobiography*. But we shouldn't assume that an African American is inevitably going to be more responsive to Malcolm than to Marcel Proust. If, on getting to college, I had encountered professors convinced that I needed to read James T. Farrell, Mike Gold, or some other designated "proletarian writers," I would have rebelled instantly. At the same time I was glad to read Farrell, among many others, and found in him something of an ally. One's literal identity—the product of race, class, gender, and socialization—is not the sole, and very often not even the central, ground for literary identification.

Multiculturalism

Know the other, says the multiculturalist. I agree. A segment of the humanities curriculum *should* be devoted to studying the literature and arts of cultures that are so resolutely different from the West's that what we confront is less likely to be live options than it is bracingly different modes of being. It is a good thing to know and respect difference, if it is worthy of respect, and to understand other cultures in their own terms.

Such knowledge may impede cruelty and exploitation, granted. But shall we know the other without knowing ourselves? If we learn only of difference, without taking the time to find, or begin to compound, the inner being, we risk being walking voids, readily taken up by, say, commercial interests, ever ready to use our college-won knowledge of others for the purposes of exploiting them. Where the inner void was, the unbearable lightness was, there the corporation may well drive its roots. Knowledge of the other without a corresponding self-knowledge is a supremely dangerous acquisition.

There may be no better training for the global economy than multi-culturalism. Students who are immersed in this curriculum will find that they are able to pose as "citizens of the world," moving among many sorts of people. But in whose interest? Who benefits? Will the world?

Writing on the rise of multicultural education, David Rieff asks a sharp question: "Are the multiculturalists truly unaware of how closely their treasured catchphrases—'cultural diversity,' 'difference,' the need to 'do away with boundaries'—resemble the stock phrases of the modern corporation: 'product diversification,' 'the global marketplace,' and 'the boundary-less company'?" Later in his essay, Rieff observes: "The more one reads in academic multiculturalist journals and in business publica-tions, and the more one contrasts the speeches of CEOs and the speeches of noted multiculturalist academics, the more one is struck by the simi-larities in the way they view the world . . . Both CEOs and Ph.D.'s insist more and more that it is no longer possible to speak in terms of the United States as some fixed, sovereign entity. The world has moved on; capital and labor are mobile; and with each passing year national borders, not to speak of national identities, become less relevant either to conscious-ness or to commerce."

Martha Nussbaum, one of the few thinkers now who is willing to suggest that literature and art matter because they can help people to live better than they do, argues that becoming a citizen of the world is the objective of liberal arts education. This goal she attributes to the Greeks. But what Socrates, primary among Greek thinkers, taught first is to know yourself. And when you do, through literature and history, you will begin to see whether being a citizen of the world is the right thing for you to aspire to be at this point in time. Perhaps the goal of world citizenship is too abstract. Maybe we need to be more pragmatic. How, precisely, does one wish to connect to the world at large? Maybe the best relation to the existing world, if global capitalism is the prevailing game, will be pure opposition, anti-world-citizenship as it were.

But multiculturalism, well understood, remains one of the joys of current humanistic study. The scholarly work of bringing together East and West, for instance, is of the greatest consequence. The religious thought and the medical knowledge of the East have a great deal to teach us in our present state. Never have we had a chance to learn so much from the study of others, including a humane, but not a blindly comprehensive, tolerance. And some texts that initially seem embodiments of pure differ-ence will turn out to be exactly the ones that future students respond to with a shock of recognition. The young upper-middle-class woman from Ohio may turn away from Virginia Woolf's *To the Lighthouse*, a book she's supposed to adore, and find that Chinua Achebe sees the world almost precisely as it is. Once we've opened up the possibility of direct literary connection—connection with great authors in the search for truth—all sorts of marvelous and unexpected meetings of mind become possible.

Pop

The spirit of education I affirm is well expressed by Harold Bloom: "We all of us go home each evening, and at some moment in time, with what-ever degree of overt consciousness, we go back over all the signs that the day presented to us. In those signs, we seek only what can aid the conti-nuity of our own discourse, the survival of those ongoing qualities that will give what is vital in us even more life. This seeking is the Vichian and Emersonian making of signification into meaning, by the single test of aiding our survival." This is what we do, or ought to do, with books— turn their signification into meaning, and so into possibility, in the hopes that so doing will better our lot.

The test of a book lies in its power to map or transform a life. The question we would ultimately ask of any work of art is this: Can you live it? If you cannot, it may still command considerable interest. The work may charm, it may divert. It may teach us something about the larger world; it may refine a point. But if it cannot help some of us to imagine a life, or unfold one already latent within, then it is not major work, and probably not worth the time of students who, at this period in their lives, are looking to respond to consequential and very pressing questions. They are on the verge of choosing careers, of marrying, of entering the public world. They are in dire need of maps, or of challenges to their existing cartography. Perhaps most of all, they seek ways to unfold their promise, to achieve the highest form of being they can. Works of art matter to the degree that they can help people do this. Books should be called major and become canonical when over time they provide existing individuals with live options that will help them change for the better. A democratic humanism can have no other standard for greatness.

The most beautiful statement of this ideal of literary education that I know of is Oscar Wilde's and comes from "The Soul of Man Under Socialism": "So he who would lead a Christ-like life is he who is perfectly and absolutely himself. He may be a great poet, or a great man of science; or a young student at a University, or one who watches sheep upon a moor; or a maker of dramas, like Shakespeare, or a thinker about God, like Spinoza; or a child who plays in a garden, or a fisherman who throws his nets into the sea. It does not matter what he is, as long as he realizes the perfection of the soul that is within him. All imitation in morals and in life is wrong. Through the streets of Jerusalem at the present day crawls one who is mad and carries a wooden cross on his shoulders. He is a symbol of the lives that are marred by imitation. Father Damien was Christ-like when he went out to live with the lepers, because in such service he realized fully what was best in him. But he was not more Christ-like than Wagner, when he realized his soul in music; or than Shelley, when he realized his soul in song. There is no one type for man. There are as many perfections as there are imperfect men." Such perfections are the aim of literary education, and if perfection is rarely the actual result, the process is no less noble for that.

Popular culture, which is more and more taught at universities, usually cannot offer such prospects. The objective of a good deal of rock music and film is to convey the pleasing illusion that people can live in the way that the singers and the actors do when they're on. Occasionally, I suppose, a performer comes through. Keith Richards seems to be, in life, the Keith he evokes when he's onstage. Most people probably don't have the guts or the constitution. When Terry Southern came to interview Richards, he laid three Quaaludes on him as a gift. Keith swallowed them all, took a slug of bourbon, and woke up two days later. No interview for Terry. But I'm not sure that this moment, taken as representative, can point to a plausible life for much of anyone except Richards himself.

Yet what David Denby says about movie love—and by extension the love of popular culture overall—still strikes me as true: "Movie love puts people in touch with their own instincts and pleasures. Movies can lead to self-reconciliation, and that is one reason they have inspired an almost unlimited affection." Putting people in touch with their instincts and pleasures: movies and many other popular forms tap into the fantasy life, and insofar as desire is being drowned by the gray waves of the reality principle, we need it to be restored. (Not to be able to fantasize at all is probably even less healthy than fantasizing all the time.) A little bit of tolerant thinking about the sorts of erotic and adventurous fantasies that we're drawn to can tell us a good deal about what's not present in our own lives. The message may be hyperbolical; fantasy is an exaggerated genre. But perhaps we need such exaggeration to be awakened from the spell of the day-to-day. Fantasy can inspire us to search for ways to satisfy hungers we didn't know we had.

By far the best inquiry into pop culture I know of along these lines is Simon Frith's essay on the Stones' *Beggar's Banquet*. "I've always lived a decent, sober, careful life," says Frith, disarmingly enough, and then he goes on to describe what it means to him to be drawn to the woozy, reckless life the Stones purvey. By the end of the piece, Frith can say that "*Beggar's Banquet*, so intense in its pursuit of pleasure, lays bare the weight borne by our notions of love and sex, the secret melancholy of life in the consumer collective. These are as much effects of current capitalism as dole queues and boring jobs and material squalor[,] and the Stones' pleasure perspective gives us a new sense of them . . . In other words, the function of the Stones' rock and roll dedication . . . is not self-indulgence or escape but defiance. *Beggar's Banquet* celebrates the reality of capitalist pleasure and denies its illusions. No expectations, a lot of laughs—the Stones' strength derives from their prodigality, from their denial of consequence." That said, the "decent, sober, careful" author has probably got to think about some riskier, more pleasure-prone ways to live.

Once we have made contact with fantasy, we need a new, larger self-synthesis that pays heed to refractory desires. Self-knowledge means knowing what we want, even if those wants are embarrassingly grandiose, or socially despised. But fantasies cannot generally be a direct blueprint for life, the way that the work of Henry James, say, can conceivably be.

Denby's article on film is related to Freud's radically undervalued essay "Creative Writers and Daydreaming." Here Freud, always competing with literature, wants to associate it with the id, giving psychoanalysis pride of place as the best way to develop the sane ego. Freud says that creative writing is simply a form of wish-fulfillment. In fiction and poetry of every sort, we find pleasurable fantasies to enjoy. What keeps us from seeing literary texts—not some, but all—as the fantasies that they are is form. Form, to Freud, is a distancing device. It offers the ego something to occupy itself, a kind of fore-pleasure, preliminary to the id's immersing itself in wish-fulfillment. In other words, form plays the role for literature, and presumably the other arts, that the dream work—the mechanisms by which the desire at the center of the dream undergoes distortion—plays in dreams.

Surely, though, it's not only form that makes John Milton definingly different from the latest pop bestseller. One can still live out of Milton's *Paradise Lost*, a poem that has a word, however harsh, to say about virtually every subject that matters. What ought to make a work survive is that it can be lived, can function, as Milton very much wished his poem to do, as a Bible of sorts. *Paradise Lost* was Freud's favorite poem, and, like all of the major works Freud pondered, from *Oedipus Rex* to *Lear*, it is a basis for psychoanalysis. Those works are far too tough-minded to be written off as wish-fulfillments, just as psychoanalysis is far too sophisticated, at its best, to boil down to the worship of one more spectral figure of authority, Sigmund Freud. Pop culture is by and large where wishes thrive, and knowing as much reveals pop culture's great value, as well as its limits.

Of course pop culture can be an area for productive disagreement. Given the work at hand, different people will respond differently to the question of whether you can live it out. Some will say yes to Bob Dylan (as I would, with reservations), yes to Muddy Waters and the blues tradition he works in, yes to Robert Altman or Stanley Kubrick. But you'll find far fewer people, I think, who'll be able to say an unequivocal yes to the Rolling Stones or to Britney Spears. That doesn't mean that the Rolling

Stones and, who knows, maybe even Britney, are without their value (fantasy matters). But teaching such work to people who're looking for answers to primary questions may not be the best way to use their time.

Not long ago, I met a student who told me an illuminating story. The student, now in college, had a high school English teacher whom he'd greatly admired, and that teacher admired Faulkner above all writers. For his part, the student admired Stephen King. He read everything King wrote; he loved his work. The teacher detested King. Why? Because, the teacher said, unlike Faulkner, King did not write "works of universal human significance."

The student walked away angry and unsatisfied, and I don't blame him. How does this teacher know what is "universal" and what is not? How does he know what something called the "human" might be? Only God—if he exists—knows what "universal human significance" is.

What the teacher might have said is something like this: "King is an entertainment. King is a diversion. But when you try to take him as a guide to life, he won't work. The circles he draws on the deep are weak and irresolute. And this is so in part because King, for all his supposedly shocking scare tactics, is a sentimental writer. In his universe, the children (or at least the pack of nice kids, the ones the bullies prey on) are good, right, just, and true. (In Wordsworth, the child is a much more complex being, appealing but not without his dangerous limits.) When King's kids see It—whether It is a spaceship, a slasher-clown from the deep past, or a ravenous vampire—It is truly there. Just about all adults who are not in some manner childlike are corrupt, depraved, lying, and self-seeking. This can be a pleasant fantasy for young people and childish adults. Facile Rousseauianism has its temporary pleasures. But bring this way of seeing the world out into experience and you'll pretty quickly pay for it. Your relation to large quadrants of experience, in particular those where you have to encounter adult authority, will likely be paranoid and fated to fail. On the other hand, Faulkner's tragic humanism is tough; it could stand the test of time. There's a lot to be learned from Dilsey, the black woman in *The Sound and the Fury*, who above all things endures. But that's not because she illuminates some 'universal human significance,' but because she does her work and lives righteously in the world."

When we teachers stop giving self-inflating answers to our students, and become clearly articulate about what the humanities can and can't offer—they may help you live better; they won't help you be a god—we'll be on our way to justifying our work to the public and attracting the students who most need us. Students now live in a bubbling chaos of popular culture. They need a way to navigate it. They need to know what's worth taking seriously, and what's a noisy diversion. We in the humanities can help them make this distinction. The mark of an educated person should be the ability to see the differences between entertainment and more nurturing, vital stuff. We need to help the public see how to make use of what great books offer. When people can do as much, they'll be able to take plenty of harmless pleasure in pop.

Many humanities teachers feel that they are fighting for a lost cause. They believe that the proliferation of electronic media will eventually make them obsolete. They see the time their students spend with TV and movies and on the Internet, and feel that what they have to offer— words, mere words—must look shabby by comparison.

Not so. When human beings try to come to terms with who they are and describe who they hope to be, the most effective medium is words. Through words we represent ourselves to ourselves; we fix our awareness of who and what we are. Then we can step back and gain distance on what we've said. With perspective comes the possibility for change. People write about their lives in their journals; talk things over with friends; talk, at day's end, to themselves about what has come to pass. And then they can brood on what they've said, privately or with another. From that brooding comes the chance for new beginnings. In this process, words allow for precision and nuance that images and music generally don't permit.

Our culture changes at an astounding velocity, so we must change or pay a price for remaining the same. Accordingly, the powers of self-rendering and self-revision are centrally important. These processes occur best in language. Surely there is something to be learned from the analysis of popular culture. But we as teachers can do better. We can strike to the central issues that confront students and the public at large, rather than relegating ourselves to the edges. People who have taught themselves how to live—what to be, what to do—from reading great works will not be overly susceptible to the culture industry's latest wares. They'll be able to sample them, or turn completely away—they'll have better things on their minds.

Democracy and Faith

This book took off from some lines of William Carlos Williams's: The new is in despised poems, he said, and men die every day for lack of what is found there. What is found there that prevents death, or death-in-life, is meaning—more precisely, meaning that can do something like what religious conviction can.

"The future of poetry is immense," Matthew Arnold wrote, "because in poetry, where it is worthy of its high destinies, our race, as time goes on, will find an ever surer and surer stay. There is not a creed which is not shaken, not an accredited dogma which is not shown to be questionable, not a received tradition which does not threaten to dissolve. Our religion has materialized itself in the fact, in the supposed fact; it has attached its emotion to the fact, and now the fact is failing it. But for poetry the idea is everything . . ."

Arnold tells us that if religious faith wanes in the world—or in a given individual—then the next likely source of meaning will be literature. The literature we have come to value, most especially the novel, is by and large antitranscendental. It does not offer a vision of the world under a deity's guidance. It suggests, though often it doesn't assert, that we humans have to make our own way without the strains and the comforts of faith.

The teaching of literature I believe in does not argue that always and for everyone, a secular, imaginative vision has to replace faith. My sort of teaching assumes that a most pressing spiritual and intellectual task of the moment is to create a dialogue between religious and secular visions of the world. Many of my students leave class with their religious convictions deepened and ramified. They're more ardent, more thoughtful believers than when they arrived. The aim is not conversion. The aim is encounter between the transcendental and the worldly. The objective is to help students place their ultimate narratives in the foreground and open themselves up to influence.

Religious faith in America now seems very strong. Somehow, in a culture that has disenchanted everything, a culture where cool prevails, religion has remained relatively intact. But I continue to feel that, as Freud expressed it in his 1927 book *The Future of an Illusion*, the promise for a large-scale turn away from religion is near at hand. There is simply too little evidence—at least by the relatively scientific standards that we now rely on in other areas of inquiry—that the miraculous tales that come to us in the Scriptures are true. Religion has attached itself to the fact, as Arnold says, "and now the fact is failing it." Efforts to prove God's existence materially and logically have never been fully satisfying. Just so, to believe intuitively in an all-loving, merciful, and omnipotent God is difficult for many of us after a century of closely documented horrors. Why didn't this Omnipotence intervene? Why didn't he prevent the horrible deaths of children and of relatively innocent women and men?

It may well be a matter of time, as Freud suggested, before lack of hard evidence combines with the absence of experiential proof to turn great masses of people against religion. But there is also the fact that many of the people in America now who claim to be religious have what is at best a tenuous purchase on faith. Their religions, often self-concocted, are Religion Lite, narcissistic investments in guardian angels and smilingly bland deities. There are few resources in such faiths to deal with tragedy and horror. When those things come to pass, how long will our current fragile faiths—think of my student's Catherinism—actually last? And if religion fails, what will there be to replace it? How will we give a meaning and shape to life? How will we tell ourselves stories, collective and individual, about our time here that can make life worth living?

Freud, for his part, commends a bleak stoicism as a replacement for faith. We need to face the fact that this life is full of undeserved, unredeemable suffering. We need to alleviate as much of that suffering as we can, not for any transcendental reason, but because it is in our interest to live in societies that do all they can to ease pain. Beyond that there is simple endurance. In his marvelous elegy, Auden commends Freud for achieving a fully compassionate regard for humanity: "Every day they die / Among us, those who were doing us some good, / And knew it was never enough but / Hoped to improve a little by living. / Such was this doctor."

Nietzsche, another major source for these thoughts on teaching and learning, felt the absence of God far more dramatically than Freud did. He saw God's death—by which he meant, among other things, the passing away of God's perceived presence from day-to-day life—as a traumatic event in human history, one whose full impact was not yet clear to most of humanity. It has still perhaps not reached us. The presence of God compelled human beings to quest for an ideal. They had to strive for something to win God's blessing—even if what they strove for was often not at all congenial to Nietzsche. Nietzsche feared that with the passing of God even that striving would stop. No one would think it worth his while to try to overcome himself. People would live happily with their own limitations. To move from a world peopled by Homeric heroes striving for the first place, to a world in which the best men and women struggled to please God by abasing themselves was cause for lament. But worse was life in which humanity had lost all interest in ideals. This was the world epitomized by "the Last Man." This creature who hops and blinks on the earth's crust, small and self-seeking, lives with the most pitiable credo: "One still works, for work is a form of entertainment. But one is careful lest the entertainment be too harrowing. One no longer becomes poor or rich: both require too much exertion. Who still wants to rule? Who obey? Both require too much exertion." The Last Man has his "little poison now and then: that makes for agreeable dreams"; he is cautious, self-absorbed, noncommittal. "We have invented happiness," the Last Men say, and then they blink.

What happens now and in the future if our most intelligent students never learn to strive to overcome what they are? What if aspirations to genius, and to contact with genius through Keats's immortal free-masonry, become silly, outmoded ideas? What you're likely to get are more and more two-dimensional men and women. These will be people who live for easy pleasure, for comfort and prosperity and the satisfactions of cool, who think of money first, then second, and third; who hug the status quo; people who believe in God as a sort of insurance policy (cover your bets); people who are never surprised. They will be people so pleased with themselves (when they're not in despair at the general pointlessness of their lives) that they cannot imagine that humanity could do better. They'll think it their highest duty to have themselves cloned as often as possible. They'll claim to be happy and they'll live a long time.

Against the coming of the Last Man, Nietzsche had little to recommend. He said that we might place ourselves thoroughly on the side of fate, and affirm the eternal recurrence of the same thing, no matter how horrible events might be. Our objective would be to turn the past ("Thus it was") into a function of our own desire ("Thus I willed it") and so come to love our fate. Our goal would be to take any event, no matter how horrible, and use it in our project of self-creation. We might use such events as a motive for growth or as raw material for works of art that would enlarge the mind. "What does not kill me," Nietzsche said in a self-vaunting moment, "makes me stronger."

But who could really affirm the eternal recurrence of everything? Who would have the demonic strength to wish for the Holocaust to happen again? Who could find possibilities for human expansion in that? And if you cannot affirm all events, including the most horrible, then surely the doctrine of the eternal recurrence dwindles in its power.

Neither Freud nor Nietzsche has Arnold's faith in the capacity of literature to create meanings that might, at the least, make life bearable. To

Freud, literature was illusion, mere wish-fulfillment. To Nietzsche, the lure of large-scale philosophical answers, answers that might be for everyone, or for everyone who mattered, such as the commitment to eternal recurrence, pushed the prospect of literary response aside.

Literary response is individual, particular: to put trust in literature affirms the antiphilosophic view that there are as many ways of living well as there are individuals disposed to do so. Nietzsche and Freud are aristocrats by temperament. The turn to literature for multiple truths is a democratic turn. The conviction that each of us has a particular genius to unfold is a democratic conviction.

Some will object to an open-ended vision of education in which we pursue our own visions, our own truths. People can become distressed when they imagine a world in which all of us, inspired by poets and other artists, create our lives, with only the inhibitions of community welfare and of our perceived failures to rein us in. They fear chaos, they say. They fear disorder. But perhaps what they fear, most truly, is genuine democracy.

And there is a sense in which they are quite right to be wary. For understood in its full implications, democracy is a gamble. People educated to enjoy the freedom of the poets may not always make the right choices, and surely they will not always make choices that we ourselves would approve. Jean-Paul Sartre says that no great work of literature could ever be anti-Semitic. It's pretty to think so. Consider Christopher Marlowe's *Jew of Malta* or Shakespeare's *Merchant of Venice*. Both are great imaginative achievements; both, whatever ingenuity a director may deploy to stage them, madly anti-Semitic at their cores. The fact is that literature can do us harm. It's a gamble to put our faith in it. It's a gamble to think of leaving religion behind.

Democratic humanism is a risk. We are betting that people will prefer life to death, creation to destruction, freedom to servitude. They have not always shown a will to do so.

All through time the consensus has been that people cannot rule themselves. In the great mass, they're depraved. They need to be controlled. The people at the top of the heap know best. But in America, we've decided to defy that long-standing wisdom. We've taken many steps toward the goal of full franchise for all, but there's further to go. We need to begin educating people now with full respect for their powers of determination. We need to give them the resources of the best that has been known and thought, and then stand back and let them make the decisions that matter.

The more chance that people have fully and freely to unfold themselves, the more chance, ultimately, that they'll find their own happiness, and the more chance that they will enlarge the scope of the possible for others. In every life-affirming human mutation, however apparently odd, there lies the chance that something new and wonderful will arise that will act as a light to future generations. If America leads and inspires the world in the years to come, it will not be because we have the most potent armies, or create the most alluring entertainments, or manufacture the best products, or even create the most wealth. It will be because here more than anywhere, people are free to pursue their own hopes of becoming better than they are in a human sense—wiser, more vital, kinder, sadder, more thoughtful, more worth the admiration of their children. And it will be because they are free to become who they aspire to be after their own peculiar fashions. They'll feel a just pride in themselves and they'll feel a tough and enduring pride in a country that trusted them enough to let them flourish. Democracy wagers that when you put human beings together and give them every opportunity to express and develop themselves, then their virtues will exceed their faults, if only by so much. To be part of that experiment, and to contribute to its success, that is something that a man or woman, however humble, can take a vast and honest pride in.

Democracy, and the democratic humanism that can make it unfold—these are my religion. These are the sources of my faith and hope. For the promises of democratic humanism are without bound. Imagine a nation, or world, where people have fuller self-knowledge, fuller self-determination, where self-making is a primary objective not just in the material sphere but in the circles of the mind and heart. ("It tends outward," that heart, "to immense and innumerable expansions.") We humanities teachers can help create such a world, a world of rich, interanimating individuality, in tandem with flourishing community. A renewed democratic humanism can take us there. We should begin, now, to heed that humanism's highest promise.

PART 2: *WHY WRITE?*

To James Naismith and His Game

Why Write?

Why write?

Why write when so many forces in the world seem pitched against writing?

Why write when it sometimes feels that so few people really read? I mean read slowly, tasting the words: read deliberately, as if their lives might be changed by what they're reading.

Too often now the public reads for information, not enlightenment. People read to be brought up to date and put in the know. They want telegraphic bursts of prose. They want the words to be transparent, not artful or arresting. They need to get right to the truth, or failing that, directly to the facts. It can seem now that writing is a service: the writer dishes up information the way the counterman dishes lunch at the fast-food restaurant. In his worst moments, the writer feels that the world doesn't really want writing: if by writing you mean thoughtful, nuanced interpretations of experience that could actually shift some basic perceptions—maybe even change some lives.

And if that is the case, why write? Why try, with as much selflessness as you can, to enlarge the contours of your mind—and to give others what real writing always has: pleasure and instruction, beauty and truth?

The world wants to be informed not enlightened, and the world wants to be entertained not inspired. Fiction writers now are supposed to give the readers exactly what they want. Novelists are to provide well-crafted, modest explorations of modest but badly crafted lives. Poets are to speak of themselves and themselves only (no big reach—no justifying God's ways to man, or man's to God) and speak in a timid whisper of a voice. To be a poet in America now is a slightly shameful condition, like having a mild drug habit or talking occasional smack to other people's kids.

In America what once were artists are supposed to be entertainers. They shouldn't offer tough or potentially dispiriting work to the world: they need to shake their rattles and jangle their bells. They live in a culture that measures success by the number of copies sold not the number of spirits touched. They have to shorten their sentences and compress their sentiments to the common bandwidth. They ought to stop worshiping low-sale losers like Virginia Woolf (a suicide) or Herman Melville (died in despair) and begin to model their careers (writers now have *careers*) on palatable entertainers.

Get this straight, too. In America what once were essayists and critics are now consumer guides. They write not to tell us what art *they* favor. That would be elitist and narcissistic to boot. They write to let us know what we would like. They are in position to reflect taste (our taste) and not to shape it. They must use small neat words; they must pretend to like what the mass of their readers do; they must never make anyone feel dumb.

The artist is a glorified entertainer; the critic pens consumer reports. Under these conditions: Why write?

Why write when every day words seem to mean less and less? We are, it's said, becoming a culture of images. Developments in video technology have created wonders. A flat-screen TV delivers a vision that can seem more real than reality. The soft green landscape out my window can't compete in intensity with the high-def football game playing on the TV just below it. On the screen, life seems to be on fire. Every figure and every object appears to exude internally generated light. At the movies, we see that directors can put any image they wish on the screen. Dream it and your dream comes true. Would you destroy the Earth? Say the word to the special effects team, seated like obedient gnomes at their computers. Will you restore it all before the end of two hours? Done.

How can writing compete? How can shadowy etchings on the surface of soon-to-yellow paper or bug-like squiggles on a screen touch the glittering image? The TV producer has become a demiurge. The film director is Jove. How can the inch-ling scraping along with his stylus ever compete? It's an open question now whether any traditional art can have the impact of the most modestly produced and conceived video diversion.

And if that is so: Why write?

There is another simpler and perhaps more serious objection to be made to writing. There is already too much of it. We live in a torrent of words that are already written and words fast coming into being. The Internet has made everyone a furious scribe; that much is understood. But beyond the Babel of words that flows daily into the world there is the accumulation of the most distinguished words—the best that has been known and thought. Libraries overflow with them and the Internet, for all its excesses, has brought us within a few strokes of *Paradise Lost* and *Regained.*

Why write when Shakespeare has already written? What has already been composed and is now there in the public domain is daunting in its magnificence and plenitude. An entire lifetime isn't enough to read all of the literature in English, or English translation that is worth reading. More lifetimes would be needed to take in the best of the sciences, law, social thought, and political reflection. Why try to add one's bit to this amazing horde of words, a treasure we can now see and enjoy online, with less exertion than it took the Arab merchant to whisper "open sesame"?

And why write when it is so damned hard to do? There really is no writing, one is told time and again. There is only rewriting, and in this there is some truth. The ones who have come before have set the bar high and every writer knows that no matter how lucky a day it has been, how smoothly the first draft rolled out, there will still be dozens of revisions and re-revisions. Writers often look at what they have done and say simply: "It doesn't work." When a mechanic says as much about the engine, he usually knows what's wrong and what needs to be done, or he can narrow it down to three or four possibilities. But the writer often has no comparable clue. It's broken; she knows that. But what's the fix?

Walt Whitman implicitly compared writing to the work of "a noise-less, patient spider." The spider is constantly sending strands of filament into the void to create his web. Sometimes the strands catch and hold, but mostly they don't. The spider, undaunted, keeps letting the filaments flow. Whitman's suggestion is clear enough: the writer's efforts come from deep inside, out of his guts. When he fails, it is not language that is failing or the genre or the culture: he is the one who is failing and it is (dare one say it?) very much like a spiritual failure. Yeats says it as well as anyone ever could:

> A line will take us hours maybe;
> Yet if it does not seem a moment's thought,
> Our stitching and unstitching has been naught.
> Better go down upon your marrow-bones
> And scrub a kitchen pavement, or break stones
> Like an old pauper, in all kinds of weather;
> For to articulate sweet sounds together
> Is to work harder than all these, and yet
> Be thought an idler by the noisy set
> Of bankers, schoolmasters, and clergymen
> The martyrs call the world.

Yeats is right (and amazingly eloquent) but I doubt the lines have ever changed the mind of a single banker or priest about the writer's lot.

Writing is backbreaking, mind-breaking work. So, one might readily ask: Why bother?

Why write when the work is as lonely as it is? A writer is isolated in two senses. There is the obvious sense: she works all day (if she can) and she works alone. There is usually no one around to talk with; there is no one to complain to after you've bored your wife or husband near comatose for the thousandth time. We're told now over and over again that human beings are social animals. Life is about the group. People who don't have a thrumming circle of friends and don't get out much are the ones who grow readily depressed. They become anxious; they entertain poison thoughts; they find themselves stuck with all the maladies that loneliness brings. We're now disposed to think collaboration is the name of the game: The best products are team efforts. Hit TV shows are created by committee. It takes a village to raise a child and it takes an army to make a film. Let's pool our talents. Let's all have a say. Let's put it to a vote, then e-mail and tweet until we've arrived at revelation. Meanwhile, the writer slogs on in her slightly toxic and highly suspect isolation.

There is the literal isolation of the writer: a room of her own can become a private cell, to which she's somehow lost the key. But the writer also takes her isolation into the world. Browning calls the poet God's spy and that's a complimentary way of putting it. We could say, more neutrally, that writers are almost always spies and have the kinds of lives that spying creates. They are constantly collecting information, making mental notes. Henry James said that often the foundation for a tale or even a novel of his was "a glimpse." A woman steps out of a tram in tears; an otherwise well-dressed man has holes in his shoes. In a crowd, writers are by themselves; at the party they may laugh with the group but often seem, both to themselves and to others, to be laughing alone. Once they've committed themselves to the writing game there is always a measure of detachment. Whitman said that he—or the part of himself that mattered most, the Me-myself—was never fully present. He was perpetually "in and out of the game and watching and wondering at it."

People live to achieve total absorption in the life around them: they want to be immersed in happy circumstances and feel calm and contentment. They find this state with their families, with their friends, watching a ballgame, or playing a round of golf. Writers out in the world almost never seem to achieve this condition; they are always watching and wondering at it. They rarely manage to disappear happily into their own lives. The only time most writers can reliably get in sync with themselves is when they are writing—and then only when it's going supremely well. Outside the study (the cell) they are prone to feel that life is out of joint. And inside the cell—there they are alone, too.

There are so many reasons not to write and so many of them good: So why?

Because writing is one of the best acts a human being can turn his hand to. With all of these objections on file, and more besides, the case for writing remains overwhelming. Writing is a great human good, even a higher good than most of its best-known and most articulate advocates have told us. I mean real writing of course: writing that rises from the desire to give other people pleasure and instructions. I mean writing done with as much detachment from desire and purity of motive as possible. (Though no one could ever ask for that purity to be complete.) Ludwig Wittgenstein famously said that the limits of one's language were the limits of one's world. By coming up with fresh and arresting words to describe the world accurately, the writer expands the boundaries of her world, and possibly her readers' world, too. Real writing can do what R. P. Blackmur said it could: add to the stock of available reality.

There are plenty of bad reasons to write, and I'll be talking about them here. But mostly this book focuses on what seem the best reasons for giving oneself over to writing. Writing to make money and writing to possess the status of having written won't do much for you in the long run. But that's not all there is to writing. Writing can enlarge the mind and strengthen the spirit. It can improve character (if you let it). The process of writing can make you happy—or get you as close to happiness as people of a certain disposition are likely to come.

Writing—to highlight one of its benefits—can teach you to think. Doesn't everyone know how to think? Can't all of us reflect? We human beings are called the rational animals after all. But no, the truth is we can't. There's jumble and senseless rumble in our minds most of the time. We live in a stream of consciousness, and that stream doesn't always go much of anywhere. Writing disciplines the mind the way hard workouts discipline the body. Writing compels us to reason and to give reasons. Then, after we've written we have to go back and check our work with a cold eye. We have to strengthen what's weak and reframe what's faulty. We strive to *make sense* as the saying goes. The saying touches on a truth. For sense is made not by coercing the facts or pumping up the rhetorical volume. Sense is made by sifting through the sand of our ignorance to find, here and there, the words and thoughts that persuade ourselves (truly) and perhaps consequently to persuade others.

I'm not sure how, without writing or intense conversation, we could ever learn how to think. Oh, we could learn to plot and scheme, all right. As human beings we are driven by desire—and usually we choose to try to satisfy that desire. So the practical mind comes into play, sometimes fiercely. But I persist in thinking that one hasn't really lived unless one has tried to think about a matter that doesn't touch on one's own immediate profit. We may never answer grand questions about human nature or what the best way of life for a man or woman is, but we are at our best when we pursue such questions. And to think well, we must train the mind much as the athlete trains the body. I sometimes think that to have been born with that majestic faculty, the mind, and have never truly thought and written is like having been born in our bodies but spent our entire lives on a mattress: no sports, no sex, no dance, not even a leisurely walk across the park.

Writing is thinking; thinking is writing. But if that sounds like too gray and utilitarian a reason to make writing part of your life, or to live for writing straight out, there are other reasons for writing that are of a more delighting sort. For once you're at home with words there are few more pleasurable human activities than writing.

"How do I know what I think until I see what I say," says E. M. Forster, and this is probably true of many of us. We don't know our views until someone asks us. Writing is a way of asking ourselves. What comes out can be dismal: it's true. Whenever I try to write something about American politics I'm forced to remember that the political is something I'll probably never understand. Is it all about the needs of selves, or collections of selves? Does soul ever enter in? Does something like a spirit of benevolence? I never know where to begin. Though at least I know that I do not know, which the ragged philosopher Socrates thought a good enough condition to spend his entire life endorsing.

But sometimes, for everyone who writes, words tantamount to wonders pour out. Truth comes forth: or at least the truth that is true for you. And sometimes the shivering soul who says never—never could I write a poem or conceive a play—by sitting down and putting a word on the page then another discovers that there are worlds inside him he never knew. Is it good? Is it bad? Sometimes it's enough if a piece of writing simply *is*. It is. *It is and I did it.* Through writing people can sometimes say along with Wallace Stevens's persona in the marvelous poem "Tea at the Palaz of Hoon": "And there I found myself more truly and more strange."

Who am I to write a book about writing? What qualifies me to take on this difficult matter? I suppose I could point in the direction of a stack of books, a few sheaves of articles; I could flourish an advanced degree or two. But really, I think what chiefly qualifies me to write about writing is that I've been a slow learner. I've gone by small steps. I didn't publish a book until I was nearly forty and I drafted that one so many times that when it was done I felt like I'd written ten. But traveling by foot has its advantages. You get to look around and take in the territory, see where you are and plot out where you're going. Maybe taking the gradual overland route has put me in a position to be a guide for others, to help them out in ways that those who have flown over the same ground in a gleaming silver jet never could.

This book is organized around themes: writing and memory, writing and thought, writing and sex, writing and fame, writing and (cue the gnashing of teeth) being reviewed. But it's also a lightly drawn writer's autobiography. I start with issues and events that dominated my early period of writing (or trying to write), move through some meaty midphase issues, and end with thoughts about the writer's later life, at which I've now more or less arrived. Writing can bring your mind to birth—and it can also let you carve your own tombstone if you're so inclined. And in the middle years, writing can help you reach many other goals, infinitely worth reaching. So here it is: some autobiography, some inspiration (I hope), and even a dose of how-to.

There's so much to be said about writing (real writing, I mean) and in the pages to follow, I'm going to say some of it. I'll draw freely from the great ones who came before me, and of course add something out of my own experience. Many wonderful words have been written about writing—words about the joy and pain of composing words—and I'll rely on some of them here. But I'll add something to the mix, a thesis if you like. As much praise as writing has gotten through the years, it has still not gotten enough. We are still not entirely aware of what writing, good writing, can do for individuals and for the collective. We have at our hands' reach a skill that is also a spiritual discipline. Writing is a meditation; writing is as close as some of us can come to prayer; writing is a way of being, righteously, in the world. And this is something that everyone ought to know.

GETTING STARTED

To Catch a Dream

For a long time, I tried to figure out how I was going to get started as a writer. I knew that a writer was what I wanted to be—though it wasn't clear exactly why. Surely it was in part because I was certain I'd never be very good at anything else. But how was I going to get started?

All right, I'd done some writing. I'd composed some essays for my college classes and those had been received well enough. But assigned writing wasn't really writing. Writing, I thought then (I was about twenty I suppose), was something you did because you wanted to do it, maybe because you had to do it. It was a form of self-expression and it was self-initiated, not commanded by anyone else. Writers were "self-begot, self-raised, by [their] own quick'ning power." Or so I believed.

I began carrying a notebook with me everywhere I went. I was waiting for lightning to strike. And sometimes something did strike. Though on examination it always proved to be something that didn't really qualify as lightning. I'd get an idea for a story, some lines for a poem, a concept for a movie script (I wasn't particular; I'd start anywhere). But then I'd think about it. This? This is going to be the *first* entry in my writer's note-book? This is how I'm going to get my start as a writer? It's too thin, too clichéd, too boring, too trite, too something or other. This can't possibly be the way *I'm* going to start.

Is it possible that I was thinking of posterity? Could I have conceivably believed that future scholars would find my first scratchings and connect them to my later work? Maybe I was thinking of Keats, whose juvenilia has traveled with him through literary history like a broken can on the tail of a dog. *Vanitas. Vanitas.* I had a bad case of it. What more is there to say?

But how bad could these early ideas of mine have been? I can show you, because as it turns out I remember one. It came in the form of a "poem." I concocted it sitting on the front steps of my parents' house in Melrose, Massachusetts. And on first consideration, I thought it pretty darned good. I had my notebook with me at the time. (I had my notebook with me at all times.) I even had a writing implement, a pencil as I recall. I reached into my pocket, pulled out the notebook, which was not imposingly made. It was not a leather number with my name engraved on the front, or even one of the sternly bound black items they sold at the bookstore of my college, where they were much in demand (for many of my contemporaries were poets; some were visionaries). No, mine was a much-sat-on pocket-sized once-royal-blue notebook, with a spring across the top that had sprung loose and looked like a strand of unkempt hair from a very curly head. Had it been red, it would have been a spring of Raggedy Ann's. My pencil was a pencil.

I drew forth the notebook and flourished the pencil and there, sitting on the doorstep of my parents' home in Melrose, I took a long breath and tried to begin to begin as a writer. It was just before dinner. The sun was more out than not, but it had put in a solid day's workmanlike performance and was ready to set; the grass had been cut (though not by me—allergies and indolence); and the birds from the cemetery down the street were gathering (they must have been, since they did this every fair-weathered day at the same time) in a massive oak tree beyond the cemetery wall, a tree that no doubt knew the secrets of the ages, having seen (maybe) Pilgrims and Indians and even a stray Salem witch or two.

Nature held its breath, or at least I did. I looked down, addressed the blank page, the white ghost-like page that haunts writers, or haunted them constantly until its job was taken by the screen of a computer that contains inside it news of the world, sports clips, pornography, and many other diversions: I addressed the page and I wrote absolutely nothing. That's what I wrote: nothing.

And it's not hard to understand why. What I had in mind was a poem. It was an untitled poem, inspired probably by all the existentialist philosophy and fiction I had been reading in college. The poem, or anti-poem, or non-poem (yes, I think that's it), ran this way: "There is a deity at the essence / of which, of what, I know not. / Only this: that the essence is lost."

Somehow I was both very proud of having concocted this and fully aware that it was abstract, boring (if you can be boring in three lines you truly have a gift), and ridiculously pretentious. Yet I was proud of it. And yet I knew it was vile. Knowledge defeated narcissism—and I wrote: nothing. A few days later the empty notebook disappeared and beyond school essays, which were tough for me to compose as it was, I wrote nothing for oh, two or three years.

The moral of this story is pretty clear. I should have torpedoed my doubts and written my pompous lines. I should have made those words my beginning and the hell with it. Starting takes guts. It usually means putting something down, looking in the mirror that is judgment, finding yourself ugly, and living with it. If a fool would persist in his folly he would grow wise, Blake says. And sometimes he is right. But I looked and I was scared and I ran away like the timid kid in the horror movie who manages to get slashed or gobbled up anyhow. I went cold and icy and dead. He who desires but acts not breeds pestilence, Blake also says. I ducked down that day and bred a little pestilence in myself, the pestilence that comes from wanting to do something worthwhile and being too timid to stay at it.

It's surprising how rarely accomplished writers are willing to talk about their initial efforts. Or maybe it's not: sprinters are never game to tell you how hard it was for them to learn to walk. Robert Frost tells a melodious story about how he "made" his first poem. He spent all day making it he says. He became so transfixed that he was late to his grandmother's for dinner. "Very first one I wrote I was walking home from school and I began to make it—a March day—and I was making it all afternoon and making it so I was late at my grandmother's for dinner. I finished it, but it burned right up, just burned right up, you know."

It's well told. (Frost always tells his stories well.) But it smacks a bit too much of the Immaculate Conception for me. I like Frost's other earthier story of where his poems come from. It's as though, he says, you're walking down the street in your hometown and coming toward you is a fellow you've known all your life. You and he are fond enough of each other—though not too fond. What you usually do when you cross paths is to exchange insults. And this time you see him before he sees you, just a moment or so, and on the back of your tongue (I elaborate a bit here) there arises the taste of the most tangy, civilized but nasty insult you've ever conceived. And it feels good and when the time comes the delivery is a perfect strike. You score, 1–0: point, game, match. They tell you that you don't have to score, Frost says. But you do. Today, with your insult you do. And that's what it's like to make a poem. "It's him coming toward you that gives you the animus, you know. When they want to know about inspiration, I tell them it's mostly animus."

That day sitting on my parents' porch, watching the grass go golden green in the twilight and aspiring to Keats-like thoughts, I imagined that writing came from the impulse toward sweetness and light. That's the impulse Frost seems to attribute to himself in the first example. I wanted to summarize the world for the world and lament its sorry state in detached and compassionate terms. A deity at the essence! Alas, the essence is lost.

But I should have realized that writing doesn't always come out of pure motives, at least not at the start. (Though I think that finally it's best when it does.) Writing can be analogous to playful insult (or semiplayful), to invective, to curse, and to rant. Milton, Blake says, wrote best when he wrote from Satan's vantage. The Puritan poet was of the devil's party without knowing it. It's necessary early on not to idealize the process too much, or to idealize yourself. (Though later on there's room enough for high aspirations.) You want to get a sail up, even if it's a ragged one, and plunge into the bay. I jumped in, Keats says. Rather than staying on shore and taking tea and comfortable advice, I jumped in and maybe made a bit of a fool of myself with *Endymion*. A critic named Croker laughed at Keats. But who has heard of Croker now, beyond knowing that Keats's friend Hazlitt called him "the talking potato"?

I think that eventually writing should be about truth and beauty, right and justice and that it should seek to profit others more by far than the writer himself. But get in by any door you can. Keep composing the lachrymose sonnets, full speed ahead with the "proud bad verse" (Keats again, though from the later, better *Fall of Hyperion*). Forward march with the inelegant essays; spring off the line on the first hut with the miserable rewrites of *Les Miz*. As long as you can in time recognize that they are bad and need work and that you must (and will) get better, you are triumphing. Virginia Woolf said that you should never publish anything before you are thirty anyhow. But get rolling now, even if you are thirteen (or seventy).

I wonder sometimes how many aspiring writers there are wandering around in writer limbo, hoping to make an august start, unwilling to touch pen to paper or finger to keyboard until they have achieved the inaugural mot juste, the Flaubertian word for just exactly right. I wish I could reach out to them and pat them on the shoulder and tell them it'll be all right, and that there is no time for starting like now. Take some courage from me. Take some spirits. And if you're truly desperate, I have some inaugural lines never really used that I offer gratis. Start with them if you want. "There is a deity at the essence . . ." From here, there is nowhere to go but up.

So how did I start? How did I get to the business of writing? I owe it to Hunter Thompson and to the invention of the electric typewriter. And oh yes, to drugs: I also owe it to drugs.

At a certain point in college I became enamored with the writing of Hunter S. Thompson. Thompson was the gonzo journalist par excellence who steamed himself up on drugs and wrote wild, scabrous, trenchant pieces on Richard Nixon, the Hells Angels, and other outlaws in American life. (Nixon and the Angels really do belong on the same page.) The archetypal photo of Thompson shows him bent like a vulture over his typewriter, long neck in a downward curl, bald head poised over what looks like a meal of bad meat but is really an exposé on Greedheads or that swine of a man and jabbering dupe of a president Richard Milhous Nixon. In his eulogy for Nixon he averred that the former president's body should be burned in a trash bin.

Everywhere Thompson went in America he experienced fear and loathing and tried to create some, too, through the engine of his prose. He was a mannered fellow, actually a bit of a dandy, with his cigarette holder and his tinted yellow sunglasses and his bald dome before bald domes a la Michael Jordan became the thing. He looked manly, more manly almost than Hemingway, who did all he could to fuse writing (a lady's parlor game, the fellas feared) with grand-safari masculinity. Hunter even had the right name: he pursued big game with the avidity of a trained woodsman.

He also spent much of his time high as a monkey, or at least his persona did. He suggested that without a closet full of drugs—uppers, downers, sliders, smackers, and blasters—there would be no writing from Hunter S. Thompson. He wrote the way Andretti drove a race car—full out, balls to the walls, into the wind. Later on I'd learn that Hunter was a bit of an eleven-year-old, living off and alone near Woody Creek, Colorado, getting

high and shooting off guns and going *wow*. And I'd also learn that when
he was just starting out as a writer, he spent his time copying page after
page of Faulkner and other writers to see how it was done. Nothing especially gonzo about that.

But what my twenty-three-(or so)-year-old self got from Hunter
Thompson was the image of a guy who fueled himself like an expensive
engine with high-octane drugs, threw himself down in his writing chair
like a bull rider hopping on the brahma, then opened the chute (which is
to say wrote a word) and let the bucking start. Thompson (my Thompson)
wrote the way Rocky Marciano fought. Full out, throwing everything
he had into it until covered with sweat and maybe bleeding from the
nose, he flung his hands over his head—victory!—and collapsed in a
winner's heap. The man went at it.

I was not Hunter Thompson to be sure. And even then I had an inkling
that Hunter Thompson was not Hunter Thompson either. But I followed
his lead, or what I imagined to be his lead, and threw myself into writing
sessions the way I had thrown myself into playing football: all out, head
up, and body on the fly into the tide of the oncoming.

I had a Hunter Thompson sort of subject at my disposal, too. I was
working as a stagehand and security guy at rock shows outside of New
York City at the time and my life was full of rock bands and drugs
and bikers and girls who stood up in the crowd partially clothed and
danced to the music the way serpents do to the charmer's pipes. I'd seen
riots and backstage fistfights and a knifing (maybe). I'd watched (from
under the safety of the stadium eaves) as a Hispanic street gang heaved
down lumps of concrete on my front-gate security crew, like the denizens of a medieval town fighting off attackers. (Get under the eaves, you
dopes!) We had refused to let the gang in for free (or I had), even though
the concert was taking place on their turf and so they were expressing
their sentiments. To complete my Hunter Thompson experiential
bacchanal, the Hells Angels turned up for our Grateful Dead shows.
One show got canceled because of foul weather even though it said "rain
or shine" on the back of the tickets. The Deadheads rioted. (One would
have thought they were too stoned to manage anything as active as
rioting, but they proved proficient at it.) The Angels ascended to biker
heaven when it became clear they were expected to put down the riot
through any means they wished. The image of a large Angel standing
at the front of the stage urinating down on the Deadheads clambering
to get up and destroy Jerry Garcia and his guitar and steal his drugs

(presumably) is one I won't forget and one that seemed sent by the gods when, a few weeks later, I sat up late in my linoleum-floored room on West 187th Street, up near the George Washington Bridge, trying to get it all down.

I pulled a complete pseudo–Hunter Thompson. I opened an envelope full of white powder—which might as well have been talc from the pool room, so potent were the powers of suggestion alive in the air—laid out a long sequence of lines, turned on the electric that had been willed to me by my writer buddy Michael Pollan, and I went to work. I wrote for seven hours running—Thompson hours—flying full force, headlong break-neck, amok in drug and sports imagery. I did not stop typing except to roll in another slice of yellow paper. I hit the keys so hard I blew holes in the yellow sheaves where the *o*'s should have been. It must have sounded like an all-night gun battle.

And from time to time I'd look down as if from a great height and say to myself, "I'm writing. I'm writing. I am writing!" It was like learning to ride a bike. It was like nailing three-pointers one after the next from the corner. It was like getting the hang of sex—if one ever gets the hang of sex. It was like magic.

I was so happy with what I'd done that a few days later, after a cursory redraft, I sent the manuscript—spilled on, fat, and sloppy as a pile of old bills—to George Plimpton at the *Paris Review*. (Michael and I had taken turns working there, basically failing to sell ads for that distinguished journal.) I knew for certain that Plimpton would love it. He'd been into the experiential journalist thing before Thompson even, though he was a bit too much of a white man—Exeter, Harvard, Hasty Pudding—for my newly fledged wild self. I did not think much about the response that was coming from Plimpton. I more or less figured that after my burst, publication was a done deal. I could now get some more ideas and write more.

What had happened? How had I finally—if a bit absurdly—done the thing I so much wanted to do and could not? How had I managed to begin, or at least begin to begin? Well, I'd made myself into something like a battering ram—a heavy, fast-moving force—and I'd rammed my way through my inhibitions. The inhibitions were a well-made, heavily cemented wall of rocks and even boulders. I was quite simply afraid that my stuff would be terrible. I was afraid that I'd see that I had no talent. I was afraid that deprived of my writing ambition I'd have no other ambition remaining and be left wandering in the void.

So it took a lot of horsepower—some of it manufactured, some of it absurd—to break through. I had to pretend to be a guy I was not. And from what I could tell, he himself spent a good deal of time working on his gonzo persona, pretending to be a guy he was not. I had to counterfeit a counterfeit. I also needed the audience of my two roommates who stayed half-awake that night in awe of my amazing dedication to the craft. And the drugs! Later on in grad school I'd settle for coffee to get my writing done—so much of it that in time it part ruined my stomach. But this time I needed the devil's dandruff, as Robin Williams illuminatingly called it. Though I expect it was more the outlaw feeling of cutting those lines and laying them out that amped me than the drug itself. My roommates turned up their noses at it—which meant it was poor quality indeed. And perhaps it was truly nothing but talcum powder. (But coke: a deathtrap. We didn't know that then, so stay away!) To write what I thought to be the truth (my truth!) I needed fictions, fabulations, creative swerves from reality, dreams! But I started writing that night and from then on knew I could at least participate in the game. I might never be a *writer* like Hunter Thompson, but I would write.

So many young aspiring writers out there—or older or simply old straight out—escape the trap of silence any way they can. One guy I know did it by putting a woman's name at the top of the page and running free; one by dictating his tales; one by three days' meditation preliminary to the first, first draft; another by putting the pencil in his left hand, his off hand, and grinding it out. To get started you can use any means necessary, though crazier means probably won't work over the long run. Pretend, pretend, pretend, if you have to, in order to get to the real.

You're breaking out of jail. If you do it digging with a spoon, that's fine; if you trick the guard that's OK, too; maybe you simply have some rich friend buy the dungeon and turn you out. By any means necessary. Because once you're out, you're out. A toast to you—my hand greets yours.

The rock-and-roll piece? A month later I got a letter back from George Plimpton beginning with the words: "It's not very good. At least not publishable." I walked around in misery for a while, feeling as put-upon and resentful as the Count of Monte Cristo when he left the dungeon after the years of wrongful imprisonment. But like the Count I also felt free. I was out and I was on my own. I was writing.

And Plimpton was wrong (give or take). My riff about the Grateful Dead show and the Angels anti-riot rioting did get published, albeit after a bit of revision and some patient reconsidering. It's in the first chapter of what in many ways is my favorite of my books, *The Fine Wisdom and Perfect Teachings of the Kings of Rock and Roll.* So what if it took thirty years to see the light of publication!

Often a benign invisible hand presides over these matters. Hey, there's a deity at the essence, right?

To Do It Every Day

Writers—especially writers who write books about writing—tend to do a lot of talking about the blank page and lately about the blank screen. It's a frightening prospect this blank space—looming up at us like the void. Every day, in a manner slightly heroic, we have to enter this void and make it pregnant with feeling and thought. Daunting of course: scary, harrowing. Each morning (or if one is prone to stay in bed as long as Dr. Johnson and a few others did, every afternoon), you've got to rise and fling a lance at your own version of the great white whale: the pale, empty page.

Well, that's overdoing it of course and writers—and especially when they're writing about writing—tend to do that. They like to make of the regular encounter with their work something rather epic. Male writers are especially prone to this I suppose, often wanting to make of the writing game something within hailing distance of war, or at least lion hunting. We don't always like to think of Jane Austen, sitting in a room with her family, her page beside her needlework, chatting and sewing, and by the way creating the most exquisitely tempered sentences to be found consecutively in English.

But there's truth buried in all the whale-hunt-style hyperbole. Writing is *hard*. It's tough to get up every day and have the wherewithal to sharpen the pencil or hum up the machine, and then set in. How does one do it? How is it achieved? How do you go from being, on any given morning, someone who is not writing to someone who is? Even after you have *begun* as a writer, you must every day contrive to *begin*.

Virtually every writer I know has a ritual or, to play it down a bit, a routine that guides him or her into the act of setting words on a page. (Page: yes, for a while let's stick to the old idiom.) One claims to sharpen half a dozen pencils to start; another gulps down a can of beer (before noon?); a third meditates (the sound of chanting from up in her lair gets the kids scrambling off to the school bus—that noise is *embarrassing*); a fourth needs espresso; his cousin requires Darjeeling (or not a silent verbal peep will be made) straight from China; a last goes outdoors and marches for a while to the beat of a different drummer: marches, literally, around the backyard.

What these rituals prove is that you've got to have an entry strategy, a way to open the door. But where exactly are you when you begin? And where are you trying to go? And why are there so many different keys with which writers open what amounts to the same door?

If you're a beginner, how the heck do you find the key that rightly belongs to you and to the door that happens to stand between you and your dream of writing every day? "We think of the key, each in his prison," says Eliot. "Thinking of the key, each confirms a prison." It's beautifully eloquent and no doubt with multiple applications. But on the matter of writing there is a prison (self-enforced silence) and there is (I think) a key. Though each person probably has to grind one to fit his own lock.

Even after you've made the grand initial leap—as I did I guess with my Hunter Thompson masquerade—there's still the work of getting up for it and into it every day, or at least five days a week or so. On the matter of how often to write, I'm a follower of Stephen King, who says he only takes off Christmas and his birthday. I take off Christmas, Christmas only. (He just writes faster than I do.)

These writers' rituals: what exactly are they for? Some people simply like the idea of being eccentric and so they try to be. They're home alone, working alone, and they can ignore office-like protocols and cultivate a little weirdness. But I don't think most writers' rituals are mere affectations. I think them quite necessary. The writer needs the right room, crowded or bare; the right drink, soft or mildly spiked; the right ambient noise or a dose of earmuffed silence. And the writer needs a way to go from what I call (borrowing from Keats again) habitual self to some other state.

There's nothing wrong with habitual self. It's a state we need to inhabit most of the time, unless we're saints or warriors or artists who never stop creating. (Picasso seems to have come as close to this condition as any mortal ever has, and even he needed to pause for some food and more than occasional fornication.) Habitual self drives the car and gets bodies, including its own, to various places at agreed-on times. It gathers the groceries and chops them and marinates them (though if cooking is truly an art, maybe habitual self doesn't *always* cook the dish). It pays bills and takes care of kids and parents and schmoozes at the post office. It takes the obligations related to death and taxes with some degree of seriousness.

But habitual self cannot write to save its life. Habitual self is good for a grocery list, a laundry list, a note to the mechanic, or a note of thanks for the spotted birthday tie or the fruit-scented candle. But habitual self cannot write. It is worldly, pragmatic, geared toward the fulfillment of desires, and fundamentally boring—at least to others. At base, habitual self is the Darwinian side of us that wants to survive and thrive and procreate. When habitual self wants to read, it reads Grisham; when it wants to write, it sounds like a machine. It sounds the way your computer would sound if it had a voice of its own.

I think sitting down to write is about getting loose from habitual self. If you're going to tap into what's most creative inside you, you've got to find a way to outwit the pressures of the ordinary. Think of habitual self as a barrier that blocks you from getting where you want to go as a writer. It's not that massive wall that most of us have to smash through to get ourselves going the first time and make ourselves able to say we've *begun* as writers. It's a smaller, less imposing but still potent version of that wall, and it rises up to some degree every day.

There are two ways to deal with that wall I think. You can go over it and you can go under it.

Most of the people I see and work with every day are professors; most of them write. And when they prepare to write they usually gear up to go over the wall. They attempt to speed themselves up. They rev themselves internally until their minds are whirling at a higher velocity than they habitually do and with the strength that speed brings, they leap the barrier and they begin to write.

And like all writers they have their rituals. Not surprisingly, those rituals tend to be caffeine based. They drink two or three (or five or seven) cups of the strong stuff and it helps them burn through their inhibitions. Their fingers itch, smoke pours out of their ears, they taste gunmetal in their mouths. They feel confident, a bit aggressive, focused. And so of course they usually write in an authoritative way, which is more or less what they want.

I understand the desire to leap over inhibitions—to try to Evel Knievel over the wall. It was more or less my method through graduate school, when I used to come off a bout of writing sweating like a prize-fighter. I had barbells on each side of my chair—heavy ones—and when inspiration flagged, I pumped them, up and down, up and down, until I was back at fighting pitch again.

I took this form of getting started to an extreme: along with the barbells there were hideous amounts of coffee and occasionally a small white pill that will go unidentified.

And I think this way of starting, this flying over the wall, works for a lot of people, including people who don't think all that much about it. They drink a cup of coffee, then another and another, and they set to work. It's a ritual really, but by now it seems simply like a routine. Writing is tough and whatever works, works. But I'm tempted to say that writing that begins by speeding through habitual self is fraught with dangers. It tends often to be two-dimensional and bureaucratic sounding: linear, flat, and unsurprising. To use Freudspeak for a minute, you're turning yourself over to your superego, the inner agency of authority and command. Whatever you can say positively about the superego, it's not genuinely a creative agency. (Unless you mean creative in the ways it can torment us. Then it can get pretty flashy.) Left to itself the superego powers through in search of a potent and univocal truth. That may be the kind of writing some people want to produce—editorialists and bosses and policy experts and theorists of this or that. And it's probably a good thing to be able to produce writing from above when you need to (probably, maybe). Though when I see all those kids (people under forty) sitting in Starbucks and juicing their screenplays and novels while hypercharged on java, I fear for the future of entertainment.

I prefer writing that slips *below* habitual self and taps other regions of mind and spirit. But getting there is probably a little more complicated than drinking three cups of black, or buying the full display case of Red Bull and rationing it to two, three, four—OK not more than five cans a day. To fly under the radar of habitual self, and its harsh older brother, authoritative self, you're going to need some skills of a subtler sort.

I think most of the best writing comes not from staying pat (habitual self), or speeding it up (authoritative self), but from slowing it down and making contact with a dreamier, more associative part of the mind that— if you connect with it just right—will in certain ways do your writing for you. You can fly over the radar on coffee or speed (or in-chair barbell pushing), but flying (or cruising) under it is more complex.

How do you slow yourself down? I think you've got to hypnotize yourself a little. That writer who loves to sharpen six or even a dozen pencils before she starts is, I'd bet, using a repetitive action to get a little way into a dream state. That's what's going on too, usually, when a writer does some meditation. (It's not that hard to learn. The Gita teaches us the rudiments, right down to what kind of animal skin we should slide under our bottoms.) The idea of meditation is to calm habitual self and get it to stop planning and worrying. (Habitual self loves planning of course and can go into ecstasies of worry.) You can charm habitual self to semi-sleep with music, too. Though you need to find the right kind of tune to get you started. I especially like the *kirtan*—chanting—that a deep-voiced, spiritual-sounding fellow named Krishna Das, KD to his admirers, can do. Most of KD's chants have about five or eight words in them and those are in Sanskrit—making it easy enough for me to hear hypnotic sounds rather than words. I don't usually continue to play music once I've gotten started, though a lot of writers do. I tend to lose my own writing rhythms in the rhythms of the music. If I play anyone while I'm writing it's often the glorious jazz pianist Bill Evans. Evans is melodious, clean, and original in his riffs in a low-key, non-show-off way. He never overwhelms you. His music is almost kind; you might even call it understanding. Ah, if I could write the way Bill Evans plays! But mostly I save Bill for early evening and try to write in the flow of my own inner music, such as it is.

Get under the wire, get under the garden wall, and see what happens. The romantics believed that the unconscious mind was a creative mind. Coleridge brought the idea of the unconscious over from the German romantics: the term is *Unbewusste* and Coleridge and most of the other major British romantics believed that tapping the unconscious could produce wonders. In his own case, Coleridge may have been right. His Unbewusste (along with a dose of opium) seems to have given him the beginnings of his weirdly majestic poem "Kubla Khan"—which for whatever reason, the Unbewusste declined to finish.

You don't have to believe in an apocalyptically creative unconscious to believe that making contact with the part of the mind that produces dreams (and occasionally unexpected jokes and—recall Frost—tangy insults) can also help you produce good writing. Of course there are dangers in trying to go under the wall, just as there are in flying over it. Listen to too much chanting, or do too much on your own (yes, I sometimes chant along) and you may find yourself falling asleep and waking up refreshed but guilty at the end of your allotted writing time.

But there are subtler challenges, too. Get a little too deep into the twilight state and writing loses almost all shape and direction. You commit automatic writing—more illuminating to your therapist than to a reader. You want to be at least two-thirds awake and alert to write, and that's usually not so hard. The simple physical act of typing or scrawling or cursively lettering (if you're that much an aesthete) will probably keep you in the game.

The members of the health service complex are always going on about the value of a good night's sleep. But it's possible, just possible, that they are not really talking to writers and other artists. I often find that when I've slept too well, I have trouble getting through to the more creative side and getting on with my work. After I've slept miserably, I may start out bleary, but once I get going I'm often more fertile than when I've had a standard good night's rest. Maybe a big deep sleep gives you lots of room for dreaming and that satisfies the unconscious well enough. When morning comes, the creative spirit doesn't need to come forward: it's done all it wants to during the night. I know by now that when I sit down to the computer or the pad feeling jagged and cranky, I may well be in for a good writing day.

Anyhow, I suggest you skip the coffee and leave the black beauties on the shelf and see what comes out of a lazier, calmer approach to getting writing done. Go for a run first—a long run. Have a dropper full of vale-rian in water. (But watch out. It's surprisingly potent for a drug they sell at health food stores.) Chant, meditate, chill by any means possible. Then see what turns up.

The key to all this is to find the approach that unlocks writing for you. It surely varies from person to person and even for a given individual it changes over time. Somehow the door gets moved, or the old key gets rusty, or the landlord (god Apollo?) changes the lock. A lot of trial and error can be involved. But it is trial and error of an interesting, I might even say revelatory sort. There's something to be learned about yourself as you find what mode of shifting consciousness works for you. Writing involves a bit of shamanism, in which you're both guiding shaman and space-traveling, time-traveling subject. What you need to travel tells you something about your version of habitual self and also about the kind of writing you're born to do. And it demonstrates your resourcefulness in getting to the place you need to be in order to do it.

There is, according to some, a guaranteed way to shift consciousness and to slip into the zone. This method not only gets you into your game, but it also does much more. If what its devotees say is true, the method will get you writing as you never have before. It will help you pass through the gates of habitual self (that's a given) and also enter the empyrean of brilliant ongoing creation. Through this method (if method is truly the right word), you will be re-created and that re-created self will be something of a miracle for all to encounter and (more importantly for our concerns) for all to hear and to read.

The method I have in mind doesn't involve drugs, even of the most potent sort, unless you think of matters metaphorically. It surely doesn't involve religion and it doesn't entail magic, though its effects, we're told, are magical enough.

I mean falling in love. Not just any love of course—you've got to fall in love with the man or woman who is your soul mate. This is the person who completes you and makes you whole: the yin to your yang, the moon to your sun, the day to your night, and all the rest. When you meet the one, or the one who is the one for a while, your powers are augmented. You breathe in a little truth and light; you see, as Wordsworth put it, "into the life of things."

Percy Bysshe Shelley seems to have felt that he could only really write when he was in love and what he wrote when in love was majestic. My grad school prof Harold Bloom called Shelley "the most intense and original lyrical poet in the language," and I agree. To Shelley, being alive meant being in love and he was in love almost all the time. ("I always go until I am stopped," he said of himself, "and I never am stopped.") In the state of being in love, Shelley wrote *Prometheus Unbound* and *The Witch of Atlas* and *Ode to the West Wind* and more and more. He was, as all true romantics are, inspired by Eros. It breathed new life into him as nothing else could. And he seemed to breathe new life into his beloved, too. Mary Shelley wrote what's probably the most potent and adaptable sci-fi myth we have when she was in love with Percy: *Frankenstein*.

Did I say Shelley's beloved—beloved, singular? That's not quite right. There were many: Mary and Jane and Harriet and others, too. He loved them with fervor; they inspired him and he them. But he was also inclined to leave them when the inspiration ran out. That's the downside of romantic writing; the love runs its course (a little like a fever) and the inspiration disappears with it. Then it's on to a new beloved. The fire needs fuel. Shelley left plenty of human wreckage behind him, as well as the miraculous poems.

But it works, or at least it worked for P. B. Shelley and Keats and Blake and Coleridge (in a way) and rather weirdly for Wordsworth (who loved nature as though it were a living human being, reveled in its powers to inspire, and feared that it would in time "betray the heart that love[s] her"). Love inspires Hart Crane and Allen Ginsberg and Bob Dylan and Joni Mitchell, and thousands of rockers male and female and in between. Though rock—and a certain sort of romantic poetry—can also be all about tearing down the perceived illusions of romantic love. Who can hear the J. Geils Band's magnificent "Love Stinks" and not be at least temporarily moved?

"As high as we have mounted in delight, in our dejection do we sink as low," says Wordsworth. He's not talking directly about romantic love here, but he could be. After the rhapsodies of discovering the soul mate and reveling in the powers you impart to each other, there almost inevitably comes the fall. You drop out of phase with each other: she loves another; sickness intervenes; death. The aged archons, the patriarchs and matriarchs of convention, get in the way: "Your papa says he knows that I don't have any money," cries the frustrated lover. The papa in question is the papa of the (probably fictive) beloved of Bruce Springsteen, the immortal Rosalita. Springsteen outwits papa: he has a new record deal and just got a big advance. But does it always work out so well?

The writer who relies on love for day-to-day inspiration is taking his chances. Some of us, the Wordsworth types, need a long, long time to recover from erotic failure or loss. Others, the Shelleys among us—if any still exist—bounce like a flaming ball from love to love and never touch the ground, much less dunk beneath the flame-eating waves. If you are one such: All honor to you! Beauty and light and truth and good times may be yours.

If not: meditation, chanting, the ritual sharpening of the pencils. Or coffee: have a cup of coffee if you really, really must.

THE NEW WRITER

To Have Written

"The truth is," a friend told me when we were young and in the habit of going around telling people that we wanted to be writers, "the truth is I don't really want to write. I want to *have written*." It took me a while to figure out what my friend meant, but eventually I got there.

Even at the time, he was something of a young gentleman. He had an apartment with bay windows; he had what qualified as a small library worth of books, the majority of them hardbacks; he occasionally, and without any provocation I could discern, put on a bow tie of lepidopteran elegance. He had a lovely girlfriend. He was a bit of a dandy, but a very bright and industrious one. Still, he did not so much want to write as to have written.

He wanted what he imagined as the life of the writer. He wanted to spend a lot of time in New York (we were trapped in dowdy New Haven) and to attend cocktail parties with people from *Partisan Review* and *Paris Review* and the *New Criterion*. He wanted to appear on panels; he wanted to be on TV to comment on the cultural emergencies of the day; he wanted to be invited to benefits and sit at head tables and schmooze with dignitaries. He wanted to have Carlos Fuentes's phone number in his book and to call Susan Sontag "Susan" and Gore Vidal "Gore." (Who can blame him about Vidal, who had a dash of real wit. Asked to be godfather to the child of friends, Vidal replied, "Ah, always a godfather, never a god.") My friend would have wanted to be able to call Robert Lowell "Cal." (If he was an up-and-comer now, he'd want to be the first guy in Brooklyn to get a beer with Martin Amis. He'd want to have been loused up once or twice, but not too fiercely, by Emily Gould.) He surely wanted to appear in the *New York Review of Books* both as reviewer and reviewed—and for this honor he was willing maybe (just maybe) to do a little writing. Still, Bartleby-like, he would greatly prefer not to. Perhaps for Robert Silvers, the esteemed *NYRB* editor, he would be willing to dictate something.

When he went to a party he wanted to be recognized. He did not want to be pointed at across the room (it would not be that sort of party), but he did want to be known from his TV appearances and from the cover-sized photos on the backs of his (already written) books. He wanted what Freud said all writers want: fame, wealth, and the love of beautiful women. He wanted fame in particular. When I told him he already had some share of these prizes (he had a rep as a brilliant student and teacher; his girlfriend really was wonderful), he would scoff at me and tell me I knew nothing of the world.

Perhaps he was right. When I thought of the life of the writer, which I very much wanted, it was something out of Balzac. It involved a five-story walk-up, crumpled balls of paper, and ink all over my hands. It involved many rejection letters and a girlfriend who threw crockery. I imagined I would commit some rather distinguished works that would be roundly ignored and some tissue paper efforts that would succeed. (Not long before, I had betrayed a shocking ability to compose a respectable *restaurant review*.) I didn't want to have written. I wanted to learn how to write, and to write something more lasting than a prickly dismissal of some poor restaurateur's escargots. "You know nothing of the world," my friend informed me when I told him my aspirations and anxieties. I had trouble disputing him.

My friend—who turned out to be quite a literary success, though alas he actually had to write to become one—was closer to the common mark. Many, many people wish to have written. They know writing to be work, especially in the early phase when one is learning the art. (In my experience, the early phase can last about ten years.) But when they have written, they believe that they will take on a new, larger identity. People will look at them with awakened eyes. Their daytime aura will glow more brightly. At noon they'll cast a bigger shadow. Face it: human beings want respect and then more respect, followed by adulation.

Writing a book can still count as a way to cop some of the esteem we require. It's been said that to survive all we need is food, clothing, shelter, and a healthy feeling of superiority over our fellow mortals. Alas, probably true.

There are by my count four troubling horsemen that ride through the beginning writer's thoughts, offering motivation for his quest. There is writing to have written, which is to say writing to achieve fame. There is writing for sex and erotic ascendancy. There is writing for cash: no man but a blockhead, Dr. Johnson said, ever wrote but for money. And finally there is writing for revenge. Fame, sex, money, and revenge: this is the four-headed beast that faces the beginning writer. (It faces all writers, but over time most make some kind of peace with it.) Indulging one of these motives or another isn't necessarily fatal—revenge in particular can be a fiery, fertile muse. But all are dangerous. I'll talk about them in turn.

Some writers are motivated by the hunger for fame. They want to be known; they want to be recognized. When they walk down the street they want the cameras to click; when they enter a restaurant, they want to see cell phones raised high as though in a toast. They've never read Schopenhauer, or if they have they've ignored him. The dark sage says that a taste for fame is like a taste for seawater. A hit of recognition satisfies at first; maybe it ravishes. But quickly the satisfaction dissipates, and a compounded thirst cries out for more, more.

The most unlikely people want to write books—or to have written them. Movie stars need to tell the world their life stories or to put it on a diet. Politicians have at least a half dozen books in them, though it is almost always the same book. Spiritual teachers need to send their teachings abroad: even the admirable Dalai Lama gets about a book a year into circulation and though it is not always the same book per se, there are potent resemblances down the line. All sorts of human beings who are, I dare to speculate, not terribly prone to *read* books are gung ho to write and publish them.

And often—no secret here—these are books they never had to write, but only to have had written for them. The books are composed by people who are not quite people, writers who are not quite writers. They're written by ghostwriters, written by *ghosts*. The celebrity or the athlete or the politician almost never sits down with a pencil or hums up the computer and stares into a blank white rectangle. Instead the very important personage relaxes into a puffy black chair, pulls his sleeping mask over his eyes, and begins free-associating on his childhood, his principles, or the dangers he's discerned in eating too much overprocessed wheat. The ghost records and jots notes and fires questions and tries to prime the rusty but elegant pump. Then the ghost writes draft upon draft, which the personage (who reads rarely) attempts to read. The personage likes the text not at all. It's time for round two, draft two. (Then three, then four.) That either the ghostwriter or the personage survives the ordeal is not unsurprising. But in time, the personage can say with a smile: "I have written. Here is my book."

I've often wondered about the term "ghostwriter." And now I think I understand it. The term is based on a reversal. For it is the personage who is the ghost: it is the personage who is too much of a cipher to sit down and organize his ideas and to render them in cogent prose. He's been leading a half life, a ghost's life—though society is prone to see it much differently. Society has given up on figuring out what the good life might be; society is interested in the enviable life the writer Adam Phillips observes. A certain sort of person does not pause to say, "Is this good or not?" Rather he asks (often subliminally) if this or that action, this or that acquisition, will prove to be enviable. Will it make my neighbors green? If yes, I must proceed. Writing a book and publishing it is, in many circles it seems, an element of leading the enviable life.

The personage who puts a book out has not actually composed it. And in some cases he may not really have read it either, or not all of it. (I once watched the former basketball star Charles Barkley listen with admiring interest as a fellow TV commentator told him what was in one of his books.) He hasn't composed it; maybe he hasn't even read it. But he has written.

There is still magic to the making of a book. The man or the woman who can do as much is still something of a Prospero. In the world, even in the current world, there are two kinds of people: there are those who have written and published a book and those who have not. The fact that people who do not read and aren't even prone to think much would want to join the ranks of book writers says something about the enduring allure of the book.

It's occurred to me too that people who cover themselves with tattoos—of whom there seem to be more all the time—are themselves aspiring writers, composing their autobiographies in hieroglyphics on the parchment of their skin. There one can find a record of their lives, assuming one knows how to read and interpret the signs, or that the tattooed personage is willing to be one's guide, which in my experience they're usually willing to do, often at exhaustive length. Here are records of past loves and deceased friends, tributes to family members and to athletes and prophets and superheroes who have somehow inspired the wearer. The tattooed personage has become a walking text. She doesn't just wear her heart on her sleeve, but her whole history and maybe her destiny across her entire body, which calls out to be read and understood—and then, with luck, accepted and loved.

It is a sad fact of the world: books that truly are books are written by writers. The books worth reading are books by people who have given their lives over to learning the art and the craft of composing. "The life so short the craft so long to learn," says Chaucer. He's talking about love, but he might as well be talking about writing. Almost no one turns aside from a distinguished career as a statesman and composes a brilliant treatise. Marcus Aurelius did it, but there have not been many such people in creation. Churchill received his Nobel Prize in Literature for tomes he at best partially wrote. John F. Kennedy found himself with a Pulitzer Prize for a book to which he made, at best, a minor contribution. But human beings wish to live *and* to write.

They want to be actors in the world. They want to be players. But then too they want the capacity to reflect and to turn their experience into melodious words. It happens, it happens—but not very often.

And the writer? Surely the writer would like to live. But from the time he throws himself into the game of making worlds with words, his actual life can become a secondary piece of business. At best, what others call his actual life is the sap that feeds the flower (if it is a flower) of his mind. He stops living and he begins observing. All that he sees exists first to stock his mind with images and metaphors and tales. I hoed beans to gather tropes, said Thoreau. A comely sight turns into a Henry Jamesian glimpse, food for a short story or a sketch. The writer doesn't always have what's called a life!

Hemingway grabbed the attention of the world because he appeared to solve the riddle. How could a writer have a *life*? He seemed to do it by being a man who was more than a man: hunting, fishing, drinking, brawling, marching through Africa in colonial state, getting married and married and married again. He became a figure of amazing allure: Papa, the Old Man of the Jungle; Papa, the Old Man of the Sea. Every man of the world could imagine being Hemingway; every writer could imagine himself being a man of action and man of thought, equally at home in the study and in the lion's seat at a legendary bar.

Maybe it happened: maybe Papa did manage to square the circle. But Hemingway is Hemingway—and not many others have managed to pull off the feat.

The aspiration to be both author and full-fledged actor in the world may be a trap. But at the heart of the desire to have written lies something more than mere vanity. My friend wanted to be recognized at the party on the Upper East Side, to "Susan" Susan and to "Gore" Gore (as did many, come to think of it), but he probably wanted something more, too. It's something that the usually oblique poet Wallace Stevens evokes in a rather simple phrase. Stevens probably didn't feel he embodied this condition, though it was one he aspired to. He looked with admiration, he tells us, at "the man who has had the time to think enough."

Who is this person who has had time to think enough? This is the man (or, surely, the woman) who has taken the time to step out of the main road and to read and to ponder and finally (probably) to write. This is someone who has observed life carefully and on his own terms and drawn some conclusions. It's the sort of person that Emerson celebrates in "The American Scholar." It's a young person who has decided not to chase after early success. He's stepped aside from the throng and become a reader and a watcher. He's read carefully (and not in a slavish, overreceptive way), for as Emerson says, "There is then creative reading as well as a creative writing." He's developed for himself a sense of proportion: he knows that a popgun is only a popgun, even if the venerable of the earth say that it's the crack of doom. Then comes Emerson's great sentence: "In silence, in steadiness, in severe abstraction, let him hold by himself; add observation to observation, patient of neglect, patient of reproach; and bide his own time—happy enough, if he can satisfy himself alone, that this day he has seen something truly." He compounds his observations, this American scholar, and he collects his truths. And in time he knows: he knows who he is (as Socrates said he must) and he knows what the world is to boot.

Has anyone ever actually achieved this exalted state? If he has I have not met him face to face, though I've encountered a pretender or two, as most everyone has. But surely there are those with real claims to the distinction—human beings who have had the time to think enough. The divine Plato, as Coleridge liked to call him, may be one; Schopenhauer is another; and Emerson himself (provided you will sift and straighten him a bit) may make a third—or so I think. They found their truth and then made it manifest; their innermost became outermost, something

Whitman too makes happen in *Song of Myself.* And the result of their efforts was a book, or a set of books. (Real books.)

I think many of us aspire to this kind of culmination and fulfill-ment. We want to have our say, let the world know our truth. But first of course we want to know it ourselves. The aspiration to have written is in most of its manifestations a silly one. "Hello Susan!" "Hi Gore!" But alongside the silliness rides a serious purpose. She who has written (and done it well) has figured it out. She's come to her own conclusions. Such a person possesses what we call character, in that any day we approach her on a matter of moment she is consistent and sure: she is always herself. And there is something true and admirable about this self, something that compels affection and respect even from the most wayward.

Imagine the person who has written and now finally needs to write no more! She's done her work; she's laid it down. And now she enjoys the view from the promontory, however high or low others take her partic-ular vantage to be. A few writers nail it and then quit. William Blake stands out: he spent the last years of his life largely silent, his magnificent visionary poems all written and illustrated with engravings. He even began to get a bit of the recognition he deserved. He resolved his relations with his wife; his finances got more stable. On his deathbed he said that though he was weak in body, the entity he called the Real Man, or the Imagination, was as potent as it ever had been, maybe more so. He died a happy and fulfilled man.

Most writers don't make it there. When most of us talk about wanting to have written, what we mean is that what we'd like is to take a lifelong vacation, at full pay (or at what we imagine full pay ought to be). But there's another way to think about the state of having written as well: some, if only a very few, will be able to walk out of the game telling them-selves that they truly have taken time to think enough and then to write it all down. To be one of them is no small matter; nor is it a small thing to aspire to be.

To Get the Girl / To Get the Guy

What writer has not dreamed that writing could lead to a glorious erotic life? I'll get famous the writer says to himself. I'll become rich and well known and then I'll get the girl or the girls. I'll write a bestseller and then another one the novelist says, and men will lay treasures at my feet. I'll have my pick and I'll take my time choosing. Freud suggests that people write books for three reasons: fame, wealth, and love. They want to be loved in general: they want crowds to admire them and to cast envious looks their way. (They want the wages of having written.) But they also want to be loved specifically, up close and in a personal fashion, by this or that alluring individual.

And surely there have been writers who have been erotic champions. George Gordon, Lord Byron, was one. Byron was the original celebrity. After the publication of his first book-length poem, *Childe Harold's Pilgrimage*, Byron attained a fierce notoriety. "I awoke one morning," he said, "and found myself famous." He was already rich. Byron inherited an enormous fortune from his father's side of the family. And he was handsome as well. More than handsome really: men and women alike thought of him as beautiful. He had skin of alabaster, liquid brown eyes, auburn curls like sea spume, and a long white neck, like a swan's. The fact that he was rather short, inclined to put on weight, and had one clubbed foot apparently took nothing away from his erotic allure.

I awoke and found myself famous—and he was. Everyone, it seemed, wanted to go to bed with Lord Byron. He was much more seduced than he was seducing. Women got themselves rolled into carpets and smuggled into his rooms; they hid themselves in savory teak chests and popped out at propitious moments; they leapt into his coach and would not be pried loose—or so the legends tell us. He was besieged by men, too. Byron was bisexual it seems, and sometimes the male besiegers broke down the walls. He was especially prone to homosexual liaisons when he was traveling in the East and wrote about them in veiled—and not-so-veiled—form in the poetry, his letters, and his journals.

Byron could look something like an angel with his riot of curls and his upturned gaze—often seen because he tended to be shorter than his interlocutors. But he had a demonic side too, or at least he affected to have one. He was eventually branded "mad, bad, and dangerous to know." He probably committed incest with his half sister, Augusta Leigh, and he demanded that his wife perform what she considered unspeakable acts. Anne Isabella Milbanke, his wife, was a lady with a predilection for mathematics. Byron called her the "princess of parallelograms" and tormented her to no end. Probably what he wanted was anal sex; it's not entirely clear. Whatever it was, she was not having any. Byron didn't seem to mind letting the world know about the more scandalous elements of his nature: he assumed, and rightly, that they made him more intriguing. Or at least they did until word about incest with his half sister got around. It became advantageous then for Byron to leave London. He died of fever in Greece, where he went to aid in the Greek war of independence. He was in his later thirties—weary of life, and ready to leave it. One of his last poems is about the nearly insupportable pain of having turned thirty-six years old.

Byron's poetry is the kind of poetry that could make almost anyone fall in love. He's melodious, fluent, perfectly pitched, ironic, and, when he wants to be, quite funny. ("But O ye lords of ladies intellectual / Inform us truly, have they not henpecked you all?") He claimed to write best when he was on horseback moving at a steady canter, and he claimed almost never to have blotted and infrequently to have corrected a line. Whatever the truth of these statements, his poetry *sounds* like it broke perfectly into the world. For all its art, *Don Juan* has a richly conversational quality; it's as though you are being talked with (though never talked at) by the most spirited, charming, and worldly man in existence.

And—this is perhaps the most salient quality—the writing does not put any real demands on you. Once you've picked up Byron's idiom, it's all sailing on a glassy lake. Byron isn't out to change the world: if he has a moral purpose, it's to soundly spank those who are. He detests Wordsworth for being a pill, with his rabid nature worship; he thinks Coleridge is a raving obscurantist. (There's some sand grain of truth in this, though it's also true that Byron had little more ability to make or follow a philosophical argument than your pet Airedale.) Byron doesn't like people with big ideas or major theories or programs for universal reform. He idealizes nothing. If he grants integrity to anything in the world, it is first love—and for him and most of his rather worldly readers first love is clapped in the book of the past and locked away. Byron is a merry debunker. He skates over the surface of life; his verse skips like a stone. He defies gravity, in all senses of the word. When he felt as though he was growing heavy and ponderous and homely and old, he contrived to bring his life to an end, in the most romantic way available, fighting in what appeared to be a glorious and lost cause.

The contemporary writer who hopes to be an erotic force should no doubt study the life of Byron with care. He or she should consider that it doesn't hurt at all to start off both beautiful and rich. Those qualities may not be necessary, but surely they aren't beside the point either. After that, what should the erotically ambitious writer cultivate? A sense of ease probably. You'll never want to let them see you sweat, unless your particular form of perspiration results in a golden glow. Yeats's thoughts come to mind again here: "A line will take us hours maybe / Yet if it does not seem a moment's thought / Our stitching and unstitching has been naught." So even if you do labor hard to write, as Yeats did, or labor hard to be beautiful, as his two women friends in "Adam's Curse" purportedly do, you've got to hide it. The world loves a natural. Byron was one (it seems) and Yeats, a brutally hard worker, understood the allure.

The writer with an erotic goal tends to be a demonic angel, in something of the way Byron was. Noble as he may appear, he also carries a whiff of sin. He's been tapped on the shoulder by the devil's hand. An erotically alluring writer seems to be a fetching mix of innocence and experience, to borrow terms from Blake. He's the lamb and the lion in one. Any number of recent writers have tried this persona on: one thinks of my bow-tied friend's paragons, Gore Vidal, Susan Sontag, and of Bret Easton Ellis, Martin Amis, and even in his way David Foster Wallace.

But I think that the key element in being a writer with an erotic aura is the one that Byron understood so well. Don't put burdens on people. Don't ask them to be better than they are. Don't challenge their world-view and their habits. Don't even go far in subtly undermining their idiom by having the nerve to write in a different one. Norman Mailer said he hoped to effect a revolution in the consciousness of his time; that doesn't sort very well with the kind of clownish hijinks Mailer the celebrity writer had to perform in order to stay on the front page of the newspaper, or at least somewhere below the last entry in the gossip column. Mailer wanted to be significant and something like glamorous at the same time—good luck. To be sexy and a writer you've probably got to be light and you've got to be swift—and how well those qualities sort with genuine writing is an open question.

I'd daresay that genuine writing—the attempt to delight and instruct and to change the world or some quadrant or speck—is probably antithetical to erotic success and allure. I'd even say that the person writing makes you become doesn't have much chance to win and win in the erotic sweepstakes. This is in part because writers are often rather—well, scary. They may or may not have figured it all out; they may or may not have had time to think enough. But to other people who use their minds sparingly and almost exclusively to get what they want out of life, someone with a developed mind who thinks freely can be frightening. Such people talk in full sentences. Occasionally a complete paragraph emerges. Writers are deft with language. When they're off work it's still their running track and their jungle gym. These capacities are intimidating; these powers make other people self-conscious. They wonder, "Am I dumb?" They wonder,

"Can I keep up?" Feeling dumb and feeling self-conscious are not states that go readily with feeling erotic attraction. "He's so sexy—he makes me feel stupid." This I daresay is a sentence that is never true. It may never have been uttered; it may be appearing here for the first time.

Writers are also prone to the deployment of irony. They may not know what irony is in any strict sense. No one may know what irony is. But they *sound* ironic nonetheless. There is, perceptibly, a double sense to what they say. They mean it and they don't mean it. To fall in love (or lust) people need to feel comfortable. They need to feel whole and at one with themselves—so they can get on with the business of becoming one with the person across the table. Irony is a duplicitous business: there is the overt sense, but then there is a secondary or subtle sense. But what the heck is it? This state of not knowing but guessing and speculating may have its pleasures, but it is probably not an erotic state.

One of Philip Roth's characters is trying to learn the art of seduction from an erotically successful friend. The friend lays it down. The average woman, the woman on the street, is not charmed by complex literary references; she does not rise to a quick flick of allusion to Melville. And she is not well disposed to irony, not at all. The woman on the street, the seducer says, hates nothing quite so much as she does irony.

The man on the street is not so well disposed either, especially when the ironist is a woman. It is no news to anyone, especially intelligent women, but men can become terrified of a woman who seems to know more, who clearly speaks better, and who maybe, just maybe scored higher on the SATs. Men like to be the boss in matters erotic. They like to primate around. They want to stand on the highest branch and holler. Anyone who interferes with this desire, though she may have to be tolerated, is unlikely to become a figure with shimmering erotic appeal. Byron who should have been the most secure of men erotically is himself afraid of those smart women: "Have they not henpecked you all?" (The implication being—they've pecked me more than a bit.) Maybe he married the Princess of Parallelograms with the intention of putting her and through her all thinking women in their places. It's hard to say.

Surely there are great poets who are also great lovers; they do often possess the gift of the gab and all that. But many of them fall more deeply in love with their verbs than with the panting virgin before them. They love the approach—the culmination much less, sometimes not at all.

Writers spend a great deal of their time alone and are in a certain sense always alone. They joy in the productions of their own minds and when it comes time to break out and connect with another person in the intimidating, arousing, confusing flesh and blood form, things do not always go well. And there is this, too. Writers can almost always *imagine* a lusher erotic paradise than any they might find or create in the actual (the merely actual) world. Too often they live in the land that Blake called Beulah, the world where all benign wishes come true, good things are got for nothing, and there are no contradictions.

Love—and erotic conquest—may also be bad for writing. (Though there are those writers—Shelley!—who cannot write without love.) We're told that history is written by the winners. Maybe. Surely literature is largely composed by and about the other constituency. We do not want to hear stories in which the protagonist moves effortlessly from strength to strength, conquering world upon world. At least we don't after the age of six or so. The story of the man who gets the girl or girls simply by wearing the right shirt, combing his hair just so, and showing up is not one that bears repeating. We may want to hear about victory from time to time, but it is the saga of defeat that draws one to read—and that is also the best subject for real writing. Writers are melancholy. They tend to silence, exile, and cunning—not empty noise, angling for invites, and the compounding of a solid game plan. Writers see the downside: when the sun's out they say it obscures their field of vision. To be a writer you may not have to exude death, the way Poe could do. But it helps to be, as Frost says he was, one "acquainted with the night."

I heard an interview with the guitarist from a band; it was called the Black Crowes I think. He said that for a while he wanted to be a writer so he could get girls. But then he noticed that all the writers he knew were guys whose teeth were going black because they couldn't afford the dentist, and who stuttered when girls walked into the room. I'd never heard of the Black Crowes, but I was assured they were huge. And the guitarist affirmed matters for me: the rock route worked just fine. He was a-swim in sex. So if sexual paradise is your game, you probably should turn off the laptop, turn on the guitar, and pen some lyrics. Keep them simple and keep them sincere. Let the love come through!

To Make Some Money

There is little choice. When one decides to talk about writing and cash flow, it is virtually impossible not to begin with Dr. Johnson. His pronouncement on this matter has gathered renown. "No man," he famously said, "but a blockhead ever wrote except for money."

Johnson had a notoriously hard time getting his writing done even when money *was* involved. He said that whenever he attempted a poem (which wasn't terribly often) he would establish at the start how many lines he was going write. He would squeeze out a few. Then he would stop, chew his quill for a while, and begin counting how many lines were still left to be written. He may have spent as much time counting as he did composing. He was devoted also to working to the very tick of the deadline. When he wrote up the parliamentary debates of his day—debates he did not attend but that he had paraphrased for him by someone who had—the printer's boy was often left waiting at the door, while Johnson (now finally inspired) took up his work with a furor. Johnson was a great procrastinator, as great perhaps as Coleridge, and his muse was compounded of equal parts guilt and the need for pay.

For after a certain point in his life (and that point came rather early) Dr. Johnson lived off his pen. He was a denizen of what was then called Grub Street, though even from early on in his career he was a rather distinguished denizen. Eventually Johnson found himself rewarded with a royal pension and took no small pleasure in it—despite the fact he had maligned pension givers and pension takers in his famous dictionary.

Through most of his life Johnson wrote for money, didn't make much of it, and believed that only a fool would put himself through the grinding labors of composition for free. He tended to think that writing performed a service: some of it gave pleasure, some instructed, and some (the very best) did both. Johnson looked at his work as instructional. He taught people what they did not know. Or he reminded them of what they had forgotten, but should not have. "Men more frequently require to be reminded than informed," he said.

What did Johnson remind them of? He reminded them about their moral duty. His essays are about ethical behavior. He went on in his papers the *Rambler* and the *Idler* (the name of the latter must have been a cause of some unpleasantness to him) about the duties of husbands to wives, children to parents, rulers to ruled, and the ruled to the rulers. (Mostly he went on about the latter: Johnson was a royalist and a conservative.) Johnson strove to offer his readers material that was—a favorite word of his—"useful." When he thought about writing, he could readily compare what a writer did to what a table maker did. He said that he could freely criticize a craftsman who made him a faulty table, even though he himself could not make a table to save his life. The same was true of poetry. He might not be able to write it brilliantly himself, but as a reader—as a customer and consumer—he could very well criticize the product.

Johnson could stand in something like awe of the writers who gave you more than a mere product and who seemed actually to be inspired rather than workmanlike. He loved Pope; he revered Dryden; he disliked Milton's personality and his politics, but he read many passages of *Paradise Lost* with amazement (as anyone must). And he was amazed by Shakespeare— by his invention and variety and his capacity to draw "just representations of general nature." But Johnson largely saw himself as a craftsman, not an artist. People needed instruction—in manners, in morals, and in the appreciation of literature. Very well, Samuel Johnson gave it to them, or rather sold it to them, at so much per line. "No man but a blockhead ever wrote but for money."

Instructive writers write for money—and of course writers who give pleasure do, too. The men and women who write the books you see in the airport racks succeed when they are responsive to the needs of their customers. They do not sit at their desks thinking, "What will interest me to say today?" They think (on whatever level), "What does my reader, my customer, truly want to pay for and be diverted by?" The reader on the airplane does not want a work that tells him in the manner of the Apollo bust in the famous Rilke poem that he must change his life. No, he wants a book that will, say, take the anxiety that he feels as his plane hums down the runway toward takeoff and do something about it. He wants his anxiety turned into suspense. Hanging and hovering in blue and cloud-swamped space the prevailing question ought not to be: "What will happen to me?" The reader should be asking, "How will it go for Sam or Jose or for Esmerelda"—who has perhaps given in and slept with her new boyfriend a hundred pages too soon.

And are we not always hanging and hovering in some kind of at least slightly foreign space, the way we are in that airplane? "We hang in anxiety," Heidegger the philosopher of being says. By which he means, in part, that anxiety is always with us, or at least thrumming on the margins of our lives. Heidegger insists that living with anxiety was part of what we could do to make life "authentic." But many of us don't want to be authentic, at least in the philosopher's sense, at least not all the time. We would rather be calmed and if possible charmed—so we use a pill, a mantra, a drink, or a book. An effectively engaging story that doesn't challenge the reader at all delivers the equivalent of a half glass of wine's worth of buzz. Should a writer be paid for providing this service? Doesn't one owe the vintner and the waiter some quantity of coin? Only a blockhead would give his wine away for free. (Only a blockhead would write for nothing.)

Alcohol and writing, intoxication and reading—these subjects come together in a memorable poem by A. E. Housman called "Terence, This Is Stupid Stuff." Housman's friends have been taxing him for writing verse they find hard to stomach. It's too harsh, too bitter, far too pessimistic. The boys at the bar would like something much merrier. "Come," they tell him, "pipe a tune to dance to lad." Housman replies, telling them that the kind of poetry they want to hear is a form of intoxication—a way of getting to see the world as the world is not. Now Housman is not against getting drunk. "I have been to Ludlow fair," he says, "and left my necktie God knows where." He's apparently tied a few on—until "the world seemed none so bad, and I myself a sterling lad." Two drinks, it's said, will make a new man out of you. There's only one problem; the new man wants a drink. And then the inevitable comes: "Down in lovely muck I've lain." And when Housman rises, "The world it was the old world yet: I was I, my things were wet." Housman says it's his business to write the kind of poetry that prepares you for a world in which there is "much good—but much less good than ill." And so he does.

Yet for stern medicine like Housman's not many people are willing to pay, and those who are often can't manage a high price. Housman is an accessible poet, but his pleasures are the harsh pleasures of contact with a stern principle of reality. He knows as much and is willing to accept the fact that he may never be the most popular of writers and that his work may not make him rich.

To write for money one must understand one's game. Housman writes for himself. He writes to express his own harsh view of the world: he wants to get it down as he sees it. If others want to partake of the vision or to learn from it, that's fine. But the writer who writes to make money puts his reader first—and he sees the reader in his day-to-day guise. He writes for the reader's self and not his soul. He gives the self a vacation from the real and transports him to a lotusland of one sort or another. Or he gives the reader practical advice that will help him buy the right stocks, eat the right food, vote for the correct party, seed his garden, or repair his perforated roof. He gives him the inside story about how the world works: Why did the market crater? Why did the Soviet Union collapse? How did the war start and why did it end? Such subjects the writer who serves his reader may cover and expect to be paid for.

But there are some writers for whom the subtitle of the book is always "The Way It Is for Me." They write to explore the lairs of their thoughts, they write to deploy and maybe to enlarge their imaginations, and they write to find out who and what they are. They ask for readers who will share—or at least entertain—their sense of things, in all its complexity and (usually) its harshness. And then—sometimes—not quite knowing themselves, they put out their right hand, palm up, and wait for the world to drop its coin. Often they wait for a long time. Writers who write to change the world go begging. The world does not want to be told to change itself—and if it tolerates the insult to its ongoing state, it surely will not willingly pay much of a price to be so insulted.

A sadness at the heart of writing! Serious writers constantly expect the treasure to fall in their laps for the strong medicine they dispense. They do not see why their higher, more serious work should not be rewarded.

A sketch cartoon I saw (or imagined) once: an artist wearing a beret and puffing a Gauloises stands at his easel contemplating a half-completed drawing of a plutocrat in top hat and tie. Beneath the sketch the words: BOURGEOIS HOG. Standing askance by the easel is the very man, the plutocrat (or hog). The artist stares expectantly at his model and says, "Could you give me a grant to finish my artwork?"

A sadness of writing! Writers who mean to give practical instruction or easy pleasure want to be acknowledged as artists. They want to be spoken of in the same breath as world-changing poets and sublime novelists. Virginia Woolf and Stephen King on the same stage, on the same Parnassus, in the same sentence. In our culture at least they have largely succeeded. The pulp fictionists appear with the high-minded poets. They cop some of the same awards, are washed in the same limelight. But on some level, the pulpists must feel themselves to be frauds. They have bought their way into the game—for they support their publishing houses, support other poorer writers (or so we are told). The entertainers must know the medals they wear are not theirs. They skipped the true campaign, never went under fire, never heard a bullet whiz up close. They are like those Soviet generals who are covered with decorations but have never been brave.

This is not to say that those who write for money don't have powers of their own—and humanly useful powers, too. I recall once sitting in a restaurant in my town when one of the most successful authors—successful in monetary terms—walked through the door. It was John Grisham wearing a bespoke suit of what appeared to be linen—with his beautiful wife, with his kindly manner, with his easy Southern confidence. Grisham writes a book a year. He spends six months writing, and then he spends six months enjoying the manifold fruits of his labors—or so the story goes. He does not claim to be Shakespeare or even Dickens, but someone who can give you an enjoyable hour's reading before nodding off or before your train arrives.

At our table one of my colleagues—we were all English profs—looked up as Grisham made his entrance and said, "John Grisham, the novelist. Sold a lot of books." A pause, a moment for reflection, and then with the best will in the world, my friend said, "We could all do that if we wanted to. We could all write that sort of book." There was nothing harsh or resentful in my friend's voice. He's not that sort of guy. But I have to confess he pushed me into mild shock.

We could all write that sort of book—that sells a half-million copies? We could all write turn-the-page, turn-the-page until a mild sort of windstorm rises from the scene sort of book? We're literate and even literary: we've read a lot (more than Grisham, I'd bet), and if need be we could do the job.

Really! Really? Because from my point of view there is no chance that any of us could have. It's hard to write for money and succeed—hard to create plots and characters that are just the right fit with the audience's need for diversion. It's tough to put the language at the right level—those lines of clichés that are not quite clichés, words that have been used often together (so as to be familiar) but not so often as to really bore the reader. Such books are hard to write. If there has ever been a writer who could go from writing for himself and expressing the world as he sees it, and doing it well, to writing popular books for money, I have never encountered him or her. That person may not exist.

Schopenhauer said that the moment you write for money or even accept a dime for your work, you are going to compromise it. You stop writing the truth as you see it (or the truth proper) and begin to write what your audience, in its most banal and commonplace guise, wants to read. To the commercial writer, money is the measure of success. To earn well is to write well; to write well is to earn well. To the more serious writer, every nickel earned with the pen should make him question whether his work is genuine. Even a readership that is too large, or not the right quality, should give him pause. Most men and women cannot bear all that much reality—and reality in concentrated and often harsh form is what the authentic writer frequently delivers. Or so at least says the noble Schopenhauer, lord of all pessimists past and to come, and also a true lord of philosophy.

Socrates knew that money and the truth did not sort well with each other. He took no cash for his teachings and castigated his enemies, the Sophists, for their money hunger. Socrates knew the score—the writer in search of hard truths cannot expect money—or much love either. (For that he should join a rock band.) No accident that the people of Athens rose up and condemned Socrates to death for disturbing their mental peace. Schopenhauer says that the young man who has studied and prepared and thought, thought, thought will break into the world with his book expecting fame, wealth, and the love of beautiful women. What he'll get is irritation and maybe anger. He'll be lucky, Schopenhauer says, to escape with his skin. As to his hopes for cash—those are hopes in vain.

To Get Even

People write to get even with others; they write to get even with the world. There's not much doubt about it; they do. The desire for revenge—along with the desires for fame and wealth and erotic satisfaction—are the four most alluring (and potentially destructive) motives for writing. It's been said that writing proceeds from a narcissistic wound. (Edmund Wilson and Harold Bloom say it, albeit in their different ways.) Someone or something gores the writer's sense of who he is and what he deserves and he takes up his pencil (or puts fingers to keys) to settle the score. Who ever feels that he gets what he deserves? Who ever feels that the world loves him enough? Who truly believes that all of his virtues have been perceived and rewarded to the right measure? We all, at least at times, are creatures of injured merit.

How does the writer get even? A thousand different ways! The most common way, perhaps, is through fiction. He relives his family life in his imagination and he gets the chance to call it as he sees it. All of the culprits are there: feckless mother, monster father, the siblings who crushed the tender author's tender sensibility—or tried. (Freud tells us that when we dream of flourishing insects we are probably dreaming of brothers and sisters.) They are all disguised thinly enough. How many people have gotten the gift of red hair or a large nose through the generous bequest of the family author?

Writing to get even is sometimes the specialty of the youngest child in the family. The youngest is the fairy-tale child. She's the one who under other circumstances might be rambling into the world to traverse the enchanted forest, slay the fiery dragon, dig up the pot of gold, and save the kingdom. But in actual life she may have felt herself to be Cinderella before the Prince came—and the Prince never really did come. She was squashed by the mean sisters and banged around like a paddleball by the nasty older brothers. So it's time to get even. It's time to get square.

I know of a writer who made a great success of a first novel based on her family. The little girl in the corner had apparently been storing up a record of all the familial insults like an angry accountant. She published her book. It sold. And naturally some of the kids in the family felt they had been tossed and gored unfairly. Brothers and sisters drank toasts in blood to her comeuppance. Reconciliations came slowly if they came at all. One of the kids, a girl, responded more vehemently. Word was that she left her job and entered a creative writing program (at rather large expense) at a well-reputed university. The objective? "To write a family novel that features a neurotic younger sister who never washed her greasy hair." I hear she wrote it and got it published, too.

Revenge can be a powerful muse. At a certain point in his career, Philip Roth found himself divorced from his wife, the actress Claire Bloom. Not long after the divorce was final, Bloom stepped forth with a book about life with Philip Roth. She had not cared for that life much at all. He was selfish and cheap and philandering, controlling and cruel. Roth got to read this himself and then, no doubt, he got to discuss it with his friends, or remaining friends. What did he do?

The blow of the Claire Bloom book—a bit of revenge in its own right— might readily have knocked him off and out of writing for good. It's not all that commonly mentioned, but writers expire all the time. They perish as writers, but maybe they perish a bit as humans, too. Keats was said to perish from a bitter review—a piece of nonsense if taken literally, but not without significance as a metaphor for the life and death of certain artists. To write poetry on the highest level (or even on the rather modest level of Keats's early volume) requires a degree of sensitivity. One must be responsive to the more subtly turning nuances of language and of life. But that sensitivity also inclines one to be readily hurt by reviewers with their poison-tipped darts. For surely no one is more likely to write out of the spirit of revenge—the desire to get even—than the book reviewer.

Book reviewers pretend to review the volume, but one knows that the volume is always the man or the woman. He who touches this book, touches a man, Whitman says. Claire Bloom did more than review the book that was Roth—or the books. She reviewed the Roth that was Roth and found him bitterly wanting. Roth might well have wound himself into a twisted shape and inched back inside a conch shell. But he didn't.

He answered back with a volume called *I Married a Communist*. In it, Claire Bloom becomes Eve Frame. Her daughter Anna—who seems to have sowed rich discord in the house—becomes an unlovable being named Sylphid. Roth is relatively gentle with Eve/Claire, but with Sylphid/ Anna, not terribly. It seems he may have gotten just the right amount of revenge in the novel. And though it's far from his best, it did probably serve to discharge his spleen and let him move on to other work. A little revenge—a little but not too much.

Still, it's clear that throughout the book Roth is not only enacting a certain measured revenge, but also contemplating it. One character says, "Revenge[:] nothing so big in people and nothing so small, nothing so audaciously creative in even the most ordinary as the workings of revenge. And nothing so ruthlessly creative in even the most refined of the refined as the workings of betrayal."

On came *The Human Stain, The Plot Against America, Exit Ghost, The Dying Animal*, and a string of splendid late-career books. The work poured forth in a shimmering profusion. He was doing strong work late into life—and it is hard to imagine that the books were not an act of revenge, or a vengeful anti-revenge to the Claire Bloom book. His ex-wife may have imagined he would respond with an overt and appalling coun- terblast, maligning her and at the same time firing her career. He went back into his writing studio and toiled away and created—as a revenge that wasn't one—the sort of book that showed the world that what his ex-wife had had to say about him did not matter much at all. And as to Claire Bloom, maybe her book was a balm to her as well. In time she appeared in the film *The King's Speech*, playing the Queen of England.

Saul Bellow, slightly older than Roth, had a taste for literary feuds. He seems to have been on the border of one with Roth himself. Addressing the prowess of his younger competitor he simply said, "What hath Roth got?" (Plenty it turned out.) Bellow sometimes seemed to love a literary feud above almost all other things; he got into one with William Phillips, the rather prosaic second banana at *Partisan Review*. He thought Phillips was a long-winded bore. "One of the nice things about *Hamlet*," Bellow said, thinking of his antagonist, "is that Polonius is stabbed."

The urge for revenge can act as a muse for some writers. It apparently did for Bellow in what some think is his best book, *Herzog*. Herzog, the title character, more or less stands in for Bellow. He is a well-intentioned, radically unworldly, erotically avid professor of intellectual history. While he's up in the Berkshires with his wife, straining to finish his book, his life falls apart. He can't get his writing done, he can barely read, he can't think straight. His wife, Madeleine, has fallen into an affair with his best friend, Valentine Gersbach, and Herzog/Bellow is destroyed by it.

It happened that way in life—or some version of it did. But the man who stole Bellow's wife away was not a radio personality in Pittsfield, but a SUNY English professor named Jack Ludwig. Even now, one runs into Ludwig endorsers who thought he got a terribly raw deal in Bellow's depiction of him. And of course Ludwig wrote a novel of his own answering back to Bellow. It's called *Above Ground*.

But debts must be paid—at least for certain writers. To these writers, the art of writing is the art of combat. They model their careers on the careers of boxers and generals—though they are not always willing to say as much. They believe on some level that writing is a test of virility and manliness. (Hemingway may have taught them as much.) They are like boxers in the ring. When someone catches them with a shot, as Jack Ludwig did Bellow, they have to repay. They can't let an insult pass. They lie in wait to rap the guy who gave them that scorcher of a review all those years ago. When Mailer first met John Leonard, Leonard was a pup, reasonably new to literary New York, and Mailer was busy being Mailer, king of Manhattan. The encounter went like this, give or take: "I greatly admire your work," Leonard said to the great man. And then: "What are you working on now?" Mailer went into his Texas accent, usually not a comforting sign: "Well, Leonard, I'm doing a new collection of poems, since I know how much you admire my poetry." Leonard didn't quite know what Norman was getting at. Then he remembered. He had reviewed a volume of Mailer's verse five or six years earlier on his radio show in Berkeley, California, and he had not been pleased with Mailer's effort, not at all. Mailer tracked all his reviews and he remembered them. Mailer kept score.

You have to keep the ego in shape. You have to exercise it and give it the diet it needs—maybe sex, maybe money, and maybe revenge, too.

And then it will repay you with endless creative juice. Or so some writers think. You have to be like Achilles, an Achilles of literature. Never let an insult pass; never take a tap on the chin you do not requite.

Even a writer as benevolent overall as George Orwell owned to a having a vindictive streak. In "Why I Write," he admitted that one of his motives was to get back at the schoolteachers and bosses who had thought too little of him, or thrust him aside. The settling of scores! In "Such, Such Were the Joys," Orwell takes aim and fires at the grotesque crew who caned him and tormented him at an English public school. It's a splendid essay—and a model for my own writing about education, for what it's worth. Would it have existed without the spirit of revenge?

Then there is book reviewing. To hear some writers tell it, the most vindictive people in the world are book reviewers. But they are not paying back this insult or that. It is nothing so specific. No, the angry book reviewer's gripe is more existential. They have a gripe with the world and with nature. Their gripe is with their own talent or lack thereof. They are enraged at having been left out in the disposition of true gifts and wish to puncture every man or woman who has been endowed. They damn with faint praise; they damn with loud imprecation. They love to take down the best and see them squirm in the dust. They show their fair-mindedness by picking out undistinguished books by undistinguished authors and sending up hecatombs to them. They love to "discover" new and meretricious talent and denounce the old and the true. Or it's the reverse.

Recently, serious writers will tell you, book reviewers have adopted another tactic in their ongoing war against creation. The book reviewers have decided to review crime stories, romance, and potboilers full of eye of newt and toe of frog and worse. And, serious reviewers that they are, they review those books in the tone of high seriousness—or at least as seriously as they review aspirants to the true laurels. Do they ever mention that reading Stephen King is a rank waste of time? Not at all. They aim to reflect taste and not to elevate it. They echo vox populi and praise the easy pleasures of the crowd. And what is this but a long-term strategy of aggression against true talent? What is it but a form of revenge? (Why be a writer if you can't be hyperbolic from time to time?)

Writers sometimes fight back. Martin Amis seems to be the progenitor of a telling line against the book reviewers. When I get a crummy review, he's said, then I pause and I ask myself: Is that really what reviewer X wanted to be when he grew up? A book reviewer? Is that really what he hoped and dreamed? True enough, maybe. Kids want to be knights and sages and sometimes even damsels in and out of distress. Some will tell you they want to be writers. But no kid will ever say he wants to be a book reviewer. Hold fast to the dreams of your youth, said Schiller.

The reviewers: perhaps they are the most prominent of writers who compose out of a spirit of revenge. But serious writers sometimes do that, too. Revenge can be a bitter muse, but sometimes it's an effective one. So much of what the great essayist Hazlitt composed seems to come out of the spirit of injured merit. He was a failure in love—and he writes for vindication against the simple (but complex) girl who dumped him. He made himself ridiculous among the literary avant-garde of his day, chiefly Coleridge and Wordsworth. Both of them he assaulted bitterly and often on a personal level. (Yet his perceptions about their poetry are so telling that the essays live on, as Hazlitt surely hoped.) At one point he launches a fierce attack on Coleridge's nose, which he sees as pathetically small and undistinguished. And the nose, says Hazlitt, is "the rudder of the face, the index of the will." STC's is "nothing—like what he has done."

The nasty reviewers and the whole unpleasant establishment can be a goad—maybe even an inspiration. Pay them back! Harold Bloom, whose work has transcended the genre of literary criticism, cried out once in print about being reviewed in the "weakest" possible way by legions of academic detractors. But he confessed that it was all to the good. They were, he said, getting my work done for me. He was writing to show 'em and to show 'em up.

Everyone knows that the literary feud—the tit-for-tat sweepstakes—is the mainstay of a certain kind of writer. Think of Vidal and Mailer, Mailer and Buckley, Hellman and McCarthy, Naipaul and Theroux. Writing is hard. It's tough to get up in the morning and look at the white snowfield of a trackless page. How to push forward? Use anger; use rage if you have to. Settle scores. And if you have no scores to settle, then create a few for yourself, not only for the purposes of public relations, but also for the purposes of inspiration. Hot-blooded, hot-tempered, always ready to take offense: the writer as duelist. Pace off twenty yards and then turn, word processors blazing. Anger can produce eloquence. That much anyone who has ever been in a spousal tiff knows. Rage is inspiration. But what it inspires— that's another question.

For the dangers of writing for revenge are manifold. How easily the vengeful writer loses distance and irony. How quickly he exposes the smallest version of himself. Despite its marvelous prose, the undersong of *Herzog* is too often a protracted masculine whine. Oh those women! Oh the false friend! Looking back at an exchange with Mailer that became physical, Vidal called it "the night of the small fists." He was embarrassed by it all and so in time was Mailer. It brought them both some attention, but lowered the esteem and expectations with which people approached their work. Even Dante, grand as he is, suffers from his vindictiveness. He settles too many scores when he populates hell and purgatory. He undermines his sense of proportion when he places his petty contemporaries in the pit beside figures from myth and legend. Dante even installs two figures in hell—Fra Alberigo and Branca Dora (traitors to guests)—who are not dead at the time he is writing the *Commedia*, so hungry is the master for retribution. Yet still, the poem will live eternally.

Writing for revenge may not be as dangerous as writing for money or fame or love. It can get you moving in the morning, give you a jolt. But in the end the purer and more detached spirit, the spirit of a Tolstoy, who writes to elevate mankind, is the one most likely to prevail.

In pragmatic America, results are everything. That you get where you want to go is what matters—so long as you don't break the law or get caught doing it. Success is all. In the East, matters tend to be different. The Buddha cares far more for intention than he does for result. If you do things for the right reasons, you will emerge with a benevolent smile, even if the results appear to be stamped by failure.

On the matter of writing, I think it best to listen to the wisdom of the Pali texts: intention matters. There are good intentions and bad and some that abide in shades of gray. The beginning writer ought to ponder the issue.

To Strengthen the Mind

The mind is a muscle. The people who say so most often—football coaches and geometry teachers and the like—aren't always the most sage. But that doesn't mean there isn't truth in the idea. The mind's a muscle and writing can make it strong. Writing can mess you up, too—no doubt about that. It can send you deeper into desire for cash and fame and no-point sex and revenge. But it can do some fine things for you, too. It's time to focus on some of those.

In order to write, you have to think. You have to take what's in your head and put it into coherent sentences: there needs to be a subject and a verb. Adjectives often help (though not too many, we're told). One sentence has to follow from the next, not like boxcars on a train. That's too strict, too predictable. But one has to be in strolling distance from the next. In her journal, Susan Sontag asks herself when she can claim that she's truly and actually thinking. She has to admit it. Only when I'm writing, she says. Or when I'm in conversation with someone I like (or love) and respect. (Plato's dialogues are built on such a premise.) But the rest of the time?

Sontag's mind was alive and alert and large enough, and she was interested in almost everything. (She once described herself as having ASD—attention surplus disorder.) But Sontag would admit it: not writing, not talking, the best that she or most of the rest of us could hope to produce is what William James described perhaps too kindly as stream of consciousness. Along it goes burbling and babbling and looping back on itself. It's not a pure stream, this stream of consciousness. It contains all sorts of figments and trifles, old memories, partially atrophied grudges, semiplausible hopes, and, not the least, fantasies, dreams, aspirations, and frustrations of a sexual sort. And the stream seems to flow where it likes. It lazes from one topic to another, and then simply slows down, pools up, and becomes gummy swamp.

Sometimes this is fine. A writer, as García Márquez says, must know how to relax. But the stagnant pool and the brook that babbles something close to nonsense—those are not the mind's ideal. When a fine writer is composing, when a splendid talker is holding forth, when a rich conversation is in gear, an almost athletic beauty and grace come into play. "How noble in reason" we can be, Hamlet says. And it is true. Yet given the chance, most of us will let the mind lie fallow for days on end.

We use it when we need to use it, which is to say we use our minds to advance our causes in the world. We plot to fill our desires; we scheme to get what we want (and usually, as Mick and Keith tell us, end up at best with what we need). We play chess with life. We try to push forward our pawns, protect the king, develop bishops and rooks, with the idea of winning this or that practical victory. We want a new job/house/car/lover. And there is satisfaction in deploying the strategizing mind. It can be a pleasure to get the best price or even from time to time to ride free. There is a practical statesman, a Ben Franklin type, dwelling inside each of us.

But we want more than a mind that's a stream of consciousness or a sloshing swamp; and we want more than a mind that functions as a consigliere, a shrewd adviser that merely helps advance our desires. We want the mind to be free to capture what is true and beautiful, at least from time to time. We want to look for truths that are going to last and don't apply to ourselves and ourselves alone. (Or we want to have the freedom to debunk what passes now for general truth.) And in this sort of quest, writing and conversation of the best sort are crucial. We may discover truth and we may disclose beauty. Or we may not. But the effort to do so strengthens the mind in manifold ways.

For the mind is more like a muscle than we think. The body of the athlete grows strong and effective under intense workouts and a salubrious diet. Where there was flab and ungainly motion, there is soon (or at least eventually) a beautiful tautness and fluidity. We can change our bodies; many people do. It is a hard fight, but a worthy one.

A man I know of had inflated himself up close to three hundred pounds. He was on the border of having diabetes. His feet hurt, his back hurt, he couldn't move without a groan, and he was barely forty years old. He'd been an athlete when he was young and one day, out of shame maybe, he resolved to get back in shape. He had young children; he had fresh responsibilities. It seemed bad form to go off and die on them anytime soon.

He started with a cymbal-clashing fall. He went out to the beach the first day and ran three miles. The next morning he could not rise from bed under his own power. When he did get up eventually, with help, a step forward brought him near tears. He had never been so sore. He slept almost all day and through the next night. But the following morning, he went back to the beach. He walked a quarter of a mile one way and a quarter mile back home. He felt horrible. But he went back and back and he never missed a day. He stopped choosing his diet from the donut-related food groups. He stopped emptying cans of beer, though he did dispatch a glass of wine from time to time. This went on for six months, then a year. He did a little more and he did it a little better every day. At the end of that time, he was not himself anymore. He'd lost seventy pounds and become reacquainted with his feet. He was another person, with a different body. That body wasn't going to live forever, but major bus accident withstanding, he was not going to die tomorrow. He had been reborn the only way non-churchly people acknowledge you can—by hard labor (which also, he testified, gave him some potent satisfaction). He had made himself a new body. Granted he had needed to use the old one for raw material and the old one was forty years old with some wear on the major parts.

The case for writing is not unrelated. It can give you a new mind. I don't want to overpromise here. Like our friend's body this new mind will use the mind you possess as its basis and it can't go worlds beyond. But you might be surprised.

For in many ways, writing is to the body what exercise is to the mind. Given sufficient provocation, or lack of it, the mind seems to want what the body wants—to regress to a vegetable state before its time. We have a tendency to inertia, both physical and mental. It is possible that in the people who appear to be most energetic that tendency is strongest. Said Macaulay of Dr. Johnson: he had a "morbid propensity to sloth and procrastination." But he also wrote a dictionary by himself. Though there was a gang of boys that swarmed around him like monkeys, running off to look matters up occasionally, it was mostly Sam Johnson of Lichfield who did the job. France had needed the entire French Academy to do it for them. England needed one fellow, the indolent Dr. Johnson.

If Johnson had had television, we might not have the dictionary, or the *Lives of the English Poets* either. For TV is a double-barreled precipitator of indolence, stalling out the mind and rendering the body recumbent. But in my experience, radical indolence of mind and body are often a sign of considerable energy that has been pent up for some reason or another. The answer: push forward. Push forward: preparatory of course to protracted rest and reward. Potentially energetic people often grow lazy because they believe that there is really nothing worth doing. Writing can wake up somnolent energies. Writing is something worth doing.

Writing can take the sloppy stream of consciousness and give it form and purpose. Writing takes what is vague and empty and slothful in our thoughts and gives it shape, so we can examine it and pass a verdict on whether it ought to stand or not. When we write, we *make sense*. The common phrase reveals something: sense will not make itself. Sense is a rather uncommon commodity. A coherent argument or an organic spectrum of images is the exception, not the rule.

It is an affront to all proponents of radical democracy and the solidarity of men and women the world over, but it is nonetheless true: most human beings do not think very much. Many are like the primitive countryman in Frost's "Mending Wall." When his neighbor asks him why there needs to be a wall between their two properties—will the apple trees on one side ever trespass and eat the fallen pinecones on the other?—his neighbor does not really think when he replies. He reverts to his father's saying: Good fences make good neighbors. And as Frost's narrator (whose own thinking has some flaws) says, it was his father's saying and he likes having remembered it so well. I find it surprising how many members of the purportedly thinking classes such as teachers and pundits seem hardly to think at all. While many carpenters and masons and waitresses have minds constantly abuzz.

When we don't offer slogans, we often produce something on the verge of mere jumble. I'm glad that in *Ulysses*, James Joyce took the time to chronicle an average man's average thoughts on an average day. But love Joyce as I do, after a few pages of it, I know why I usually want to read the thoughts of people who have passed beyond the average, and read them on their best days, for there is little time remaining to us, no matter how much we happen to have.

The mind can expand. This is Plato's point in *The Republic*. When a student walks out from the cave of shadows into the region of the sun and moon—the region of true knowing—it hurts. His eyes blink from the light; his head pulses from the strain. He feels wearied after too much exertion, much as the athlete does. It takes time to make himself worthy of his new destiny—becoming a thinker. But that is, in truth, simply to become a human being, for a human being is a rational animal to Plato, and some of us who go on two legs (some of us featherless bipeds) alas do not quite qualify. Thinking makes one a man or a woman. Plato seems to have followed Socrates in the *doctrine* that conversation is at the heart of thought. But then too Plato, against the dictates of his teacher, wrote and wrote and wrote. Make up your mind, we say. What is writing if not the best way to do precisely that? Make up your mind!

Diet and exercise, says the athlete. If writing is the mind's exercise, then reading is its diet. As a teacher I can attest to a distressing fact. There are many young people now, some with real promise, who are interested in becoming writers. They love to write. They compose and compose until the computer keys are in danger of wearing out. But many of them do not really read. Oh, they read for pleasure: dull science fiction, fantasy, and adventure. But they do not want to read books that are the caliber of the books they hope to write. Writing is reading; reading is writing. Hemingway, the figure who did the most to masculinize writing this past century, trying to pass it off as a cousin of hunting and warfare, freely confessed that he read for hours a day.

By reading you learn how it's done. You keep your standards high. And constantly, constantly, you get fresh ideas. Books are your diet when you are a writer and if what you consume are the candy and carbohydrates of the literary world, then you will probably produce nothing better, no matter how hard you work. Books need to be meat and vegetables, strong greens, ripe fruits. Is it possible to be a writer in America and never to have dropped all the way into Melville or Dickinson, the prophet Whitman, or Emerson, the sage of Concord, Massachusetts?

Emerson may have told us that genius is always the enemy of genius through overinfluence, but one deals with that through struggling with the great and making one's way both with and against them. To ignore them is to ignore the sun and the stars. The best books create the best writing—or at least the best writing one is capable of doing. The best diet helps make the best runner or rower. How many writers' work has declined over time in part because, without quite knowing it, they now subsist on a diet of literary junk food? They spend too much time at the movies. They watch a lot of TV.

Writing can also lend itself to the re-creation of character—dare one say even the improvement of character. I once heard Bernard Malamud say that he thought revision was one of the most dignified and ennobling pursuits a person could take up. By all accounts Malamud, who taught at Bennington College when I was a student there, revised fiercely. He was not a natural, though he wrote a fine novel about a man—a ballplayer— who was. He went over and over and over his work. He brought his sentences to perfection or as close to perfection as he could. And this he felt to be character building.

He was right. Going back and back and back at a project is based on a fundamental perception. Nothing is ever quite right; nothing is ever good enough. In revision the writer admits to mortality and the flaw that's at the center of being human—or at least he does if he revises with the intensity that Malamud apparently brought to the game. He deploys and he develops what may be the human characteristic most important for success in any endeavor: persistence. For everything must be worked on. Rarely does one get it quite right the first time. In a marriage, in a career, in the rearing of children, failure is the order of the day. It doesn't work right; it doesn't play correctly—whatever it is. So what is to be done? Hit it one more time. Pull your energies together and give it another shot. One could even say that character at its best is the capacity to acknowledge you are wrong, or at least that matters could be better, and then throw yourself into repair. The house is always breaking down, disorder is everyplace, and there is no carpenter or fix-it guy to call except oneself.

If we can revise a text, maybe we can revise our characters—and do so in the writer's way of making things a little bit better, one step at a time. We can bring the same hard eye to our own affairs that we bring to the words that dance (or should dance) before us on the page. Make no mistake. An essay has a spirit. Novels and short stories do, too. Maybe a text is the closest analogue to a human spirit that we have. "This is no book," says Whitman. "Who touches this, touches a man." (It is a line that I cannot get away from or do without.) The text is a self, the self a text. It is not easy to improve one or the other. But it can be done.

To revise well we have to begin by detaching ourselves. Usually we're dug deep inside the trench of self. We hide behind the earthworks; we don't want to hear a negative word, much less pronounce one about ourselves. The beginning writer quails at the first piece of disinterested criticism he receives. For he knows it is he himself being criticized; that text *is* his spirit. But in time he learns to listen bravely and to take to heart what he needs.

The critic David Bromwich says that one of the most important powers one acquires in becoming an academic is the power to listen to what you do not want to hear about your work. Graduate school in the humanities cultivates many abilities. But one of the chief ones is the capacity to sit down and shut up and listen while someone with more experience tells you how you can improve. I once asked a teacher of mine, the formidable medievalist and poet Marie Borroff, where I was weakest as a scholar and writer. I can still recount what she said, pretty much word for word. It was a hearty dish, served without sugar, and it's stood me well for a long time. One does not have to attend an academy to get this kind of nutrition. There are many sources to be found.

How do you know that a criticism made by another or yourself is valid? How do you recognize criticism that can help you to grow? It is impossible to have absolute knowledge here. But I would say that when you hear sharp words from someone, either about yourself or your work, and they sting a little, something may be up. And if you find that you cannot, however hard you try, forget those words, well then, the truth does sometimes taste a bit like salt. You've been found out by another or by yourself: time to reconsider, improve, fix—time to make it new.

To Grow

It's hard to remember everything one learned in graduate school. There are times it is hard to remember anything at all. This is so even when one has had the best teachers, which I feel I did. But at least one moment in a seminar on Shelley and Keats, taught by the wonderful scholar and critic Geoffrey Hartman, has stayed with me. It taught me something about both writing and the reasons for writing that might be arguable, but mean no less to me for that. Writing and reading can strengthen the mind the way exercise and eating right can strengthen the body. But I think writing can contribute to the growth of what I'd like to call the spirit, too.

You have to understand, Professor Hartman said, something central about John Keats. (Keats is a hero of this book, as is no doubt becoming plain.) He wants each one of his individual poems to count. He wants you to be absorbed and maybe even moved. But he wants something else as well. The poem matters to him, but what matters as much—maybe matters more—is the poem that it puts him in a position to write next.

Keats's poems, in other words, are dedicated to the growth of his spirit. He is always trying to put himself in a position to surpass himself. With every consequential poem, he is attempting to grow. He wants to get himself in a place where he can write another better poem. He wants to expand his spirit and then be able to expand it further.

The process isn't only about poetry. Keats didn't just want to become a better poet. Though he certainly did want that: he died with the belief that though his career was short he would be "among the English poets." And so he is.

But Keats also seems to have believed that expanding his capacities as a poet would entail expanding his capacities as a human being. He wanted, as Hartman put it—using the sort of avian metaphor that the romantics themselves were prone to—to "molt into a higher humanity." True or not for Keats—I think it is—people do write in order to grow. They write so as to make themselves better men and women. They write to engage in *Bildung*, or self-shaping. They write to enlarge their minds and increase the reach of their hearts. Keats writes about this process in an amazing letter in which he describes the poet's progression through phases. The poet begins in the infant or thoughtless chamber where all is mystery; and then there is the chamber of maiden thought, where the beginning poet (the young woman or young man) begins to test the world. Then there's the next chamber, which is the one that Keats believes that he is stepping into as he writes. The chamber of maiden thought is full of beauty and wonder. Its inhabitant lives there in delight. There is nature, there are books, there are friendships (Keats was a wonderful friend), and there is often the beginning of love.

But to grow as a poet (which is perhaps to grow as a human being), you cannot stay in the chamber of maiden thought forever, singing the songs of spring. You have to step away from this world of earthly delights and feel what Keats (borrowing from Wordsworth) calls "the burden of the mystery." In the next chamber we see that the world is full of sorrows and miseries. We understand that life everywhere is infected with pain. In the great nightingale ode, Keats talks about the mortal land where "palsy shakes a few sad last grey hairs," and "where youth grows pale, and spectre-thin and dies."

The line about dying youth refers to all men and women who pass away young, but it has a particular referent as well. Keats is clearly thinking about his brother Tom whom he nursed after he became ill with tuberculosis. Keats wants to be the sort of poet who can write persuasively about delight: "A thing of beauty is a joy forever," he famously begins his early poem *Endymion*. But he also wants to grow to the point where he can write about the sorrow to which all flesh is heir. He admires Wordsworth's capacity to do so: "His genius is explorative of those dark passages," says Keats in the maiden thought letter. In time, Keats will write brilliantly if obliquely about the passage of time and the pains of loss. No one who has once read the closing lines of "Ode to Autumn" is likely to forget them.

But Keats wants more than the capacity to write about the sorrows of the world. He clearly wants to be able to experience them and respond with humane compassion. He wants to come to some understanding about what suffering is and how it is best dealt with. Like Tom (and like his mother before Tom) Keats also contracted tuberculosis. During his illness he had to envision the loss of his beloved Fanny Brawne and imagine all the poems he would never have the chance to write. This he does with a dignity that is modest and self-aware and irrevocably moving. "Here lies one," his self-composed epitaph will say, "whose name was writ in water." He became the man that his poetry and his letters imagined into being. Poetry was his vocation, but it was also his school. I will call the world a "vale of soul-making," Keats says in another letter. And through his writing he made it precisely that.

When I was in college I took a drawing class. Why, I'm not really sure. Maybe it was that Bennington, the school I was attending, was an artistic sort of school and I felt the need to do something in art. I was simply terrible. My still life of dishes and pots and drapes did not look like the dishes and pots and drapes nor did it look unlike them in an interesting way. My nudes were all skinny shaky lines. When the models came off their pedestals and saw what I had done to them, they shook their heads in sorrow. But I tried. I smudged charcoal, wore down pencils, and ruined paper. I had the kind of fertility one associates with Picasso—five, ten drawings in an hour. (Drawing is easy if you don't know how.) I had the fertility one associates with Picasso, but a few of the other qualities seemed to be missing.

At the end of the term I had a conference with my teacher. She had won my heart on the first day of class by telling a story about how she began her life as an artist (a story which I shall elaborate rather freely). She had grown up in rural Vermont, and one day when she was a very young girl—three years old, four?—her parents told her that an important guest was coming. His name was Robert Frost. My teacher felt that this Robert Frost might be related in some way to a more important and more enduring being by the name of Jack Frost. Jack was to her the spirit of winter. He scattered the snowflakes from his palms and painted the windows white and sent the wind running loose over the sheeted fields and all the rest. She drew him and drew him and drew him, as she imagined him to be. The arrival of the actual man, perhaps the best American poet of his time (ask him—he would tell you, albeit archly enough), was a letdown, and his interest in the drawings wasn't what my teacher-to-be had hoped. But once begun on the artist's path there wasn't any stopping her.

So this kindly and rather high-spirited person, who was not much older than I, sat down and looked with me through my jungle of lines and shades and listened as I told her that I couldn't, wasn't, and never would. What she said went something like this: "You have no facility as a visual artist. You have none whatsoever. And this disturbs you." I agreed that it did.

"It's a mistake," she said. "It shouldn't." She told me that if I devoted myself to the medium of drawing I'd soon learn to create more plausible sketches. I would in time be able to draw a cat that looked like a cat—though maybe not one that anyone would expect to up and meow. I would learn to render shapes much as I'd learned (much as we'd both learned) to put sentences together and to write (and to think) more or less grammatically. But something else entirely would determine how far I would go as an artist.

It's the spirit that's in you that matters most, she said. It may take longer to express itself if the medium you choose is one you aren't naturally fluent in. You might come into your own faster using words than you would using forms and shapes—but you'll go about the same distance either way. It depends on your commitment to growth. I was twenty-one; I'd never heard the like of this. She said a lot of artists had to fight against their facility. She observed that a writer's glibness could stop him from cutting deep and getting to the serious matters he might want to express, as can a writer's sense of humor. (Nietzsche, who didn't come into the conversation that day, was always suspicious of facility and though at times quite funny was nervous about joking. A joke, he said, is the epitaph for the death of a feeling.) An artist's fluency with his pencil could turn him into a mere illustrator, someone who created generic images allied with commonplace perception. A facile writer would always have a chance to sell the works of his pen—and that could corrupt him quickly. The gifted illustrator would face the same perils. These perils, my teacher and I agreed, would not be mine. They would not be mine in the visual arts and, as it turned out, they would not be mine in verbal endeavors either.

But my teacher's idea—which Keats would not, I think, reject out of hand—has stayed with me. I liked then and still like the notion that a medium—paint or clay or words—can be a medium for something called spirit or soul. I like the idea that mastering the medium is important, but that it's not the ultimate task. Keats's early poetry wasn't abominable quite. But it flirted with extreme badness. No one who reads the first volume he published (and that gleaned those horrible reviews) could ever imagine what kind of work he would produce and how quickly. Did Keats simply learn his craft at a stunning velocity? He did I think. But it was the need to express something—something in and of his spirit—that compelled him to move so quickly and to achieve so much. The spirit needed a way to make itself known in the world—or so at least I, a lover and maybe an idealizer of Keats and his poetry, am inclined to believe.

The growth from *Endymion* to "Ode to Autumn" is an artistic growth, but it is a growth of spirit, too. Melville said that a whaling ship was his Harvard and his Yale. Keats used poetry as his school, and it addressed his mind and his heart. He left with the highest conceivable honors.

He expanded. Early in his career, Keats could only write persuasively about a few matters: spring, beauty, pleasure. But as time went on and he exerted himself further, his powers expanded. He became someone who knew what to say when faced by loss and by death—and by love. Most of us cannot do that. When we fall in love or lose someone we adore, we are struck mute. But growth as a writer can in time allow one to face the most complex and powerful experiences and turn them into words. Keats passed from being able to write about happiness to being able to write about almost anything in words that are fresh and full of feeling. He used words to become himself. He used words to grow. Faced with death, a human being wants to be able to say more than "she's gone." Faced with love, he wants to say more than "she's beautiful." A real writer can say more, and the more makes his life something singular and true and more worth living than it would be if he remained mute, or spoke only in generalities and echoes.

But Keats is Keats. Can the rest of us send ourselves to the school of writing and emerge new men or new women? Surely it is not easy and few of us may be able to complete the whole course; that is few of us will let writing lead us as far as it can or will into unfolding what is best in ourselves. But I persist in thinking that no one who devotes a life to writing and uses it as Keats did to make better the self that genes and fate have given him will be entirely frustrated by what he can achieve. Whether the world itself is always a "vale of soul-making" is uncertain. But writing, entered into in the right spirit, is and always will be, at least for a spirit like John Keats.

To Fail

Melville said it memorably. He told the world that insofar as he was free of his obligations to his purse—his need to make money and keep mammon half content—he was dedicated to writing those works the world inevitably called failures. He evokes of *Moby-Dick* of course, which was neglected by many reviewers and generally misunderstood by the few who deigned to take note. Melville began his writing life as a smash success with a couple of novels about his travels in the exotic Pacific islands, *Typee* and *Omoo*. The writer who brought those books out was young and dashing and fresh from his own Pacific sojourn. The literary world made much of him. He didn't have a run quite like Lord Byron's, our exemplar of the erotic writer—this was Puritan America after all— but for a while Melville got close to being an American celebrity.

But something in him rebelled against it. He began to write more poetry—and Melville's poetry is wonderful, but not for everyone. His fiction became radically demanding. His audience felt like he had sold them out. The young entertainer was becoming something else. It was an insult, an affront to those who had loved his early work. They turned their backs on him and that seemed to push him further.

Melville might have gathered himself and reconsecrated his work. He might have let his audience—rather than his strong imagination—shape what he was going to do. But Melville didn't. He repaired with his family to a farmhouse in Pittsfield, Massachusetts, the far western part of the state, and went to work full bore on *Moby-Dick*. He wrote the book in a blue heat, flying along, hour after hour, sometimes as though it were being dictated to him from some other world. He wrote it fast. It took about fourteen months by one account and when he finished he felt he had been purified. I've written a wicked book, he told his friend Hawthorne, and now I feel spotless as the lamb.

The public didn't care for Melville's demonic book. The American reading classes were not up to it. They didn't have room for an orating sea captain whose nearly insane hunger for conquest and revenge and the great white whale predicted so many part-mad American quests to come. In Ahab's eyes you could catch the gleam that would put America in war after war, compel it to annihilate its Indian population, expand west and south, and then, in time, hunger to take the entire world under its eagle's spread wings. Melville predicted Vietnam and he predicted Iraq and he predicted the slaughter of the rebel armies in the Philippines and the murder of the Indians at Wounded Knee and everyplace else the tribes went down in senseless slaughter. And he predicted our hypocrisies, too. Ahab sometimes believes that his quest is *noble*. He sometimes seems to think himself a knight errant going off to rid the world of the predator beast, leviathan. His contradictions became our own. We are the nation who sought to create an empire for liberty. What an amazing thought! An empire that would bring freedom to those we conquered and exploited. What a beautiful dream, having it both ways was. Melville's murderous multiracial crew is the harbinger of the multiracial American army that traverses the globe, blowing human beings to fleshy bits in order to save them.

Melville saw into the future in ways that his contemporaries never could have. (And in a way it's not hard to forgive them for their incapacity.) It took history (and us) some time to catch up with Melville's vision—Melville's failure.

As to Melville himself, he did not always take his lack of success in stride. He'd had his run with the great bitch goddess Success, as Henry Adams liked to call her, and it is not hard to understand why he wanted at least one taste more. With the vast novel about the whale, he surely must have felt he earned it. But Melville had to live with what over time seemed to him a rank failure. He went broke. For a long while he stopped writing. Some of the work he did manage stayed in the dark. "Bartleby, the Scrivener" was another piece of dire prophecy. The man who sits at his desk stubbornly preferring not to is a parody and a patron saint to every oppressed office worker from then to now who sits and dreams and broods and detests his life. The office slavery that Melville captured in that tale has become the order of much of the civilized world. Melville knew it. Melville knew it before we did or even could have. Prophet? Yes, but what the teacher said is true. Prophets are not honored in their own land or in their own time either. The future bears them out—or it does not.

Truly original writers, it's been said, must create the taste by which they will be appreciated. This Melville did. It was just that the taste-creation process took about a hundred years. And Melville suffered for it during his life. He didn't only want readers in the future; he wanted readers in the present, now. Some people said his failure, or what he perceived to be failure, drove him nearly mad. He surely became deeply melancholy. He surely came close to giving up writing altogether. But he did have enough faith to finish *Moby-Dick* and in time to do more work. "Bartleby" is a wonder—and then came *Billy Budd*.

And I suspect that despite the sorrows there were other times in which Herman Melville's main sentiment was defiance. He was surely feeling defiant enough that day he spoke to the far more timid Hawthorne about the demonic whaling book. Melville was Ahab's creator after all, and I think he partook in Ahab's faith that the best way to confront a bitter, predatory world is to strike back at it—or to hit first. "Thy right worship," Ahab says, "is defiance." *Moby-Dick* was a defiant book, far darker than anything America was ready for, and Melville not only paid the price for his defiance but also reaped the bracing pleasures. After Melville died, the story goes, they came to move his desk. Carved far back on the great wooden vessel, the vessel that had gone over all those seas with the writer, were written some words from a poem by Friedrich Schiller. They were simple and direct: "Hold fast to the dreams of your youth."

But I'm not Herman Melville, you might say. I don't want to dare failure the way he did. I can't revel in possible failure in Melville's way. "No! I am not Prince Hamlet nor was meant to be," T. S. Eliot's Prufrock says, "am an attendant lord, one that will do to swell a progress." How many of us feel worthy of a Melville-like destiny? He was great and we are small. There is no reason to court failure the way Melville did. The probability is that we will fail twice. We'll fail once in the present (as Melville did) and then again in perpetuity. No bad books are remembered down through time, Auden said; but many good ones are forgotten. Chances are that one way or another we will be forgotten. No, we are not Prince Hamlet, nor Herman Melville either.

But Herman Melville was not Herman Melville, at least to begin with. He became so over time and well after he died. When he lived he was simply another writer trying to achieve what he could. He was overshadowed by numberless less accomplished figures; he was shunned by his publishers; he was insulted and maligned and all the rest. He was also loved and supported. Even in his darkest days he had friends, or at least some of them. But he did not know for certain that it was his destiny to live on through time. When he said he was devoted to failures, he meant that he was out to write books that were so large in scope, so ambitious and so original that they would have to fail, at least in some measure. No human being could realize the project that was *Moby-Dick* to perfection. There was joy in this feeling of taking on matters that were too big. Attacking something massive raised up a warrior's spirit in Melville. Emerson talks about the how young men sitting in libraries read the works of the great who have come before them and cower at their originality and force. What they forget is that those great authors were once young men sitting in libraries themselves. But they did not do much cowering—or if they did, they overcame it in time.

Part of the dignity of writing is that it allows men and women to take on tasks that may seem overwhelming and then do their best knowing that what's being attempted can't but end with some measure of failure. The critic Randall Jarrell once defined a novel as an extended fictional narrative with which something significant is wrong. In general it is more than merely one thing. You can keep yourself awake all night counting up Charles Dickens's literary crimes and misdemeanors: the sentimentality, the sloppiness, the overwriting, the sententiousness. But then you get up from your half slumber and read the opening passage of *Great Expectations* or *Bleak House* and you know that what he achieves is still magic. You are in his world in an instant and you do not want to leave.

One is tempted to echo Eliot. Good writers borrow; great writers steal. We might say that good writers fail small time; great writers are constantly failing at a rather grand level. If you're not failing, you're probably not setting your sights high enough. I know there are some works that we think of as flawless: Jane Austen's and Alexander Pope's come to mind. And they are wonderful writers, but put beside them Charles Dickens and that massive failure John Milton (God's lines in the great poem are beyond being merely embarrassing) and they become something a bit less. It's wonderful to see chunky Babe Ruth whack one out of the park. But he misses the ball with almost the same relish as he slams it. The swing is all.

Writing is always a lost cause. To stay with baseball for a second, you can always see much further than you can hit. You've read the very best of literary artists and you know you are not there, cannot get there today, maybe will never get there. But this knowing lends dignity to what you're up to. You've entered a world in which there are no limits to excellence—and accordingly a world where everyone fails and there is failure everywhere.

Mailer is not Melville, but on the subject of failure the sage of Brooklyn has some worthwhile thoughts. Mailer was a devoted reader of his reviews and in time he became a close student of what reviews meant about the nature of a book. He suggested that if your reviews broke 60 percent thumbs up and 40 down, then that was fine. He implied that probably the reverse was OK, too. Though he knew that when matters went that way his next advance would suffer. But Mailer also suggests that when the reviews are unremittingly positive, you haven't done what you should have. You haven't pushed hard enough against the boundaries of conventional opinion and conventional consciousness. In other words, if you have succeeded too well you haven't failed nearly well enough.

I've only had one book that was anything like an across-the-board critical success. It was called *Teacher* and its ostensible subject was a terrific and very eccentric philosophy teacher that I and my buddies were lucky enough to have at our proletariat high school. (Its non-ostensible subject? Growing up. America. The sixties. Rock music. My father.) Man, did reviewers love that book. I must have grabbed around forty reviews, almost all positive—with some gushers thrown in. Never have I been so much kissed in print. Everyone seemed to like that book, which made me feel grand—and also crummy. I'd read Melville; I'd listened a little to the sage of Brooklyn. I wanted to write books, not Hallmark cards.

In time I was rescued. It turned out there was a constituency who hated *Teacher*—or at least looked at it with a wary eye. Teachers! Many teachers who picked up the book were made unhappy by it. In the war of us against them, kids versus teachers, I was too much of the party of the kids it turned out. I'd aligned myself with the kids in their rank rebellion against the way it was and the way it had to be. I was using my adult mind and my expensive education to say in rather more polished ways what the students at every slave-system high school coughed into their sleeves. Down with boredom. Down with submasters and disciplinarians and the people who're running a jail when they pretend to be running a school. The great thing about our teacher Frank Lears was that he was not really a teacher at all. He was one of us. Real teachers read the book—it was a frequent Christmas present to them I fear—and they let loose some bile.

I heard about it—letters and e-mails and stand-up well-rehearsed harangues at lectures. I took it with a smile. You might even say that I was happy. I knew I wasn't playing for the biggest stakes. But finally the oddly delectable, acrid burnt-coffee scent of failure had entered the room.

To Change the World

Should you try to change the world—or some small corner of it—with your writing? Ultimately every young writer must decide if she will make the attempt. Writers achieve gains for themselves, or they try. As we've said, they can develop their minds and expand their spirits, and they can fail in the most satisfying and profitable ways. But what about the writer and the world outside her head and heart? Can writers change the world? Should they even try?

Percy Bysshe Shelley was accused once of writing books for the purpose of changing the world. Shelley wasn't long in responding. He wanted to know exactly what purpose his detractor had when he wrote his books (or his essays, or his squibs). Ultimately, Shelley asked what purpose there could be to writing if not to change the world.

Shelley was that way. Every time he picked up his pen, he was out to save humanity. He believed in the transforming power of literature; he told us at the end of his treatise in defense of poetry that "poets are the unacknowledged legislators of the world." Well, after Shelley they shouldn't be unacknowledged anymore. According to Shelley, everyone should understand that much of what we call human progress owed and owes to the exertions of imaginative writers.

How do writers change the world? For one thing, they reinvigorate the language. If poets don't come along with their metaphors and their verbal twists and turns, then language will become inert. It will be dead, as Shelley says, "to all the nobler purposes of human intercourse." Language is the most intimate medium of human exchange and it must be kept vital. Language must reflect the mystery, beauty, and sadness of life. Those are abiding facts, and when language flattens out, we can no longer perceive them.

Literature is also a source of virtue, or so Shelley says. In the great books we come up close to images of the best of all possible human beings; we meet the ideals of a good or true or beautiful life. Shelley tried to offer such images himself all through his career. His paragon of humane excellence is Prometheus, the hater of tyrants: not only a poet but also a scientist, architect, physician, and inventor whose contributions transform human life for the better. For Shelley all forms of productive invention are related to poetry. The source of great writing is imagination to be sure. But scientists and rulers who genuinely want to help mankind draw on the same ennobling faculty. They conceive the world not only as it is, but (through imagination) as it ought to be, and they work for the necessary changes.

Above all Shelley was an apostle of freedom. Everywhere he looked he saw that his fellow men and women were in chains—and he did what he could to help snap them. But the chains were not always material. Often they were what Blake, who would have loved Shelley's work had he read it, would have called "mind-forg'd manacles." For Shelley believed he had made a discovery. People were addicted to their own servitude: over time they came to love being in thrall to this absolute power or that. They were often physically constricted but the constrictions that mattered most were mental. And Shelley believed that by writing with passion, energy, and daring, he could liberate his readers. He wrote to spread the truth and to change the world.

His Prometheus isn't only oppressed by the gods; he's also oppressed by himself. Chained on the rock, Shelley's Prometheus is the victim of the horrid god Jupiter's wrath, but he's also the victim of his own. When we first encounter Prometheus (who is surely a version of Shelley) he is suffering harshly and a bit operatically. "Ah me," he says, "pain ever, forever." Not only is he locked down to a rock in the barren Caucasus Mountains but also every day an eagle comes to feed on his liver. What keeps Prometheus going at the outset of the poem is knowing that his foe's days are numbered. A prophecy has told them both that one day

Jupiter will fall. Prometheus spends his time pining for that day, and imagining what horrors he'll inflict on Jupiter once he, Prometheus, rules the world.

Shelley's implications in this, perhaps the greatest of romantic poems, are clear. As soon as he ascends, Prometheus will set to work becoming a Jupiter figure. He'll torture Jupiter in the same way and eventually with the same thrill with which Jupiter tortured him. Prometheus is in thrall. He's in thrall to the horrible king of the universe, but he's also in thrall to his spirit of revenge. He doesn't want freedom; he's not pining for the liberty to create and to love. Those matters are at best secondary. He's pining for the chance to exact revenge and to get the whole cycle of domination, submission, and rebellion going again. In the course of the magnificent poem, Prometheus will learn better. He'll see that the true reward for breaking free from Jupiter's chains is anything but becoming another Jupiter. He'll make himself into a genuinely loving and creative figure and what he achieves society may achieve along with him.

Everywhere men and women are in chains. It's a sentiment that's close to Shelley's heart—and almost all the romantic writers share it. In their different ways Wordsworth and Coleridge and Keats and Whitman and Emerson and Thoreau and Emily Dickinson all wrote to break chains. Dickinson wrote in part to liberate herself from the oppressions of her Puritan faith and straitlaced culture: but many readers who have encountered her over time have been set free from their own bonds—or so they felt. The romantics write to enfranchise men and women. Romantics write to change the world.

But the poets are not the only professed chain breakers. Rousseau and Marx, two of the major political thinkers of the modern period, also saw humanity in chains; the metaphor occurs and reoccurs in their work. For Marx the manacles are forged by capitalism; in Rousseau the culprit is society with its rules and regulations and its swerve away from the humane and just life that nature offers. Rousseau and Marx both wanted to change the world. They wrote to liberate; they wrote to enfranchise.

There are not many now who will say that Marx did the world palpable good; most will, in fact, say quite the opposite. And Rousseau? He is still esteemed in France. Almost all French writers who have achieved any measure of renown are still esteemed in France. But few of our contemporaries can rest easy with his view that human beings are *naturally* good—not after Darwin, not after Auschwitz. And his centrality to the

men who fomented the French Revolution and sent streams to the guil-
lotine will always make him suspect.

Face it. We now often look askance at writers who think of themselves
as chain breakers. We are not comfortable with scribbling liberators of
mankind. So many of the monsters of the last two centuries have come
to us trailing their ideologies, their cruelties, and the books they authored
to make it all seem justified. Somewhere in an ugly squat of hell Mao
waves the Little Red Book; Hitler reads aloud from *Mein Kampf*; Lenin
rages on about imperialism and the death throes of capitalism. Perhaps
Rousseau and Marx are there with them.

Are Blake and Shelley on hand too: not for the content of their doctrine,
which is humane and generous, but rather for their hubris? For by writing
to change the world they contributed to the pernicious illusions that
books and authors really are the legitimate legislators—rather than, say,
custom and usage. Or maybe they are there in hell simply because they
asked too much of humanity—when we all know that one of the best
ways to make people explode in resentment and then maybe succumb to
regression is to make demands they cannot fulfill. Sublimation—the
turning of basic energies into refined, civilizing energies—can only go so
far the psychiatrists tell us. Eventually the old demons break through and
often with redoubled force.

"Poetry makes nothing happen," W. H. Auden famously said. By which
I think he means that true poetry, the sort he aspired to write, makes
nothing happen. Authentic writing makes nothing happen in part because
it can never be confused with propaganda. Poetry—real poetry—is too
enmeshed in complexities ever to be turned into policy. Auden can be a
didactic poet, no doubt. (Saying that poetry makes nothing happen and
saying so in the midst of an elegy for Yeats is evidence.) But Auden was a
close enough student of politics and history to see that it was raw simplici-
ties that most often swayed the world. He once declared that a person who
felt he had a lot to say—a good deal of advice to dispense to humanity—
would probably amount to nothing much as a poet. Rather, Auden said, it
was the sort of person who liked to play with words to see what they might
be able to do and how they could sound together that would have the best
chance to write poetry, or at least to write poems that W. H. Auden would
want to read.

Well, you may say, that was Auden. But—if one can venture a gener-
alization this large—most postromantic writers of consequence have

followed his lead, the lead of writers we call modernist. Virginia Woolf wrote a partially admiring essay about Shelley in which she said that he was "not one of us." By "us" she probably meant most all women and men, who cannot readily say of themselves what Shelley once did of himself: "I go until I am stopped and I never am stopped." But Woolf was also talking about the denizens of Bloomsbury, her fellow artists and writers, who were prone to be ironic, urbane, and interested more in cultivating their own gardens and developing the rigors of their art than in changing the world. The headlong nature of Shelley's art was anything but Bloomsburyan.

Do writers now want to change the world? Should they? I think most writers now shy away from the great romantic project, which comes along with multiple risks. They are afraid of sounding too grand; they are afraid of being mocked. They write from their own vantage point—but they resist the general perspective. They don't talk about "we"—both as we are now and as we might with work and luck become—in the way Shelley and Whitman so freely did. Even those writers who want to do more than entertain are cautious, tapping ahead like unsighted men and women over uneven ground.

They're nervous. How can they speak for all when, as they see it, we're all so different? Maybe there is one truth for women and one for men. Maybe the black truth is not the white. And maybe the Asian truth subverts both. What about the times in which we live and how they condition our perceptions, maybe to the point of determining them? What's so now will be untrue tomorrow—and in need of being unsaid. Wittgenstein made a famous claim: The world is all that is the case. But won't what is the case and what makes up the world shift and slide like a city built on water and sand? Writing that describes a far-gone and past world—and the news media tell us the world is new every fifteen minutes, or after the next commercial interruption—can't be of any value and can only in time be a humiliation to the author.

Does anyone write to change the world anymore? Does anyone still write to break the chains?

I think they should. William Carlos Williams said that he understood it was hard to get the "news" out of poems—especially, he implied, modern poems like his and those of his lifelong friend and antagonist, Ezra Pound. The poems tend to be difficult and dense and (in Pound's case) frighteningly allusive. But, Williams went on to say, it's important to keep at it; for men and women die miserably every day for lack of what is found in poetry. He wasn't talking about poems that feature the poet, the teakettle, and the kitchen curtains. He was talking about poems of sweep and daring, poems that come in like thunderstorms at sea and send the waves into a reeling dance and make the clouds leap in the sky. Williams wrote some of those poems, or at least he tried. He tried in his own behalf and, as his famous line shows, he tried in behalf of his readers.

Prophetic writers have done their harm. The ones who have seen themselves as coming down from Sinai with a tablet in hand rather than down from the attic with a fat yellowed manuscript have sometimes made mischief. But it is not as though without writers there would be no mischief.

Without some waking up, human beings would die of self-suffocation; they'd lie down and push the pillow over their own heads and press, press, press. The spirit of the self takes us over very easily. We are inclined to back away into existences that are not much better than animal. We horde and sleep and feed. We become creatures of appetite, not much more. Writers say everything under the sun. But I think that all real writers are constantly saying one thing. Wake up!

Wake up: stop sleepwalking. Put an end to the death in life, the comatose come-along that most of us engage in most of the time. Wake up and smell the coffee, the flowers, and the air. (To breathe the air is sheer delight, says Shelley—or at least it can be after Prometheus effects his revolution.) Wake up! And then what? Well, what you do when you open your eyes is up to you. But, the writer (the real writer) continues, I do have a few ideas.

HITTING YOUR STRIDE: PERILS AND PLEASURES / PLEASURES AND PERILS

PERILS AND PLEASURES

To Drink

Writers drink. There's no way around that. They do. It's one of the main perils of writing. Writers as a class probably drink less than they once did, but they can still hold their own against most any professional group, no matter how bibulous. They do drugs too and for all sorts of reasons. But why do they? And should you?

Alcohol is a mystery drug. We don't really know what it does for the imbiber, either on the psychological level or the physiological. If there is a more puzzling everyday mystery than what happens when people get high (a little or a lot) on alcohol, I'm not sure what it is. I do think, though, that we can say something general about what happens when you take in smallish amounts of booze: one drink, two, or (if you happen to possess a stevedore build) maybe three. But probably not three. No, probably not. The poet George Herbert tells us to avoid the third glass and there's almost certainly something in what he says.

It's hard to avoid the third glass, though, especially when you use alcohol the way I think many writers do. They use it to relax. All day they've been using and overusing a muscle, their minds. And rather than getting looser, as bodily muscles will, the muscle that is (metaphorically) the mind seems to have a tendency to grow tighter with focused (and often profitable) use. The basketball jock and the tennis player exhaust the muscles of their bodies and when they're done, so long as they haven't pushed themselves too far, feel pretty good. They get what people like to call "deliciously tired." They sprawl out on the old gray overstuffed and they listen to some music or watch TV or read a book or simply claim a benignly vegetative state. This according to many is happiness.

Mental exertion seems a bit different. If you've figured out your entry protocols—your meditation, your drink of choice, your nonfattening chocolate bar (which someone should invent soon)—then your initial feeling on sliding into your work is loose and easy. You're on the field; you're warmed up and ready to play. And play it can be. When the ideas are rolling out and somehow the (approximately) right words are appearing and forming (roughly) the right order, then you feel a little like you're flying. And even if you're not flying or even gliding yet, there's still a sense of untapped energy. The wind is in your sails, and all that.

This goes on. The wind lasts for different lengths of time for different people. For a given individual it may vary day to day. While the breeze blows it's all lovely. But then, imperceptibly, the breeze cuts back a little and you have to start rowing. Rowing strains the back and the legs and the gut, but the craft is still sliding forward and all's well. But then it gets hard. It gets very hard. You taste the sweat on your face and the oar blisters your hand. You're puffing. And so it can be with writing. You're sailing, but then in time you have to push it. You have to row.

Even if you have the sense to quit before you melt down completely, you've still tired out your mind and probably your spirit, too. And there you encounter one of the catches of writing: it doesn't always relax the mind the way physical exertion relaxes the body. The elastics get tighter and tighter rather than loosening. Why this is I'm not sure.

No doubt there are writers who finish a pair of sessions in a day and feel cleansed and pure and ready to go off and do complex math in their heads. But I'm guessing not. What comes after the writer's play and work is often painful mental compression. Writing can intensify the tensions in the mind to a potent degree.

Writer's tension doesn't only come from exertion it seems to me. There's also the pressure of doubt. Is this any good? Should I keep working on it? Am I wasting my time? For the novelist, this must be an especially tough issue. For novelists, practiced as they might be, are always liable to make wrong turns. Suddenly the love interest's car veers off the road and into the ditch—ambulance, emergency room, doctor, body cast. Body cast! Body cast? Was that really such a good idea? A body cast has the power of inhibiting a plot as well as anything. But I've gone twenty pages down the body-cast path. To backtrack or not to backtrack? There's cause for a headache.

Now add some financial insecurity to your mind fatigue and artistic worry. You're hearing the ping of e-bills as you write. Add a daughter with a high-mucus cold and a son whose proclivity to share toys at day care by flinging them at other kids has been revealed only yesterday afternoon. Enough said.

And, as all writers know, there is an elixir that can relax those tensions with a few swallows, then a few more. It really is something like magic. Writing long and hard the mind becomes aching and taut. But then, a little like Alice on her journey through Wonderland, we come upon a magic bottle that says DRINK ME. (Actually we know very well where the bottle is.) We do, and the iron hand that's been squeezing our brain relaxes its hold a little. I'm not always sure why the Greeks made devious Hermes a god; and jealous Hera can be exasperating, always running down Zeus to spoil his fun. But two or three swallows of red wine after a hard day's writing and I am ready to contribute to the building of a local temple for Lord Dionysus.

Damn is red wine good stuff. (Recast that sentence using your own drink of choice and see how well it works.) I even like the red wine that comes in flagon-sized bottles and that's what I drink most of the time. Twelve bucks' worth—lasts me three nights—no it lasts four, five, honest. But I don't need prime vintage. I'm with that character in Iris Murdoch who had only one thing—one thing only—against a dear friend. She introduced him to high-priced, grand-tasting red wine, which made his day-to-day vintage (the vintage he could afford) seem dull. It's red wine itself that's wonderful and Lord Bacchus be praised for even its modest manifestations. As to the top-shelf stuff, I'll drink it from time to time. Good wine is my default celebration flourish. But really, I'm always most happy to return to backbench, down-home, plain and simple red. Lord Bacchus, be praised one more time!

The drug is magic. It does what the imaginary label says it is supposed to do. It makes calm what was turbulent; it makes soft what was steel; it slacks the ropes and lets drift the craft. If any drug was ever concocted for the weary writer it must be wine. It's as though Bacchus, a junior god, made a kind offering to his older brother, Apollo, lord of arts and artists. This is for all, Bacchus might have said, but especially for your children, children of the reed. (Or pen.) What Apollo gave in return I'm not sure, but it could not have been small.

Wine (or beer or whatever) loosens the screws, and they can get awfully tight. That's one glass. That's two. But then the *peril*.

One glass, two—it gives you more than relaxation. It gives you something just as important. Wine (or whatever) gives you a dose of self-acceptance.

Let's say—along with Freud and Plato and plenty of other thinkers— that human beings are not unified in their inner lives. Let's say we're made of relatively separate pieces, relatively separate agencies. Freud called them the I, the over-I, and the it. Plato called them mind, spirit, and appetite. At the very least, almost everyone who has seriously considered the question understands human beings to be creatures split at least in two. The dualists see us as divided between nature and culture or between nature and God. Plato and Freud are more complicated (and for my money, more illuminating). To most who have paused to think hard about it, we are not united creatures. We want more than one thing at a time and those wants collide to create confusion (Plato) and anxiety (Freud). Division hurts. In Freud the I wants to survive, the over-I wants perfection, and the it wants all the pleasure it can get. One can readily see the problems that inevitably arise. We're three-headed beings clamoring (and sometimes whispering and sometimes scheming) for three (at least three) different objectives.

It's not surprising that we seek unity. For in unity we find calm. Plato says the exercise of reason can bring us such calm, but admits there are few who exercise reason terribly well. Freud says calm is the exception, not the rule and we have to learn to live with internal discomfort. Being human means accepting a measure of anxiety. Writers tend to be lively, even turbulent spirits—hungry for life, hungry for the perfection of their work, and aware (sometimes) of their need to get on in the world. The agitators in the machine can seem to churn without ceasing.

A passionate nature, the fatigue of writing, and the desire for some resolution and calm: no wonder writers and artists of all types (as well as people who think the first step in becoming an artist is to get messed up a lot) are prone to drink. And—marvel of marvels—it works. One glass of wine, then another (or the equivalent), sipped slowly creates a soft sea of tranquility. As my former teacher David Lenson describes the experience of being a little buzzed in his great book *On Drugs*: "What *is* simply *is*." But when we have the couple of cups, we are (to get a little high flow about it) like a Moses who has seen the promised land and maybe stepped foot inside. We want to stay there. We want to abide forever in the sphere of self-acceptance and calm. And then our troubles begin. Gore Vidal expresses the hunger for inebriation trenchantly, if darkly enough. In Michael Mewshaw's *Sympathy for the Devil*, Vidal speaks of the desire "to sink myself into whiskey where one's sense of time is so altered that one feels in the moment immortality—a long luminous present which, not drinking, becomes a fast-moving express train named . . . Nothing." Did Vidal bemoan the fact that he was always a godfather never a god? It seems that drink made him feel just a bit more deific.

There have been many fine observations about getting high—that is, elevating ourselves over the human landscape of bumps and ruts, sorrow and pain, and then cruising along as if on wings. But there is none in my view to touch a line by George Carlin, which I'll adapt to the subject at hand. Glass of wine, great stuff. Makes a new man out of you. Only one problem: new man wants a glass. (New woman does too.) Once we've touched the promised land of peace and plenty, we want to stay there, or go deeper inside and so the perils begin. The only paradises are lost paradises the man says. And a booze buzz makes us feel that we are returning to some life of fullness and plenty (in the womb, in Mom's arms?) that we've lost. New woman wants a drink. New man does, too.

And if your inner life is especially active, if the weather front tends to shift four or five times a day, then no doubt a little release feels fine. And then it fades and you go running after what you had like a kid who's lost his grip on the tail of a gorgeous kite of many colors. Trouble begins.

And the trouble can continue on a long way. Booze gives us a dose of happy consciousness, and that's not so easy to find. But booze can also deliver smashed dishes, smashed cars, smashed marriages. Booze has been compared to rope, for which there are many fine uses. You can use it to secure ship to shore; you can use it to tie the load on tight; you can have a high-spirited tug of war with it, too. But you can also put a hangman's noose in your rope and throw it over a branch or a beam. And then what happens does. As Lenson says in *On Drugs*, "Beneath alcohol's icons and institutions lie its familiar wastes: broken glass, a body in the gutter, the wreckage of cars, promises, families, and dreams."

Booze creates all sorts of troubles, from great to small, starting of course with the hangover. One glass extra, two or three too many and you begin waking up with mild and not so mild symptoms of flu. You've got a dose of what they used to call the ague. Tired, sore, dry throat, sluggish, irritable—there you are. Does your husband have to jam so many of those loud consonants into his sentences? Does your wife need to sing with so much gusto? Ah, the hangover—a subject in itself, but for another time.

One might only say this. As grievous as a hangover can be, it has its advantages. It tends to make you hypersensitive, critical, suspicious, mildly annoyed at the world, and maybe a little more than mildly annoyed at yourself. It's the perfect state, in other words, to experience a certain difficult *pleasure*. It's the perfect state in which to revise your work.

Like many other facts of the midgame writer's life, drinking is a double-edged matter. At extremes it can quicken and it can kill; in moderation it can brighten a sallow world. But even in moderation booze is a complicated business, with all the twists and loops of a demon's tail.

Writing is full of glorious oases that turn out to be alive with toothy monsters, and those sites that appear to be nothing but woe can often yield unexpected possibilities. You're alone all the time—and that's often a trial. But when you get in the habit, and cultivate it well, loneliness can morph into deep pleasure at being alone. You have to change your ways of reading from complete and joyous immersion to something more detached, and that too can have its long-run satisfaction. As a spy in the world of the normal and the ostensibly nice, you'll sometimes be compelled to silence. But you'll be able to redeem that silence when you get back to your desk.

And the immediately good things about writing can have a dark underside. That book of yours that sells and sells can taint your mind in strange ways; that beautiful new word processor, your personal genie, can maim your possibilities as a writer but good.

The writer's middle distance is a land of ambiguities. There are no pleasures but a little pain comes along to salt them. Almost no losses but they have their salutary side.

The key, I think, is to develop a double vision that sees both dimensions of life and never to be terribly surprised when the sweet suddenly goes a note sour; and never to be shocked when what seems the worst turn reveals some expanding possibilities. To be a successful midgame writer, you have to master the art of what the poet of Hibbing, Minnesota, once claimed was the only thing he really knew how to do: keep on keeping on. (Like a bird that flew.)

To Get Reviewed

Emerson did not care for his reviews or his reviewers. He said once that when he looked up at the sky and took in the glories of the firmament and brooded on the majesty of the universe and of the bounties of the creator (I elaborate a touch here) then (and probably only then) could he forget that he had been reviewed. One knows the feeling. Reviews are a peril. Reviews—no matter how high hearted about it all one claims to be—are a danger. They're one of the reasons for writing it (whatever *it* may be) and putting it in the drawer, maybe not just for Horace's recommended nine years, but forever.

Reviews are an inevitable peril (by and large) in the writing game. But in times past one could hate or disdain or fear a select few sources: the human hatchets at *Newsweek*, the meat cleaver who chops bones for the *Post*, the hangmen at the *Times*. (A writer friend of mine comes to visit the newborn of mutual pals. The writer leans over the crib and intones a melancholy blessing: "May you never be reviewed by Michiko Kakutani.") But now everyone is a reviewer, thanks to the Internet and the democratizing of the review. And all can do it anonymously. (Reviewing a book anonymously, Schopenhauer said, is not unlike addressing a political gathering wearing a mask.) The Internet gives license to galloping hordes of reviewers, where once there were but a few.

Said Heraclitus: Life is a child playing with dice: the game is to the child. Well, in the lifetime feud between writers and reviewers, the game is to the reviewers. From time to time someone on the writer's side will get a good one off. Martin Amis asked us to ponder the simple question: Is that what he wanted to be when he grew up? A reviewer? But that's a well-aimed sniper shot discharged from the concrete and steel wreckage; the reviewers deliver the bombs.

Even when they like—even when they love—what you've done, there is usually something at least slightly wrong with what they say. The review of your book describes something not unrelated to what you take yourself to have written. There are the characters; there are the themes; there is a word about the style that's not irrelevant to the book as you believe you know it. But something is wrong here. Something is badly wrong. They wrote about your book and they made it much smaller than it is. They made it much, much smaller. What they failed to see were the implications. They missed the ripple effect. They didn't understand how your book, though ostensibly about one thing, was actually about many things. In fact—whisper this; don't say it aloud—your book was about *everything*. Oh, it may ostensibly be just a memoir, but in that memoir was an implicit story of America, the whole shebang, circa the time of *you*. It was large. It contained multitudes—both spoken and implied.

That's what the bad reviewers do. That's what all but the very best reviewers do. They cut off the connotations.

The reviewers took Melville's gargantuan book (this is every writer's favorite example isn't it?) and they thought it was about whaling and in whaling it turned out they were not terribly interested. Nor did they expect the American literary public of 1851 to be. What they didn't see—the connotations, the resonance!—what they did not see was that this was a book about America. (Most all of our books are about America aren't they?) No reviewer will ever give you your penumbra, your halo, your ripple effect. Good books are about what they're about, but they're about more, too. Reviewers seem never to get to that "more." Melville's didn't; they left him angry and distressed. In time he wrote "Bartleby" about someone alone and unhappy and misunderstood, and he wrote *Billy Budd*, which would break the devil's heart if he chose to read it.

I've learned a great deal from my reviews says the magnanimous writer. Hah! Many writers stop reading their reviews at a certain point in their lives. They get their wives or husbands to give 'em the gist and that's enough. Sometimes they request the gist with a bit of sugar on top. It's said that Thomas Hardy's wife having read a review of her husband's latest in some shrine to literary respectability called out: "Thomas you have to read this. There are a great many fine criticisms of your work here." "Criticisms, criticism," Hardy purportedly said. "What I want is praise!" So Frost asked his readers and reviewers to be more responsive to the feats he accomplished in his poetry. "The whole thing is performance and prowess and feats of association," Frost said. "Why don't critics talk about those things—what a feat it was to turn that that way, and what a feat it was to remember that, to be reminded of that by this. Why don't they talk about that? Scoring. You've got to *score*. They say not, but you've got to score, in all the realms—theology, politics, astronomy, history, and the country life around you." Frost scored and scored, at least to his own mind (and mine). But the scoreboard the reviewers controlled never quite gave out the right totals.

Even a good review can leave you reeling and a great one (those exist, don't they?) can leave you growling quietly to yourself. (No one wants to hear those particular growls.) They shrink your book. And accordingly they shrink you. Whitman (as one cannot say too many times) had it right: he who touches this book touches a man. The book *is* the woman who wrote it, soul and body. We're all trying. We're all doing our best.

Why don't reviewers understand as much and occasionally dispense the benefit of the doubt?

I quit writing reviews. I had sinned a few too many times (though not that many) against literary faith and love and the spirit of Melville. But during my reviewing time, who knows how many true writers I may have pushed off course, or gored so deeply that they had to spend a month on the couch waiting for the wound to close. I am sorry to one and all.

The writer James Atlas talks in his fine and undervalued memoir about what it was like to get his first (and only—mark that!) novel, *The Great Pretender*, reviewed. It was a set of killers: Lehmann-Haupt in the daily *Times*, Jonathan Yardley in the *Washington Post*, Leslie Fiedler in the *Times Book Review*, and the one that even thirty years down the line I still remember—Sven Birkerts's in the *New Republic*. There's a moment when Saul Bellow enters Atlas's book for a cameo. He places his hat down on the kitchen table. The hat! Bellow's hat! The narrator idolizes Bellow and the sight of the great man's haberdashery on the table propels him into a moment of bliss. Bellow's hat!

Birkerts's finding: The novel was timid as a cheese-seeking mouse in daytime, flat as your palm, and derivative, mostly derivative. It emerged from the Chicago laureate. It popped out of Bellow's hat.

The reviews were apparently about as easy for Atlas to get over as a case of dengue fever. Atlas started with a period where he was supine, suffering, and near delirious. Then he rose unsteadily and stumbled around the room and finally out into the light. But the thing about dengue—the thing about this bad review—was the recurrence factor. Atlas assumed that everyone he knew had read it. So when he emerged from sick bay, still shaky, he was always ready to hear a nasty crack from someone: always nervous, always distressed, and ever ready to cut and make a retreat. And some of his friends (so-called) did want to talk about the reviews. They wanted to congratulate him for being considered at length in the pages of prestigious journals. Or they wanted to discuss the nuances of the denunciation. They did not, in other words, want to do the one thing the author needed: forget it, or if not that, at least shut up about it.

Atlas took it all to heart. His invitations dwindled (and he knew why). Acquaintances crossed the street when he came trundling their way (and he knew what for). His phone sat silent as an abandoned black anvil, it being the days of black anvil phones I guess (and he knew the reason). No one asked for his next novel (and he knew why and this time maybe he was correct). And then he went on to write about it all in a funny, deft, absorbing memoir, in an often silver-throated voice, and probably got some redemption. Probably—*some* redemption.

Maybe the reason Atlas's life got bleaker was because he got bleaker: postreview he became more of a trench coated alone-goer, a Dostoyevskian lurker in his own life. And who wants to hang out with that guy? But still, one has to sympathize. He writes that "eventually after a few years of therapy, I came out of my depression." Years! Of therapy! Years!

I suppose you could say the nasty reviewers are the wolves that cull the herd. They lie in wait for the weak and unwary and pounce when the moment comes. They open up space for younger, or simply stronger (or more tone-deaf) aspirants to enter the writing game. They send the gimpy players off to the sidelines and exile them, sometimes permanently. Still, I cannot love reviewers. They can rarely imagine that the book they are reading is better than the books they have written or could write.

Yet see it from the reviewer's point of view. Buying a book and reading it is an investment: an investment of money, yes, but more than that an investment of time. Shouldn't readers be forewarned when they're on the verge of acquiring a lemon? If the fruit on the stand is rotten or the king is buck naked, shouldn't someone say so? A bad movie blots out two hours of your life; a bad novel can blacken two weeks. Yes, yes, I suppose so: there are reasons for bad reviews. But should the reviewers take such ostentatious joy in producing them? Denunciations are easy to compose (ask legions of secret police and spies). Praise is hard. One must be modest; one must admit the book (the woman, the man) is better than you are.

Don't laugh about the effects of rotten reviews. In his elegy for Keats, Shelley talks about the destructive power of the arrow that flies in darkness. He's referring to the negative and anonymous reviews that he suggests had a part in the early sickness and death of Keats. Northrop Frye, one of the wisest of critics, claims that Shelley is being figurative. What Shelley means to say is that the indifference and the disdain of the public can have an ill effect on writers. To which, lover of Frye that I am, I have to say: No, sorry, I don't think so. Shelley knows more than you do. That reviewer who told the young physician Keats to stop writing and get back to his pills and his camphor ought to have been brought up on charges. In a way, he was. Keats's older friend Hazlitt took him to task in an essay that will live eternally in the vindictive hall of fame. But that did nothing to save Keats.

Souls are like bodies; you can hurt them with a blow. Unearned violence against them can cause trauma. Earned violence can, too. I more than half believe that if it were not for those reviewers, Keats might have gotten sick later than he did. We might have had a few more poems like "To Autumn."

One believes in compassion. Freud said he was a godless Jew. As to me, I think of myself as a godless Christian. I believe in the teachings of Rabbi Jesus—or most of them—but not in worshipping the character who drowned the world because it annoyed him, and who wiped out the first-born of all the Egyptians to show his might. So that means I believe in compassion. As Blake put it, "I forgive you, you forgive me / As our dear Redeemer said / 'This the Wine and this the Bread.' "

Still there are certain stories about encounters between reviewers and the reviewed that I don't mind hearing more than once. Dale Peck, a human hacksaw, reviewed Stanley Crouch's novel *Don't the Moon Look Lonesome*, and he did not care much for it. ("*Don't the Moon Look Lonesome* is a terrible novel, badly conceived, badly executed, and put forward in bad faith; reviewing it is like shooting fish in a barrel.") Crouch apparently caught sight of Peck at a restaurant in the Village, crossed the room, and identified himself. Crouch reached out his right hand and Peck took it. Crouch, who is a sturdy fellow, grasped hard and harder. With his left, he slapped Peck twice across the face, with force. Unfair, you'll say, uncouth. But isn't this a version of what reviewers sometimes do? Clasp your book in their hands, embrace it, and then slap you across the face?

I understand that the *Times* reviewer Michiko Kakutani (may you never be reviewed by MK) never disseminates her photo, rarely goes out in public, rarely makes herself known. No surprise—she has written some memorable appreciations. But all professional reviewers have it in them to be killers of souls, and she is no exception. Occasionally, just occasionally, they should have to answer.

Emerson was right and so was Shelley. The best reviews are tough to take: they're like dessert pies made of spinach and green beans. The worst are unspeakable. They're made of barbed wire and dead bolts. Eat them you must—even if because merely hearing of their existence, you up and compose them yourself. In general there are no great reviews and there are no great reviewers.

Oh, every now and then some large soul who does not frequently review makes his way into a periodical and writes with something like love in the heart. But once he has revealed the capacity, the authorities take care to have him eliminated in a midnight purge. From time to time a generous review gives true pleasure. The writer feels finally that one of his highest hopes has been fulfilled. He wrote to be *understood* and now at least one large soul has done it.

Too many reviews are studies in resentment. They condense the rancor of the reviewer who cannot write and calm the envy of those who wish to write and cannot. The reader of reviews will have to read between the lines to find out if he will actually enjoy the book and profit by it.

Writing is its own reward. Do not write with an eye forward to the day of publication and review. Write with an eye to the next word that you'll put down. Reviews are like divots in the playing field; insignificant in themselves they can still cause injuries if you let them.

Step out into nature, stare up at the teeming sky, full of stars that glow like the works of the writers who've come before us and inspire and incite; they are your true company, not the company of reviewers. (Melville shines down. Keats does and Shelley, too.) Follow Emerson. Forget you've been reviewed or ever will be. Then come inside and start writing again.

To Learn to Be Alone

Pascal's got it right I think. People get into trouble because they are unable to stay in their rooms. Pascal stayed in his and recorded his thoughts about our mortal state and also invented a geometric system or two. But Pascal was the exception and knew it. (Did he spend some time in a hair shirt? Highly possible.) Pascal—who did not think much of humanity; he called a man a thinking reed—was wary of the mischief we could get into when we worked our way through the locks and inserted ourselves into the outside world. So he stayed home and slept in his narrow bed and asked nothing of his servants and thought his usually rather chilling thoughts.

Pascal got things done. He did not leave his room. But not leaving one's room is a peril, as bad as being reviewed—as bad as the third glass can be. Though staying locked down inside has a few sweet pleasures, too.

I'm sure Pascal was abetted in his stay-at-home ways by his proclivity for writing. When you are isolated inside your room, you need something to do. Pascal, like every other writer, had to acquire the art of being alone. It's a good art to acquire and it's not terribly easy.

Everyone knows that a writer is a self-sentenced prisoner. For a certain part of every day, he must repair to a small walled enclosure. Whether it's a room of his own or rented from someone else is beside the point. There he is and there he stays. For a while, I wrote in a large, book-lined ship's-cabin-like structure. It was freestanding; it was rustic; it was full of books growing dusty and plants growing hardly at all, since plants must be watered and this was beyond the scope of the prisoner. But still, there was a certain rude luxury about the place. I had a music system to turn on and to juice myself with when inspiration failed. I was especially prone to listening to the live record by Dylan and the Band: *Before the Flood.* ("But time will tell just who has fell and who's been left behind / When you go your way and I go mine.") That amped me up pretty good. In grad school I lived in an apartment that was smaller by half than the place where I ended up writing my first books. In my studio, I had bay windows, I had wood floors, and after a while I had a bathroom. There was a bed I could conk out on and sometimes did. For a while a belief persisted among my sons that a horrible grouchy old man lived there. Then they found it was only their dad, and visited quite regularly.

Visiting too were friends who stopped by to say hello. All of them wished me well in my writing ventures; almost all of them mooned over my writing space. If only I had this, they said. If only I had this superb cabin of my own, then I would write. (Everyone it sometimes seems wants to write.) Then, truly I would be happy.

I like having friends. And since I like having friends, I did not let go of the words that were pushing against my lips with the force of souls trying to escape torment. Sure, I wanted to say: On Day One, you'd love it here. You'd put on some tunes, sharpen a few pencils, get a cup of coffee that's exactly right. You'd settle in in three bears style. You'd kick it all off with a little meditation, maybe Buddhist style, maybe the kind you learned at that workshop where they gave you a personal mantra in a quiet initiation ceremony. One more sip of the delectable brew and you'd sit down and begin to write. *Scratch, scratch/scrape, scrape.*

And by about noon, either that day or the next or the next, you'd be in the process of becoming a wreck. Not because you're dumb, not because you have nothing to say, not because you aren't "serious about writing." But because you, public persona, people person, rooster on the collective roost, have little experience in being alone. To write, you have to be able to countenance your own company. To write, you've got to be able to hang by yourself. You've got to go azul azul, as the Italian has it—or at least the improvised Italian that was spoken in the Hillside section of Medford, when I drank Bud and white port there with various and sundry, including Bova and Scialoia, and Castle and Carbone, circa 1971.

People can't stand themselves. They get all alone and they freak. They make a phone call, check their e-mails, click on the flat screen. In a pinch, they're even willing to pick up a book. But if you ask someone who has no experience in the game to write, even if you send him to his writing-room heaven, he's probably going to have a rough time. I surely did. I looked around my studio and saw that it was all I'd ever wanted as a writing hideaway and set to work. But then—an hour later, two at the most—I'd be itching for action, itching for people. I'd be out and in my car and on my way to town. Like most aspiring writers, I hadn't acquired the basic art. I hadn't learned the power that writing both relies upon and in the long run teaches. I did not know how to be alone.

I bored myself. That's the long and the short of it. And so does most every gal or guy who sits down to write. With all of his hustling in the world, he has only learned to use his mind as an instrument for success and the fulfillment of his desires. He has not learned to reflect and consider. When left alone, without anyone to talk to, he does not know what to do or say. He panics. And pretty soon the writing vocation or avocation that he's both affected to envy and made a little fun of begins to look daunting. After a week in the little room, it begins to look down-right frightening. He will do anything to get out.

Adam was alone in the garden and smarted keenly about it. In Milton's rendering, he spends more than a little time petitioning God to bring him a partner, mate, and confidante. God seems to be in a bit of a playful mood (rare for Milton's God), and he teases Adam about his neediness. Look, I've made a paradise for you. What more could you want? Then God comes to his main point. Look at me. I have been alone here all through eternity and I'm not pining for release. Adam points out the gap that divides him from the Lord on high and God relents. When Adam is asleep, the Lord pulls a rib from Adam's side and fashions Eve. Then there's bliss, at least for a while.

But the point shouldn't be lost on us: there is something a touch godlike in the capacity to be alone. Of course we humans can usually only achieve a small-time version of the state. We're not alone for eternity as writers, but simply for two or four or six hours a day. Still, for us this is a feat. (Aristotle said that only a god or a beast could live entirely by himself.) And for others who are not adept in the art, it's rather undoable.

For to be alone, you have to be able to put up with yourself. Not for nothing does Jonathan Franzen suggest a challenge when he titles his book of essays *How to Be Alone*. Being alone is a skill. You've got to be able to move your mind away from worry and obsession and plain noodling and focus on what's in front of you. You have to focus on what's before you, and that may be an empty page. But it also might be a gutter running with rainwater, a bird feeder alive with hyperactive wings and beaks, or a winter sky about to go into tantrum mode. You've got to be able to be where you are and not with any intense alpha wave, front-of-the-brain intensity, but rather in a loose, easy, appreciative way letting what will come, come and enjoying it as it does.

The condition that exists when you write a leisurely first draft might well be an apt model for the best condition of consciousness in us all. Take it easy, as we used to say down at the Hillside park between pulls from the brown-bagged bottles and cans. Take it easy, but take it. Writing demands, from many, from most, a soft, easily suspended attention that is both alert and receptive. Receptive: Whatever comes, comes. Let's look and let's see. Alert: You've got to have your eyes open. You need something like an internal road map, though it's not good to peek at it too often. You have to be sharp but drifty and a little dull at the same time. You've got to receive and also to impart.

One of the most useful instructions a yoga teacher ever gave me was to cut the energy coming out of my eyes by about half. He had the right guy on this. I'm a practitioner of what feminists used to call the male gaze, though it's a touch more complicated than they say it is. I like to look at beautiful women, sure. But I also just like to look, stare, burn a hole in almost anything that's in front of me. Writing, for me at least, is way more compatible with the state in which you let it happen and let it flow. And that mode in turn—half in the game, half out of it—helps you to be alone in life. Or so I learned after a lot of false starts—a lot of sitting down at the computer, then running to the car and into town for an espresso and a chat.

When we're by ourselves our minds can get too busy. We think and rethink. We overprepare the event. We obsess on what will happen and might happen and could happen. Writing, with its relaxed focus on what is in front of you, and its combination of interest and receptivity to what's there, helps you to create the habit of mind that will let you be alone without the anxious semi-freak-out we sometimes suffer when we close the door behind us.

Presence: That's the habit of mind I think writing helps develop. It's a soft discipline that lets you be where you are—both when you're actually writing and when you're not. We humans are cursed (and I suppose blessed) by our knowledge of the future. Unlike the animals, we know the future actually will *exist*. So we're always on the lookout for what's coming—and not without reason. We're all looking ahead to old age and sickness and death. It's no easy trick to take your eye off the fiery ball that's coming our way and live in the present. In this pursuit writing can help, at least a little.

To be alone, you have to able to stand yourself. To stand yourself, well that requires the ability to soften and aim your mind. Writing helps you to do that. It's like a physical exercise that's salubrious in itself, and then pays you again and again as you go about your daily business.

The first days of being alone as a writer are tough. But you want to know yourself, you want to strengthen your mind, you want to learn to remember. (You may still also want to get rich and get famous and get the girl or the guy. But I'm betting those things will pass.) And so you begin the discipline of being alone, which ends up in time being something you need. As for myself, I need four to six hours of time azul azul in a given day and if I don't have them, I'll swipe 'em by staying up too late or getting up too early. I'm addicted to being alone, but that's better than being addicted to company. After all, I'm always there. And so are you.

To Read as a Writer

Are there any days that are better than the days of early reading? I mean the time, usually in youth, when you first fall in love with books. Every book is a fresh intoxication. Every author who matters to you (and there are so many!) initiates you into a vivid, unbroken dream. Reading delivers you from your all-too-fixed position in space and time and takes you to a world elsewhere. It's a form of magic, isn't it? No matter where you are, almost no matter what's going on around you, you can leave and go to some other place that is richer, more complex, and stranger yet also somehow more your home.

Books can cast spells, especially for the young. Every writer who matters to you (so many, and more to come) is a generous Prospero. He fills the island with wonders. She conjures the aurora borealis in the sky. I remember the bliss I felt when I learned that Shakespeare had written more than the three or four great tragedies one studies in high school. There were dozens of plays left! And all of them were there waiting for me.

The experience of reading in youth is one of total immersion. You become one with the author. You are no longer your ragged everyday self, but instead exchange minds and hearts with Walt Whitman or Nathaniel Hawthorne or Emily Dickinson. Suddenly our consciousness is expanded as we become identical if only for a while with a spirit larger than our own. We may not always be quite up to comprehending the splendors we encounter, but even in that sense of inadequacy there can be a feeling of optimism: There is more to learn, space to grow. There's more to being alive than I thought.

Reading early in life—or reading with the ardor of youth—is what we might even call a form of reincarnation. Suddenly, we are born again as another. We are reborn into a spirit larger and more intricate than the one we possessed.

We lose contact with our quotidian selves, and all our daily worries and desires swim back into the recesses. We are then other than we are—and we feel all the better for it. To read deeply when young is to see the world anew: to read, really read, while in the first phase of life is to be doubly young.

I remember the first time I picked up Thomas Wolfe's *Look Homeward, Angel*. What a revelation that book was for me. It was above all things a young man's book. Wolfe has a genius for rendering two drives in particular: ambition and desire. He is simply superb at chronicling what it is like to be young and to want to roll the world into a ball and have it as one's own to toss and catch as one might please. Desire: desire for sex and love and belonging; ambition: the urge to be the best, to do what hasn't been done, to be known and seen—no one could give that to you the way Wolfe could when he depicted Eugene Gant. No matter what Eugene was doing in the story, I somehow pictured his avatar behind him, legs spread, back arched, arms thrust upward to the sky, and crying out the words: "I want!" The emotions that fed the book were turbulent, but Wolfe gave you enough distance from them to look on with an assured tranquility. It was a serene dream of a beautiful, surging life, a life that might in time become one's own.

Was I indulging some wishes in reading this way? I probably was. But what's so wrong with indulging a few wishes, especially when you're young? Most people are conscious enough of wanting, often wanting in an aching sort of way. But what do they want? They frequently do not know. Part of reading when you're young involves putting yourself in touch with your desires. You identify with the protagonist, and what she wants you want, too. And so in her hopes, and the sorrows she goes through to fulfill them (or maybe to modify them or even to cast them aside), you shine a light down your future life.

But mostly I think early reading makes and elaborates a more general discovery and it is simply this: There is more to life than we had ever dreamed before. There is more to know and enjoy and fear and experience. And there is more—far more—to understand especially about the lives of others than we had ever thought. Safe within the mediated world of words we explore at a distance that is not too far and not too near the world as it can be. And we are enlarged—quietly but surely—by the experience.

Hypnotism, mild inebriation, dreaming, dropping into the preconscious mind: these are states we associate with early reading and they are wonderful. There is perhaps nothing like them in life. Sex can be what it can be, but it can never last as long as a good book can, no matter how slowly you proceed.

Early reading is wonderful. But if you're going to become a writer, you are going to have to stop doing it. You are going to have to take from yourself one of the great pleasures in your life. You're going to have to exchange a relatively easy pleasure for a far more difficult one. But isn't that a half-decent definition of what growth entails? Exchanging easy for difficult pleasures?

When writers want to lose themselves in a vivid continuous dream, I think they usually go to the movies. No doubt a few have sustained the power to read like boys and read like girls, as some have sustained the power to do what Wolfe said you never could do: go home again. But not many.

What do writers read for? Many reasons, I suppose. But surely there is always a tutorial going on when a writer reads, especially when it's work in her own genre.

How did he do that? How did he make that happen? Can you really get away with that? Another narrator, this far into the book? Can she really bring that off?

At a certain point writers read a little the way pro ball scouts watch a game. There's pleasure and often admiration, sure. But there's also constant evaluation. Can he hit a curve? Can he throw a guy out from the warning track? Can he beat out an infield hit? But the scout is only compiling information. The writer drafts an internal report and then puts it to use for herself. She wants to learn what she can. Maybe she even wants to steal what she can. Good writers borrow, Eliot said. It is the great ones who manage to steal. (And, one might add, who manage to get away with it.) Writers read with their eyes wide open. Writers read to make a grab and then run off with what they have captured.

There is also the matter of competitiveness. Norman Mailer swore he never read novels when he was attempting to write one. He said it was as though he was out in his driveway repairing his car. There are parts scattered on the tarmac and even on the lawn. There's grease on his hands and there's grease on his pants. There's even grease on the grass. Then from the corner of his eye he catches a mint roadster, tuned to perfection, purring just right, and turning the corner like a cat. That's bad for morale. That's bad for the spirit. Avoid looking at that slick set of wheels. Get in the garage and go to work. Get in the garage, close the door, and stay there until you're done.

Mailer says that when he finished his own novel, he turned to the stack of his friends' books that had mounted up and up, and he read with a level of pleasure—and a level of generosity—that he savored. Maybe then he read as he did as a kid—swimming in James T. Farrell and John Dos Passos—if only for a day or two. But most of the time, he stayed in the garage.

He has a new book out! He does! He just published a book! Where did this one come from!

Writers, I fear, utter such words—if only under their breaths, or beneath the searchlight of their direct awareness—when they pick up the *Times Book Review*. And sometimes, if they're feeling wounded or pernicious, they turn a few pages or click the cursor and slide their eyes down to the final paragraph, hoping to see a little fire and brimstone rained down on the fellow too-fast author who up to this point they rather believed they liked. But no—it's a good review, a better than good one. Off goes a quick congratulatory note. (Easy to do with e-mail.) Now it's time to hunker down and get something of one's own done. Will our writer read his friend's just-trumpeted masterpiece? Not very likely. Not likely at all.

I have a writer friend who simply will not read Jonathan Franzen's novel *The Corrections* or, dammit, *Freedom* either. Though I think my friend would prefer to take up *Freedom*, being that he understands it to be a less accomplished book. You see there is not only reading as a writer, which is perilous. There is also not reading as a writer, which is perilous as well.

But why does my friend boycott Franzen? He does it for something of the same reason that Freud boycotted Nietzsche. Freud's rationale had been boiled down by Samuel Weber to a simple sentence: I will not read Nietzsche; I know he will be far too interesting. This writer does not read Franzen because he fears that Franzen might be far too good. He fears that Franzen might be a writer who has squared the circle: written good books (my friend has written good books) while at the same time writing books that sell (my friend's books have not really sold). Franzen's books can be real, if flawed, pleasures. (What novels are not flawed?) And my writer friend deprives himself of a genuine bounty by boycotting a fellow writer for (potentially) being too good and too interesting.

This may not happen to you, when you turn from reading to writing. One of the major themes of the book is the need to work against the inevitable dangers of writing and the writing life—envy, anger, the hunger for revenge, the desire for fame and wealth and copious untethered sex. But envy is a major pitfall. You can't be envious of the writer at hand and live fully in the world of his vivid and continuous dream.

In one of my favorite books, unread by almost everyone, a woman named Ann Marlowe uses her ten-year engagement with heroin to brood not only on drugs, but also on sex and music and time and anxiety and family and philosophy. Though her first time trying heroin could have killed her—she snorted too much—she says that she has never felt bliss in her life anything like it. All of the anxiety in her body and mind melted, and it was only then that she saw how much anxiety she had locked down like poisoning kryptonite in herself. She rose above time. She stopped time. (Thus the title of her book: *How to Stop Time: Heroin from A to Z*.) She loved it.

And then, not surprisingly, she went out to try to find that feeling again. No matter how many times she snorted dope, she never quite did it. The only paradises are lost paradises she came to think, and in time she stopped doing drugs. But she spent a decade looking for the lost paradise of the first time with the drug. "Ah," she says, "for the time when heroin felt instantly, overwhelmingly wonderful. If I had to offer up a one-sentence definition of addiction, I'd call it a form of mourning for the irrecoverable glories of the first time."

I've never done heroin, though there was a time when I was interested. When I worked at rock shows in the seventies, it was around but it never quite came my way. But when I think of times I have felt like a voyager in lotusland, void completely of anxiety, I think of my early days of reading. When Thomas De Quincey depicts his idea of terrestrial nirvana, he includes a snug room, a fire, a soft chair, snowflakes dropping like tiny white angels from the sky, and a book, a good book. Needless to say opium is involved, too. Reading and opium, it's said, go well together and it is no surprise. Says De Quincey: "Opium always seems to compose what had been agitated and to concentrate what had been distracted." Sounds a lot like reading, early reading.

And it's not surprising that people pursue the paradise of early reading with all of their might. I still do. I take home half a dozen books from the bookstore and library almost every weekend, hoping that one of them will cast the perfect spell. And sometimes, sometimes, it happens. I don't leave the couch. I forget to eat. I stay up half the night. Novels tend to do this for me, when it *is* done. Smith Henderson's *Fourth of July Creek* made it happen not long ago. But it's rare, rare. And then when it does happen, I go running off trying to find another dose and usually, of course, it doesn't work so well. As Marlowe says (though she's not talking about reading, not quite): "Yes, once in a while there's a night when you get exactly where you're trying to go. Magic. Then you chase that memory for a month. But precisely because you so want to get there it becomes harder and harder. Your mind starts playing tricks on you. Scrutinizing the high, it weakens."

Perhaps most people eventually find themselves exiled from the paradise of reading whether they become writers or not. They become too enmeshed in the world and its doings to be lost in the bliss of a perfect story or an exquisite poem. Or they go too often to the enchanted spring, the way Marlowe went too often to her drug, and they look to recapture an un-recapturable past, if they can.

But committing yourself to the life of writing is almost certain to drop you from regular access to the paradise of reading. You may be able to overcome your competitive envy. (I hope you can. I hope my friend will. He'd love Franzen.) But you'll probably never be able to overcome the detachment that being a practitioner entails. When a magician sits in the audience and watches the Houdini of the moment, he really has no choice but to look for the slips and the slides and to figure out how it's done by keeping his eye off the most obvious ball.

No one loves being exiled from paradise. Eve and Adam took it hard indeed and it's been that way down through time. But as the angel told them, they'd be compelled henceforth to create a paradise within themselves, assuming they could. The angel even said that the inner paradise could be "happier far" than what they had possessed when they were garden dwellers. The paradise the writer seeks when he's cast out of the paradise of early reading is the one that writing can provide. For ultimately the pleasure of real writing outstrips the perils and pains of casting yourself out from the world of hypnotic reading, beautiful as that world was. Now, perhaps, as a writer you are providing entrance to that beautiful world for someone else.

To Do *Something*

One of the facts that's affirmed constantly in the history of writing (which probably bears some relation to the history of literature) is the odd affiliations writers have. Writers don't usually feel themselves to be the spiritual kin of doctors and lawyers and corporate chiefs. They don't tend to feel at home in a room full of dedicated professionals. Most writers don't care for insurance salesmen or car salesmen or real estate brokers. In an auditorium full of junior trainees for middle management positions (with plenty of potential to ascend) they are like plants on time-lapse film, wilting for lack of water. At the end of the first presentation they are parched; at the end of the second they are a clump of dismal brown.

Writers don't usually fit in; there's no denying that. They are often the ones who hung wraith-like in the corner at the high school dance watching and pining (and judging) and feeling all the while like they had an invisible wound somewhere in their midsections. But then, of course, they didn't do what others of their disposition tended to do, which was to run home or to skip dances from then on. No, they came and they watched and they ached and they cultivated their loneliness and they hated their loneliness, too. There's a story by Thomas Mann called *Tonio Kröger* and Tonio is the artist as a very young man. We see him at dance lessons watching the beautiful movements of a perfect blond girl ("blue-eyed, laughing Inge") and feeling uncontrollable admiration and desire. She hardly knows that Tonio exists. The girl who does know is a little fräulein who is "always falling down in the dances," Magdalena. "She understood him, she laughed or was serious in the right places; while Inge the fair, let him sit never so near her, seemed remote and estranged, his speech not being her speech."

Has there ever been a writer who was an equal half of the perfect blond couple? And even if the writer wasn't one who fell down in the dance, he surely feared being relegated to the society of the clumsy and the unfit. The writer is often an outsider, as much by his own volition as by the designs of others—who frequently do not notice him much at all. He is unfit for social life, but he often is unfit—or makes himself unfit—for almost every other form of life as well. He tends to think of himself as a loner and maybe an outlaw, as someone who knows the rules and despises them. As Keith Richards sings it: "Always took candy from strangers / Didn't want to get me no trade."

Keith's alienation may not apply to every writer term for term: maybe he does know how to hold on to a book; maybe he's been afforded a second chance and a third; maybe he's got a fancy degree with which to decorate his wall (though no writer would do such a thing). Yet he feels a kinship to the semi-outlaw life that the Stones like to squall about. He doesn't want to play the game. He isn't like Mom and Dad and Buddy and Sis.

And often, he doesn't become alienated because he is a writer. He becomes a writer because he is alienated. Writing gives him somewhere to go when he thought there was nowhere. Despite perils, writing manages to give him some pleasure in a life he thought would be mostly pain.

He may have no early interest in language or getting matters down on paper. He's probably a reader—all half-decent writers are. But it may be— it often is—that a writer turns to writing because he's not capable of doing anything else.

This was surely the case with Henry Miller, who didn't turn to writing until he was about forty and had screwed up every other endeavor he'd undertaken. He was, he attests, horrible at business, a miserable husband, a wash as a son, even a crummy friend if you wanted to know the truth. (Don't leave your wife alone with Hen.) Miller went off to Paris not mainly to be an artist but because he could live the vagabond's life more cheaply there.

If there is any vocation with which writers have an affinity, it is prob- ably that of the vagabond. When a writer sees a traveling hobo, a rambling guy with a guitar in a cardboard box, a street singer roving from town to town, he feels immediate kinship and at least a dram of admiration. Here is someone who has taken it all the way. He couldn't find anything to do in this futile, ridiculous world either. But rather than stopping at the last step before the cliff—I'm a writer, a writer!—he stepped directly over and went into free fall. A writer has just enough anxiety in him about what other people think and just enough fear of radical and prolonged discomfort not to make the final move, pack his comb and harmonica in a handkerchief, tie it to a stick, sling the stick over his shoulder, and begin rambling off to the beat of an endlessly looping Hank Williams song.

Now granted there are middle-class writers who want all the comforts and speak about writing as a profession and themselves as practitioners of a noble calling. These are women and men who can have dinner with a table full of rich bankers and businessmen and listen to their pompous opinions (they must be smart; they are rich) and not fall out of their chairs laughing at their self-importance and servitude to riotous jargon. Such writers exist and they write novels about the suburbs and live in the suburbs on occasion, too. They want to be normal and they try to be nice. By and large it doesn't work and they pay for it.

Real writers are at least in some measure outcasts. They are wandering Jews—and wandering Christians and Muslims and nonbelievers, too. They can't fit and they can't do what they are supposed to do. They don't always fall down in the dance, but often they can't stand the music. So why do they have to express their sorrows? Why can't they just shut up about it—like most of the other pariahs of the world do?

The question is not an easy one. Why must they make a record of their own and wave their hands at the world: Look at me! Listen! Here's my book! I hate you all! Why do this when the writer's initial feeling about the human world, the social world, is often one of at least partial rejection? Why not simply roll with it?

Perhaps writers who write from the edges are trying to compound an explanation. And what they are trying to explain is nothing so much as themselves. They wish to explain themselves to themselves. Why am I as I am? Why always in the corner? Why will none of the common pursuits do for me? Is it sheer vanity that makes me this way? Is it stubbornness? Is it at bottom a fear, a fear that if I really did immerse myself in the game of life I would be one of the hard-trying losers? Every lyric poet and almost every essayist and a few novelists and story writers to boot pose these impossible-possible questions to themselves. These are the questions that Montaigne asked himself and Proust, but also the questions of Emerson and Thoreau and Dickinson and Whitman. ("I and this mystery here we stand," Whitman says.) It is also the question of ragtag bobtail writers all down through the centuries.

But then why publish the results to the world? You could just as well lock your journal and toss the key, or declare to yourself that it is not for nothing that "essay" means "attempt" and that trying to make permanent what was meant to be transitional and notation is forcing the issue.

Writers often publish out of vanity, vanity and the desire for a dollar. But an author can be generous, too. A writer can mean well not only for himself but for others. He knows there are many people like the self he once was (and continues in certain ways to be). There is no end of people equally confused and lonely and distressed and looking to understand why this is and if it truly must be. It is simple humane generosity that makes certain kinds of outcasts writers. They write, as the great outcast Socrates told them to, in order to know themselves. But they also write to open the doors of understanding to others—and especially the young, who stand outside.

People surprise themselves all of the time. People shock themselves all of the time, especially when they are young. They think thoughts, feel feelings, experience impulses that are radically strange, and when they do they ask the inevitable questions: Am I alone? Am I some sort of freak, some sort of monster? Has anyone ever felt this way before?

But then they find writers who can unlock their isolation for them. They're sprung from the prison cell of self. They see that the world is more complex and varied and strange than they had imagined; in fact the world is as complex and varied and strange as they are themselves. They see there are others like them who don't believe the commonplace and can't stand the hype and the cant and the jive. These people are writers, very often.

As puerile as the Beats can sometimes seem to me now, when I read them at the age of seventeen or so they were deliverance. Jack Kerouac had one dream, one aspiration above all the others. He wanted to get the hell out of here. Nothing pleased him about stable life; nothing made him happy on Main Street, with the people passing and greeting their everyday greetings and sighing their everyday sighs. He wanted out. He was only happy when he was on the road and on the move, listening to the chants of his manic friend Neal Cassady. The only freedom was in motion. No one ever read *On the Road* all the way through without wanting to take to the highway. No one ever read the book with sympathy without seeing the trudging life around him with new eyes, and with more confident eyes. To do the same thing every day in the same place! Wasn't this hiding from life?

Kerouac saw that habit and routine and repeating, repeating, repeating were dumb counterspells. They were ways to pretend that time wasn't passing. We could think today was yesterday and both would be tomorrow. We warded off thoughts of death and change but did so at the expense of dulling of the spirit. We got grayer and more tired in our timidity. America, maybe, was getting grayer and more tired in its timidity. So Kerouac and his pals—silly, charming, bumptious, sly, occasionally smart—took off for the territories. Their only pleasure came in movement. "Power ceases in the instant of repose," says Emerson. Power is in movement; power is in transition. "It resides in the moment of transition from the past to a new state, in the shooting of the gulf, in the darting to an aim."

Then the sage adds a critical perception. "This one fact the world hates, that the soul becomes." The world hates the people who try to change for the better. It hates the people who remind it that it has grown stale and old and is now in the habit of congratulating itself for doing so. The world came to hate Kerouac in time. No writer in my memory was so roundly mocked. And he did not take it well. He turned up on TV drunk and slurring; he insulted his enemies or those he imagined would be his enemies if he gave them half a chance. But he had his reasons. "It's not writing, but typing," they said of *On the Road*. Tell that to a generation of kids, me included, that the book shook out of dull sleep. We loved that book then and in my experience students and young people of all sorts have continued to love it for over fifty years.

But Kerouac paid the price for what I have to see as his generosity. He was a working-class kid from Lowell and he was an athlete, a star football player. Yet he had the heart of a poet. Ginsberg says he learned more about poetry from Kerouac's short lyrics than he did from any of his contemporaries. Allowances made for friendship: this is still no small accolade. But Kerouac had too many internal tensions to stand up to the abuse he took. He crumpled and drank some; got hit, crumpled, came back, wrote more, and drank some more. He wrote with the kind of fury that someone who is being chased by ridicule and can't stand it must often do.

I suppose Kerouac may have wanted many of the conventional rewards writers strive for. I'm sure he wanted to make a dollar and see his name in the paper—though once one has seen one's name in the paper in a certain manner, it is a wish that declines. But I also think that he—lonely in himself, and writing out of a protracted loneliness—wrote for all the other isolates and brilliant sad cases that dotted America. What a godsend to me and my friends he was. He was born only a few miles away from us and he lived in Lowell, Massachusetts. Lowell! A city we cruised to on Saturday nights to hear rock bands and drink and maybe pick a fight. Kerouac lived a twenty-minute car ride from our two- and three-decker houses. Kerouac!

He got himself in trouble at Columbia. Though he was a terrific student and a fine athlete he consorted with bums and ne'er do wells. He even let Allen Ginsberg sleep over! And he sent his writing out to us. Even excoriated by those who were supposed to know—not writing, but typing—he kept at it, telling us things about what we could do to break out. Travel? Sure, of course. But there's nature and the mountain climb. There's Zen. There's the holy spirit of jazz. There's the kind of friendship that's about more than networking and small-timing it to the top. I think Kerouac was a generous writer. I think many writers are generous writers.

He wouldn't have lasted a minute with those great lawyers Dylan talks about, discussing lepers and crooks. He wasn't management material. He was one of nature's warmhearted vagrants. He ended up a sad overweight drunk, living with his mother back in Lowell. And this in some part was because he reached out to the other lost souls in America and they heard him. None of the professors liked his books—not the way they did F. Scott Fitzgerald's anyhow—and they let him know about it.

Kerouac wrote because there was probably nothing else he could do in this world and he wanted to figure out why that was. And he wanted others who were in the same fix to breathe a little easier and feel a bit more at home in America. If they didn't like what they saw around them, they could always take a ride. I hope that on some level, despite the sorrows, Kerouac from time to time took some pleasure from what he'd done for us. It's a pleasure all writers can aspire to, though the pains attendant are real enough.

To Hold Your Peace

Has the world always been as full of talkers as it is now? I can't imagine it has. We would have had more testimony down through time about the plague of chatterboxes that was besetting the human race—filling the air with their clamor, polluting all public space and most private, and drowning out the music of the spheres. Alexander Pope seems to write about a comparable situation in *The Dunciad*. But so gifted and to the point was Pope that almost anyone outside himself and his esteemed circle of friends (Swift and Arbuthnot and the rest) might seem a clamoring dope. Plutarch wrote an essay on nonstop-talking bores. Yet it is, rather shockingly for that fascinating writer, a bit of a bore itself.

No, the plague of yackers that besets us seems to be something of a current phenomenon. It is, maybe, a sign of our era. Everywhere you go, people seem to be pinning others, often (nominally) their friends, to the mat and having at them with words. Listeners are tied to the track and run over with nonstop discourse. What is a dinner party now but a site where all the alphas present (and everyone now aspires to alpha status) vie for the position of king of the oratorical hill? This status is usually achieved not by being the most articulate, the most learned, or the most original. It is achieved by being the loudest, the most aggressive, and the least sensitive to the desires of others to be—every hour or so and ever so softly—heard. But there is an upside to this. At least there is for the writer: you can convert this pain to pleasure. You can take it from gap to gain.

True to the spirit of the original child's game, the grown child who seeks to be king of the oratorical hill pushes other aspirants down by talking more—and more loudly—than anyone else. He goes on and on and on. Challenge him and he raises his tone higher until it sounds like he is bellowing in a church. Or he resorts to subtler stratagem to hold the floor. I have witnessed a man make adept use of his stutter to call attention to himself, to incite sympathy and thus silence, and then to take over the dinner table like a mutineer captain taking over shipboard.

Is it necessary to say that the most common dinner-table mutineer captains are male? A woman may do it from time to time, but it seems often a political gesture, a drive for equality, or an object lesson to show the males around the watering hole exactly what it's like. But usually the orator is phallic.

There is, from what I can tell, a genre of book that aids and abets this practice. Such books are found in airports and often composed by contributors to various glossy magazines. They tell you how the stock market really works, why there is so much poverty in America, what the next wave of computers will be like, what's hot in real estate, and why in football the left tackle means as much as he does. From what I can tell, males buy these on the way home from business trips, skim them on the plane, arrive home at six, and by eight thirty, fork in one hand knife in the other, are regaling a set of relative innocents with a summary of the book's contents. Often they do not cite the author. They claim, implicitly, that this knowledge has been compiled by none other than themselves. They never shut up. In small cities, the table toppers may often use *New York Times* articles to hold the fort; in big cities it seems only a book will do.

These usurpers are, as I say, most often male. I have heard a story about a young woman who put up with one of these dinner party disquisitions for as long as she could stand it. But this time the perp actually named the book he was citing—a breakthrough for him no doubt. She informed him quite directly that she knew the book well. She had read it multiple times. He continued talking. She knew the book she claimed inside and out. On the elocutionist went. This was a book, she averred, from which she could quote freely. Didn't stop the dude. She then declared to him and all others listening that she had in fact *written* the book.

The orator took this in. He contemplated the fact. He did not doubt her. After a decorous pause, he spoke again. He took up where he left off, explaining the author's book to her and all others who could bear to listen. Now I'm not sure I believe this one out and out. But let it stand as an emblem for the current discursive situation in certain provinces of American culture.

The urge to orate is not limited to dinner tables at present. It is everywhere and it is not easy to account for. If Tocqueville were to come back from his aristocratic grave in France and tour America once more, he might well tell us that it all owed to the factor that the author of *Democracy in America* believed explained most of what mattered in the states—the rule of the people. Sometimes Tocqueville thought that the rule of the people, democracy, brought you uncomfortably close to anarchy. So why does everyone want to talk? Maybe because he who speaks is king, or at least rules for the present. If nobody rules, maybe anybody can. As Springsteen says, "Poor man wanna be rich / Rich man wanna be king / King ain't satisfied 'til he rules everything." So everybody wants to hold the floor. And I mean everybody. I've listened to interminable monologues by people still residing deep in their teens about their (brief) lives and (thinly perceived) times. At discourse's end, they inquire to know what my name might be so they can send me a daily chorus of tweets. Tocqueville warned me. I didn't listen. George Steiner wrote the essay "The Distribution of Discourse" in which he bemoaned the passage from the day when Dad talked a lot and Mom talked a little, but to potent effect—and everyone else simply jammed a fist between his teeth and listened.

There's also, I think, the self-justifying business. Again, it has to do with democracy, a little. To wit: no one knows anything. No one knows with certainty what's good or bad, right or wrong in the way of the conduct of life. Sure there are laws. Sure there are mores, even a few manners. But people often feel uncomfortably like they are making it all up as they go along. Am I who I say I am? Am I living the right way? Does my life make sense? In the current random, these questions can feel up for grabs.

A lot of what the yackers do in my experience is to justify the peculiar and often rather contingent forms their lives have taken. They are not only telling you, and the rest of the unfortunates standing by with the ice melting in their drinks, who they are. They are telling themselves. When there are not a lot of templates out there, when the Ten Commandments could be nine or four, but probably not fourteen or thirty, it's hard to figure out who one is and why that matters. Did Mailer write a book called *Advertisements for Myself*? In our time it seems everyone is advertising for himself. Everyone needs the microphone, everyone needs the floor, everyone is perpetually clearing his throat to set in, and once in he will not conclude until the Dog Star rages (which, I gather from Lord Byron, is quite a long time). The era of the orator is upon us. Everyone wants to be a (relatively benign) dictator—which, as Northrop Frye reminds us, is nothing other than a speaking machine—a nonstop talker.

It's no pleasure spending one's life as an ongoing audience. When one of the self-justifiers or front-table monarchs is rattling down the tracks like an empty train with all its couplings loose, you feel crummy. There's something diminishing about having someone let loose a monologue in your face. You can feel your sense of self shrink a little with every fresh dependent clause. The candle flame of ego begins to splutter. How long before it winks completely out? That's what the talker wants, naturally. They grow and you shrink. It's a zero-sum activity. Has anyone ever spoken of castration by conversation?

But. However. Consider.

Once you've gone over and become a writer, at least in your own mind, all of this changes. And the purgatory of eternal listening can become something like a pleasure. Now you know that after the storm of discourse is over, you can go back to the room of your own, or to your corner of the coffee shop, and set the truth down as you see it. You can write and rewrite and compose and recompose, and indulge in all the necessary visions and revisions, and have yourself some latte or some hot chocolate while you're there. In other words, you will get your turn.

Now this may be small comfort to some, but there is more. While being regaled you can stop feeling that you are suffering in silence and realize a critical truth. You are not a passive victim any longer. You are in the role of God's spy. Whether you write poems or novels or plays or blog posts, you are gathering material. This will be of use. This will pay off.

My wife, the most socially kind person I know, endorses listening to bores with rapt attention. She finds it to be an exercise in Zen self-effacement—good for the modesty, good for the soul. But she is also always on the watch for a fine phrase—fine because it's artful or (more often) fine because it illuminates a certain personality to perfection. This fine phrase will reappear in an arch short story of hers somewhere down the line. And so will the phrase's—I was going to say originator. But often the speaker is simply channeling the latest in some form of pop patois: medical, political, environmental, what have you. And the speaker may turn up in her story, too, though charitably disguised.

The final truth about the situation of the writer in the world of windbags is still yet unspoken. Ask Jane Austen about it—or ask her works. And there you will encounter what can only be highly civilized, exquisitely refined writer's reparation. (Which is something not quite like the wholesale kamikaze revenge I spoke of earlier.) I would eagerly bet that each and every prosing gasbag in *Pride and Prejudice* had a proto-type in the realms of what people sometimes foolishly call Austen's "limited experience." I'm guessing that the bumptious social-climbing Mrs. Bennet had one; and that the insufferable parson, Mr. Collins, got his start on a pulpit not far from Ms. Austen; and the drably ferocious dragon, Lady Catherine de Bourgh, spent some time posing for Austen in some sublunary form before she made it into the celestial pages of the novel.

And then all the Mrs. Bennets and Lady Catherines and Mr. Collinses down through time had the pleasure of seeing themselves in the novel—or at least their associates did, since people like Mr. Collins and company are inclined to avoid anything resembling a mirror.

Revenge? Revenge is too strong a word. There is no poison in evidence, no dagger, not even a lawsuit with a well-buttoned advocate pleading one's case. But there is a measure of mild retribution and it has its savors. The writer may not get the first word at the dinner party, or many of the words that flow in the middle like bland lava. But if she's anything like Jane Austen, she can always get the last.

PLEASURES AND PERILS

To Learn Something

I have been a teacher now for thirty-five years and when people ask me why I love the job (which I do) I sometimes lie—or at least I leave the main motive out. I tell them how much I like students (and I do) and how much I love the feel of colleges (they often seem like ideal cities to me) and how well I get along with my colleagues (true, most all the time). But what I leave out is that I love teaching because it is the only way I've ever found to learn anything that mattered to me. When I want to know more about something—philosophy, religion, movies, books—I arrange to teach a course about it. I'm a passive reader (half the time I'm dreaming away) and when I go to a lecture I one-third listen at best. But when I have to give a lecture or present a class, the mental beams (such as they are) go on high (or as high as they get) and I actually learn what I am supposed to teach.

There are writers who write to learn not what they already know (on some level) but those who write to discover new aspects of the world outside themselves. (They write for much the same reason that I, and many others like me I'll bet, go into teaching: without what we taught ourselves teaching others, we'd be dopes.) I love writers who are perpetual students, the sorts of people who become hungrily curious about one thing or another and go to work to learn all they can about it. What they write for is to discover something new. The writing can almost be an *excuse* for the learning. A person suddenly becomes possessed by the idea of learning about gardening or fly fishing or architecture or the way Wall Street works (and doesn't) and then goes to work, chugging down facts and metabolizing them at a velocity that often leaves me stunned. I'm the archetypal slow learner and I'm pleased and grateful when a quick learner comes along and dives headfirst into a fascinating subject and acquires triple time what would take me years to capture, and then serves it all up in sterling silver prose. Such writers find pleasure themselves and yield it in no small measure to their readers.

Such writers tend to be optimists. They tend to love the world. Though they are often critics of what they consider (Wall Street!), they have an abiding faith that change will soon be tinting the horizon. "If winter comes," says the poet, "can spring be far behind?" They write slashing exposés like *Fast Food Nation* and they do hyper-overtime research and holler expertly at the banks. And then they pop up two or three years later working on some only partially related subject having gorged themselves again on facts, facts, and more facts. They are the servants of humanity and they are perpetual students.

Walter Benjamin says the correct attitude toward life (which means it is surely the correct attitude toward writing) is that of children in fairy tales—cheerful, confident, and resourceful, ready to take on whatever comes. Anyone who has read the Oz books (the movie is a slightly different matter) knows that Dorothy is a wonder. Weird things are always happening to this American Alice in Wonderland, but unlike perpetually nonplussed Alice, the polite English girl, Dorothy is never taken completely by surprise and always knows what to do. She's curious, warm, and ready for anything, a perpetual student of the bizarre world of Oz. Writers who learn and teach are students of our own often Oz-like world of marvels and they often lack nothing of Dorothy's doughty spirit.

A certain sort of writer is a perpetual student. Writing is his excuse to educate himself. Where other men and women are satisfied to go off and read a book about the president or the latest war or the way we eat now, this kind of writer goes out and writes one. He travels and he reads and he interviews and he researches. He spends as much time away from his desk gathering materials as he does sitting down and composing the book. He's a sociable sort of person, the educating writer, and he has the very rare capacity of being equally at home with people and at his desk. Hannah Arendt said that to be a politician you had to be able to spend protracted periods of time with people you fundamentally do not like. Many writers—I'd even say most—don't like much of anyone and live a sort of self-imposed internal exile. This kind of writer, the writer who writes to learn and teach, has a gift for liking everyone, or at least everyone who can help him enlarge his base of knowledge. He can cruise a cocktail party to find the staffer who'll tell him what's up in Congress, or cold-call a scientist to learn all about nuclear fission (or fusion), but then he can repair to his home, turn off the phone, recede from the Internet, and get working. Unlike other writers, who often spend the three hours of a dinner party watching their hands, the educating writer can chat nimbly with all comers. Norman Mailer saw this quality in his contemporary Dwight Macdonald, who, Mailer said, could immerse himself in deep discourse with an Eskimo making his first visit from the tundra within five minutes of being introduced. Most sociable people can't write; most writers can't schmooze. This kind does both.

The persona of the student is one of the most attractive of human identities and one of the most pleasure yielding. Not only does it often yield much-praised literary results, but it also feels good to inhabit. You can roll through life like a feisty cub, asking questions, smiling, and doing the dance of deference, which people naturally love you for. You can be a terrific listener because a little like old Rumpelstiltskin, you'll soon be spinning the conversational straw into gold. People love to hold forth, especially insecure intellectual types, *male* types in particular. And there you are to catch their words in a pearl basin. Then back to the office and the desk and the Herman Miller Aeron Chair to kick back and put it all in order.

The persona of writer-student doesn't only work well in the research phase. People love to hang out with a literary learner. That's what reading his books can feel like—hanging out with him or her. He doesn't make them insecure or nervous. He doesn't make them feel dumb, the way old-time writers like Milton and Spenser do. If anything, readers maybe feel a bit sharper than he is. He is so earnest, so modest, so solicitous of their attention, and so determined to feed them the material in tasty (and nutritious) bites. He puts himself in the readers' place and asks all the questions they want to ask; he anticipates their feelings and addresses them in humane, nonstuffy ways. He writes profiles and features for the *New Yorker* and bestselling books for every outlet that pays. What he does is hard to do, and the world thanks him (if he does it well) with coins by the chestful and trophies and plaques.

But the peril is this: the writer who writes to learn often doesn't write that well. He hasn't had time to metabolize his material, so he writes out of the front of his brain and not out of the feelings in his gut. He goes off and finds subjects, rather than letting subjects find him, bubbling up from the bottom of the cauldron that is his creative source. Yeats, very late in his career, says he's searching for a subject and can't find one, just can't. He pines and even grieves a bit, but he eventually comes to a solution. He's going to go back down to where all of his work has always begun: "the foul rag and bone shop of the heart." The business about his creative unconscious being foul seems to me to be simply Yeats's everyday being—his selfhood—talking. He doesn't want to descend into the mess of memories and dreams and fantasies. It's damned embarrassing. But Yeats, great poet that he is, knows that true subjects are in you and have to be dived down after—or simply waited for.

Writing a book or an article about something you get interested in for the purpose of writing a book or an article is often going to result in thin gruel. People may read the book once for the information, and the timely buzz. But they won't go back to it time after time. The best writers, I think, don't only want to be read; they want to be reread.

The late Christopher Hitchens was a writer who could take the events of the day—even a particularly brutal or strange day—and spin them into sense overnight. Hours after the attacks of 9/11, Hitchens was churning out reasonably astute, reasonably thoughtful reactions. And Hitchens could write a book in a trice. He blazed into a subject, got a grip on it, and produced something lively and smart. He attacked religion; he attacked Bill Clinton and Hillary; he even went after Mother Teresa. He savaged Lord Elgin for stealing the marbles from the Parthenon. Hitch's fires flared brightly, but they were often fed by paper and sticks. Try rereading any one of these books and you'll see how glib they are. One feels he is in the hands of a man who wants to make his word count for the day, have a drink, and get paid. I loved Hitchens the journalist. When something of note happened, he was the one I wanted to read first. I just didn't want to read it again the next day. Hitchens was a teacher and Hitchens was a student—glad to learn, glad to teach. But even in his memoir, you can't say he wrote from the guts. That sort of thing just wasn't in him. He was in a major hurry, always running like Alice simply to stay in the same place.

Yet there are days when I—and I suppose many others—would trade a good deal to be this sort of student-writer. Such people have a connection with readers that one envies. They really do work for their constituency. They find the subjects that will interest the public; they go at them in a direct way; they answer all questions and leave nothing unsaid. They are like literary lawyers and doctors, performing a service the world seems to need—and for which the world sometimes rewards them munificently.

Do they ever *shape* taste, or expand consciousness? Not very likely. When they hear the poet say that the writer must create the taste by which he will be appreciated, they nod dismissively. They don't want to enlarge consciousness or question existing protocols of thought. They want to please and instruct, with the pleasing always coming first. They want their readers to feel hip, knowing, and at home in the world. They are all too often the equivalent of a warm blanket and a cup of tea, however insouciant they may pretend to be. And yet I have no doubt that without them the world of writing would be a far poorer place. Write to learn; write to teach. It brings pleasure (and yields pleasure), but it's got its perils, too. It's not the noblest way to butter one's toast I suppose, but it's far from the worst.

The midgame writer has to decide if he or she will go this route or not. Will she walk over the terrain of current culture with the equivalent of a divining rod, hoping to be drawn to the next big topic that's just slightly buried but ready to surface? Or should she follow her heart, and write what she most wants to write? That way has perils, too. One knows what it is like when your interests simply do not line up with the existing interests of the world at large. One has had the experience of composing the right book at the wrong time. But insofar as you are free of the exigencies of your purse, I think it best to write about what you love, and leave the journalism, even the higher journalism, to the fast and the fluent, and those hoping to make the literary slot machine pay out with a hooting of whistles, a clanging of bells, and an avalanche of brass tokens. Love is hard to find—and harder as life goes on and one enters the middle distance. To be able to do something—anything—from the heart is a pleasure and a gift not to be denied.

To Stay Sane

Everyone knows the line about how great wits are near to madness aligned. One might add that at times moderate and minor wits are, too. Hitchcock's Norman Bates mutters once that everybody goes a little mad sometimes, and in this, if nothing else, Norman is probably not far from the truth.

Writing is not likely to cure a haunting depression or a truly torturing case of anxiety and as for the more serious psychological maladies— schizophrenia, bipolar disorder and the like—writing will do no more for the suffering soul than persistent whistling would. But I think for many of us who want to retain sanity—keep our balance, stay in the game— writing is not a half-bad form of therapy. I'm not talking about writing at length about one's sorrows and sufferings. I'm not thinking about writing as a mode of defining one's inner maladies. But I do think the habit of writing can help many people in the quest to be reasonably balanced on an emotional or—why not say it?—a spiritual level. And sanity—what greater pleasure is there than that, especially when one contemplates the alternatives, or has experienced them.

Harold Bloom says that the major trope used by American writers is the trope of surprise. They did not specialize in irony or metaphor, but in the surprising of others and themselves with what came forth on the page. It's not hard to imagine Walt Whitman waking in the morning after an evening's bout with the poem that would become *Song of Myself* (in its first manifestation it had no title). Reading over his efforts from the night and day before, Whitman couldn't but sigh and laugh a Broadway laugh and say something like: "I did that. I Walt Whitman wrote those words!"

For Whitman's arrival as a poet was to say the least surprising. He had no formal education; he knew no literary people; he had failed in almost everything he'd tried to do. (He'd flunked as a schoolmaster purportedly because he failed to beat the boys.) At the ages of thirty-one and thirty-two he had a heroically bad temperance novel to his credit (it was called *Franklin Evans*), a stint as editor of the *Brooklyn Eagle,* and some skill as a printer. He was working as a carpenter. No one expected much of anything—though on some level he surely did himself. When he began to write the entries in his notebook that would eventually become *Leaves of Grass*, he was framing two-room houses in Brooklyn.

What he wrote in that journal could only have surprised him. It still surprises most anyone who reads it now. In one entry that (probably for the better) doesn't make its way directly into the poem, Whitman imagined himself sauntering down the streets of heaven. Whitman never rushed, never trotted. He was always taking it slow, looking at what was around him, a saunterer extraordinaire. On the streets of heaven,

Whitman sees Jahweh, Lord God of Hosts, deity of Abraham and Moses coming his way. Whitman is suddenly struck with a major perplexity. What's he going to do in regard to the hat issue? To wit: Is he going to tip his hat to Yahweh before Yahweh tips to him? (Yahweh wears a hat?) Is he going to show the Lord *that degree* of deference? For Walt Whitman is part of a singular species of being. He is, as he will say in the poem, "Walt Whitman, an American." At length, Whitman decides he'll tip his cap to the creator of the universe if the creator makes the gesture first, or at least signals willingness to bring off a simultaneous cap tip.

More than a decade later, during the Civil War, Whitman worked as a male nurse amid the wounded, both Union and Confederate, in Washington, D.C. On his morning walks, Whitman occasionally used to see the president of the United States, Abraham Lincoln, out alone taking the air. One wonders who was the first to touch his hat.

Whitman is playing a bit (one hopes) when he talks about meeting Yahweh in heaven and withholding deference. But how could he have imagined he would ever create such a scenario, even right up to the moment of composition. Even afterward, he must have been filled with surprise bordering on awe. I said that. I wrote that. Walt Whitman, an American, who turned out to be more than the son of Walter Whitman, the drunken Quaker carpenter who mistreated Walt and his brothers when they were growing up. Surprise.

Writing when it is going well is all about surprise. We laugh and sigh and whisper and look in a kind of awe at the strangeness of what we are occasionally moved to put on the page. Who is speaking when the voice we hear is both ours and not ours? Where do utterances like Walt Whitman's come from?

The answer perhaps is obvious. We are not one self but many. We teem with different voices, different attitudes, different founts of appreciation and judgment. In certain sorts of writing, we let these ancillary and antiselves get out and take the air. We let them strut and fret their hour on the stage and be heard in due measure.

Psychoanalysis teaches us that what is not available to consciousness abides in the realm of the repressed and is therefore toxic, pathological. The material that comes forth on the couch, in free association, rises from a personal Tartarus. It's a twisted and tormented discourse, infected with wayward desires. But writing suggests that that which is not present on the surface isn't necessarily pathological. We have voices in us, dreams and desires that have been banished or pushed to the rear not because they are poison. At their worst they are inconvenient. They don't help us get on with the day. They aren't practical. They don't help shake fruit from the tree or grind the wheat or ferment the wine. But they are waiting nonetheless. What they wait for is to be expressed and the expression I believe is healthful. It creates a higher sanity.

Psychoanalysis is right about this. Much is latent; much goes unsaid. And the pain of the unsaid is real. It makes for anxiety, too much needless buzz in the psyche. But what is unsaid is not always poison or harmful; it's not always a black acid rain that requires a therapist on hand to open an umbrella. Much of what lies unspoken, as Whitman's great poem shows, is benign or even benevolent, albeit sometimes rather peculiar.

In *Song of Myself* the poet travels through life like a demiurge: "I pass death with the dying and birth with the new washed babe and am not contained between my hat and boots." He shows up at a frontier wedding between a trapper and an Indian girl; he's there during what he calls an old-time sea-fight and also present at a massacre during the Mexican-American War. He watches people doing their jobs—ploughmen and singers and bartenders and factory workers and carters and printers like himself. The list is almost endless. Whitman loves to watch people work—though one senses that concentrated physical labor is something the poet himself shies from a bit. He watches a well-bred woman watch twenty-eight handsome young men frolicking naked in the water. And then he watches her imagine jumping in with them and he becomes her (and gets to frolic with those young men himself). He watches animals and talks to them (in the way a child can do) and says at one point that he could happily go and live among them because as far as he can see they don't complain all the time or try to foist religions on each other. (Whitman likes everyone just about, minus priests and occasionally, alas for me, minus schoolteachers.) He runs off with the runaway slave and feels the sting of the rifle ball as it penetrates his leg and he hears the yelp of the pursuing dogs.

As any reader of the poem will know, this is only a sampling of what Whitman does and sees. But if he is fascinated by the life of the world—and he is—he is also fascinated by the life of his spirit. "I and this mystery here we stand," says Whitman, and he's not kidding. His internal life is a mystery, though he intends to explore it and does before the poem finishes. Whitman isn't one person, unified and alone, far from it. Besides the being he shares with other Americans there is an interior being, too.

"Apart from the pulling and hauling stands what I am," he says. This self, whom he calls the "Me-myself," is "amused, complacent, compassion-ating, idle, unitary . . . Both in and out of the game, and watching and wondering at it." Whitman's Me-myself is quite shy, sensitive, observant, neither male nor female—and in fact perhaps beyond the beckoning of desire. There is no precedent for such a being in any prominent map of the spirit before or after Whitman, at least none that I know about. Freud surely has no use for a Me-myself, and even devotees of Whitman, like Ginsberg and Crane, don't adopt the persona.

Through writing, Whitman discovers an as yet undisclosed aspect of himself and then deploys it to discover fresh qualities in the world. It is, we might think, the uncovering of the Me-myself that makes Whitman as patient and observant as he is. Part of what appeals about *Song of Myself* is its slow-motion indolence: the poet rambles and looks and ponders. He's never in a hurry. The Me-myself will not be rushed.

I think this opening up of the inner life was conducive to health and sanity for Whitman and I think similar opening can be good for almost all of us. What rises to the surface when Whitman expands himself through writing isn't usually forbidden material. His poetry isn't about the return of the repressed. It's about new discovery—new thresholds, new anatomies, as Hart Crane would say. It feels good to expand the mind and to get the results of that expansion into words and into the world.

By following Whitman and expressing what's latent inside we can give ourselves a marvelous sort of peace and tranquility. Freud was right when he said that putting thoughts and feelings into words brought peace. We only need to amend him to say the thoughts and feelings don't have to be of a forbidden nature. Simply to give expression to what is latent in us can be a source of calm joy. Wallace Stevens has a marvelous phrase that bears on this process. He talks about "the hum of thoughts evaded in the mind." By giving expression to those thoughts, the evasions stop. And the hum, which can at times sound like a construction gang at work, or at least a major case of tinnitus, goes quiet. We've earned some peace.

Whitman suffered some hard days before he became the poet Walt Whitman. He had trouble getting work and holding on to it; he may have been prone to depression. But his struggles with the health of his mind were not as severe as those of Virginia Woolf, whom I consider perhaps the most heroic of writers.

On at least three occasions in her life, Woolf went completely mad. She succumbed to bouts of what was probably schizophrenia. She suffered from illusions and delusions; she heard voices. She believed that the people who loved her most—and she earned a great deal of love in her life—were her enemies and were out to destroy her. She had to be confined in her room and watched twenty-four hours a day. When her husband, Leonard, whom she clearly adored when she was sane, came into the room she was capable of screaming the vilest execrations at him. She hated herself and she hated the world.

Writing did not make Virginia Woolf sane. To be honest, the strains of writing might sometimes have pushed her into mental turbulence. But Woolf lived to write. Her productivity was spectacular: novels, short stories, brilliant book reviews, and polemical prose like *A Room of One's Own*. Beyond that there were her diaries: five thick volumes that contain some of her sharpest (and her funniest) prose. And letters. Woolf adored the act of writing. She threw herself into it like a warrior into the fight.

When she broke down, there was one goal that was preeminent in her heart: to get well so that she could write again. She fought against madness, hung in, suffered, and persevered, so she could get back to doing what gave her life fullness: writing.

Eventually Woolf succumbed. Her suicide note says that she could not put Leonard through another round of madness and she did not think that she could sustain it either. She dropped thick stones in her pocket and waded into the river.

But she lived long enough to write *To the Lighthouse* and *Mrs. Dalloway* and the essays that have brought hope to what are now generations of aspiring women writers. (And a few men too, dare I say?) Woolf fought to stay sane and fought to write. No athlete coming back from injury, no politician returning after defeat to try it one more time could possibly possess the guts that Woolf showed in her hunger to be sane and to write.

She and Papa Walt, two of the strangest and most idiosyncratic writers who ever lived, have a great deal to teach us about writing and the achievement of sanity. Honor them for their works, of course. But for their example, we should honor them, too.

To See What Happens Next

Walter Benjamin tells the story of an impoverished schoolmaster who lives far out in the countryside—which I'll elaborate just a touch. Every season the catalogues from the great publishing houses in Berlin and

Munich arrive in the mail. He reads them through with avidity and with awe. Wonderful books, wonderful—there are so many he would like to read. His salary is miniscule, though. He can barely afford his rent. But these books—one way or another he must have them. The titles promise amazing thoughts, revelation perhaps. But he looks down at his frayed cuffs and wonders if his linen will hold out one term more.

So what does the schoolmaster do? He picks out a choice title or two from the catalogues. These are the books he would give anything to read. He writes the name of the first one down on a sheet of paper and then he sets to work. He sets to work writing the book for himself.

The story of the schoolmaster may sound like the tale of an eccentric— and a hyperbolical tale at that. But the more one thinks of it, the more one sees it is a tale of the writer proper. Or at least it is the tale of many writers. They write because the books they most want to read are not available to them. They write because they are not really disposed to read exclusively what is on offer in the library. They write because they are curious. They want to know, somewhat as we saw Whitman did, what kinds of stories and essays and poems lie latent in their own minds and spirits. They write to find out what will happen next.

For truly, in writing one often does not know. Writers who make outlines and graph it all down to the most minor character's most negligible utterance tend to be assembly-line writers. They are often writers for money—not the worst identity in the world, but not the best either. They are like dictators for a state yet to come into being. They want to exert control over the whole production. And the production then feels overmanaged, overcontrolled. In genre writing this may be the idea. But the authentic writer wants to surprise her readers. More important than that maybe, she wants to surprise herself. This sort of surprise, as I've suggested in the last chapter, is one of the greatest pleasures in writing.

"I never know what I think until I hear what I say." True—often too true—for many of us. But the writer is someone who can be surprised and delighted by what comes unexpectedly forth when she sits down to write. We know more than we think we know; we feel more; we have observed more and even thought more. There is, we think during our good runs, something like a creative unconscious. While we've been going about our business, it's been gathering perceptions and organizing ideas and preparing fresh forays. When we get on a roll, that part—whatever it is, wherever it is—seems capable of endless invention. The birds wake early and they sing until noontime. Then maybe there is a bout of melody in the late afternoon or even under the approving silver face of the moon.

There is a part of us always eager to let us know what happens next, always ready to surprise us with the depth and heft of its perceptions. It is—dare I say it?—a source of (potentially) endless pleasure. Real novelists wake up in the morning and when it is rolling well they wake up and tell themselves a story. They are parent and child. They write the tale and enjoy the pleasure of its being told, too, for they do not really know what is going to happen next until it does. They never know what they think and feel and trust, until they hear what they say or see what it is they write. A writer is her own Scheherazade. She spins a tale for her own enjoyment that delights the world. Or it doesn't quite—but to her on those perfect mornings it was the best tale in town. It was better than reading Tolstoy, superior to immersing herself in Proust, and far in happy excess of the mutterings of the gossip down the road, in the phone line, or on Snapchat. Inside the writer lies the child who always wants to hear the tale the writer herself has to tell. The child does not know what is going to happen next— and neither does the writer.

But for this to go on—for the writer to find out what is best in him simply by sitting back and hearing what he says next—conditions must be met. There are often, as we've said here, rules to the game. There is frequently a price for the ticket. That which is most creative in the individual is a god, or at least a feisty little demiurge. Anyone who would write does well to learn the ways of his inner god, and to observe its favored forms of gratitude, sacrifice, and recognition.

I heard a story once about the poet Theodore Roethke that went this way. Roethke's work had not been going well. He had been drinking extensively. It is no secret that Roethke was given to drink. He often drank as a prelude to writing and then as a reward. There were apparently periods when he drank as a substitute for writing. But in the midst of an especially hard period, Roethke received a pure visitation. The poem unfolded itself from end to end; it came as if it were a piece of dictation. It came something like the way the lines of *Paradise Lost* came to Milton. The blind poet woke early and they seemed to appear out of nothing. When he had twenty or thirty lines in his head, he would call one of his daughters to take dictation. I need to be milked, he called out. From what I can tell, this is Milton's only recorded joke, unless you include the one about vegetarianism in the middle of the great poem. "No fear lest dinner cool," the poet says about a fresh-harvested vegetable feast. But that's about it.

Roethke's poem, my storyteller told me, struck him like thunder, lightning, and finally fresh spring rain. He wrote it all down and he felt cleansed and light and pure. Then what did you do, his friend asked. Oh, Roethke said. I did what I usually do when I get a poem like that. This was to fall down on his knees in the middle of his living room, burst into tears of joy and gratitude, and thank whatever power it was that had given him the gift.

Few writers go quite this far; Roethke seemed to have gone all out in many things. But I strongly believe it is important to say thank you. It makes sense to express gratitude to the force that is both you and more than you and that enables you to create stories and make sense and conjure a trope where before there had been nothing. Academic literary critics like to say that past writing begets writing. They think there is a template for a novel of a certain sort or a poem or an essay and that writers internalize those templates and then give them a twist or a tweak. (Bloom, more generous to creative souls, talks about the "swerve" away from past creators.) From this vantage, writers are plagiarists. They find much more than they make. But ask one of those critics to give you a passable sonnet. No dice! He's read a few thousand. Why didn't he manage to internalize the template? The empty page is just that—empty. And people fill it with the effusions of heart and soul. (Though often they'd better revise to make the effusions a bit less effusive.) And after they do so—after they've enjoyed the vast pleasure of creation—I think they are well advised to proffer some form of thank you.

The force that is inside the writer and that is him and not him—the force that makes it worthwhile to hear what you say—needs to be thanked, just as it needs to be coaxed into action in the morning with this ceremony or that. (Sharpen six pencils—not five, never, never four!) But I think the internal spirit of writing needs more tending to than that: a writer, like a lover, has to go beyond hellos and good-byes.

The writer Sven Birkerts says (in sum) that he may write for an hour or he may write for three—or he might write for a mousing fraction of sixty minutes. It doesn't really matter. All the rest of the day is dedicated to making that writing time possible. Maybe he needs some hard exertion—classes taught, walls mended, other peoples' essays whacked into shape. (Sven's an editor.) Or maybe the preparation is gentler—so-and-so many football games to be watched, hot baths taken, walks in the woods during which one does not walk terribly fast. Gabriel García Márquez had it right—and it is maybe *the* central piece of writer's advice. "A writer," says Gabo, "must know how to relax." But her relaxation is a different sort than the other woman or man's; her hammock swings for a purpose. The writer has got to learn how to make the force of writing available to himself—to hear what he says so he can know, for the time being, what it is he thinks.

But what precisely is this force that begets writing? Is it possible to define it? One might begin again with Freud, who did a lot to define the unconscious, though the definition is partial and thus rather misleading. If you invert much of what Freud said about the unconscious, you begin to get at the truth of the writer's creating force. Freud believed in the unconscious, of that there's no doubt. His first real book, *The Interpretation of Dreams*, affirms the centrality of an unknown region of the mind. It's unknown, yes, but it is also potent: it may even determine the course of our lives. The pressure of the unconscious is what causes us to dream. Then comes Freud's justly famous formulation: "A dream is a disguised fulfillment of a repressed wish."

Why repressed? Why isn't the unconscious available to the conscious mind? Because the wishes clapped down in the unconscious are forbidden wishes. They are murderous, sexually perverse, oedipally charged. We can't allow them into consciousness because they are too disturbing. If we were compelled in the middle of the day to entertain a fantasy about sex with mother, father, sister, or brother, we would be deeply disturbed, pushed to the brink of fear. At night, the dream censor—the bar between the unconscious and the conscious mind—becomes slightly more tolerant and the forbidden wishes make their way into our minds, albeit in disguised form. And that, naturally, is why dreams are so weird. They are always submitted to partial censorship.

Freud wanted to protect us from the unconscious, or at least from being influenced too much by it. Every now and then he slips and admits that something fresh can come out of sleep and dreaming. He remarks casually that often when he gives himself a problem—even a tough intellectual riddle—before bed, he wakes up and finds he's untangled the knot or (being Freud) that he's cut the rope with a stroke the way Alexander did with the Gordian knot. How did this happen? His unconscious did the work for him. But then he goes on to forget that he ever said as much or felt so. Mostly the unconscious is a danger; it leads us back over forbidden grounds. Its desires are the desires of childhood and it behooves us to have adult desires. Take your cues from the conscious mind, Freud says. Respect the unconscious, but don't be directed much less determined by it. Acquaint yourself with the creatures of the night, but don't let them drive the vehicle or even fill out the trip plan.

Freud affirmed again and again that the unconscious is regressive and fundamentally pathological. It is not creative. Thinking so, Freud suggests, was the error of generations of poets, and in particular the romantics. Coleridge, who did not interest Freud at all, but is the preeminent philosopher of Anglo-American romantic poets, strongly believed in the creative unconscious. For him, it was clearly linked to the imagination, which "dissolves, diffuses, and dissipates, in order to recreate." That sounds like Freud's dream work—except that for Coleridge the result can be magnificent poetry rather than disturbing dreams. The wonderful Coleridge poem "Kubla Khan" rose up from STC's unconscious as a dream—assisted of course by a bit of opium.

Writers tend to know that both Freud and Coleridge are right. There are toxic dreams; we all have them. And there are times when the unconscious, or whatever in there does the writing, grows ill. It produces only stale images, tells only stories it has told before, lets the judgment overmanage the product, turns writing into assembly-line work. There supervenes the horrid condition called writer's block, which is, truly, too unpleasant to talk about. Though when a student who is producing nothing, *nada*, and *rien* claims to be down with the malady I think of the wise words of a certain longtime writing instructor. They go something like this: You? Writer's block? No, sorry. Writer's block is for people who have *written* things, and usually pretty good things. And then for whatever reason, they can't write anymore. You don't have writer's block. You just aren't writing. A touch harsh, but there it is.

That's the downside—the debilitating side of the unconscious. But when the unconscious has been made healthy and strong—by whatever means you use to make it so—then one feels there really is something creative that is both oneself and other than oneself. Granted it has its own strange ways and often needs extensive care and feeding, sometimes with multiple naps included. But anyone who has worked away at writing has experienced those days when something else within is doing all the work. Before Saul Bellow started writing *Augie March*, he was in Paris on a Guggenheim Fellowship and he was genuinely blocked. He was on a novel about two men in adjoining beds in a hospital, and the streams were all clogged up at the source. (It's a premise that might even block

Shakespeare, unless he thought to make a comedy of it.) Suddenly a new idea, a new voice came into his head. "I am an American, Chicago born— Chicago, that somber city—and go at things as I have taught myself, free-style, and will make the record in my own way: first to knock, first admitted; sometimes an innocent knock, sometimes a not so innocent." Well, you know the rest, or if you don't you have a treat coming when you crack that book.

The point is that by whatever work of quotidian magic, Bellow opened up and made contact with the source and let it have its way, he said of *Augie*. "The book just came to me," Bellow said. "All I had to do was be there with buckets to catch it." That doesn't mean writing isn't about rigor and training and all the rest. It doesn't mean hard work doesn't apply. But there does come a point for some writers when the work has been done, some discipline's been acquired, the desk's clear, and the unconscious is tipping, if ever so slightly, in Coleridge's direction rather than Freud's. Then it's time to play around a little, write freely, find out what the spirits have on their minds this morning—see what will happen next. It may be hard to get to that fine point, but when you do, what greater pleasure is there?

To Find Your Medium

In my experience, if you've just met a writer and want to have a rich conversation with him, ask him how he writes. (Or ask about cats.) I don't mean the entry strategies (meditation and pencil sharpening and the rest). Those are too personal. You're trespassing on the writer's spiritual life when you try to pull that. I mean the implement question.

Do you use a pen? If so what kind? Is it a jazzy Montblanc or a Bic with the nether end chewed just so? A pencil. Well, OK. But a No. 2 or a 3? And what sort of paper? For a long time I was disposed to the yellow lined legal pad. Makes me feel official—lawyerly. But I'm also free to make plenty of mistakes. It's yellow, throwaway paper. I'm just practicing / this doesn't really count.

Does your dinner companion use a computer? Probably so. But when in the process does she, as it were, go electric? Does she write drafts on the machine? But then isn't it hard to redraft, given that it's all so well laid out and authoritative looking that it would seem a little sacrilegious to mess with it?

And if your new acquaintance uses a computer, what kind? And what's the best of all possible programs for composing novels or screenplays or stage plays or epic poems or haikus, as the relevant case may be? If you really want to get on the writer's good side, and maybe learn something to boot, ask about the *history* of her writing technology. Yes, even the pencil is a form of technology, if you understand technology as McLuhan did. Technology is the extension of man, the sage of Toronto said. So a pencil might be said to extend the hand and likewise with a pen—and give the hand a capacity it doesn't possess, the marking capacity. And a computer—what does that extend or enhance? The whole human brain maybe (at least once the computer has been connected to the Internet), or at least a significant part of it.

Why does a writer use one implement rather than another? Why should you? Is it possible, vaguely possible, that you can improve your writing, or even get it going, simply by using the right tool? Picking your tool can be nearly as important as deciding whether it will be fiction or nonfiction, short stories or poems. Getting the medium right is one of the great pleasures of writing—but it's often a pleasure that needs to be renegotiated through the middle distance of a writing career. What worked early may not work quite so well as the road winds on and the clock goes around and around.

The writers I grew up admiring all seemed to have the same method. They wrote in longhand. They slaved away with pencil (or pen) and paper, sweating and steaming, as though they were humping crates in a factory. This writing was *work* dammit. They blotted their papers and crossed out and shed ink over them as though it were their heart's blood. Then they crushed the papers like tiny cannonballs and sent them flying across the room. At the end of the day, it looked like the room was full of tiny boulders stained blue with angry ink. But there was something left—a page or two that might be keepable. And then? And then?

Then they had it *typed up*. They gave it to their typist, who tended to be a girlfriend, a wife, or a secretary who had been with them for two decades. Early that evening, or maybe fresh the next morning, the writer has a clean, clean copy in hand, which he then proceeds to scourge with his pen, until rents open up in the skin that is the paper. Then it goes back to the typist again. Even if the writer types himself, he sends it off to the typist to retype, so it's clean as a freshly laundered Brooks Brothers shirt, which he will then, of course, submit to war-time trials.

What was up? Writing technology used to be a lot more primitive than it is now. Sure. Anyone entering the game could feel certain he was going to engage with a lifetime of Wite-Out and correction tape, as well as with machines that commonly threw off one letter from overuse, inevitably a vowel, almost inevitably one's favorite vowel. (If one may have a favorite vowel.) But to remedy this situation there was for the writer, or anyhow for the successful writer, the typist, who turned your volcanic flow into the cold, authoritative word.

That was a guy thing, to be sure. Males have almost never been confident in the writer's role, especially when what they wrote was fiction or poetry. They needed to make the game more masculine. Hemingway helped us out of course with the fishing and hunting (and the remarkable early prose). But maybe it wasn't enough. The business of passing on one's pages to an indentured typist—which still goes on, I can attest—was in part the business of trying to seem like a man of business with a secretary, or maybe a high-ranking personal assistant of some kind. But whatever rationale existed for the scribble and pass it off technique is now gone, usurped by the computer, which is not only an expansion of the writing hand, but a marvelous expansion of the human brain.

Writing on the computer gives you everything that possessing an amanuensis ever could have and more. It is magic, or about as close to magic as writing can get. Press a button and the letter appears; press a few more and you have a word. More still and sentences are inclined to appear. In not long a paragraph is what you have. How do you write so much someone purportedly asked Lytton Strachey. I write one word and then I write another, he sagely said. On the computer, writing that way is as easy as pie. Your shoulder doesn't hurt (usually), your back feels fine (you can half recline when you write), and if you take some precautions, your hands won't succumb to this syndrome or that. And—most magical of all—you can erase without effort and without defacing your paper in the least. You can edit with ease. Try this! Try that! See how it sounds. Keep a half a dozen drafts of the piece and then compare. The computer is quite simply a writer's genie. You call it by simply opening the screen of your laptop and then it goes magically to work for you. Your password is the only alakazam you need.

And it will correct your spelling. No small thing if you happen to be, say, me and could spend ten minutes trying to piece out a word like, oh, amanuensis. If you don't have a fact or quote at hand, turn to Lord Google and lo! The computer is a demigod—and it is completely at your disposal.

It does your bidding over land and water like those angels in the Milton sonnet. The computer is a miracle.

But should you use it? The problem with writing on the computer—or rather *a* problem with writing on the computer—is that writing can quickly turn into typing and typing into writing. Truman Capote of course said something like that about Kerouac's *On the Road*, and it supposedly bothered Kerouac for the rest of his days. That's not writing; it's typing. The writer who uses a computer for the first draft is maybe creating an illusion for himself. It looks so finished. It looks so clean. It looks publishable. Darn it. It looks virtually *published*, and all after a first draft. The softness of the keys, their responsiveness to touch, the bright almost glamorous light that comes off your page—it's all so easy and so (why not say it?) beautiful. How can you not fall in love? How can you not tumble head over heels with what is nothing better than a first draft?

The form and the content, we might say, are at radical variance with each other. The form is slick, smooth, and lovable. The content on the other hand . . . Well, the content is the content of a first draft. The quality of the computer manuscript can sing you sweetly into feeling that your work is all done when it is anything but.

If you use a pencil and pad, or even a manual typewriter, your first draft will look like what a first draft most probably is: the dog's dinner. OK, no big deal. Time to fix it. But when your first draft looks almost like a sculpture in marble, why should you mess with it? Once you have something that looks that good it's hard not to let it stand as is. Oh, you'll go back through the manuscript and tinker of course: rearrange sentences, check facts, crush a few tiny, bug-like mistakes. But you won't be likely to do what many writers feel goes a long way to deepening a work. You won't start over with the raw first draft at your side. The cake looks to be already baked and iced. Add a cherry and a few sprinkles and you're done.

But for many writers what they want and need to say lies a few layers below the level of immediate articulation. Their first drafts come too much from that everyday self that does the laundry and takes the car in for servicing and goes to the movies to relax. For them, a first draft, even a promising one, stands there blocking their access to what genuinely matters. It's a barrier as much as anything. Hart Crane rewrote his poems so often that sometimes no really significant terms appear in the final draft that were present in the first. That's extreme. Still, for some writers the first draft, though welcome, is a little like Ahab's pasteboard mask.

They have to smash through it to see what's on the other side. Tinkering is not smashing. Fixing the grammar will not blast them through the pasteboard to make contact with the real.

Do one draft, I tell my students. Then set it beside you and go into the second from the top down. I'm guessing that since the advent of the computer this advice has been observed largely in the breach. But it is the right idea, especially for the beginning writer. When Henry James—a master in his own fashion—entered his late phase he was able to dictate his novels. Joyce did much the same with *Finnegans Wake*. But one is not Henry James, and surely one is not Joyce, James, either.

Writing overall may have actually declined because of the computer: less consideration, less compression, more sheer text let loose on the world. They call it word processing. What's in a name? Word processing sounds like what they do in a word factory where volume and speed and efficiency overrule other values. Write your words. Don't process them. Computers are a pleasure, but a peril, too.

Posture is part of your medium as well. Hemingway wrote standing up. He brought himself to attention in front of his desk every morning and went at it. And what came out at least early on is what you might expect—clear, sharp, exact prose. He wrote prose that was *disciplined*. He stood at attention or something close to it, and he wrote prose that was also often at attention. He seemed to write the way a sentry on guard duty would, observing the scene with a cold, discerning eye. Not every writer's work lines up with his writing posture the way Hemingway's does—or the way I'm imagining it does.

But in writing, posture matters. It doesn't matter quite as much as your direct writing medium, maybe. But it is important what your body is doing while you do your work. For what it's worth, I tend to write first drafts half reclining on a couch. I want as much bodily ease as possible hoping that will translate into as much mental freedom as I can get. Body relaxed: mind and spirit relaxed and receptive. Or that's what I'm hoping for anyway. I think a lot of first-draft writing is associative; one idea leads to another and then to one more. What guides the associations? Who knows? I think if you've read a lot and thought some about writing, there are templates in there. You know what an academic argument feels like; you know how a short story can go; you have a feel when to glide into your ending if you're writing a poem. Those templates, I find, usually undergird your free, or almost free associations.

I, and probably most people who try to write, find a sense of ease and dreaminess more useful than what Hemingway seems to have wanted: discipline and distance. And I use posture to try to get that. Later on, doing a second draft, I'm more likely to sit up straight in a chair and focus. Sitting gives me a sense of schoolroom seriousness and I sometimes expect to see my old sixth grade teacher, Miss Smith, much beloved by me, though only in retrospect, looming over and judging what she sees. I'm glad I'm working on a computer; she won't have to see my spidery handwriting.

Dress can matter too, though it sounds strange to say so. A fine critic who teaches in New York could, it was said, only do his work—reviews for the *New York Review of Books* and such—after he'd showered and shaved close and put on a three-piece suit and adorned himself further with tie and cuff links. And he did possess a rather official-sounding voice—good for a critic no doubt. Though isn't writing supposed to be an alternative to a soul-chewing day job? I couldn't put on the tie and the links, unless it would buy me an essay like Eliot's "Tradition and the Individual Talent" (Eliot was perfectly capable of writing in a three-piece suit) or Trilling's on Keats (Trilling was wearing a jacket and tie even when he wasn't).

Most writers I know list in the other direction. One I've heard of teaches writing at a large state university. He's jammed his classes into a two-day intensive and when three thirty on Tuesday comes, he rolls into his house, climbs into his bathrobe, raises his hands over his head in caesarean triumph, and cries: "Weekend!" It's said that he writes all the rest of the week long and only really emerges from the robe when it is time to shower, sleep (nude, naturally, all emperors sleep in the primary), or fornicate. He needs to be relaxed and he is.

So check your wardrobe. If you write best as an emperor, then dress as one. Some no doubt are prone to athletes' togs—and if I'm right, the old line is true and athletes and writers have more than a little in common. And if you're hoping to be a cultural statesman, by all means look the part.

But more important is the transcribing medium. I'd think twice about falling first into the computer, especially if you're just starting out. Get a pencil; get a pen. Get your papyrus of choice and have a go at a first draft that goes from brain to arm to hand and then flows onto the paper like a magic spell. (Writing *is* magic when you think about it. Words that were in your mind come out and stand in place on the page and all can read—read, as it were—your mind.) Words are holy: direct connection with them is sublime.

To Skip Writing the Great American Novel

There are times when I wish I had been alive in 1814. There is to be sure a good deal I would miss: I appreciate penicillin, advanced dentistry, and the power to hear any rock song I want (just about) anytime I want (nearly). But 1814 had its advantages, one of which was that it saw the publication of Jane Austen's *Mansfield Park*. However bad the food was then, however rotten the English weather, whatever the worries about Napoleon's resurgence and war with the French, one still had something. One had Jane Austen. At least the few people lucky enough or shrewd enough to read her did.

As everyone knows, all of Austen's novels are about the same subject: young women getting happily and advantageously married. Both words matter—happily *and* advantageously. Emma and Fanny and Elizabeth find the man who will fill their lives with joy, but they also manage to get, or in Emma's case to stay, rich. (The plot of *Persuasion* is a tad more complicated and *Sense and Sensibility* is not quite readable to me, though almost.) The plots are similar, but the characters are different, fascinatingly so; the dialogue is exquisite; and the texture—the lived experience of the young women and their suitors is rendered with such precise detail and such near to bursting intricacy as to make you ask aggressive and disagreeable questions. How could this person, this Jane Austen person, see so much of the life around her (and a few miles away from her) while the rest of us see so little?

For Austen's novels are contemporary, contemporary to her. She is looking out on her own social scene. She is writing about her times. The dresses her heroines wear are the dresses in the windows of the shops Jane Austen passed. (She could see those dresses in the milliners' windows; though she probably could not have afforded them herself.) The papers they read are the current papers; in Austen's provinces the London paper is a few days late and so it is for the newspaper readers in her books. At Austen's balls her dancers dance the right dances to music by the composers of the day; they eat what was served. They ride horses or coaches or walk (there's a lot of walking in Austen) as they would in the contemporary world at large. The soldiers wear red coats; the women wear muslin; the servants make their servile ways in homespun. The plantation Sir Thomas goes to visit in the Indies—leaving the young people to frolic (rather dangerously) at Mansfield Park—is the sort of plantation replete with slaves that a British nobleman might have owned in the early nineteenth century.

It's all there. Austen's world is Austen's world. She does what truly great novelists can do: takes her own time and metabolizes it into fiction. She turns the external into the internal. From reading newspapers and chattering with people and watching what passes before us, we gather a sense of the world we inhabit. But it is an external sense, a journalistic sense, a detached and small sense. We do not *know* what it feels like to live as we do, and we do not even know what it is like to know what we know. Thought and feeling, ideas and experience are unjoined.

Austen famously compared her work to minute carvings in ivory, and to this there is something. Her world is small. But she can make it feel quite central. If you've traveled with her and paid attention (Austen requires a great deal of attention), then you can know by association much about the life of her times. She hits the center of the bull's eye—though almost anywhere she aimed would become the center of the bull's eye, so much significance would she find there.

Great fiction writers offer many bounties, but one of them is to take their time and render it in words that let readers know what it is like to live—in their own moment. Don't we all know that? No. Absolutely no! Not in the least. We swim blindly through our days; we sleep even when we are awake. But there are some who *are* awake. They see what is before them and they have the added gift, combined with the discipline, to render it in words. Of these few Jane Austen was one. She wrote the great British novels—at least two of them, *Emma* and *Pride and Prejudice*— circa 1800.

The "circa" matters. No other form of writing is as time bound, time responsive, and time sensitive as novels are. The proclivity of the form, its grandeur and limitation, is encoded in its name: novel. It seeks to give you something new, something new about that which is new. Novels, good ones, turn the news into a form of secondary lived experience. They wrap up your time for you and hand it to you in a box of many pages. And as your time passes away, the power of the novel does, too. Novels are of their time. Lyric poetry may aspire to duration. Shakespeare made claims of longevity for his sonnets, but not his plays. And philosophers seek to speak truth to the ages. But a great novel is now.

It doesn't mean that a novel of the past can't be read with pleasure and profit in the present—far from it. But I think the power of fiction usually diminishes as time passes. The miracle is to take the present and find its significance—disclose its meanings—in the way no journalist or blogger or newsman or newswoman is in a position to do. The best time to read *Mansfield Park* would have been the day it was published. On that day its light would be strongest and most subtle and it would illuminate more areas of experience than at any other moment. Novels are news that are more than news. But they don't usually stay news forever.

Some are so strong as to shrug off the wear of time—or some of it anyway. We still want to read Proust and James and Woolf and Austen. But we would much rather read the Jane Austen of our times (if we had one) than the Jane Austen of her times. There is much that stays true over time and great novels can capture that truth, but we want the eternal matters joined with the immediate—and real novels do that.

That brings us to the great American novel—and your relation to it as a writer. I love the lines that are beneath the Statue of Liberty in New York Harbor, the lines about giving us your tired and poor, the huddled masses yearning to breathe free. And I love Woody Guthrie's "This Land Is Your Land" and think it should be the national anthem and be inscribed from place to place across the country. But I fear we Americans have another side and would find another fit motto if we dared. Americans: We want to have our cake and eat it too. Have you ever heard of the longing for the great African novel? The great novel of Asia? Nope. But the great American novel? You hear about that all the time.

Have our cake and eat it too: that's about what we want in almost anything and almost everything. We want to have complete domestic security all the time, but never infringe on anyone's civil liberties. We want complete national security all the time but never to mistreat a prisoner or to commit an aggressive military act. We want to spend all the money in our coffers and be certain that our kids will be able to pick up the tab when their turn comes. We want to have our cake and eat it too. We'll consume it with champagne and gusto. The having—the possessing—satisfies the good little citizen in us; the eating satisfies the spoiled little kid. Fun to be both—if you can manage to bring it off.

The dream of the great American novel is an instance of the cake-both-ways desire, albeit a fairly minor one. What we want is a novel that does two nearly incompatible things. First it takes its own moment and turns it, to use some shorthand, from journalism to art. The literary writer Northrop Frye tells us what happens. The historian tells us what happened. And the philosopher tells us (or presumes to tell us) what must happen. We want our fiction writers to tell us what happens now. They must let us know in sensuous and specific detail how it is with us here in the present. This is work enough. Years pass in which, one might argue, no novelist succeeds in doing this. At best, very fine novelists become contenders. They never get full agreement. There are those who believe that Jonathan Franzen rang the bell with *The Corrections*, those who believe that David Foster Wallace slammed down the hammer, sent the missile high, and maybe shattered the sound piece with *Infinite Jest*. But there will be no consensus. Philosophers talk about holding your time in thought. Fiction writers could talk—if it wouldn't spook them—about holding it in both feeling and thought nicely merged together. (You might call it, after Schiller, the merger of the spiritual and the material through play.) And that is a lot to achieve.

But the quest for the great American novel asks for more. Not only must the book summarize now, but it must also last for all time. It's got to capture the moment and every moment to come; it needs to be litera-ture (what happens now) and philosophy (what must happen) simultane-ously. This is virtually impossible. We want to have our temporal cake and our eternal (never spoiled) gateau on top of it.

There are novels that defy this difficulty. Joyce's *Ulysses* may be the most local, specific, time bound, historically evocative novel ever written, being as it is about one day in the life of Leopold Bloom, Stephen Dedalus, and Dublin, Ireland, the third protagonist of the book. Ah, maybe there is a fourth hero, the day in question, June 16, 1904. There is no more bril-liant study of the way we are now—at least if you were alive in Dublin on what ought by now to be a holy day of obligation for all lovers of literature.

Joyce is of his time, emphatically. But the book's technique, or rather techniques, reach out ahead of June 16, 1904. *Ulysses* is written in every literary mode known to humanity and a few that are still not quite understood. You get overt narration (some), collage (in the wandering rocks), stream of consciousness (Bloom much of the time), drama (Nighttown), catechism (a chapter of seemingly endless Q&A), and in Molly's chapter, the last of the book, what's surely the grandest novelistic monologue both heard and overheard (Bloom's are overheard) of all time. Every fresh form of writing in *Ulysses* reveals new possibilities for literary technique that we can still learn from. But they also explore the workings of consciousness (in *Finnegans Wake* Joyce will explore the unconscious, though an unconscious much unlike Freud's). Expand the resources of consciousness; blaze some trails for the development and the fulfillment of the mental powers. I think Joyce does that, too.

So OK, OK, one instance: not the great American novel, but surely the grand Irish novel. And maybe, maybe there is someone out there who can complete the American task. (Maybe *Moby-Dick*—but maybe that was more a book of the future than of its 1850s present, and as such a stunning anomaly.) But it's a high mountain to rope your way up and even Joyce (shh, don't say a word about this to anyone) can sometimes be in his attempt to merge the eternal and the temporal with all the literary razzmatazz what one can only call—well, you know, oring—with a *b* up front. Put it this way: when we go to Nighttown, I reach for my pillow. And Joyce's decision to yoke his book to Homer—which I'll bet came late in the composition—makes things more mannered and dry than they need to be. Eliot lapped this stuff up in his essay on Joyce and the mythic method—but then Eliot was using Joyce to try to teach us to read his favorite author, T. S. Eliot. Jane Austen, on the other hand, is entertaining and instructive every moment of the way in *Emma* and *Pride and Prejudice* and *Mansfield Park*. She's great, a wonder. I only wish I were alive in 1814, to read her as she truly deserves to be read.

So don't be bothered by the beckoning of the great American novel, or the beckoning of greatness, period. Remember that sloppy, inviting immortal beginning of Bellow's *Augie March*. "I am an American, Chicago born—Chicago, that somber city—and go at things as I have taught myself, free-style, and will make the record in my own way."

Freestyle. That's right. The novel's a mess and probably won't outlast its time by much. But freestyle: that's how you do it. Free. And what pleasure is greater than the pleasure of freedom?

To Find Beauty and Truth

Who can do justice to the subject of writing and beauty and truth in a few pages, a few books, even a few lifetimes? Surely not I. Others with greater powers and larger claims to achievement (by far) have dropped their buckets into this well and often what they've come up with has been impressive, though not yet (as I see it) definitive. One thinks of Horace and Longinus. One thinks of Blake and Shelley and Hazlitt. One thinks of T. S. Eliot and of Virginia Woolf. This is stern company and one does not seek entrance to it readily.

But one might say to start that writing's ultimate goal should be to do something for others as well as for oneself. Writing is about enlarging the mind, the expansion of consciousness, the addition, as the critic R. P. Blackmur liked to say, to the stock of available reality. We're told that writing is about finding the truth and infusing it with some beauty, too. But what does that mean?

The philosopher—the pure philosopher, the follower of Plato—seeks ultimate truth, Truth with a capital *t*, if you like. He aspires (it usually is a he) to capture truths that will be true in all cultures, at all times, in all places. If Plato's depiction of the three parts of the human soul—the rational, the spirited, and the appetitive—does not hold as bindingly true for Americans in the twenty-first century as for Athenians in the fifth, then Plato fails.

It's impossible you say. We know now that truth is contingent on history and culture—and on race and class and gender to boot. Maybe, maybe that is so. But why then do we still read Plato? Why do young people all over the world still open his book and find there not a subtle indication of ancient attitudes, but instead a vision that thrills them with its aptness—its candor, its shrewdness, its (why not say it?) claim to truth? Plato is a contender for the ultimate palm. Of this I at least have no doubt.

But while Plato can be poetic, he is not quite a poet. That is to say that his truth is not always beautiful. The Myth of Er and the story of the ladder of love that Socrates imports from Diotima in *Symposium* have their glamor and allure, certainly. But there can be—there often is—a slight brittleness to Plato. He smacks too much of the logician. There's a whiff of the schoolroom. Above the door of his academy, it's said, there was a sign posted: ONLY THOSE WHO KNOW GEOMETRY SHOULD ENTER HERE. Is all truth geometric, or based on geometry? Some, no doubt. But there may be more—and that more, that other kind of writer's truth—may be what inspired Plato to banish the poets from his Utopia.

What do we mean when, in Keats's spirit, we want to fuse truth and beauty? Or—in Horace's version—we hope to intermingle instruction with delight?

What the romantic poets offer is a version of truth that is personal. This is how I see it. This is how it is and was for me. (And here too is how I hope it may be for you!)

What some writers do, the romantics among them, is to let us know what is true for them. The question of how it is becomes how it is for me. Do they risk self-indulgence? Solipsism? Sure—and worse: this way madness can lie. But who knows that perhaps Plato was wrong about universal truth and the best we can hope for is to see the world as it truly is *for us.* Perhaps there are only individual truths—and by affirming our own we open up the possibility for others to go on similar quests. My exploration of my own mind widens the area of the possible for the minds of others Mailer tells us (and rather apologetically tells himself). Who knows? Stranger things have been true.

The writer who seeks personal truth almost always seeks something along with it. He seeks something that might be called a writer's beauty. By that I mean he not only wants to unfold his vision—his truth—but to convey the *feelings* that are part of seeing the world as he does. He is not detached but immersed, not authoritative but questing, not godly but human, as the sage says, all too human.

Literary beauty is distinct, it seems to me, from the beauty of a water lily or of Monet's rendering of one. It does not offer the possibility of detached contemplation that Kant commends. It doesn't offer alluring purposiveness without any purpose and lift us above the push and toss of the world as it is. Rather literary beauty may give us the feel of the belief it infuses. The work sees the world a certain way—all right. But what is it like to see the world in that way? How does it feel? Tolstoy and Virginia Woolf differ not only in subject, emphasis, and scope, but they differ also in the music they make and the music that makes their visions what they are. Tolstoy is stern and strong and somehow both passionate and detached. (This happened. This will pass.) Woolf is alert, immersed, present, and very nearly participates in the dramas she unfolds. She lives and joys with Mrs. Ramsay. She dies with Septimus Smith.

She does it (and he does it) through something it is not quite right to call style, though style may be the best word we have for the phenomenon. What I mean is the braiding of the sound and the sense of a piece of writing, so the way the author sees and the way the author feels about what she sees become united. Frost says that style signifies the way the author took himself in relation to what he has to render. Did he believe it fully? Partially? Did it fill him with joy? Loathing? Some impossible but possible combination of the two? Style is too external a word for this power of fusion. You put on the right pants or pantsuit and you have a sartorial style. But I think the beauty of writing—the fusion of sense and sound—doesn't involve put-ons of any sort. Rather it involves what one might call an integration of character.

Truth and beauty (even if it's the author's particular truth, the author's beauty) fused together suggest a mind that knows itself as far as minds can do. The mind of this kind of writer not only knows what it sees and understands, but it also renders what it feels like to see the world in such a manner. When Woolf writes a description of Mrs. Ramsay, we feel not only her powers of perception of a character but also the spirit of admiration and sorrow and exasperation and love, mostly love for this figure. It's there in the prose—in its music and in its metaphors—though it is not easy to isolate it and break it down into elements.

An imperfect illustration: look at the movies. All movies are scored. Music plays virtually all the time through virtually every film. And generally, alas, one *hears* the music. At best it is mildly agreeable. At worst it is an intrusion; it feels too overt, manipulative. I don't need to be *told* how I should feel. Just make me feel that way, if you can. But sometimes matters are different. Sometimes the images and dialogue on the one hand and the score on the other manage to fuse. You don't really hear the music; you don't know it's going on. It's part of a unified piece.

The analogy doesn't fully work because a movie score is still much more extraneous to a film than literary beauty is to writing. The expressive beauty of writing—the melding of sound and sense—is what nonutilitarian writing is all about. It's what lifts a piece of writing up from being just adequate to being something special and memorable. Few works of verbal art that do not possess it in some measure have a chance of surviving.

But this all sounds rather high-flown. What could it possibly have to do with anyone who is just starting out as a writer? Or even someone who is in the middle distance of the race?

Most people, I think, feel that sense comes first. We figure out the plot, the argument, the central metaphor, then on we go. This is no doubt true sometimes. But I think there's another truth that's often allied to composition—one less commonly understood. That is that sound can create sense. What I mean is that when we start writing, what we're looking for is the right voice: the right degree of irony, the right level of sobriety or exuberance. And then tone leads to text.

I'm inclined to work quite a while until I have a first sentence I like. (Or in a longer piece, a first paragraph.) And by "like" I mean like the sound of it: that sings, that jumps, that rocks, and maybe rolls. Or at least it doesn't pancake down on its face. And once the voice—what I think of as the literary beauty—is there, then the words usually come. The voice is the key that opens the door to sense. Music makes the movie happen, not the reverse.

This may be why a lot of writers listen to music while they write. They want to purloin a rhythm, grab a sound. I'd rather find my music myself, but on this, each to her own.

Yet this is worth underlining. In writing, beauty can bring on truth; sound can be the creator of sense. Why this is is hard to say. Do we have different voices living in our spirits? Do we possess—and are we possessed by—different selves? Where do they come from and what are they? They surely don't have a place in Plato's map of the mind or Freud's or St. Augustine's.

I've never dowsed for springwater and despite temptations (I live on the site of an old farmhouse) I've never taken a metal detector to the grounds around my house. But writing is sometimes a little like dowsing and prospecting. We search for the right voice, the right tone, the right rhythm. Then, led by the music, the ideas come pouring in. Or they stay in abeyance because we approached a piece in the wrong key. It's not that our ideas were bad per se. We couldn't get to the good ones because we did not find the song of the inner oracle that spoke to the matter at hand.

For a long time, I wrote books and essays that were—give or take—literary theory. My wife, a fiction writer to the tips of her fingers, couldn't really give a toss about literary theory. But I always showed her the opening paragraphs of anything I might do on Derrida or Foucault or their compeers. She'd read it, maybe not quite know what was being said, but with great confidence be able to say: "You're on!" And also, from time to time: "You're not!" This had nothing to do with the content—only with the music, or lack thereof. "Not custom or lecture, not even the best," Whitman says, "only the lull I like, the hum of your valved voice." When you hear that hum, some truth may be on the way.

I think one of the reasons we care about literary writing and prefer it by far to what we can get in the newspaper or the review is this attempt to fuse feeling and thought. The reviewer and the newspaperman want to get the feeling out of the way. They often want to sound universal, authoritative, imperially anonymous. The literary writer lets us know how it feels as well as how it is, and in a unified and intelligent way.

In a famous essay, T. S. Eliot told us that fusion of thought and feeling had passed away from literature sometime around the English

Renaissance. He called it "the dissociation of sensibility." Before that point, Eliot says, writers commonly thought and felt at the same time. His crucial example is John Donne (the essay is on the "Metaphysical Poets") who conceives a blush and conveys the experience of it at the same time.

Eliot claims to be cross with the modern world for doing away with the possibility for this sort of cohesion. But I'm not at all sure he's right. The idea is a part of his overall polemic against the current world. But the truth may be that for most of us the unity of thought and feeling may have been broken. We are pragmatists in our public lives, romantics in our private. But putting it together—that is no easy matter. In fact, it never was and never will be. It seems to me, for what it's worth, that Eliot (among many others) does so again and again. He had the mind of a metaphysician (his thesis was on F. H. Bradley) and the heart of a religious quester. Poems like "Little Gidding" do a fine job of recomposing that dissociated sensibility. For it is a state that bothers us all and has, I suspect, from the start of rationalized and overrationalized civilization.

Writing that takes as its ultimate goal the integration of feeling and thought can create fine results, and on two levels. It can provide us with work that truly lives, the kind Keats says we could prove upon our pulses. And it also brings us together into something like unified being. When we laugh we know why; when we weep we do, too. Feeling never goes far from intellection, intellection from feeling. We are, insofar as a human being can be, united within ourselves.

THE WRITER'S WISDOM

To Mine a Fresh Experience

I sometimes like to think that writers age backward, a little the way Merlin was supposed to do in the Arthurian legends. Up to a certain point, they get younger over time—at least if you attach a certain meaning to the word "younger."

Quite simply, you get better at what you do as time passes. Writers often don't peak until they get into their forties and fifties. And if Yeats, who exploded creatively in old age, isn't exactly representative, he clearly shows us what can be done by an old writer—even when he takes that apparently most depressing of periods, old age, as his subject. Yeats sometimes loved being old; he had always pined to be wise and now he has some claims to be. He has seen much and he has thought it over. And words—Yeats is never at a loss for glorious words. When he says that this everyday world is "no country for old men," he takes us to a new land, Byzantium, that's richer yet in imaginative possibility.

It's here that the analogy between the writer and the athlete falls apart. The beginning writer and the athlete just starting out have much in common: they're both acquiring their craft, learning their moves. By the time the athlete reaches her peak, the writer will probably be nothing more than an advanced beginner, still stuttering, still stammering, still not sounding like herself. But days go by. The big-time passer hurts his arm; the running back pulls up lame; the lineman's knees wobble. But the writer surges forward, getting stronger as she enters her thirties and forties, getting her game on when the athlete is relegated to the announcer's booth or the brown card table where he sits signing the memorabilia. Writers do fade, but they enjoy long-stemmed growth, often into old age and sometimes to the end. Old age is harvest time for the writer, and if he has written and read with integrity, the harvest will be rich in yellows and crimsons and gold.

Old age provides subjects for the writer. There is the world around her as seen from the vantage of long experience. There is also the life of the aged man or woman as it is day to day. People have never lived as long as they do now. They have never counted as many years. This gives all of us aged and aging writers access to fresh experience—the experience of being older than people (or at least people outside the pages of the Hebrew Bible) have been before.

Writing in old age, or late in life, has another advantage, too. What people commonly say about aging and memory seems to have some truth in it. We elders may not know where we put the car keys, our car keys, but we can wake up remembering the cars our mothers and fathers drove, and what it felt like to lie supine in the backseat, on the way to get ice cream, or to visit a relative in a parlor or a cemetery. Though the present has faded to a lighter shade, the past opens up. It's as though we've stepped inside one of the photographs that was left in sober black-and-white silence in the picture album. And then, suddenly, suddenly, all is color—the way it was for Dorothy when she whirled out of Kansas and came down in the kingdom of Oz. Suddenly, we are children again—children who see with both childish eyes and the eyes of experience, too.

Everyone who is disposed should try, when she reaches the season of ripened memory, to write a book about her past. If the gone world truly opens up for us as the present world recedes a bit (those keys, those keys), why not acquiesce and be students and connoisseurs of our own early days? Who knows what discoveries we will make?

For the writer who has been at work a long time and has mastered some part of his craft, old age can also be a blossoming time. He's made the right moves. He's begun to begin. He's slammed through the wall that separates writers from nonwriters. (Even if he had to, well, do something as bizarre as making like Hunter S. Thompson to do it.) He's got his set of rituals and incantations to get flying above the walls of prohibition and commonplace mind, or to let him slide elegantly below. And he's learned all the things writers need to know, or at least that he as a writer needs to know: he's got the right device (and it's probably not a computer, or not exclusively one); he's comfortable being alone; he's jazzed at the thought of knowing what he thinks by hearing what he says, not scared; he's aware that sometimes it's the music that matters most when you start to write and so he listens, or asks someone he loves to listen, for his proper melody. In other words, he's learned all this book has to teach and probably a lot more.

Then he can sit down, get into gear, start writing, and see that the face reflected in the words on the page is his own, and no one else's. He is his words and his words are him, even when—and maybe mostly when—they surprise him the most. That happens in old age, if it happens at all, and even then it probably does not last. But when he writes and he sounds like himself and no one else, and does so without trying all that hard—well then, something very good has happened. The writer has made it home to himself.

To Beat the Clock (A Little)

I'm an old writer, and really it's not too bad. Being most other things when you get old is less than wonderful from what I can see. Old movie star, old athlete, old CEO, old construction worker: usually not so good. Old writer: so far not half bad.

They talk about laying money aside for your later years. I've tried to do some of that, yet I haven't done nearly what I should have. Though I plan never to retire from my job teaching at the University of Virginia, factors larger than our own desires can intervene. There's sickness; there's growing so far out of touch with students that you can't really understand them, nor they you; there's the possible insane desire of one of my younger colleagues to possess my large-windowed office, which might result in who knows what. But barring those events, or my ability to negotiate them (that younger colleague who wants to bask in my sunlight better know what he's getting into), I intend to stay with my job. And just as important, I intend to stay with writing. Because writing is something you can do when you're old—and if you could do it passably when you were younger, you can probably do it at least semi-passably during the gold (or gold-plated) years. Surely in time the workings of the mind will slow and slide to the point where even you can't make much out of what you've put down on the page, but that may not be for a very long while.

So I'm not saving much money for retirement—and what's left in the account when I go I hope that my sons (both artists) will get. But I consider writing to be a sort of socking away of pennies for the purposes of the future. By writing I'm investing in at least a partially livable old age.

Now I'm not talking about the prospect of a late-career blast, like the one Henry James had when he dictated those three astonishing semi-readable late novels. I'm not even talking about a run at the bestseller lists like the ones Bellow and Roth managed in late or latish innings.

I mean writing as a consolation, vocation, and pastime for late life. I'm also talking about it as a form of mental health sustenance, especially well suited to the old. The mind's a muscle. (This much has been a premise of the book.) And though I haven't a single scientific study to back me up, I'll advance the hypothesis that writing can help keep the mind sound in old age. Physical infirmity is one sorrow; we've all had a taste of it before we've been old. The back goes out; the leg twists and the next day we're lurching forward on crutches; the dentist looks inside our mouths, doesn't like what he sees, and does three hours' work, only to release us with the promise that we'll be back in three days for another round. We've all had a taste of the physical infirmities, an amuse-bouche as they like to say, even if we've been pretty lucky.

But of the sliding mental powers we know little. We've lost our keys many times, even if we're twenty (especially perhaps if we're twenty), but we know what the damned things are. They're keys, for goodness sake. (Babies love keys: they open the portal to adult life, or adult life under capitalism. Keys matter.) To forget your husband's name, to not know your four-year-old grandson when he races down the driveway to show you a new gizmo you have every right not to know about, to be unable to address an envelope, to be confused every point of the waking day: this is harsh punishment.

I'm not sure. No one in a lab coat is behind me on this. But I'm betting the exertions of writing can cancel some of the mental sorrows of old age, or at least postpone them for a while. If you do not use it, you lose it. And to write well (write and revise and laugh at it and improve it) you've got to use it. There is no other way. The cliché doesn't lie. (One of the joys of getting old is that you can use clichés with almost full conviction and near abandon.) You *make* sense. You make sense through writing and you make sense through talk—good talk. But there isn't always someone around who can hit the conversational ball back over the net with the right velocity and challenging spin. So writing is the best default. It only requires you, a pencil, and a sheet of paper. (What inventions they are:

paper and pencil. I sometimes look at them both, pencils in particular, and smile with strange gratitude.) Writing helps you learn to make sense. And when you do that and you get good at it, or as good as your lights allow, you may keep doing it long after the investment banker and the real estate mogul and the doctor who told you that you had better live better than you do are slipping into the twilight. Maybe. I'm not a scientist and I don't know. But Socrates (greatest conversationalist on record, maybe) was sharp enough at seventy to talk rings around the citizens of Athens, and Sophocles was still writing topflight plays into his eighties. The playwright competitions held in Athens in Sophocles's extreme old age? He won one at about the age of eighty-seven.

But maybe the best thing about writing in old age is that you can write as yourself. This sounds a bit strange and isn't easy to explain, but here goes. Old age (of which I'm a fairly youthful exemplar) is as Schopenhauer and others have told us the time of self-acceptance. We've become who we are going to be and that's pretty much that. The writer in old age doesn't need to get up on stilts. He's tried that before. He's tried to write what the superego demands. (The death of most academic writers.) Or he's tried to write in the voice of the superego. (That's the death of his reader.) In old age, he is no longer aspiring upward. He can write as himself.

Himself? Who might that be? The most optimistic lines I know of about identity in old age come from Confucius. It goes this way: at fifteen I set my heart on learning; at thirty I stood firm; at forty I had no more doubts; at fifty I knew the will of heaven; at sixty my ear was obedient; at seventy I could follow my heart's desire, without overstepping the boundaries of what was right.

Confucius is Confucius—one of the sages of all time. But the point for all of us is that in old age he became himself. He no longer had to strive and strain. His deeds and his sayings as they came at the moment and off the cuff were his own and they were, all things taken into account, quite good.

What the old writer writes, when his faculties are still intact, is himself. He's not pushing it too hard. He's not trying to grab the fruit at the top of the tree, which may not be ripe at all—or if ripe, not terribly tasty. He's happy with what falls into his lap. He doesn't revise all that much, except to correct the technical mistakes his fading eyesight makes inevitable. (More on this in the next chapter.) Keats was surely thinking about writing as a young poet when he made his famous observation about the way poetry ought to come into being: "If Poetry comes not as naturally as the Leaves to a tree it had better not come at all." But such easy coming for poetry is a sign of self-acceptance—something the old writer is more likely to possess than the young. He's already had his shot at matching Tolstoy, if that's what he's wanted to do. Didn't work out, in all probability. (Though I persist in thinking that some of the best of current novels have probably never seen the light of print.) And now whatever blooms on the trees of his imagination, he finds himself grateful for, grateful and glad.

Shuffleboard, whist, bridge, hollering at editorials in the *New York Times*—all these pursuits have a couple things in common. All are penchants of the reasonably upscale elderly; all are dismal. Doing the crossword puzzle is no joy either I'll bet. But if you can write, you can engage in something that is dignified, serious, potentially humorous, and maybe even noble. Looking back and writing about what one knows, or believes one knows, putting one's life into words—this is dignified activity. This is worth your time. Does writing keep you young? Now there were only two real young writers that one can think of offhand—that is writers who have written with *genius* from the position of extreme youth—Keats and Rimbaud. But the rich detachment and absorption that writing demands are qualities of deep and thoughtful middle age. Thus this chapter's slogan. Writing: it keeps you middle-aged.

And perhaps giving the green light to oneself in old age might help one hit one's stride. It's possible that one of the best goals for a writer is to become *identical* to his work. That means he's the same person in life that he is in his writing. He talks like his books—which speak modestly and generously and sometimes even wisely. (The young Susan Sontag expected her idol, Thomas Mann, to talk like a brilliant book. Instead, she said, he talked like a book review.) And when you meet him on the street or the subway he's got some of that good stuff to give you, too. Holden Caulfield talks about wanting to call up the authors of the books he likes and ask them a few questions and make friends. And how many young readers have wanted to call up Salinger and have an intimate chat after finishing *The Catcher in the Rye*? I surely did. But Holden figures that the authors probably put the best of themselves into their books and he'd be disappointed. Maybe he's right. Probably so. At least for the young writers: the man or woman you encounter in their books is a self-projection into a desirable future, a persona. But the old-man writer? Imagine encountering Montaigne. The great old essayist called every spade a spade, and every tool a tool, and talked of the most exalted things in the most available words. He was someone who could talk of simple things in simple and memorable terms and complex things in the simplest and most illuminating terms possible. I'll wager that Montaigne talked the way his books did, even if J. D. Salinger never could have. Montaigne's essays constitute a prolonged memoir; and we might say that a prerequisite for such writing is the self-acceptance that old age can bring.

That would be something—talking like your books and getting away with it. It would take time to achieve that status; you'd need to accept yourself, sure. But the self in question would have to be well worth the acceptance. It'd have to pass muster, survive judgment. The young person becomes himself when he leaves professional school and takes the first job or opens a business or buys his mother's farm. The writer may not fully become himself until old age: the moment when he and his books become one. And that is something worth working (and waiting) for.

Another way to describe the self-acceptance and wholeness that writing in old age can bring is to say that in old age one can sometimes all but stop revising. (It's a scandal, but I believe it.) More of that next.

To Stop Revising

Revision is the god of many writers and the god of all writing programs. And I admit that I have been—and in some measure still am—a congregant in the faith. Revision builds better writing. Revision can not only build character in itself, but it can also provide a template for how character overall is built. (Try it again. And again. And again.) People who achieve a lot usually start with some ability, and then over time develop a tolerance for failure that's not unlike a champ boxer's tolerance for getting hit. (A tolerance for failure is different from an attraction to failure, or an addiction to failure; those proclivities are far from uncommon and tough to kick.) Revision is all about failing, acknowledging the failure, and hitting it again (and again). The devoted revisionist knows that nothing is ever quite right and nothing is ever quite finished. You never really finish anything, Truman Capote said. At a certain point they come and take it away. (Capote was lucky to have a "they" who wanted to take it away and then pay him for it, but that's another story.) Revision is about goat-like toughness, and character and fortitude. It draws on and enhances almost all of the cardinal virtues. Who then can speak a word against revision? Who then, especially having spoken more than a few words on revision's behalf, can gainsay this noble process?

Well, why not? Here we go.

One of the virtues of writing in old age, I'll dare to suggest, is that one can dispense with a good deal of revision. Self-acceptance and experience, the virtues of the old writer, can sometimes make revision superfluous. It is what it is—because we are what we are.

To teach writing, one understands, is to teach revision. Join a writer's circle or an MFA program or an online school that gets you corresponding with a writer (for a fee), and the emphasis will be on writing and then rewriting. Your teacher will boast about how she redrafted a story ten times, or a poem fifty. Your fellow students will be seen slug stepping out of the coffee shop, looking like they're just over the flu. But no flu—it's simply that, as they'll proudly announce, they just completed another draft. Are they done? You ask them with full solicitude. In some writing environments, being "done" is the equivalent of siphoning money from departmental petty cash, then spending it all on a lavish lunch. No one is ever done: they simply come and take it away from you. And if no one comes—which is likely—then are you ever done? Tomorrow the coffee shop sloucher will be at it again: revising, revising, and revising.

Isn't there something a tad Puritanical about it all? Isn't there something a bit masochistic going on when you take revision to the point where you become a member of the holy church of revisionism? You can leave it to Americans to take an activity as potentially joyous as writing and turn it into a soul-slamming job. We don't feel good unless we believe we're earning what we get, earning in triplicate. There's too little belief out there in the god of writing, the god who simply drops one in your lap from time to time, the way the god did for Roethke. And for no other reason than that she feels like it.

When that drop occurs (if it does), have the character not to sit down and start revising wholesale. Because in writing there is such a thing as grace, such a thing as blind good fortune. You get the right subject, and the right genre, and the right weather (I like fall and spring) on the right day. Maybe you're in love and maybe you're just out of love. Maybe you fasted and prayed and maybe you ate and drank and made as merry as your belly and heart would allow. But now you have it, and this time, aside from adjusting some spelling and checking a fact or two (Bucephalus or Bellerophon: which is which, really?), you're golden. There are times when vision does not require revision; ask the visionary saints and they'll tell you.

And sometimes the best thing to do with a piece that isn't working is not to bring it into the factory of revision, turn on the assembly line, get on your goggles, bring out your welding tool, and start sweating. No, sometimes the best thing to do when you've laid a bad egg is simply to walk away from the nest. Get gone. Throw the darned thing out and start something new. You can advance by leaping from endeavor to endeavor, as well as by trying to repair the broken-down model that's on blocks in the driveway. As Ralph Waldo Emerson, the sage of Concord, tells us: "Power ceases in the instant of repose; it resides in the moment of transition from a past to a new state, in the shooting of the gulf, in the darting to an aim . . . The soul becomes."

War wasn't the right theme for you; iambic pentameter isn't your music; you sound too much like T. S. Eliot for this to be yours. So run away. Be like that follower of Jesus in the Gospels who is with the Savior in Gethsemane. When a Roman soldier grabs him by the cloak, aiming to arrest him probably, the young man takes off. He slips his way out of his cloak and runs naked into the dark. So try it. Run naked into the dark and soon you may see some light.

We all know about the Indians' ceremony, much observed all through these states, of potlatch. At a certain point every year the tribe got together and burned everything its members did not need and many items they thought they did. They burned lodges and they burned clothing and they burned saddles and they burned their weapons. They wanted a new start and they knew that you cannot make a new start in old circumstances.

If the tribes could nobly burn their all, then surely some of us can afford to burn a manuscript, especially one that has been giving us nothing but misery. Print it up, take it outside, light a fire, and feed the flames. And by the fire's light it'll be very surprising if you don't conceive of something new, or at least hear a fertile whisper or two around your ear from the crackle of the flames.

When the fires were over, the Indians had a great feast (I commend this part passionately) then set to making their lives again, better than before. The computer has many advantages, but it's not as easy as it should be to jettison a textual weight once and for all and *start again*. The text simply looks too good—too clean, too polished, too publishable. In fact it looks to be almost already published. Still, sometimes one must cut it loose.

People stay in rotten marriages; they maintain rotten jobs; they live in crap neighborhoods. And sometimes this is out of grim grinding necessity. But no one needs to make the killing interest payments on a so-so piece of work that will never get really much better than it is. Declare bankruptcy in the court of yourself; tell the judge to cram it and hit the street.

I think the current love of revision has much to do with that grand MFA and now undergrad institution, the writing workshop. There's much to be said for the MFA in fiction, not least that it gives writers a home, some bread and milk and maybe a little wine, and keeps them from having to work ten hours per in the bowels of the dry cleaner's. (Whenever I enter a dry cleaner's and look in the back and hear the thrum and smell the chemicals and feel the steam, I say a prayer of thanksgiving.) But the MFA has its downside, too.

There must be something called workshops. To these workshops you bring your story or poem, as if it were a busted-up automobile, and the senior mechanic and the mechanics in training surround your ride and while you obey an enforced silence tell you what must be done to repair it. (Truly, you are not allowed to talk as they analyze your vehicle. This is something I could abide for ten seconds or until the first truly flat-brained comment, whichever came first.) Then you go off and commence repairs. Occasionally I'm sure your colleagues will tell you, though not in so many words, to take your vehicle to Moe's Scrap and Salvage. But mostly it's all about repairs, which is to say revisions.

No religion of revision, no MFA programs: I think that's pretty much the truth. No MFA programs, nowhere for experienced writers to go and make decent coin and no place for young writers to hole up and work. I'm all for the hideout for the kids and the decent coin for gramps. But at a certain point, our cover stories risk becoming our stories and we get serious about our deceptions.

There's much to be said on the side of revision. And earlier in this book I hope I've said some of it. But there are limits to the religion of *once more unto the breach*, and for all writers—beginners and pros—they are worth keeping in mind.

But so far in doubting revision, I've employed what the sage calls "a poor external way of speaking." There's something truer and maybe more profound to be said about putting the revision religion aside in the late game.

Isn't there a sense in which all revision is lying? That's putting it hyperbolically, but maybe revealingly, too. Shouldn't the writer be able to present himself as he is, rather than as he can make himself appear to be after endless sand-and-buff sessions? Whitman says—and he's said it plenty in this book—that "This is no book. Who touches this, touches a man." He means himself of course, and it was true for that first volume. It simply poured forth: life and all it means (here in these states) according to "Walt Whitman, an American" as he calls himself partway through the poem. There is no author's name on the title page of the 1855 edition of *Leaves of Grass*, just a picture of Walt in open shirt and slouch hat, "one of the roughs," as he likes to call himself.

In certain forms of writing, I want the writer coming at me direct and unprocessed. Reading some overedited books is like listening to studio jazz albums—too highly produced, too short, too unwilling to let the tattered flag of the self fly. (Whitman calls the grass "the flag of my disposition, out of hopeful green stuff woven.") I like writers who show you the holes in their elbows and knees, and who ramble and even rant a little sometimes. I like Montaigne in his essays and Emerson in his journals and strange spontaneous-seeming books like Ann Marlowe's *How to Stop Time*. Critics are accused of breaking butterflies on the wheel. Too many writers break their own butterflies. They try to hit the street with a factory shine. They smell too much of new-car interior, for me. Whitman of course liked to talk about a part of himself he called the "real Me": the part that stands both in and out of the game, "compassionating, idle, unitary." And he gives us that part and its perceptions as immediately and crudely and sweetly as he can. Later on Whitman went to work trying to write Walt Whitman poems and he seems to have revised them until they could all be dropped into glass bottles full of formaldehyde. Against revision? I'm at least against the sheen that comes from the *appearance* of too much revision and that appearance is everywhere. Turn a page or two in the *New Yorker* if you don't believe me.

But there's something deeper at stake here. I think the evolution of a writer into his final phase can be an evolution beyond revision. That is to say he has become identical with his voice and writing sensibility. He doesn't have to strain; he doesn't have to struggle. What comes out when he sits down on a pretty good writing day is his and that's that. Tinker as he will, it won't get much better and maybe it will get worse.

All his life, he's been trying to find a way of speaking and writing that fits with his sense of the world. For a while that involved a lot of tinkering and messing and fooling around. He had to stand on tiptoe to sound the way he wanted to; he had to find a soapbox and get up high. But late in the game he can echo both Popeye and Ralph Ellison's Invisible Man (and a larger creative force that doesn't need to be named): I am what I am. This is the moment of quiet and assured self-acceptance, the moment when striving stops, the self is unified, and no longer lives as much in becoming as it does in simply being. The palm at the end of the mind, as Wallace Stevens calls it, has been reached, and there is nowhere further to go—which is both a sorrow and a blessing. You've done your work; you've figured it out. You've become yourself, as Nietzsche liked to say. But you're also the old man or woman sitting on the dump. "One sits and beats an old tin can, lard pail. One beats and beats for that which one believes." Everything you say and write is your own, and yourself and you are at home in your mind—and that's a fine thing. But the next change is the last one.

To Remember

Faulkner famously said that "memory believes before knowing remembers." Though no one is terribly certain what he meant. What Faulkner *may* mean is that there is a deeply sunk layer of memories we are connected to and committed to, and that exist on a level beyond conscious knowledge. We don't *know* the past; we feel it in our bones and blood, and we live it out day to day. (Especially, no doubt, if we live in the South.) We all have pasts, both personal and collective, and writing is one of the best ways to recover them. Whether what we recover bears much direct resemblance to any kind of objective truth (assuming one exists)—well that, as Faulkner suggests, is an open question. On a level too deep for ready questioning, memory is disposed to believe.

Is there a value in remembering the past, putting it in some kind of order, maybe turning the events of our lives into a story—or maybe finding the story that is latent in those events? I think there is and especially so for the writer in old age. Is there a genre more fitting to late life than the memoir? The material is all there before you. You probably have the time. Why not let it rip?

There are obstacles, of course. And perhaps they are more intense for the old writer than for the young. Will anyone care about my book? That is a way of asking: Will anyone care about my life? Will anyone, does anyone, care about me? The ultimate form of getting someone else to care, according to many, is getting one's book published. And the fear of failing at publication may be at the root of failing to write the book of one's life. I'd like to zap that fear away, for the young, but for the old in particular. Writing is not about publication, though publication *can* be a splendid event. Writing is about writing. Some of the richest writing is about the life and times of the writer. And unless you are a superb and rather long-winded talker, with an audience of patient, loving listeners, then writing is the only way to set out the story of your life.

I applaud the memoir genre. I like it that individuals sit down and try, usually in something like the way Aristotle commends, to see their lives as having a beginning and a middle and at least a provisional end (the end supplied by the moment of composition). Many of the narratives handed down to us through culture and history don't really work anymore. Many people can't attach their lives to a religiously based story about salvation, or a patriotically based story about their place in the drama of the nation. They may take some sense of identity from their families, but it doesn't prove to be enough to give them what all of us, I believe, crave: a sense that our lives have meant something and continue to.

We want to believe that our lives have a shape and that they add up to more than what our bank accounts and tax returns and school degrees testify. We want to feel that we progressed toward a goal or goals. We tussled with this dragon or that; we overcame obstacles; we pulled matters into place. And then, from a resting spot, however temporary, we can pause and look down at the progress of our lives and feel a sense of unity and order. What better time to do this than in old age?

Some literary critics will tell you such order is always imposed, and that it has been fabricated and falsified. Really all there is to any life is a string of chance events. We don't make our own histories; history makes us, or race does, or biology, or social class. But more than likely it's all a matter of chance, a spin of the wheel. And we don't know what's going on. We never see the wheel; most of us don't even know we're in a casino.

But I see it differently. Those qualities of plot that Aristotle valued so much have been around for a long time. Stories that matter have protagonists: The protagonist has a task or tasks to do. He enters into combat, enters into strife. He finds he doesn't know what he thought he did about the world or himself. But then in the long run, he emerges, knowing more than when he started and feeling the pleasures and the sorrows of his experience. There's no way to prove it, but it seems to me that conventional ideas about plot reveal important truths about life. We do struggle and strive, we do exert our wills, we do desire to make ourselves better women and men. But *how* we wish to do this—through getting money or status or getting very high and staying that way—can often be flawed.

The premise of what we call the life story or the memoir is that we are creatures who seek to learn. We want to educate ourselves in the ways of life and we believe that we often do. We screw up, granted. We make messes and then compound them. But humans are united (just about) in their wish to learn from the messes they have made and to improve. We all want to attend the school that is the world, and in deciding if we pass or fail its manifold tests, we finally want recourse to only one schoolmaster, and that is ourselves.

Poetry, John Stuart Mill said, is not heard but overheard. And memoirs, the genre of our moment I think, are usually overheard: it is not a man speaking to men, but a guy talking to himself that makes a memoir. The reader of the memoir is often a bit of an eavesdropper, and not every conversation one hears from beneath the eaves is an edifying one. I often find that certain memoirs don't matter enormously to *me*. I have different dragons to fight and the author can't make his bestiary into anything close to a universal one. But I love the *idea* of memoirs.

Everyone should write one, or everyone who has even a tinge of an appetite for it should. Anybody who is drawn to writing and is in search of a subject could probably not find a better one than himself or herself. Writing personally teaches many virtues—among them, how to take oneself. You can't sound like a monarch, but you can't sound like a clown either. You've got to develop a degree of irony about yourself that fits the narrative you're unfolding. How much skepticism is due your younger self with her dreams and plans? Or maybe it's the older self more prone to concession that needs to be treated with a slightly harsher tone than the young aspirant. You have to figure out your life, or a significant portion of it. You have to look back and see who really mattered to you and how. You have to see what incidents shaped your trajectory. In short, you have to brood on what you've become and how. You need to take a few steps toward knowing yourself. And then—well, you have a pretty good base for figuring out what you might try to do for the rest of your life. Or maybe you see that the past has been all about fate and chance anyhow and you relapse into a kind of opiated ease in regard to future plans. Don't bother chasing your destiny the Bedouin saying goes; your destiny is always in pursuit of you.

One of the best things about memoirs is that they are not autobiographies. Most autobiographies are written in stone—chipped away with care and precision, concerned about how posterity will feel and what the neighbors will think. They are self-justifying, posturing affairs that usually read as though they have been translated (badly) from the Latin. An autobiography is an attempt to deliver your own eulogy—in fact, to be completely in charge of all your last rites. It's a posthumous piece of writing. Memoirs come from the middle of the journey. Or often better still they come from the later phase—and they don't set out to get the writer elected to high office. The people who write the best ones *try* to be honest. Oh, they may fudge this or that detail and swell a story beyond its verifiable bounds. But emotionally, they try to get it right. Emotionally, they are usually willing to let it rip.

Hey, the memoirist says, this is how it feels to be alive. It hurts! It's grand, awful, amazing. But mostly: It hurts! Pleasure comes and goes. Pain is a guest that checks in and stays around—and sometimes monopolizes every room in the house. Autobiographers are topflight politicians and scientists and Nobel Prize winners (and near-miss runners-up who're still pissed). They are always looking for significance—their significance in particular. Memoirists are Frankie and Mary and Joe and Kashi and Mohammed and LeDonna; they are groping around the way real humans do for some meaning. It's a noble quest, or at least an admirable one, even when it doesn't go all that splendidly line to line.

When people finish their memoirs they rush to the publisher's office, or they try to. Most publishers throw heavy bars across their doors. Everyone wants to publish his book and if he can't, he feels himself a failure. Not true! Bad idea! Are musicians not musicians because they never cop a record deal? Is there something ignoble about the jam session and, as Joni says, "Playing real good for free"? Not a bit. People should be able to write and feel proud without ever being published. Writing is a human right (the pun tells us so) and humans should be able to do it without being judged as failures for not making the professional cut.

In that sweet rock song, Joni looks at the one-man band by the quick lunch joint and she envies him. She says that she plays for fortune and what she calls (with nice irony) "those velvet curtain calls." But the guy on the street sending sweet sounds out of his clarinet is a free man; he plays what he wants. And he doesn't play for cash or to inflate his ego. He gives his music to the world as a gift and he makes it for himself, for the pleasure of it. "Nobody stopped to hear him," Joni says, "though he played so sweet and high." Well, OK, but he made the music and no one was telling him that he had to cut a little off the end and squelch the solo and mute the controversial stuff about death row in Texas or AIDS. No one was listening? Not really. Another real artist—Joni—was. And she was missing the days when she could do what the street corner guy could: play real good, for free.

Not writing your memoir because you won't get it published is like not playing ball in the gym because you won't be going to the NBA. The game is still there; the game is still the game. Why not jump in and have some fun. People think getting a book published is everything. Then they get a book published. And so they think this publication ride was a bumpy one. My editor got fired midproject, my agent got into crack, my publicist got a divorce. Next ride will be better, so they work hard and think only of the glorious day when the book will come into the world. Books aren't babies. For the mother (and father too I hope), the birth is everything. For the writer the gestation is the wonderful part. The putting of the words down on the page and then fussing with them and fussing some more. If you like that sort of thing, there is nothing like it. Asked about what his life as a writer was like, Tobias Wolff reportedly answered: Boring unless you happen to be me. But if you are me (the implication goes)—not half bad, even rather amazing.

There are primary rights in this world that aren't specifically mentioned in the Constitution. You have the right to pray and to make music and to make love without being graded on a skill scale of one to ten. You are also fully licensed to write under exactly the same standard. (Or so say I.)

Writing strengthens memory. One of the most enjoyable aspects of writing a memoir (I confess to three of them, with another in embryo) is the way the mind opens its doors for you if you'll stand outside patiently and offer an occasional soft knock. Screaming "open sesame!" probably won't do it. You have to show up every day with your bowl in your hand and wait. But lo, in time, one door swings open and a corridor appears— the past being as it is a mansion of many apartments. And down the aisle you walk.

Some of what they say about old age and memory appears to me to be true. One suddenly has access to the early years. I can now recall the snowsuit I wore when I went out to play when I was four. (I was wearing it when I pancaked down on my face and could not get up.) I recall the shape of the driveway at 68 Main Street and I can see that policeman walking reluctantly up to tell me that my dog, with the unremitting seal bark, has got to go. These recollections have not been available to me for fifty years and more. Now at sixty, here they are. But don't ask me, please, where I put the title deed to the old Volvo two weeks ago.

Life can feel thin day to day. We do our duty, we complete our errands, we repeat our repetitions. We feel sometimes as though we spend all our time skating on surfaces and that we do not truly live. (As the poet Matthew Dickman says, "I made my plans. / I never arrived. I ate my food. I drank my wine.") People use journals to solve this difficulty. They make every day a word-worthy occasion. They delve keenly into what is before them and they find the meaning they can in buying baby formula, shopping for groceries, reading a snatch of a story, catching an installment of *Game of Thrones* on TV. Here in everyday life the journal writer gets at what Wallace Stevens called "the plain sense of things."

The memoirist adds density to his life through recollection. The repetition compulsion that is daily life gives way to a complexly layered sense of being. Freud compared the psyche to the ancient city of Rome, in which building was built upon building: there's the Forum and the Palatine Hill, under which the ruins of a mud-hut village are there to be detected by the close observer. So it is with the self. The person we are sits atop different phases of identity, different layers of being: all of them shape each other and the first layer is shaped by the simple contours of the land from which it rises. To begin to excavate those layers is to begin to touch the mysteries of living in the world and to make our lives as miraculous to us as they deserve to be. The memoirist restores wonder to the day to day through the patient and supplicant art that is memory. For the old writer there are more layers, more revelation, more gold.

The mind strengthens itself though writing. The more we use our memory the stronger the muscle becomes. We think better than we did, for in certain ways thought is memory and memory is thought. When the seminar was puzzled by a line of Wallace Stevens or Hart Crane (so difficult he must at times have been a puzzle to himself), a teacher of mine asked us a question: "What instance in literature or in life does this remind you of?" That question, simple as it is, always had the virtue of getting the group unstuck and moving. Memory creates analogies that enable us to see what is in front of us. Yes, I've been here before give or take and (give or take) I know what to do.

Frost said, with a certain measure of exasperation, that he could do with a bit more praise from critics. They needed to understand that writing could involve feats that ought to fill them with admiration. They should see, said Frost, what a feat it was to be reminded of this by that, what a feat it was to think of the perfect metaphor at exactly the right time. And it *is* a feat too, to be thinking about climbing a birch tree all the way to the top, being careful not to lean forward too hard and send the slender birch groundward before you reach the top and to be reminded of filling a glass with liquid to the very top and then (you know what this looks like) over the top, but without spilling a bit. The metaphor—and what is metaphor but being reminded of one thing by another?—occurs in "Birches" and it is, genuinely, a feat of memory and imagination.

Thought relies on memory; if you cannot remember you cannot think in any but the most rudimentary way. Writing brings memory to bear and enhances its powers. Writing is the great school of the mind, from the writer's Day One to old age and to the end of her life: there is no better one.

To Get Better as You Get Older

"That is no country for old men." That's William Butler Yeats looking back at the world of nature, appetite, and generation as he sails away from it. He loved that world. Yeats was a vitalist and a romantic and thought for a while that his best inspirations came from erotic love, even when (and maybe especially when) that love failed consummation. He seems to have proposed to the woman he thought to be his soul mate, Maud Gonne, at least three times, and when she said no for the third, he proposed to her sister. (Their last name is pronounced Gun. Yeats should probably have taken heed.) Still, Yeats loved being in love and thought that some of his best work came from the flowering that takes place when one is smitten with a beloved.

In "Sailing to Byzantium," the poem with the line about the country that's not for old men, Yeats is both rhapsodic and exasperated about "the young in one another's arms" that he sees all around him. They call up comparison to "the salmon-falls" and "the mackerel-crowded seas": those lovers are vital, passionate, but they are not quite human either. They've become animals, though glorious animals to be sure. Anyway, Yeats is no longer one of them. (At least for the space of this poem.) He's banished, or self-banished from their world. I find myself chanting the opening lines of "Sailing to Byzantium" to myself on the opening days of classes in the fall. The weather's warm, the young are in one another's arms (more or less) on the steps of Old Cabell Hall, the breeze is blowing. Everyone is eighteen or nineteen or twenty. The kids are wearing not too much. They're lying back—some smoking, some vaping. They are laughing even when their lips are set. This is no country for old men, or for old women, either.

That's true *overall*, of course. It's true in America; it's true in most of the West. This is not a country for old men. Youth is everything and everything that matters is young. We cherish the new, the novel, the latest, the fresh. We avoid what is fading and faded.

People peak early in our culture. The paradigmatic career is the pro athlete's or the pop star's. They flash like comets across the sky, flare madly, burn bright, and then slide downward losing light as they go, until finally they douse themselves in the brine. A few hang on, embarrassing themselves and us with their sagging bellies and plastic reconstructed smiles. They are there to remind us what happens to all things bright and beautiful and new. The former-jock-now-commentator lassoed into his uncomfortable tie, the old rocker in kicky new boots recall to us the glories of youth and the sorrows of age. Getting old is something that one ought to apologize for.

And often the old do. Oh, not in so many words, but they slink and scrape and bend and try their best to admire the latest and praise the new. They're sorry for having lived so long; they feel they're in the way. If only the young would indulge them a bit, let them live on with their remaining teeth and pleasures, gratitude would abound. This is no country for old men, or for old women, either. This is the country of the gleaming, chirping, tweeting, twerking new.

But to this rule, there is one exception. Not always, but most of the time it is true. Writers, real writers, often get better as they age. And even if their work declines a little, they can stay strong, keep producing, and keep doing what they love. They aren't like dust-binned CEOs or sidearm pitchers who have or haven't had Tommy Johns, or wrinkled race-car drivers, or admen whose careers have been added up by their superiors and found to be a few digits short. No: writers stay in the game until nearly the end, and it is not uncommon for their work to get better as time passes. Writers come in as tyros—skinny batters, easy to fool. Their gloves are bigger than they are. But while others decline from about their thirtieth birthday, the writer keeps growing stronger. He leaves the game more potent than he went in. Put it in physical terms—because, remember, the mind is a muscle. The writer starts with a stripling's physique. She works and works. She labors on and on. And in early old age, though her physical body may be declining, the body of her imagination is muscular and lithe. She's gotten better, often a lot, as she's gotten older.

"That is no country for old men," Yeats says. And he turns away from "whatever is begotten, born, and dies" and heads out—he's in a sailing ship, the sailing ship of his imagination—for something else. Which is what? What is the alternative to the life of the burbling new that surrounds him (and every writer in or nearing old age)? Before the opening stanza is over, Yeats offers some outright defiance to the culture of the new: "Caught in that sensual music," he says, "all neglect monuments of unageing intellect."

Sensual music—the music of desire is a form of enchantment to Yeats. It casts a spell upon the dancers and it is a lovely spell and it is lovely music, but the music is so strong that one cannot stop dancing. Try it and see. When you're young, you are always in thrall to desire. You perpetually want something. Most likely it is love (and sex). But all desires may in time become modeled on the desire for love and sex. All desires become similarly fierce, similarly fervid. You want and want and want and when you tire of wanting, you find that the sensual music is not only beautiful but also enslaving. You cannot stop desiring and acting, sometimes foolishly, on that desire. You cannot stop dancing.

Sensual music—it's so potent that you can dance to it throughout your whole life. When you are very young, you'll dance wildly. You'll be giddy, inspired, but also sometimes out of control. And when you're old, you'll keep dancing, especially if, as it is in the West now, the music plays as loudly as it does and is as alluring and well orchestrated as it is. You'll keep dancing even though you're out of step and you can hardly move your feet and you know you look silly and you are humiliating both yourself and the spirit of old age. But you cannot stop dancing. (I want an iPhone, I need a computer, give me some cash, I want, I want.)

A poet I greatly admire, Jack Gilbert, wrote a volume of poems in old age called *The Dance Most of All*. And Gilbert's evocation of the dance would be well understood by Yeats. I'm not going to give it up, Gilbert all but says. Even when I'm old I'm going to keep dancing, keep falling in love, keep being struck with awe, keep moving to the sensual music. He's going to be like old, old Tiresias in *The Bacchae*, who when Lord Bacchus comes to town gets out and grabs the thyrsus, sacred to Dionysus, and shuffles his feet to the tambourines and gongs and bells. Gilbert and the ancient seer go in full well knowing what they are getting into. All honor to them. They'll go out as they came in, to the beat and the melody—to sensual music. But for the old man, and the old writer in particular, there are other possibilities: "Caught in that sensual music all neglect, *monuments of unageing intellect.*"

Unaging intellect. There are forms in this world that pass away and there are some, a few, that actually last. Yeats wants to leave the sphere of passing things and to dwell if he can in the eternal. He wants to give up on love and love's music and see if he can find truths that will abide. Are there such truths? Plato told us there are and Yeats could often believe there were, too. In Byzantium, Yeats hopes to make contact with art that will last and maybe to create some, too.

There may not be eternal art; there may or may not be eternal truth. But Yeats feels that though he's lost some valuable pursuits to old age, other possibilities have opened up for him. He's not stuck in time and the concerns of the moment, so maybe he's in a position to create something that will outlast him and will outlast time. He's optimistic, in other words, about writing in old age.

Most people see old age as sheer loss. Yeats admits that age is loss, but he affirms that there's plenty of gain to be had, too. For the first time in your life, you're pulled away from desire, and that hurts. It's humiliating to be old. You feel the grief of missed pleasures. But old age is also a time when, freed from desire, you can create writings you could not create before.

You need to prepare for this moment. You almost certainly need to do some writing when you are young and make the way ready. But if you've developed a discipline, if you've learned to read and think as a writer, if you've stayed with it despite the vagaries of publication and reviewers and editors and the people in your family and out of it who think you are wasting your time, then old age need not be a time of grief and sorrow. You're at least partially freed from that "raging madman" that Plato's Sophocles says held him in bondage through the first portion of life: his desires. And you have time to consort with longer-lasting matters. You have, in other words, something new to write about.

And that is exactly what Yeats—among the greatest of artists in old age—did. In his late seventies and early eighties, Yeats wrote his best poems. In them, he wrestled with what old age took away and what it opened up; he developed new perspectives on politics and culture and money and class and tradition, and of course on love. He felt he was seeing the world afresh. He did not repudiate his past adherence to love, not entirely. He sailed to Byzantium and embraced the monuments of unaging intellect. But sometimes he wished himself away from that place, too. One of his last poems has him foreswearing politics and worldly affairs and pining to collapse in the arms of a beautiful girl who is (ostensibly) much too young for him.

Old age is rich for the writer. It has its singular subjects and it has its particular freedoms. The aged writer can get better as he gets older not only because he knows more and has seen more, but also because a new state of being, the state of being potentially beyond desire, opens up and beckons him. And from that state he can see and feel much that is new and surprising.

Our culture is pitched to youth, and this is almost inevitable. But the old writer has much to tell the young about a life lived beyond the bounds of wanting. He can show them a world that is free from obsessive chasing and grasping, from getting and spending. And he can offer them the chance to take a breath, calm down, and to live there for a while.

Yeats knows what an old man looks like from the vantage of the young. "An aged man is but a paltry thing," he says. He's but "a tattered coat upon a stick." Surely it feels that way sometimes; surely the girl passing you on the street, fresh from the dress shop, can look at you and see nothing at all. One can become invisible. An old man is "but a paltry thing," a "tattered coat upon a stick"—no face, no body.

But not all the time, no. The old man who is a writer lives not only in the world of what is begotten, born, and dies, but in another world, too. And given the chance, he'll let you hear about it. For sometimes a soul can "clap its hands and sing and louder sing." Then the new world, which is the eternal world (maybe), opens up and we live beyond time. Seeing the world with full detachment, but not without humanity: this it seems to me is what a certain sort of wisdom entails. The country of wisdom: that is a country for old men and old women—and also for the young, whom we invite, most humbly and cordially, to join us there from time to time.

To Draw a Constellation

To the ancient Romans there were three ways of living on in the world once your physical life had ended. The first was the most obvious and immediate. You could attain immortality by doing great deeds. Caesar's conquest of Gaul and his ascension to absolute power in Rome were such deeds. And as Plutarch tells us, Roman history is riddled with spectacular achievements. Or you could speak words that would last forever. Cicero did that and so in his way did Tacitus. The last way to live for all time, at least as the Romans saw it, was to have children. They could carry your name down through the ages. To the Romans this was the least noble way to keep living after death. But it was also the most tenable and the most reliable, too.

Most of us will not write or speak words that will live forever. In old age we come to see this, if we have not seen it already. Our books and essays, our poems and plays will not find the eternal. With every passing century more splendid writing gets winnowed away from what is read from the past. We want to read what was written last week, or at the most last year, and there may be good reasons for this. But that means less time for the old books. No matter how good what we write today might be, it will almost surely sink into "the dark backward and abysm of time," to quote Shakespeare—that writer whose works almost surely never will so long as humans (or technologically enhanced or atomically mutated beings that resemble them) traverse the crust of the planet.

But our writings—great or small, published or locked down in the hard drive—can still serve us when we consider ultimate things. Our writings are our spiritual children we might say—offspring of the spirit— no matter if they be (as biological children sometimes are) stunted and strange in this way or that, or perfect only to ourselves and that not for as long as we would wish, for parental narcissism has its ways of being shattered. No, our writings carve our tombstones; they are our elegies. Or, maybe a better analogy (and surely a more optimistic one): our writings create constellations. They are the way we look back (or look up) and see that we have had a life.

A first book, as the writer Michael Pollan says, is a dot shining (however brightly or not) out there in space. But when you write a second book (or string out another essay, or compose a consequential poem), something happens. You have established the basis for a line. A segment connects one point to the next, and now everything is different. There is that which is above the line and that which is below. There is the slant of the line and there is the distance between the two points—a distance composed of how far the points are from each other and how direct the movement is from one to the other.

Now you have a writer's identity. Now you have a sort of biography. A dot is a dot. But a line—or a segment—suggests a being over time. This is where I started. This is where I went. Now, where do I go from here?

Suddenly, you are writing your life story. All at once, you are composing a biography. You are charting the course of your mind and spirit over time. No one is likely to sit down after I am gone and make the connection between my second book (on literary theory—hard-core academic) and my third, on the Gothic (written con brio with lots of reference to the here and now and only a little to the then). But *I* can make that connection. For me, it was about branching out—a move into a kind of language and thinking I hoped would be interesting to profs and nonprofs, to the clerisy and the laity, to use Coleridge's trope. I wanted to handle the now; I wanted to bring literary history to bear on the present, visual as well as literary. *Nightmare on Main Street* is a book about movies as well as a book about books. I wanted to spread my wings, such as they were, and look down on spooky Gotham.

But I think I'm right to believe that writing over a lifetime creates something of an intellectual/spiritual biography. You start one place, with your first published work or at least the first work of yours that gives you pleasure and satisfaction. Then you begin to move. You go from point to point, dot to dot. And partway through, your points—which may glow with starlight, if only to you—begin to form a *constellation*, though a constellation of a private sort, most probably.

But you're not done yet. There are more stars to place, a larger outline you still might draw.

Some writers put their stars so close together that no significant shape can emerge. And some put them so far apart that it's almost impossible to see from one to the other. The first writers tend to be very cautious: they're poets, sometimes, who have scored a hit with one volume and then want to do it again and again. The second type, the ones who want to expand so far into the void that their last effort is left eons behind, are sometimes the pros, the writers for money.

That some writers write the same novel (story, poem, play) over and over again is no secret. If it worked once, it may work again and it probably will. These are the cautious ones, the ones who are tied to a simple vision of themselves and what they can do. It's usually a matter of confidence. They never imagined they could have success of any kind. They were most unsure of themselves. They worked hard and they worked hard and then—voilà: there came something well worth saving and maybe worth showing to the world. And all were pleased and some were well pleased. So what to do from here? Repeat, reiterate: say it again. If Elmore Leonard ever wrote more than the one novel a hundred times over, I have not seen much evidence. Though sometimes the guys wear fedoras and sometimes they wear cowboy hats. (I love Elmore Leonard. I truly do—but still.) Something similar goes for my kindly and generous near neighbor, John Grisham. If you like one, you'll like them all because as Shakespeare's characters like to say, "All is one." If you write the same work over and over again and it succeeds, your spiritual autobiography is likely to be written in bank statements. Or as Bellow's protagonist says of a certain greedy-got character: she's writing her memoirs without a typewriter: she's using an adding machine.

Then there are writers whose books are so much unlike each other as to defy belief: one on insects, one on chamber music, one on the career of General Sherman. (I exaggerate, but you get the idea.) This is the career of a hobbyist who is ever acquiring a new hobby and dropping the old. His autobiographical dots can hardly be seen one from the other. They are points on a map that leads nowhere. The books may be good; they may be not so good. (I bet on the latter.) But they don't really add up to a story about who the author was and why it might matter to him and to the people who know and (authors do inspire some of this; I'm sure they do) love them.

Some people keep track of their lives with their photographs and their home movies—and that's fine. But that's a record of the outer life, not the inner. They know themselves as others saw them, or as they would have liked to be seen. They've got a stack of laminated idealizations, or computer files of CIA length to click and slide through. But there's more to life than the way it looks. There is also how it feels. There's also what you did and how you changed.

Michael Pollan, whose idea of the dot-to-dot progress I've borrowed, started out writing about nature in general and gardens in particular. From there he went to architecture, studying the subject from Vitruvius to the present and building his own writer's studio to boot. Then he went to the erotic lives of plants—and the part that humans play (and are tricked into playing) in those lives. Then he moved on to food. What do we eat? Why is it as bad as it is? How can we make it a little better? This project involved the purchasing of a cow, which the author followed on its journey from the feedlot to you-know-where.

What holds Pollan's work together? Many factors: good prose, a hunger to make contact with readers, modesty, humor, curiosity. But what also holds it together is an unfolding interest in the places where nature and culture intersect: the garden, the dinner table, the roof overhead that shelters the man or woman the way trees once did and maybe will have to again. Pollan is interested in the subtle balance between nature and culture and particularly in getting that balance close to right. It's not right now—and that feeling is what tends to draw Pollan to a subject. (Our diets stink. We live in goofy dwellings.) But Pollan is an optimist, and some of the pleasure of his books comes from believing that the interplay between nature and culture can be adjusted to make us happier and sustain what's best in the world of nature. We can get it right.

Did Pollan know that was what he was going to spend his life doing when, around the age of thirty, he wrote his first consequential article for a magazine, a piece on (of all things) compost? No, he didn't. I can say that with some authority because I was there. Earlier we collaborated on a very non-Pollanian piece about *Time* magazine. We called it "De-mythtifying Time." The *Columbia Journalism Review* published it, almost. There was no grand program on Michael's part, no game plan. He just followed his interests and his nose—talked and listened to people and figured out by a kind of ESP where his interests and the interests of many others overlapped. They too wanted to improve their lives in the immediate world. They too weren't willing to go Thoreau's route and climb almost all the way back into the heart of nature. They wanted a compromise, a dialectic.

Pollan has been arguing with Thoreau ever since he was an undergrad: a longtime love-hate relationship. Part of using your writing to under-stand your past life is seeing who—truly—your influences were and why they mattered to you. Major influences are like family: they are your spir-itual mothers and fathers and just as precious sometimes in that if your parents gave you life, your writing teachers gave you motive for living. If that's too high-flown, you can at least say they gave you something to do. Part of what the writer looking at the endgame can do is construct her or his family tree: the influences, negative and positive and in between. That's another way of telling yourself who you are and who you have been. It's a matter of expressing gratitude—even to the ones that brought you to life through antagonism: negative inspirations. It's a matter of modesty. Though one might like to say with Milton's Satan that one is self-begotten and self-raised by one's own quickening power, it's not true (it wasn't of Satan either) and in the long run it's much less interesting than giving a full genealogy. The real writer doesn't have to hire a genealogist; he's already created his own ancestors. It's only fair and fitting that late in the game the writer draw the map and give credit where it's due.

And me? I recall one day a colleague telling me apropos of nothing much that my work was "all over the place." And that, of course, was more than distressing. There seemed to be something to it, at least on the surface. I had written a book on Freud and literature, one on literary theory, then that wing spreader about the Gothic in books and movies, followed by a memoir about high school, and scattered in between essays about everything else I'd ever been interested in including playing pickup basketball. How could I draw any kind of pattern with those particular dots? At best, I looked like an amateur, a well-heeled dilettante. But pattern? Map to a life—and mine was well more than half done I suppose—that was hard to find. It was as though a child had tossed a handful (a rather large handful, for I was nothing if not productive) of those stick-on stars, gold and red and blue and (I'm afraid at times) black, onto his playroom floor, let them fall where they might. "You're all over the place." Was that really me?

My friend was anything but all over the place. One of his books grew out of the next in a progression both logical and illuminating. He had started with one poet—a great one. And what he had learned meditating on that giant, he took into the field of poetry in general. Now this was someone who knew how to conduct a career—and maybe even a life. For the process of growth that is the unfolding of literary talents and interest is a perfectly fine model for the expansion of a life, and my friend's life had expanded most successfully.

And I? I was all over the place, wasn't I? It seemed I had nothing like Pollan's dialectic of culture and nature to work through in its many forms. And, a professor myself, I possessed nothing like my professor friend's trajectory of intellectual growth. Or so it then seemed to me.

Was there anything that held my work together—or was it just a repeated rattling and tossing of the dice? Did my writing (did I?) have an overall point?

Sometimes the best answers are the most obvious—and also, as in this case, the strangest. I hated school for a long time. Middle school, high school: about seven years of it were for me stretches of desert alternating with pits of muck. I hated it. I hated the teachers and the books they gave us and the way the books talked to us and the way the teachers talked about them. School was prison. I sensed that and when I heard it confirmed one day by the writer Ken Kesey, a real writer, I felt completely justified in my view. School was prison and I had been a seven-year convict.

But later when I looked across the terrain of my writing, one fact came clear. I was always writing, in one way or another, about education. I was writing mostly about individual education. I was interested in, and often moved by, the way an individual takes herself or himself in hand and goes about making changes. We're all given a life by nature; and we're all subjected to the influence of culture. But for some of us—for many I'd guess—the culture we're given by our parents and by our churches and by our towns and by our schools (by our schools, in particular!) isn't good enough. That kind of education doesn't put us in a satisfying relation to life and to others. So we've got to strike out for ourselves.

It's not that we don't have teachers; everyone needs teachers. But ours aren't the usual pedagogues, the ones who stand at the front of the class and bore us into semicomas. Our teachers are the ones we seek out. Sometimes they're attached to institutions, sure; but very often they're not. Our teachers can surprise us. Plato was a teacher for me, and Shakespeare too (though it took years to figure out what I'd learned from them). The game of football was a teacher of mine (and I've written about how) back when I was in my teens. Now the game of basketball, pickup basketball (one of the most democratic and elevating pursuits you can find in America now I think) is a teacher of mine, too. It's very good for someone who stands at the front of a class and can readily be mistaken for an unflappable authority to spend time doing something he loves but is at best so-so at.

I educated myself in my own fashion, freestyle, as Augie March says. But the process of education didn't only involve reading such and such a book or playing a sport or having two children (and so going back to school two more times than I might have liked). It also meant writing about those experiences. Because I don't think education is complete, truly complete, until you have turned your significant experiences into words and seen what the words might reveal to you. And since experience continues, there is always the possibility for further education, as you turn what's happened to you (and what you've made happen) into more sentences.

I wanted to do this for myself—educate myself through and in the medium of words. And I wanted—I'm still answering my friend here, though I'm answering myself, too—to offer the chance to others. A tenet of mine is that if you only take the paths that are unrolled before you, by the authorities, you may well be righteously screwed. There is a yellow brick road for you, I think, but you have to get to work and find it yourself. Most of the public signposts are lies; most of the guides are deceivers. Thoreau is right when he tells us there's not much to learn from most of the old: they've messed up their lives to unendurable degrees and are now seeking the appearance of redemption by posing as guides to others.

Don't I risk posing as that sort of guide? (Horrors compounded.) I risk it I suppose, but really I want to say one thing: Here's what worked, or half worked for me. What's going to do it for you? Something will. Something has to make the lives of usually quiet and occasionally noisy desperation most of us lead a little better than they are. By reading, by traveling, by playing sports, by talking to people, and by listening, you can gather the resources to make a life of your own. (That, in condensed terms, is the answer to the question: Why read?) By taking your experience and making it into words you solidify and define what you've acquired and make it the basis for further growth. And maybe you inspire a few others along the way to do the same for themselves. (That, in condensed terms, is the answer to the question: Why write?) And when you see that life isn't only about the individual (you) but about the group and community and you decide you want to live in a country and world where people aren't being produced like machines in a factory, then you do what you can do to spread the word about the marvelous chances there are to stop listening to the nonsense that's in the papers and on TV and burbling on the Internet and get in contact with the best that's known and thought (and played and sung), then you can contemplate being a teacher, one who teaches by example (flawed and funny, I hope) and not by edict. You think you'd like to stop trying to blow solos and want to be part of a jazz band where everyone can play something fresh and people like playing backup almost as much as they like standing out front and blasting away. (That, in compressed terms, is the answer to the question: Why teach?)

So you write books about education rather than about nature and culture or about the development of poetry. And (look!) your work isn't all over the place. And even if the constellation that the books and essays make doesn't glow with diamond brightness in the writers' night sky, there it is—and maybe it's still waiting to be completed. Maybe it lacks a star or two or three, sharper than the rest, more interesting to contemplate, and for others a modest but sure guide through the territory of their lives.

To Have the Last Word

Let's say, shifting the metaphor away from constellations and to something more duly modest, that the writer's career looks something like a sentence. Every significant work is for him, for her, a word, or a set of words. All good things must come to an end and even the best of sentences must find a period. (Though there are times when reading Proust, say, one might doubt that this is so.) In this case, what is the period but the writer's last word?

To be sure, anyone can write—or speak—his own epitaph. But a writer is likely someone who will ponder those last words. He wants to mold them, shape them, get them just right. He wants a final perfection. I cannot imagine that Goethe's final cry was entirely unconceived until the moment of articulation: More light! And I would be very surprised to find that the words on Yeats's tombstone or Keats's grave were but a moment's thought. "Cast a cold eye on life, on death," it says on Yeats's stone. Then the final leap: "Horseman, pass by." You could spend a profitable enough week pondering that inscription in the light of Yeats's life and work. Keats's will break your heart if you have a heart to break (and know something about his life and early death). "Here lies one whose name was writ in water." Not true, though: ultimately not true, which I suspect is precisely what Keats hoped when he wrote it. He did confess in a letter that he believed he would be "among the English poets." "He is," Matthew Arnold said of him, hyperbolically but generously, "He is with Shakespeare."

Famous last words! Are there any that are better than Oscar Wilde's? He is in disgrace, having served time for (what comes down to) being homosexual. He has lost his money, his reputation, and his position. His name is a synonym for depravity all through England. He's exiled in Paris and he is sick, badly sick. Looking around his shabby chamber he focuses on the cracked and broken crockery on the shelf, always the aesthete, always the connoisseur par excellence, utters the immortal words: "This wallpaper and I are fighting a duel to the death. Either it goes or I do."

Thoreau departs with the words: Moose. Indian. Or perhaps it was: Indian. Moose. Emerson in his grand but equivocal eulogy for Thoreau says that Thoreau loved an encounter with a "good Indian." That is, one who could swap lore with him about where trout could be caught in August and how to set a trap for beaver and where the best huckleberries might be found. Thoreau was a learner all of his life, much like Emerson. But Thoreau came to the end of it having put forward a lean but complete vision of his philosophy in *Walden*—assuming that by philosophy you mean how to live, and live wisely. A moose sighted at the pond would have been a major event to HDT, one to brood on and take pleasure from for many days to come. Moose. Indian. Thoreau was maybe the first real American, and maybe the only one. White as he was, he kept the legacy of nature (moose) and the natives who got here first (Indians) and then extended them to himself and his kind. In *Walden*, maybe the best American book (*Leaves of Grass* is not a book but a vision quest; *Moby-Dick* is a prophetic rapture), Thoreau says he aspires to fuse within himself the hardihood and resourcefulness of the savage with the refinement of the civilized man. It's surprising how much, for instance, Thoreau admired the railroad.

James Joyce ended by asking those he was leaving on earth and maybe too those celestial spirits he would meet in heaven a direct question: Does nobody understand? Surely he was thinking of *Finnegans Wake* and of *Ulysses* and maybe of his own strange nature, simultaneously so earthy and refined. Tolstoy left the world talking about his love for all things living and prophesying the fulfillment of the vision of Jesus. Not long before, he had repudiated almost all of his great works because they traduced the message of the Gospels.

The list of writers' last words goes on and will until it touches infinity and then rolls past it. But the question remains: Why are writers given to final pronouncements? Why do they seem to study and craft and refine their last words? What's the attraction to putting their own period at the end of the sentence that has been their lives and works?

One thinks of a grand pronouncement by Oscar Wilde—my candidate for the most sublime of last wordsmiths. Wilde's line about how either the wallpaper goes or he does is perfect. It condenses his aestheticism, his desperation, his claims to courage, and his capacity to exalt himself by diminishing himself.

Wilde said many other memorable things of course. A favorite of mine is very simple: "Most people," Wilde said, "are other people." Now what exactly does that mean? One can only speculate. But—one might say that most people make themselves over in the image of the crowd. They don't want to be noticed, don't want to be heard. (Unless it is anonymously, online: then look out.) They want to conform. Most people share their values and their virtues and their vices, too, with other people. They are copies of replicas of facsimiles. They pick up their senses of self from school and church and home and the neighborhood and the movies and the Internet and then have done with it. They are echoes of echoes, shadows of shadows. Writers may be these things too in the end, but they do not wish to be. If there's a flaw in the die that stamps them, they will struggle to make a virtue of it. They do not want their identities conferred by others; they will not be beholden to newspapers for who they are. They will write their story lines, and in the end they will write their obituaries, too. The genre of the self-elegy in modern poetry is anything but a depleted one.

Most people are other people. But some refuse the offer to be anything other than they are or aspire to be. They want to appropriate the discourse, as they say in lit theory 101. It matters to them that they make their own record even up to the last possible moment and maybe even beyond. The poet Mark Strand had what he thought a splendid moneymaking idea— but maybe it was more than that. It was an innovation in graveyard design. Headstones would be equipped with what amounted to an archive. And when you put a few dollars into the appropriate slot, or swiped your credit card, or (down the line) let the stone's apparatus read the bar code tattooed on your wrist at birth, you could get an encounter with the deceased. Here comes his favorite song right at you, then a passage from the book he loved best, a dozen or so of the jokes he laughed loudest at, then maybe his own last words, all recorded and sent your way. Maybe in time you could access videos. So much better than cold stone: the deceased could be there at your fingertips, or at the edge of your credit card. The proceeds? Those would go to the family in addition to (or in lieu of) any material legacy available at moment of departure. What is to be said about this idea? Much. But I'll simply observe that only a writer could have had it. If Mark Strand created such a final installation, I'd be there to take it in, credit card in hand.

Change the trope a bit. What is a book but a record of the spirit over a period of time in the writer's life? (What is a good book I mean.) So if you've created a span of books, you've created a span of memorials—call them grave markers if you like—and you can look back over them as the days wind down. But inside each one is not death but life, or all the life you might have been able to muster at the time. That life becomes manifest when the book is opened by someone else down the line. And that life is augmented when your book becomes an inspiration or a goad to another writer—or someone who wishes to be one. Writers can be competitive as Formula One drivers, sure, but beneath that there's a sense of unanimity or hopefulness that flows from one to the other, as through members of a team.

In a sense, Mark Strand's crazy dream is already alive—in that every book that's any good is likely to be full of the writer's best wisdom and even his favorite jokes and the scraps of a song or two. Open one and see. And if the book stays quiet for long years and no one taps on its door, still there is hope. The spirit is open-eyed in there (if the book is a good one) ready to jump out and perform its white magic in the world. Who cannot date a new epoch in his life to the reading of a book? The life that is enshrined in a good book waits there patiently for the right reader or readers to come along and be lifted out of the doldrums and take sail with a fresh wind. The old writer is reborn in the spirit of the new. And that is reincarnation—and immortality on the small scale, or at least as close as most any of us is likely to come.

PART 3: *WHY TEACH?*

Introduction

Midway through the last decade of the twentieth century, American higher education changed. Colleges and universities entered a new phase in which they stopped being intellectually driven and culturally oriented and began to model themselves on businesses. They sought profit; they sought prestige: the more the better. To be sure, there had always been a commercial side to American higher education. But in the mid-nineties, universities began dropping pretenses and putting profit ahead of intellectual and (dare one say it?) spiritual values. This book reports on the change and attempts to combat it.

What does it mean for a university to stop seeing itself as having something like a spiritual mission and begin acting like a commercial venture? Many things: The shift the universities underwent was complex and had multiple dimensions. There were major technological changes, changes in the intellectual climate. As this book unfolds, it will offer a comprehensive picture. But we might begin by saying that at the center of it all was a shift in the role of students. Before 1995 or so, students had about as much say in the shaping of the university as members of a fairly well established religious community have in determining its moral codes and forms of worship. Which is to say, they had almost none. The professors ran the show: What was important to them was what mattered.

But things changed. Starting in 1960, the American birthrate began to decline. In 1974, it hit its lowest point in sixty years. The baby boom was emphatically over. Twenty years later, the kids born in the seventies were ready for college, but there simply weren't enough of them to supply the schools that had so happily expanded to accommodate the baby boom population.

The university of the early nineteen nineties was still geared to the enormous swell of kids born after the Second World War. When that previous population finally made its way through—like a juicy meal passing the length of a boa constrictor—the schools began to see trouble. How were they going to complete the freshman class? How were they going to pay for all the tenured professors and the entrenched deans brought on to educate the prior generation? Colleges can expand readily enough—hire more professors, hire more administrators, build more buildings. But with tenure locking professors in for lifelong employment, how do you get rid of surplus faculty when the market declines? What do you do with the dorms that threaten to stand empty? How do you fill all those potentially vacant seats in Psych 101?

The answer was obvious. The universities were going to have to pursue students much as businesses pursue customers. They were going to have to treat their prospective students as potential buyers. And they were going to have to treat their existing students as customers too, for students can always switch brands: They can always up and transfer. So securing customers and getting them to maintain brand loyalty became the order of the day. "Most colleges don't have admissions offices anymore," a college administrator told me in 1993. "They have marketing departments." Even those schools that had more applicants than places in the first-year class had to market aggressively. They were competing for prestige and position with other schools of their caliber. They were also competing for full-tuition payers. Everyone wanted the kids who weren't going to petition them for a full ride or nag for discounts come tuition time. Ultimately, too, the schools were competing for future money: The best students tend to become successful, and then (with luck) committed donors. "The primary purpose of Yale University," a Yale faculty member said not long ago, "is the production of wealthy alumni to further enrich Yale University."

How did the students respond to being treated like customers? They didn't seem to mind at all. From what one could see, they loved it. They were long accustomed to the consumer role. From the time that

they were toddlers they'd been the targets of ads and ads and more ads. They were used to being addressed in the teasing, whimsical, and ultimately sycophantic advertising mode that the universities now felt compelled to use. The kids apparently adored being fawned on: They'd grown up in front of the television, being treated like monarchs of the marketplace. When the universities followed suit and began to address them with similar deference, the kids ate it up. On came expensive student centers, lavish gyms, gourmet dining, and slews of student service workers, deans and deanlets to cater to the whims of the customers. Universities began to look like retirement spreads for the young.

No surprise that when the kids got to the classroom they demanded a soft ride: They wanted easy grading, lots of pass-fail courses, light homework, more laughs. If the professors didn't oblige, the kids flayed them on the course evaluations. Those evaluations had an impact on tenure, promotion, salary, and prestige. By and large, the professors caved.

In the old days, when the university was a quasi-churchly institution, the professors largely called the shots. (The ecclesiastical style of architecture at Yale and Duke and numberless other schools makes the old religious affiliations clear.) The professors disseminated scientific knowledge that could improve daily life and help us to understand nature. They promulgated literary and philosophic wisdom that initiated young people into the complexities of the adult world.

But in the new university all this changed. Now the professors were the people who gave the grades, period. They needed to be humored at all times and hearkened to occasionally. But anyone who revered them for their wisdom or wanted to emulate them was tacitly understood to be half-cracked. The word *professor* intoned in a certain way began to mean "learned fool."

As the professors' influence receded, the world of consumerism and entertainment enhanced its powers. In the mid-nineties, the kids were socialized into the consumer mentality by their new, two-hundred-station TV sets (and of course by their parents). The first chapter of this book, "Liberal Arts and Lite Entertainment," describes the confrontation between the TV-driven consumer ethos that the kids brought with them from home and the intellectual ethos of the university. At the time, many commentators ascribed the decline in American higher education to the advent of programmatically debunking cultural theory. Freud, Marx, and Derrida were at the root of all evil. If debunking theory did have an effect, it was largely because of how well it rhymed with the attitude of dismissive superiority that TV and commercial culture overall tended to stimulate.

Ten years later, in the middle of the new millennium's first decade, things changed again. Now kids weren't only being shaped by the belch-and-buy spirit of TV, but by the hurry-up consumer ethos of the Internet, which they patrolled with unsleeping vigilance. (We create our tools, Marshall McLuhan famously said, and then our tools create us.) To put it crudely: The students had been sped up. Now they were consuming, watching, enjoying, buying at a hyper-accelerated pace—living in over-drive. What they couldn't do was slow down: slow down to observe and examine, slow down to think. The second chapter, "Dwelling in Possi-bilities," tells how the new computer technology administered an adren-aline shot to the already robust rebellion against real education. Now the consumer worldview was more confident, further insinuated, tougher to budge. What was actually a product of culture—the buy-buy, do-do ethos—was beginning to feel more like a precipitate of human nature. And fighting what people believe to be natural is never an easy thing.

This book tries. It's addressed not to presidents and deans and boards of directors and trustees; it's not addressed to the chair of the faculty senate or to the consortium of student leaders. Most of these people are by now part of the problem. The book is addressed to individual teachers and most of all to students and their parents. It puts a diagnosis on the table and then offers strategies for dealing with it. In these pages I talk about how to get yourself a good education at an American college or university, even when the forces of the school itself are arrayed against you. (The major enemy of education in America now is American educa-tion, university education in particular.) There are astonishing opportu-nities to be had at almost all American colleges, and this book aims to inspire students to seek them out. I also want to offer teachers some resources to fight against the current modes of dull conformity that afflict us.

For education now is not for the individual. It is not geared to help him grow to his potential and let him find out what he truly loves and how he might pursue it. No. Education now is a function of society. This is the theme of the first section of the book, "The Shift." Current schooling, from the primary grades through college, is about tooling people to do what society (as its least imaginative members conceive it) needs done. We are educated to fill roles, not to expand our minds and deepen our hearts. We are tooled to slide into a social machine and function smoothly with a little application from time to time of the right pleasing grease. Education now prepares us for a life of conformity and workplace tedium, in exchange for which we can have our iPhones, our flat screens, our favorite tunes, Facebook, and Twitter. But what we want is real learning— learning that will help us see the world anew and show us that there could be more to our lives than we had thought.

Conservative jeremiads against the university tend to declare that universities are not doing their socializing job comprehensively enough. They want higher education to feed the demands of the American economy overall and of private enterprise in particular. The authors of such tracts are inclined to feel that one idea subversive of the status quo is one too many. In my view, universities are still functioning far too much in the service of conformity. Whether the academic idiom in play is conservative or purportedly radical—traditional or post-post-structuralist—schools now educate the mind and not the heart. The curriculum has become arid and abstract: Preprofessionalism is the order of the day. What Keats memorably called "Soul-making" is absent from current higher education. It needs to be restored.

How do you educate yourself, or, if you're a teacher, how do you try to educate others? The next section of the book is called "Fellow Students," for I think of myself as being a student of my discipline, as all teachers must be. In "Fellow Students," I talk to people who are still in school and trying to get themselves an education despite the odds. I offer plenty of advice: about how to read, about how to deal with professors, about how to struggle against a decadent university culture. I talk about the kind of education you can find in a classroom at its best, which is epitomized for me by what my great teacher Doug Meyers offered. I ask young people to ponder the virtues of failure and to think about what they can gain educationally from sports—and what they can lose. I reflect on what's called global education and I let students know why I think they should all— and I mean all—at least consider becoming English majors.

The final section of the book is called "Fellow Teachers," and it's addressed to my comrades in what can often seem like one of the impossible professions. I encourage people who teach in universities—and especially in humanities departments—to stop thinking of themselves as creators of so-called new knowledge (or "fresh paradigms," as the current jargon has it) and start thinking of themselves as teachers. I'd like them

to imagine themselves as potential liberators, not only of the students in
their classes but of the people outside of school who might attend their
lectures or read what they write. I urge them to stop the professional
posturing and prestige chasing and liberate themselves and others into
the fields of joy and salutary change that the liberal arts at their best
provide. I'd like them to step up and oppose the commercialization of
their universities. I'd like them to think less about their careers and more
about the hopes that brought them to the study of great books to begin
with. I'd like some of them to cut the shit. I'd like all of us to have a little
more fun.

I'd like us to blow a hole through the university's ethos of entertainment and training for success and to bury its wearisome work-hard, play-
hard frat-boy ideology. We should blast away the customer-coddling
deans and student service hacks; blast past academic pretension and the
hunger for "standing in the field." Blast university presidents so afraid of
offending a potential donor that they won't raise a word in behalf of social
justice or political sanity. Blow away the trustees who think that they're
a corporate board of directors and will not rest until their schools
resemble Walmarts. Blast them all. And while you're doing it, have a good
time. Because knowledge is joy. Creativity is ultimate freedom. Real
thought is bliss. *Sapere aude,* as the old thinkers liked to say: Dare to
Know; Dare to Be Wise!

THE SHIFT

Liberal Arts & Lite Entertainment (1997)

Today is evaluation day in my Freud class, and everything has changed. The class meets twice a week, late in the afternoon, and the clientele, about fifty undergraduates, tends to drag in and slump, looking disconsolate and a little lost, waiting for a jump-start. To get the discussion moving, they usually require a joke, an anecdote, an off-the-wall question—When you were a kid, were your Halloween getups ego costumes, id costumes, or superego costumes? That sort of thing. But today, as soon as I flourish the evaluation forms, a buzz rises in the room. Today they write their assessments of the course, their assessments of *me*, and they are without a doubt wide awake. "What is your evaluation of the instructor?" asks question number eight, entreating them to circle a number between 5 (excellent) and 1 (poor, poor). Whatever interpretive subtlety they've acquired during the term is now out the window. Edmundson: 1 to 5, stand and shoot.

And they do. As I retreat through the door—I never stay around for this phase of the ritual—I look over my shoulder and see them toiling away like the devil's auditors. They're pitched into high writing gear, even the ones who struggle to squeeze out their journal entries word by word, stoked on a procedure they have by now supremely mastered. They're playing the informed consumer, letting the provider know where he's come through and where he's not quite up to snuff.

But why am I so distressed, bolting like a refugee out of my own classroom, where I usually hold easy sway? Chances are the evaluations will
be much like what they've been in the past—they'll be just fine. It's likely
that I'll be commended for being "interesting" (and I am commended,
many times over), that I'll be cited for my relaxed and tolerant ways (that
happens, too), that my sense of humor and capacity to connect the arcana
of the subject matter with current culture will come in for some praise
(yup). I've been hassled this term, finishing a manuscript, and so haven't
given their journals the attention I should have, and for that I'm called—
quite civilly, though—to account. Overall, I get off pretty well.

Yet I have to admit that I do not much like the image of myself that
emerges from these forms, the image of knowledgeable, humorous detachment and bland tolerance. I do not like the forms themselves, with their
number ratings, reminiscent of the sheets circulated after the TV pilot has
just played to its sample audience in Burbank. Most of all I dislike the
attitude of calm consumer expertise that pervades the responses. I'm
disturbed by the serene belief that my function—and, more important,
Freud's, or Shakespeare's, or Blake's—is to divert, entertain, and interest.
Observes one respondent, not at all unrepresentative: "Edmundson has
done a fantastic job of presenting this difficult, important & controversial material in an enjoyable and approachable way."

Thanks but no thanks. I don't teach to amuse, to divert, or even, for
that matter, to be merely interesting. When someone says she "enjoyed"
the course—and that word crops up again and again in my evaluations—
somewhere at the edge of my immediate complacency I feel encroaching
self-dislike. That is not at all what I had in mind. The off-the-wall questions and the sidebar jokes are meant as lead-ins to stronger stuff—in the
case of the Freud course, to a complexly tragic view of life. But the affa-
bility and the one-liners often seem to be all that land with the students;
their journals and evaluations leave me little doubt.

I want some of them to say that they've been changed by the course. I
want them to measure themselves against what they've read. It's said that
some time ago a Columbia University instructor used to issue a harsh
two-part question. One: What book did you most dislike in the course?
Two: What intellectual or characterological flaws in you does that dislike
point to? The hand that framed those questions was surely heavy. But at
least they compel one to see intellectual work as a confrontation between
two people, student and author, where the stakes matter. Those Columbia

students were being asked to relate the quality of an *encounter*, not rate the action as though it had unfolded on the big screen.

Why are my students describing the Oedipus complex and the death drive as being interesting and enjoyable to contemplate? And why am I coming across as an urbane, mildly ironic, endlessly affable guide to this intellectual territory, operating without intensity, generous, funny, and loose?

Because that's what works. On evaluation day, I reap the rewards of my partial compliance with the culture of my students and, too, with the culture of the university as it now operates. It's a culture that's gotten little exploration. Current critics tend to think that liberal arts education is in crisis because universities have been invaded by professors with peculiar ideas: deconstruction, Lacanianism, feminism, queer theory. They believe that genius and tradition are out and that PC, multiculturalism, and identity politics are in because of an invasion by tribes of tenured radicals, the late-millennial equivalents of the Visigoth hordes that cracked Rome's walls.

But mulling over my evaluations and then trying to take a hard, extended look at campus life both here at the University of Virginia and around the country eventually led me to some different conclusions. To me, liberal arts education is as ineffective as it is now not chiefly because there are a lot of strange theories in the air. (Used well, those theories *can* be illuminating.) Rather, it's that university culture, like American culture writ large, is, to put it crudely, ever more devoted to consumption and entertainment, to the using and using up of goods and images. For someone growing up in America now, there are few available alternatives to the cool consumer worldview. My students didn't ask for that view, much less create it, but they bring a consumer weltanschauung to school, where it exerts a powerful, and largely unacknowledged, influence. If we want to understand current universities, with their multiple woes, we might try leaving the realms of expert debate and fine ideas and turning to the classrooms and campuses, where a new kind of weather is gathering.

From time to time I bump into a colleague in the corridor and we have what I've come to think of as a Joon Lee fest. Joon Lee is one of the best students I've taught. He's endlessly curious, has read a small library's worth and seen every movie, and knows all about showbiz and entertainment. For a class of mine he wrote an essay using Nietzsche's Apollo and Dionysus to analyze the pop group the Supremes. A trite, cultural-studies bonbon? Not at all. He said striking things about conceptions of race in America and about how they shape our ideas of beauty. When I talk with one of his other teachers, we run on about the general splendors of his work and presence. But what inevitably follows a JL fest is a mournful reprise about the divide that separates him and a few other remarkable students from their contemporaries. It's not that some aren't nearly as bright—in terms of intellectual ability, my students are all that I could ask for. Instead, it's that Joon Lee has decided to follow his interests and let them make him into a singular and rather eccentric man; in his charming way, he doesn't mind being at odds with most anyone.

It's his capacity for enthusiasm that sets Joon apart from what I've come to think of as the reigning generational style. Whether the students are sorority/fraternity types, grunge aficionados, piercer/tattooers, black or white, rich or middle class (alas, I teach almost no students from truly poor backgrounds), they are, nearly across the board, very, very self-contained. On good days they display a light, appealing glow; on bad days, shuffling disgruntlement. But there's little fire, little passion to be found.

This point came home to me a few weeks ago when I was wandering across the university grounds. There, beneath a classically cast portico, were two students, male and female, having a rip-roaring argument. They were incensed, bellowing at each other, headstrong, confident, and wild. It struck me how rarely I see this kind of full-out feeling in students anymore. Strong emotional display is forbidden. When conflicts arise, it's generally understood that one of the parties will say something sarcastically propitiating ("Whatever" often does it) and slouch away.

How did my students reach this peculiar state in which all passion seems to be spent? I think that many of them have imbibed their sense of self from consumer culture in general and from the tube in particular. They're the progeny of a hundred cable channels and videos on demand. TV, Marshall McLuhan famously said, is a cool medium. Those who play best on it are low-key and nonassertive; they blend in. Enthusiasm, a la Joon Lee, quickly looks absurd. The form of character that's most appealing on TV is calmly self-interested though never greedy, attuned to the conventions, and ironic. Judicious timing is preferred to sudden self-assertion. The TV medium is inhospitable to inspiration, improvisation, failures, slipups. All must run perfectly.

Naturally, a cool youth culture is a marketing bonanza for producers of the right products, who do all they can to enlarge that culture and keep it grinding. The Internet, TV, and magazines now teem with what I call persona ads, ads for Nikes and Reeboks and Jeeps and Blazers that don't so much endorse the capacities of the product per se as show you what sort of person you will be once you've acquired it. The Jeep ad that features hip, outdoorsy kids whipping a Frisbee from mountaintop to mountaintop isn't so much about what Jeeps can do as it is about the kind of people who own them. Buy a Jeep and be one with them. The ad is of little consequence in itself, but expand its message exponentially and you have the central thrust of current consumer culture—buy in order to be.

Most of my students seem desperate to blend in, to look right, not to make a spectacle of themselves. (Do I have to tell you that those two students having the argument under the portico turned out to be acting in a role-playing game?) The specter of the uncool creates a subtle tyranny. It's apparently an easy standard to subscribe to, this Letterman-like, Tarantino-inflected cool, but once committed to it, you discover that matters are rather different. You're inhibited from showing emotion, stifled from trying to achieve anything original. You're made to feel that even the slightest departure from the reigning code will get you genially ostracized. This is a culture tensely committed to a laid-back norm.

Am I coming off like something of a crank here? Maybe. Oscar Wilde, who is almost never wrong, suggested that it is perilous to promiscuously contradict people who are much younger than yourself. Point taken. But one of the lessons that consumer hype tries to insinuate is that we must never rebel against the new, never even question it. If it's new—a new need, a new product, a new show, a new style, a new generation—it must be good. So maybe, even at the risk of winning the withered, brown laurels of crankdom, it pays to resist newness worship and cast a colder eye.

Praise for my students? I have some of that too. What my students are, at their best, is decent. They are potent believers in equality. They help out at the soup kitchen and volunteer to tutor poor kids to get a stripe on their résumés, sure. But they also want other people to have a fair shot. And in their commitment to fairness they are discerning; there you see them at their intellectual best. If I were on trial and innocent, I'd want them on the jury.

What they will not generally do, though, is indict the current system. They won't talk, say, about how the exigencies of capitalism lead to a reserve army of the unemployed and nearly inevitable misery. That would be getting too loud, too brash. For the pervading view is the cool consumer perspective, where passion and strong admiration are forbidden. "To stand in awe of nothing, Numicus, is perhaps the one and only thing that can make a man happy and keep him so," says Horace in the *Epistles*, and I fear that his lines ought to hang as a motto over the university gates in this era of high consumer capitalism.

It's easy to mount one's high horse and blame the students for this state of affairs. But they didn't create the present culture of consumption. (It was largely my own generation, that of the sixties, that let the counterculture's search for pleasure devolve into a quest for commodities.) And they weren't the ones responsible, when they were six and seven and eight years old, for unplugging the TV set from time to time or for hauling off and kicking a hole through it. It's my generation of parents who sheltered these students, kept them away from the hard knocks of everyday life, making them cautious and overfragile. It was their parents who demanded that teachers, from grade school on, flatter them endlessly so that kids are shocked if their college profs don't reflexively suck up to them.

Of course, the current generational style isn't simply derived from culture and environment. It's also about dollars. Students worry that taking too many chances with their education will sabotage their future prospects. They're aware of the fact that a drop that looks more and more like one wall of the Grand Canyon separates the top economic tenth from the rest of the population. There's a sentiment currently afoot that if you step aside for a moment to write, to travel, to fall too hard in love, you might lose position permanently. We may be on a conveyor belt, but it's worse down there on the filth-strewn factory floor. So don't sound off, don't blow your chance.

But wait. I teach at the famously conservative University of Virginia. Can I extend my view from Charlottesville to encompass the whole country, a whole generation of college students? I can only say that I hear comparable stories about classroom life from colleagues everywhere in America. When I visit other schools to lecture, I see a similar scene unfolding. There are, of course, terrific students everywhere. And they're all the better for the way they've had to strive against the existing conformity. At some of the small liberal arts colleges, the tradition of strong engagement persists. But overall, the students strike me as being sweet and sad, hovering in a nearly suspended animation.

Too often now the pedagogical challenge is to make a lot from a little. Teaching Wordsworth's "Tintern Abbey," you ask for comments. No one responds. So you call on Stephen. Stephen: "The sound, this poem really flows." You: "Stephen seems interested in the music of the poem. We might extend his comment to ask if the poem's music coheres with its argument. Are they consistent? Or is there an emotional pain submerged here that's contrary to the poem's appealing melody?" All right, it's not usually that bad. But close. One friend describes it as rebound teaching: They proffer a weightless comment, you hit it back for all you're worth, then it comes wafting out again. Occasionally a professor will try to explain away this intellectual timidity by describing the students as perpetrators of post-modern irony, a highly sophisticated mode. Everything's a slick counterfeit, a simulacrum, so by no means should any phenomenon be taken seriously. But the students don't have the urbane, Oscar Wilde–type demeanor that goes with this view. Oscar was cheerful, funny, confident, strange. (Wilde, mortally ill, living in a Paris flophouse: "My wallpaper and I are fighting a duel to the death. One of the other of us has to go.") This generation's style is considerate, easy to please, and a touch depressed.

Granted, you might say, the kids come to school immersed in a consumer mentality—they're good Americans, after all—but then the university and the professors do everything in their power to fight that dreary mindset in the interest of higher ideals, right? So it should be. But let us look at what is actually coming to pass.

Over the past few years, the physical layout of my university has been changing. Our funds go to construction, into new dorms, into renovating the student union. We have a new aquatics center and ever-improving gyms stocked with StairMasters and Nautilus machines. Engraved on the wall in the gleaming aquatics building is a line by our founder, Thomas Jefferson, declaring that everyone ought to get about two hours' exercise a day. Clearly even the author of the Declaration of Independence endorses the turning of his university into a sports-and-fitness emporium.

But such improvements shouldn't be surprising. Universities need to attract the best (that is, the smartest *and* the richest) students in order to survive in an ever more competitive market. Schools want kids whose parents can pay the full freight, not the ones who need scholarships or want to bargain down the tuition costs. If the marketing surveys say that the kids require sports centers, then, trustees willing, they shall have them. In fact, as I began looking around, I came to see that more and more of what's going on in the university is customer driven. The consumer pressures that beset me on evaluation day are only a part of an overall trend.

From the start, the contemporary university's relationship with students has a solicitous, nearly servile tone. As soon as someone enters his junior year in high school, and especially if he's living in a prosperous zip code, the informational material—the advertising—comes flooding in. Pictures, testimonials, videocassettes, and CD-ROMs (some bidden, some not) arrive at the door from colleges across the country, all trying to capture the student and his tuition cash. The freshman-to-be sees photos of well-appointed dorm rooms; of elaborate phys-ed facilities; of fine dining rooms; of expertly kept sports fields; of orchestras and drama troupes; of students working alone (no overbearing grown-ups in range), peering with high seriousness into computers and microscopes; or of students arrayed outdoors in attractive conversational garlands.

Occasionally—but only occasionally, for we usually photograph rather badly; in appearance we tend at best to be styleless—there's a professor teaching a class. (The college catalogues I received, by my request only, in the late sixties were austere affairs full of professors' credentials and course descriptions; it was clear on whose terms the enterprise was going to unfold.) As that perhaps too candid college financial officer told me: Colleges don't have admissions offices anymore, they have marketing departments. Is it surprising that someone who has been approached with photos and tapes, bells and whistles, might come in thinking that the Freud and Shakespeare she had signed up to study were also going to be agreeable treats?

How did we reach this point? In part the answer is a matter of demographics and (surprise) of money. Aided by the GI bill, the college-going population in America dramatically increased after the Second World War. Then came the baby boomers, and to accommodate them, schools continued to grow. Universities expand easily enough, but with tenure locking faculty in for lifetime jobs, and with the general reluctance of administrators to eliminate their own slots, it's not easy for a university to contract. So after the baby boomers had passed through, the colleges turned to energetic promotional strategies to fill the empty chairs. And suddenly college became a buyer's market. What students and their parents wanted had to be taken more and more into account. That usually meant creating more comfortable, less challenging environments, places where almost no one failed, everything was enjoyable, and everyone was nice.

Just as universities must compete with one another for students, so must the individual departments. At a time of rank economic anxiety, the English and history majors have to contend for students against the purportedly more success-insuring branches, such as the sciences and commerce. In 1968, more than 21 percent of all the bachelor's degrees conferred in America were in the humanities; by 1993, that number had fallen to about 13 percent. The humanities now must struggle to attract students, many of whose parents devoutly wish they would study something else.

One of the ways we've tried to stay attractive is by loosening up. We grade more indulgently than our colleagues in science. In English, we don't give many D's, or C's for that matter. (It's possible that the rigors of Chem 101 create almost as many English majors per year as the splendors of Shakespeare.) A professor at Stanford explained grade inflation in the humanities by observing that the undergraduates were getting smarter every year; the higher grades simply recorded how much better they were than their predecessors. Sure.

Along with softening the grades, many humanities departments have relaxed major requirements. There are some good reasons for introducing more choice into curricula and requiring fewer standard courses. But the move, like many others in the university now, jibes with a tendency to serve—and not challenge—the students. Students can also float in and out of classes during the first two weeks of each term without making any commitment. The common name of this time span—shopping period— speaks volumes about the consumer mentality that's in play. Usually, too, the kids can drop courses up until the last month with only an innocuous "W," for "withdraw," on their transcripts. Does a course look too challenging? No problem. Take it pass-fail. A happy consumer is, by definition, one with multiple options, one who can always have what he wants. And since a course is something the students and their parents have bought and paid cash for, why can't they do with it pretty much as they please?

*   *   *

A sure result of the university's widening elective leeway is to give students more power over their teachers. Those who don't like you can simply avoid you. If the clientele dislikes you en masse, you can be left without students, period. My first term teaching I walked into my introduction to poetry course and found it inhabited by two students, one of whom was the gloriously named Bambi Lynn Dean. Bambi and I chatted amiably awhile, but for all that she and the pleasure of her name could offer, I was on the way to meltdown. It was all a mistake, luckily, a problem with the scheduling book. Everyone was waiting for me next door. But in a dozen years of teaching I haven't forgotten that feeling of being ignominiously marooned. For it happens to others, and not always because of scheduling glitches. I've seen older colleagues go through hot embarrassment at not having enough students sign up for their courses: They graded too hard, demanded too much, had beliefs too far out of keeping with the existing disposition. It takes only a few such instances to draw other members of the professoriat into line.

And if what's called tenure reform—which generally just means the abolition of tenure—is broadly enacted, professors will be yet more vulnerable to the whims of their customer-students. Teach what pulls the kids in, or walk. What about entire departments that don't deliver? If the kids say no to Latin and Greek, is it time to dissolve classics? Such questions are being entertained more and more seriously by university administrators.

How does one prosper with the present clientele? Many of the most successful professors are the ones who have "decentered" their classrooms. There's an emphasis on group projects and on computer-generated exchanges among the students. What they seem to want most is to talk to one another. A classroom now is frequently an "environment," a place highly conducive to the exchange of existing ideas, the students' ideas. Listening to one another, students sometimes change their opinions. But what they generally can't do is acquire a new vocabulary, a new perspective, that will cast issues in a fresh light.

The Socratic method—the animated, sometimes impolite give-and-take between student and teacher—seems too jagged for current sensibilities. Students frequently come to my office to tell me how intimidated they feel in class; the thought of being embarrassed in front of the group fills them with dread. I remember a student telling me how humiliating it was to be corrected by the teacher, by me. So I asked the logical question: "Should I let a major factual error go by to save discomfort?" The student—a good student, smart and earnest—said that was a tough question. He'd need to think about it.

Disturbing? Sure. But I wonder, are we really getting students ready for Socratic exchange with professors when we push them off into vast lecture rooms, two and three hundred to a class, sometimes face them with only grad students until their third year, and signal in our myriad professorial ways that we often have much better things to do than sit in our offices and talk with them? How bad will the student-faculty ratios have to become, how teeming the lecture courses, before we hear students righteously complaining, as they did thirty years ago, about the impersonality of their schools, about their decline into knowledge factories? "This is a firm," said Mario Savio at Berkeley during the Free Speech protests of the sixties, "and if the Board of Regents are the board of directors . . . then . . . the faculty are a bunch of employees and we're the raw material. But we're a bunch of raw material that don't mean . . . to be made into any product."

Teachers who really do confront students, who provide significant challenges to what they believe, *can* be very successful, granted. But sometimes such professors generate more than a little trouble for themselves. A controversial teacher can send students hurrying to the deans and the counselors, claiming to have been offended. (*Offensive* is the preferred term of repugnance today, just as *enjoyable* is the summit of praise.) Colleges have brought in hordes of counselors and deans to make sure that everything is smooth, serene, unflustered, that everyone has a good time. To the counselor, to the dean, and to the university legal squad, that which is normal, healthy, and prudent is best.

An air of caution and deference is everywhere. When my students come to talk with me in my office, they often exhibit a Franciscan humility. "Do you have a moment?" "I know you're busy. I won't take up much of your time." Their presences tend to be very light; they almost never change the temperature of the room. The dress is nondescript: Clothes are in earth tones; shoes are practical—cross-trainers, hiking boots, work shoes, Dr. Martens, with now and then a stylish pair of raised-sole boots on one of the young women. Many, male and female both, peep from beneath the bills of monogrammed baseball caps. Quite a few wear sports, or even corporate, logos, sometimes on one piece of clothing but occasionally (and disconcertingly) on more. The walk is slow; speech is careful, sweet, a bit weary, and without strong inflection. (After the first lively week of the term, most seem far in debt to sleep.)

They are almost unfailingly polite. They don't want to offend me; I could hurt them, savage their grades.

Naturally, there are exceptions, kids I chat animatedly with, who offer a joke, or go on about this or that new CD (almost never a book, no). But most of the traffic is genially sleepwalking. I have to admit that I'm a touch wary, too. I tend to hold back. An unguarded remark, a joke that's taken to be off-color, or simply an uncomprehended comment can lead to difficulties. I keep it literal. They disturb me a little, these kind and melancholy students, who themselves seem rather frightened of their own lives.

Before they arrive, we ply the students with luscious ads, guaranteeing them a cross between summer camp and lotusland. When they get here, flattery and nonstop entertainment are available, if that's what they want. And when they leave? How do we send our students out into the world? More and more, our administrators call the booking agents and line up one or another celebrity to usher the graduates into the future. Recently Kermit the Frog won himself an honorary degree at Southampton College on Long Island; Bruce Willis and Yogi Berra took credentials away at Montclair State; Arnold Schwarzenegger scored at the University of Wisconsin–Superior. At Wellesley, Oprah Winfrey gave the commencement address. (*Wellesley*—one of the most rigorous academic colleges in the nation.) At the University of Vermont, Whoopi Goldberg laid down the word. But why should a worthy administrator contact someone who might actually say something, something disturbing, something "offensive," when he can get what the parents and kids apparently want and what the newspapers will softly commend—more lite entertainment, more TV?

Is it a surprise, then, that this generation of students—steeped in consumer culture before going off to school, treated as potent customers well before their date of arrival, then pandered to from day one until the morning of the final kiss-off from Kermit or one of his kin—are inclined to see the books they read as a string of entertainments to be placidly enjoyed or languidly cast down? Given the way universities are now administered (which is more and more to say, given the way that they are currently marketed), is it a shock that the kids don't come to school hot to learn, unable to bear their own ignorance? For some measure of self-dislike, or self-discontent—which is much different from simple depression—is a prerequisite for getting an education that matters.

My students, alas, usually lack the confidence to acknowledge what would be their most precious asset for learning: their ignorance.

One day I asked my Freud class a question that never fails to solicit intriguing responses: Who are your heroes? Whom do you admire? After one remarkable answer, featuring T. S. Eliot as hero, a series of generic replies rolled in, one gray wave after the next: my father, my best friend, a doctor who lives in our town, my high school history teacher. Virtually all the heroes were people my students had known personally, people who had done something local, specific, and practical—and had done it *for them*. They were good people, unselfish people, these heroes, but most of all they were people who had delivered the goods.

My students' answers didn't exhibit any philosophical resistance to the idea of greatness. It's not that they had been primed by their professors with complex arguments to combat the notion of genius or any other form of human distinction. For the truth is that these students don't need debunking theories. Long before college, skepticism became their habitual mode. They are the progeny of the hypercool ethos of the box. It's inane to say that theorizing professors have created them, as many conservative critics like to do. Rather, they have substantially created a university environment in which facile skepticism can thrive without being substantially contested.

Skeptical approaches have *potential* value. If you have no all-encompassing religious faith, no faith in historical destiny or the future of the West or anything comparably grand, you need to acquire your vision of the world somewhere. If it's from literature, then the various visions literature offers have to be inquired into skeptically. Surely it matters that women are denigrated in Milton and in Pope; that some novelistic voices assume an overbearing godlike authority; that the poor are, in this or that writer, inevitably cast as clowns. You can't buy all of literature wholesale if it's going to help draw your patterns of belief.

But demystifying theories are now overused, applied mechanically. It's all logocentrism, patriarchy, ideology. And in this the student environment—laid-back, skeptical, knowing—is, I believe, central. Full-out debunking is what plays with this clientele. Some have been doing it nearly as long as, if more crudely than, their deconstructionist teachers. In the context of the contemporary university and cool consumer culture,

a useful intellectual skepticism has become exaggerated into a fundamentalist caricature of itself. The teachers have buckled to their students'
views.

At its best, multiculturalism can be attractive as well-deployed theory.
What could be more valuable than encountering the best work of far-
flung cultures and becoming a citizen of the world? But in the current
consumer environment, where flattery plays so well, the urge to encounter
the other can devolve into the urge to find others who embody and celebrate the right ethnic origins. So we put aside the African novelist Chinua
Achebe's abrasive, troubling *Things Fall Apart* and gravitate toward
hymns on Africa, cradle of all civilizations.

What about the phenomenon called political correctness? Raising the
standard of civility and tolerance in the university has been—who can
deny it?—a very good thing. Yet this admirable impulse has expanded to
the point where one is enjoined to speak well—and only well—of women,
blacks, gays, the disabled, in fact of virtually everyone. And we can owe
this expansion in many ways to the student culture. Students now do not
wish to be criticized, not in any form. (The culture of consumption never
criticizes them, at least not *overtly*.) In the current university, the movement for urbane tolerance has devolved into an imperative against critical reaction, turning much of the intellectual life into a dreary Sargasso
Sea. At a certain point, professors stopped being usefully sensitive and
became more like careful retailers who have it as a cardinal point of
doctrine never to piss the customer off.

To some professors, the solution lies in the movement called cultural
studies. What students need, they believe, is to form a critical perspective on pop culture. It's a fine idea, no doubt. Students should be able to
run a critical commentary against the stream of consumer stimulations
in which they're immersed. But cultural studies programs rarely work,
because no matter what you propose by way of analysis, things tend to
bolt downhill toward an uncritical discussion of students' tastes, into
what they like and don't like. If you want to do a Frankfurt School–style
analysis of *Braveheart*, you can be pretty sure that by mid-class Adorno
and Horkheimer will be consigned to the junk heap of history and you'll
be collectively weighing the charms of Mel Gibson. One sometimes
wonders if cultural studies hasn't prospered because, under the guise of
serious intellectual analysis, it gives the customers what they most want—
easy pleasure, more TV. Cultural studies becomes nothing better than
what its detractors claim it is—Madonna studies—when students kick

loose from the critical perspective and groove to the product, and that, in my experience teaching film and pop culture, happens plenty.

On the issue of genius, as on multiculturalism and political correctness, we professors of the humanities have, I think, also failed to press back against our students' consumer tastes. Here we tend to nurse a pair of—to put it charitably—disparate views. In one mode, we're inclined to a programmatic debunking criticism. We call the concept of genius into question. But in our professional lives per se, we aren't usually disposed against the idea of distinguished achievement. We argue animatedly about the caliber of potential colleagues. We support a star system in which some professors are far better paid and teach less under better conditions than the rest. In our own profession, we are creating a system that is the mirror image of the one we're dismantling in the curriculum. Ask a professor what she thinks of the work of Stephen Greenblatt, a leading critic of Shakespeare, and you'll hear it for an hour. Ask her what her views are on Shakespeare's genius and she's likely to begin questioning the term along with the whole "discourse of evaluation." This dual sensibility may be intellectually incoherent. But in its awareness of what plays with students, it's conducive to good classroom evaluations and, in its awareness of where and how the professional bread is buttered, to self-advancement as well.

My overall point is this: It's not that a left-wing professorial coup has taken over the university. It's that at American universities, left-liberal politics have collided with the ethos of consumerism. The consumer ethos is winning.

Then how do those who at least occasionally promote genius and high literary ideals look to current students? How do we appear, those of us who imagine that if you give yourself over completely to your subject you'll be rewarded with insight beyond what you individually command?

I'm reminded of an old piece of newsreel footage I saw once. The speaker (perhaps it was Lenin, maybe Trotsky) was haranguing a large crowd. He was expostulating, arm-waving, carrying on. Whether it was flawed technology or the man himself, I'm not sure, but the orator looked like an intricate mechanical device that had sprung into fast-forward. To my students, who mistrust enthusiasm in every form, that's me when I start riffing about Freud or Blake. But more and more, as my evaluations showed, I've been replacing evaluation and intellectual animation with stand-up routines, keeping it all at arm's length, praising under the cover of irony.

It's too bad that the idea of genius has been denigrated so far, because it actually offers a live alternative to the demoralizing culture of hip in which most of my students are mired. By embracing the works and lives of extraordinary people, you can adapt new ideals to revise those that came courtesy of your parents, your neighborhood, your clan—or the tube. The aim of a good liberal arts education was once, to adapt an observation by the scholar Walter Jackson Bate, to see that "we need not be the passive victims of what we deterministically call 'circumstances' (social, cultural, or reductively psychological-personal), but that by linking ourselves through what Keats calls an 'immortal free-masonry' with the great we can become freer—freer to be ourselves, to be what we most want and value."

But genius isn't just a personal standard; genius can also have political effect. To me, one of the best things about democratic thinking is the conviction that genius can spring up anywhere. Walt Whitman is born into the working class and thirty-six years later we have a poetic image of America that gives a passionate dimension to the legalistic brilliance of the Constitution. A democracy needs to constantly develop, and to do so it requires the most powerful visionary minds to interpret the present and to propose possible shapes for the future. By continuing to notice and praise genius, we create a culture in which the kind of poetic gamble that Whitman made—a gamble in which failure would have entailed rank humiliation, depression, maybe suicide—still takes place. By rebelling against established ways of seeing and saying things, genius helps us to apprehend how malleable the present is and how promising the future. If we teachers do not endorse genius and self-overcoming, can we be surprised when our students find their ideal images in TV's latest persona ads?

A world uninterested in genius is a despondent place, whose sad denizens drift from coffee bar to Prozac dispensary, unfired by ideals or the glowing image of the self that one might become. As Northrop Frye says in a beautiful and now dramatically unfashionable sentence, "The artist who uses the same energy and genius that Homer and Isaiah had will find that he not only lives in the same palace of art as Homer and Isaiah, but lives in it at the same time." We ought not to deny the existence of such a place simply because we, or those we care for, find the demands it makes intimidating, the rent too high.

What happens if we keep trudging along this bleak course? What happens if our most intelligent students never learn to strive to overcome what they are? What if genius, and the imitation of genius, become silly, outmoded ideas? What you're likely to get are more and more two-dimensional men and women. These will be people who live for easy pleasures, for comfort and prosperity, who think of money first, then second, and third, who hug the status quo; people who believe in God as a sort of insurance policy (cover your bets); people who are never surprised. They will be people so pleased with themselves (when they're not in despair at the general pointlessness of their lives) that they cannot imagine humanity could do better. They'll think it their highest duty to clone themselves as frequently as possible. They'll claim to be happy, and they'll live a long time.

It is probably time now to offer a spate of inspiring solutions. Here ought to come a list of reforms, with due notations about a core curriculum and various requirements. What the traditionalists who offer such solutions miss is that no matter what our current students are given to read, many of them will simply translate it into melodrama, with flat characters and predictable morals. (The unabated capitalist culture that conservative critics so often endorse has put students in a position to do little else.) One can't simply wave a curricular wand and reverse acculturation.

Perhaps it would be a good idea to try firing the counselors and sending half the deans back into their classrooms, dismantling the football team and making the stadium into a playground for local kids, emptying the fraternities and boarding up the student-activities office. Such measures would convey the message that American colleges are not northern outposts of Club Med. A willingness on the part of the faculty to defy student conviction and affront them occasionally—to be usefully offensive—also might not be a bad thing. We professors talk a lot about subversion, which generally means subverting the views of people who never hear us talk or read our work. But to subvert the views of our students—our customers—that would be something else again.

Ultimately, though, it is up to individuals—and individual students in particular—to make their own way against the current sludgy tide. There's still the library, still the museum, there's still the occasional teacher who lives to find things greater than herself to admire. There are still fellow students who have not been cowed. Universities are inefficient, cluttered, archaic places, with many unguarded corners where one can open a book or gaze out onto the larger world and construe it freely. Those who do as much, trusting themselves against the weight of current opinion, will have contributed something to bringing this sad dispensation to an end. As for myself, I'm canning my low-key one-liners; when the kids' TV-based tastes come to the fore, I'll aim and shoot. And when it's time to praise genius, I'll try to do it in the right style, full-out, with faith that finer artistic spirits (maybe not Homer and Isaiah quite, but close, close), still alive somewhere in the ether, will help me out when my invention flags, the students doze, or the dean mutters into the phone. I'm getting back to a more exuberant style; I'll be expostulating and arm-waving straight into the millennium, yes I will.

Dwelling in Possibilities (2008)

At the beginning of school last fall, I ran into a student out on the University of Virginia Lawn, not far from the famous statue of Homer instructing an admiring pupil. Homer's student is in a toga. Mine was wearing wrap-around sunglasses like Bono's, black jeans, and a red T-shirt emblazoned with white Chinese characters. Over his shoulder he carried his laptop.

We asked each other the usual question: What did you do over the summer? What he did, as I recall, was a brief internship at a well-regarded Internet publication, a six-country swing though Europe, then back to enjoy his family and home, reconnect with high school friends, and work on recording a rock CD. What had I done? I had written five drafts of a chapter for a book on the last two years of Sigmund Freud's life. I had traveled to Crozet, a few miles away, to get pizza. I'd traveled 150 miles to Virginia Beach the day after I woke up distressed because I couldn't figure out how to begin my chapter. I stayed a night at the beach, figured it out (I thought), and come home. My young friend looked at me with a mixture of awe and compassion. I felt a little like one of those aged men of the earth who populate Wordsworth's poetry. One of them, the Old Cumberland Beggar, goes so slowly that you never actually see him move, but if you return to the spot where you first encountered him two hours ago, lo, he has gone a little way down the road. The footprints are there to prove it.

I headed back to my office for draft number six, or something comparably glamorous. Where was my student going? He was no doubt heading into a more turbo-charged version of his summer, a life of supreme intensity created in collaboration with the laptop slung over his shoulder. For his student generation is a singular one: Its members have a spectacular hunger for life and more life. They want to study (a little), travel, make friends, make more friends, take in all the movies, listen to every hot band, keep up with everyone they've ever known. And there's something else, too, that distinguishes them: They live to multiply possibilities. They're enemies of closure. For as much as they want to do and actually manage to do, they always strive to keep their options open, never to shut possibilities down.

This hunger for life has a number of consequences, for now and for the future. It's part of what makes this student generation appealing, highly promising—and also vulnerable and dangerous. These students may go on to do great and good things, but they also present risks to themselves and to the common future. They seem almost to have been created, as the poet says, "half to rise and half to fall." As a teacher of theirs (and fellow citizen), I'm more than a little concerned about which it's going to be.

Internet technology was on hand for my current students from about 1995, when the Netscape browser made the Internet accessible to everyone. And the Internet seems to me to have shaped their generation as much as the multichannel TV—with that critical device, the remote control—shaped the students who registered for my classes a decade earlier. What is the Internet to current students?

Consider first what it is not. A friend of mine who has assiduously kept a journal for forty years calls the journal, which now runs to about forty volumes, a "life thickener." His quotations, pictures, clips, drawings, and paintings give dense meaning to the blind onrush that unexamined life can be. He looks back through the volumes and sees that there *was* a life and that to him it meant something. To my students, I suspect, my friend would look like a medieval monk laboring over his manuscripts, someone with a radically pre-postmodern feel for time, someone who did not, in fact, understand what time actually is.

An Internet-linked laptop, one may safely say, is not a life thickener. At the fingertips of my students the laptop is a multiplier of the possible. "I dwell in possibility," says Emily Dickinson, "a fairer house than prose." My students want to dwell there with her. Just as TV and the culture of cool slowed kids down, made them languid and a bit shell-shocked, the Internet has had the effect of speeding them up.

My university recently passed an edict: No one, dammit (insofar as edicts can say dammit), is going to triple-major. Everyone now who is worth his tuition money double majors: The students in my classes are engineering/English, politics/English, chemistry/English. An urban legend in my leaf-fringed 'hood is that someone got around this inane dictum about triple majors by majoring in four subjects—there was, it seems, no rule against that. The top students in my school, the ones who set the standard for the rest even if they drive the rest crazy, want to take eight classes a term, major promiscuously, have a semester abroad at three different schools, connect with every likely person who is on Facebook, be checked in with by their pals and check in at every living moment.

One day I tried an experiment in a class I was teaching on English and American Romanticism. We had been studying Thoreau and talking about his reflections (sour) on the uses of technology for communication. ("We are in great haste," he says, "to construct a magnetic telegraph from Maine to Texas; but Maine and Texas, it may be, have nothing important to communicate.") I asked the group, "How many places were you simultaneously yesterday—at the most?" Suppose you were chatting on your cell phone, partially watching a movie in one corner of a computer screen, texting with three people (a modest number), and glancing occasionally at the text for some other course than ours—grazing, maybe, in Samuelson's *Economics* rather than diving deep into Thoreau's "Economy"—and then, also, tossing the occasional word to your roommate? That would be seven, seven places at once. Some students—with a little high-spirited hyperbole thrown in, no doubt—got into double digits. Of course it wouldn't take the Dalai Lama or Henry David Thoreau to assure them that anyone who is in seven places at once is not anywhere in particular—not present, not here now. Be everywhere now—that's what the current technology invites, and that's what my students apparently aspire to do.

Internet-linked computers are desiring-machines—machines for the stimulation of desire. But so is a TV; so in a certain sense is a movie screen. What makes the Internet singular is its power to expand desire, expand possibility beyond the confines of prior media. (My students are possibility junkies.) You can multiply the number of possible clothing purchases near to infinity and do it with stunning speed. You can make all the pleated skirts in the world appear almost all at once for you to choose from. As we talked about this in class—with Thoreau's disapproving specter looking on (sometimes it appears that Thoreau disapproves of everything, except the drinking of cold water)—something surprising came out. The moment of maximum Internet pleasure was not the moment of closure, when you sealed the deal; it was the moment when the choices had been multiplied to the highest sum. It was the moment of maximum promise, when you touched the lip of the possible: of four majors and eight courses per term and a gazillion hits on your Facebook page, and being everyplace (almost) at once, and gazing upon all the pleated skirts that the world doth hold.

This is what Immanuel Kant, were he around to see it, might have called the computer sublime. (He called something like it mathematical sublimity.) The moment when you make the purchase, close the deal, pick a girlfriend, set a date: All those things, the students around the Thoreau table concurred, were a letdown, consummations not really to be wished for. The students were a little surprised by the conclusions they came to about themselves. "It's when I can see it all in front of me," one young woman said, "that's when I'm the happiest."

Ask an American college student what he's doing on Friday night. Ask him at five thirty Friday afternoon. "I don't know" will likely be the first response. But then will come a list of possibilities to make the average Chinese menu look sullenly costive: the concert, the play, the movie, the party, the stay-at-home, the chilling ("chillaxing"), the monitoring of SportsCenter, the reading (fast, fast) of an assignment or two. University students now are virtual Hamlets of the virtual world, pondering possibility, faces pressed up against the sweetshop window of their all-purpose desiring machines. To ticket or not to ticket, buy or not to, party or no, or perhaps to simply stay in and to multiply options in numberless numbers, never to be closed down: Those are the questions.

And once you do get somewhere, wherever it might be, you'll find that, as Gertrude Stein has it, there's "no there there." At a student party, I'm told, about a fourth of the kids have their cell phones locked to their ears. What are they doing? "They're talking to their friends." About? "About another party they might conceivably go to." And naturally the other party is better than the one that they're now at (and not at), though of course there will be people at that party on their cell phones, talking about other simulacrum gatherings, spiraling on into M. C. Escher infinity.

It's possible that recent events in the world have added intensity to a student's quest for more possibilities. The events of September 11, which current college students experienced when they were eight, nine, ten, were an undoubted horror. But they had the effect, I think, of waking America's young people up from a pseudo-nihilistic doze. Before New York, Pennsylvania, and Virginia, the middle-class American teenager's world had been a pleasure dome full of rare delights. It was the reign of television: the oracle that knows everything and can take you anywhere. Television brought images of bliss, and its ads showed you the products that you needed to buy in order to achieve it. That well-known Jeep ad I mentioned in the last chapter that depicted hip kids tossing Frisbees and laughing like rock stars had nothing to do with the properties of a Jeep. It was a persona ad that advertised the sort of person you'd be when you acquired the product. The ad was an emblem of the consumer moment: Buy in order to be.

Students wanted to be cool. They wanted to be beyond reproach. There was a sense abroad that if you simply did what you were supposed to do, kept low to the ground and stayed on the conveyor belt, the future that TV promised would be yours. Everything was a mode of entertainment, or could be transformed into one after it had been submitted to Letterman-style ridicule. President Clinton was a genial boy from Arkansas who awoke one day and found himself in office. But that had not slaked his boyishness at all. He still wanted a version of what every boy did: all-nighters, pizza, and his pals in constant attendance. The president was a dog who couldn't stay on the porch. My students—the guys in particular—often found him the perfect image of success: You need never grow up; need never abandon college-boy mode. The couch where you sat, hours a day, monitoring TV in lordly condescension, would in time morph into an airship to swoosh you into your dreams.

But then there came the day of near–American Apocalypse, September 11, 2001. The prospect of hanging, Doctor Johnson observed, does wonders to concentrate the mind. The mind of America has been concentrated. No one believes that the whole edifice is likely to topple down around us soon. But everyone now lives charged with the knowledge that today, tomorrow, next week, we can suffer an event that will change everything drastically. A dirty bomb in the middle of a great city, poison wafting in sweet-smelling clouds through a subway system, a water supply subtly tainted: Such things would not only destroy the lives of those they touch directly, they'd discompose and remake America in ways that would be, to say the least, none too sweet. Tomorrow the deck may be shuffled and recut by the devil's hand. So what shall we do now?

The answer that comes from current students would seem to be this: Live, live, before the bombs go off in San Francisco or the water goes vile in New York and the new Mahdi appears on a billion screens at once to pronounce another turn in the Holy War that, for him, has been ongoing since the first Crusader scraped an armored foot on the soil of the Holy Land. On that bad day there will be, at the very least, the start of a comprehensive *closing down*. There will be no more free travel, no more easy money, and much less loose talk. Life will become a confinement, a prison, a pound. So now, as James's Strether instructs Little Bilham, you must "live all you can; it's a mistake not to." There's a humane hunger to my students' hustle for more life—but I think it's possible that down below bubbles a fear. Do it now, for later may be too late.

It's clearly a new university world that I'm living in, though it took me some time to see it. My revelation occurred a few months ago. Up until that point, I was always happy to see students bringing their laptops into class. The sight of them conjured up visions of upbeat news magazine covers: kids in ordered rows behind their computers, tapping in the new millennium. And the students who brought their laptops seemed to be the most engaged: They'd be skittering fast across the keys, alert and alive and glancing up from time to time to toss a few sentences into the conversation. These were the plugged-in kids, the committed ones. But then one day I made a rare trip to the blackboard and on the way glanced over a laptopper's shoulder. There was what appeared to be a YouTube video in one corner (Shakira? The "Hips Don't Lie" video?) and e-mail front and center, but nothing much to do with the subject of the class. How could I have missed it? This sort of thing is now the way of the classroom world.

Three thousand first-year students entered my university last year: Two thousand nine hundred and six of them—we keep some tight records here—brought laptops with them; ninety brought desktops. Four students—the incoming James Deans no doubt—showed up computerless. (Ten years ago, half of our first-year students came to school without computers.) At Virginia, as at just about every other university, almost all buildings are now equipped with wireless routers. This began to happen about four years ago, and many of us professors barely noticed it in part because we generally travel only from office to classroom. But our students are nomads, on the move all day. Wherever they sit, they set up Internet Command Central. Now students in almost any classroom can get directly onto the Internet and, given the shieldlike screens on their laptops, they can call up what they like. Especially in the big lecture classes, everyone's flitting from website to website, checking e-mail, and instant messaging. Do they pay any attention to the class? My students tell me that they're experts in paying attention to many things at once: It's no problem at all.

A romantic, says Nietzsche, is someone who always wants to be elsewhere: If that's so, then the children of the Internet are romantics, for they perpetually wish to be someplace else and the laptop reliably helps take them there. The e-mailer, the instant messager, the Web browser are all dispersing their energies and interests outward, away from the present, the here and now. The Internet user is constantly connecting with people and institutions far away, creating surrogate communities that displace the potential community at hand.

Then, too, booking by computer has made travel easier and, by eliminating a certain number of middlemen, kept it reasonably cheap. So there's an inducement to take off physically as well. The Internet is perhaps the most centrifugal technology ever devised. The classroom, where you sit down in one space at one time and ponder a text or an issue in slow motion, is coming to feel ever more antiquated. What's at a premium now is movement, making connections, getting all the circuitry fizzing and popping.

For students now, life is elsewhere. Life is at parties, at clubs, in music, with friends, in sports, and on and on through the Internet. Classes matter to them (a little), but classes are just part of an ever-enlarging web of activities and diversions. Students now seek to master their work—not to be taken over by it and consumed. They want to dispatch it, do it quickly, cop a high grade, and then get on to the many things that truly interest them. For my students live in the future and not the present; they live with their prospects for success and pleasure. They dwell in possibility.

Drugs? Drugs are a big part of the game, along with the Internet. The answer to the question "What drugs are college students taking now?" is, as it has been for some time, "All of the above." But the drugs that have most recently entered the scene are the ones designed to combat attention deficit disorder: Adderall, Ritalin, Concerta, and Daytrana, which delivers the meds through a patch. These are all pharmaceuticals, obtained by prescription, though often the people taking them have never gotten diagnosed. The ADD drugs seem to be omnipresent; they're on sale in every dorm at prices that rise exponentially as the week of final exams approaches. "Twenty dollars for a hit," one student told me, "on the night before an exam in the intro econ class." Their effect is, pretty subtly but pretty surely, to speed the taker up. They kick him forward, give him fresh juice to keep exploring possibilities, to keep buying and doing and buying and doing.

The idea is to keep moving, never to stop. It's now become so commonplace as to be beneath notice, but there was a time that every city block contiguous to a university did not contain a shop dispensing a speed-you-up drug and inviting people to sit down and enjoy it along with wireless computer access. Laptops seem to go with coffee (and other stimulants) in much the same way that blood-and-gold sunsets went with LSD and Oreo cookies with weed. (It's possible, I sometimes think, that fully half of the urban Starbucks in America are located in rental properties that once were head shops.) Nor were there always energy drinks, vile-tasting concoctions coming in cans covered with superhero insignias designed to make you run as fast and steady as your computer, your car, and—this is Darwinian capitalism after all—your colleagues. You've got to keep going. Almost all of my students have one book—an old book—that they've read and treasured and read again. It's the American epic of free movement, *On the Road*, a half century old this year, but to them one of the few things in the culture of my generation that's still youthful.

The sports that this generation has put its stamp on, X Games sorts of things like snowboarding, surfing, and skateboarding, are all about velocity, motion, skimming. They're about speeding flawlessly through space without being diverted, slowed down, or captured by mere gravity. (Gravity, in all senses, is what my students are out to avoid.) Like the drugs, the sports help to keep the kids moving elsewhere.

How about their music? It's a little hard to say. Students no longer turn their speakers out the dorm window and blast the quad with Poco's *Deliverin'*. Music now comes personally, a whisper in the ear, through the iPod, so that everyone can walk around with the soundtrack to his own movie purring. This constant music plug-in is another mode of being elsewhere, about right for the current dispensation. As to the sort of music it is, the kind of stuff that runs through the iPods is varied. Many of my students delight in listening to bands that absolutely no one but they seem to have heard of. When I ask them in class to tell me their favorite tunes, I'm reminded of the days when my friends and I would show each other our baseball cards. As you flipped over yours, the other guy responded with "Got it. Got it. Don't got it. Got it." "Don't got it" came with a wince. The coolest kid in the room now is clearly the one whose favorite bands are the ones the others wince most over—the ones they don't got.

But the students have a collective musical taste, too. When they're together at a party, when they've unplugged their iPods and put their cell phones temporarily on vibrate, what they want is rap. Whatever the content of rap, its form is propulsive forward motion—the beat, the energy pulse, is what it's about. It drives you forward, runs fuel through the motor. Rap is part of the constant stimulation that students seem unable to live without.

When a seminar is over now, the students reach their hands into their pockets and draw—it looks like *Gunfight at the O.K. Corral*. But what they're reaching for—after discussing Thoreau, say, on the pleasures of solitude—are their cell phones. They've been disconnected, off the drug, for more than an hour and they need a fix. The cell phoning comes as a relief: The students have been (give or take) in one place, at one time, pondering a few passages from *Walden*. Now they need to disperse themselves again, get away from the immediate, dissolve the present away.

But I teach at one university, the University of Virginia, known for high-powered students who are also sometimes high partiers: Is what I'm saying true for all schools? Well, I do some traveling and talking to colleagues at other places, and from what I can tell, the more high-prestige the institution, the more frenetic and centrifugal the pace. At Harvard and Yale, I'd now expect to find kids who've hit a white incandescence or maybe who've fused completely with the Internet, living within it, like characters out of *Neuromancer*, finding in their merger with the machine a kind of high that can take the place of happiness.

Skate fast over the surfaces of life and cover all the extended space you can, says the new ethos. Perhaps the greatest of all surface skimmers, the poet laureate of the way we live now at college, was William Wordsworth's arch-antagonist, George Gordon, Lord Byron. The poetry of Wordsworth, the explorer of inner space, is deliberate, slow, ponderous, like those old men of the woods he loves to depict—and that I may resemble to my fast-skimming students. The complaint against Wordsworth is that he is tiresome; he has no time for sex or violence, just muted natural beauty and a mystical sublime. Byron—rich, beautiful, glamorous, with startlingly white skin, black hair, and a swanlike neck—doesn't celebrate violence. Sex is his game. In *Don Juan*, the hero skims and skips from one encounter to the next. His desires are mobile: He can play the woman's part and the man's. Desire doesn't provoke complex ambivalence in Byron, just the need to move from one beckoning satisfaction to the next. Byron's poetry has all the velocity of this ever-moving, ever-changing desire: His rhymes are shrewd, arch, unexpected, and seem to be turned with a wrist flick's ease. Thus Byron on Wordsworth's good friend Samuel Taylor Coleridge, who had just published his *Biographia Literaria*, a book Byron disliked because it was dense and difficult, something you needed to read at least twice: "And Coleridge, too, has lately taken wing, / But like a hawk encumbered with his hood,—/ Explaining metaphysics to the nation—/ I wish he would explain his Explanation."

Byron claimed to compose best on horseback and to be able to concoct dozens of lines in an outing. Wordsworth shouted his lines aloud as he roamed through the Lake District, his dog browsing ahead of him to bark if strangers, who might hear his bellowing and think him mad, appeared on the trail. Byron disliked Wordsworth for one reason above all the rest: boring. The poet of "rocks and stones and trees" was boring. Byron wished never to be bored. So he kept moving, kept accelerating from one point to the next, not in hopes of being satisfied—that he took to be an illusion—but so as not to be overcome by the new-tide demon, ennui. In 1825, the year after Byron died, the first passenger locomotive appeared and maybe, says Camille Paglia, Byron's aristocratic spirit flew by metempsychosis into the machine. Perhaps Byron's restless demon has migrated again, this time from locomotive to laptop.

Students now are quasi-romantics—of a Byronic sort. He would have adored their world of fast travel, fast communication, and fast relationships. There is no more Byronic form of erotic life than the hookup. When after the publication of *Childe Harold's Pilgrimage* Byron became a celebrity—"I awoke and found myself famous," he said—he was surrounded with erotic opportunities. Women sent him notes begging for liaisons; they followed his carriage through the streets; they smuggled themselves into his rooms. And frequently Byron, who was probably more often seduced than seducing, was pleased to comply. In his superspeed erotic life, Byron is said to have hooked up hundreds of times.

What exactly does it mean to hook up? It means managing to have good sex without activating all the strong feelings that sex usually brings. Hooking up is a fantasy of frictionless sex—sex free of deep emotion. It's sex that lets you keep on sliding over surfaces, moving from partner to partner as smoothly as you move from site to site on the laptop. In fact, the Internet-linked computer is an erotic bazaar, a hookup machine. All of those pages on Facebook are, among other things, personal ads. (Byron would love shopping there—and, more, being shopped for.) Here students (and others, too) can find objects more alluring than pleated skirts. They can find sexual possibilities without end.

Hooking up, of course, is a kind of myth. Sex usually does provoke strong feelings, even when people swear to each other that—this time, this time—it won't. Not everyone is wired like Lord Byron. Students often find that they need continuity and comfort in what can be a harsh college world. Many of them hold faithfully to boyfriends and girlfriends through all four years of school (albeit sometimes with special spring break dispensations). And a few of those students busting out of my class, grabbing for their cell phones, are calling not the alluring near stranger who just texted them, but their parents. In every class I teach, there are at least two or three students who call home every day.

For the way that my students live now is dangerous—some of them know it, some learn in time. "In skating over thin ice," Emerson says, "our safety is in our speed." But sometimes, like it or not, we're slowed down or stopped, and then trouble begins. Last term a young woman, an art history and commerce major who was in one of my classes, stopped by my office. She's a marvelous student; I've never taught anyone who could read poetry with much more subtlety and feeling. She was pale, sleepless; her teeth were chattering softly. I invited her to sit down, and then asked some questions. "How many courses are you taking?" Five, no six, seven. "Audits?" Yes, one. "A thesis?" Almost done: She planned to knock out forty pages over the weekend, but now her father, whom she clearly adored, was sick, and she'd have to go home and then how could she—?

"It's too much," I said.

"What?" she hadn't heard me exactly.

"What you're doing? It's too much." And then came—as it almost always does when I say these words, or something like them—a feeling of great relief. Someone with a claim to authority has said that it's okay to be tired, okay to ease up. Okay to rest. When my students crash on their own, they crash like helicopters dropping straight out of the sky when the rotor stops spinning. They're often unaware that they're on the verge of trouble. They're doing what they are supposed to do, what their parents want, with all those courses and the multiple majors; and they haven't got much of any resources to look inside and to see that matters are out of joint—no one has thought to help them acquire those. Did Byron ever fall apart, victim of his own hunger for speed and space? If so, he told us little about it.

I wonder, thinking back, was it something like an encounter I had had— to take the reincarnation trope a step further—with Lord Byron that fall day on the Lawn? He was all for glamour and motion. I was all for—well, what was I for? Was it the magic of the fifth draft on a project about a thinker, Freud, about whom—let us be generous—not everyone seems to care a great deal? I admit that I love that line of Yeats's about how writing is ceaseless stitching and unstitching, but "if it does not seem a moment's thought / Our stitching and unstitching has been naught." The stitching-unstitching business fascinates me. Yet my student had been to six countries, *six!*—and that was only part of his summer's story. If you asked returning students now for that old composition standard—What I Did This Summer—they'd have to hit you with three-decker novels.

And what do I have to offer the speedsters, I, a slow person from the generation of one kind of Coke, three TV stations, one mom and one dad? How exactly do we professors teach this kind of student? What do they need to know?

Many of my colleagues have a ready answer, and its essence is this: If you can't lick 'em, join 'em. In effect, they've made the courses an extension of the Internet. Their classes are laser and light shows, fast-moving productions that mime the colors and sound and above all the velocity of the laptop. There are movie screens, sound systems, Internet tie-ins. And, these colleagues say, it works. One professor I know equips his students with handheld wireless input devices that have twelve buttons and look a lot like TV remotes. Every five minutes or so he stops teaching and polls the kids to see how well they're doing. I admire the resourcefulness that's on display here—and I admire the skill and energy that many of my fellow teachers have deployed to meet students halfway. And yet . . .

Not long ago, a younger colleague came by my office to chat and at a certain point informed me that her son, who was four years old, had a favorite dinosaur and that it was called the Edmontosaurus.

("Edmundosaurus" is what I could have sworn she said.) She remarked, with what seemed untainted goodwill, that this may be the very oldest of the dinosaurs. A few weeks later she came by again—was she wheeling a TV in front of her, taking it to class?—and ended up telling me about this Edmundosaurus one more time. Well, the kind of schooling I endorse goes back at least as far as Socrates and maybe further, though—thanks anyway for the suggestion—not all the way to the thunder lizards.

For a student to be educated, she has to face brilliant antagonists: She has to encounter thinkers who see the world in different terms than she does. Does she come to college as a fundamentalist guardian of crude faith? Then two necessary books for her are Freud's *Future of an Illusion* and Nietzsche's *The Anti-Christ*. Once she's weathered the surface insults, she may find herself in an intellectual version of paradise, where she can defend her beliefs or change them, and where what's on hand is not a chance conversation, as Socrates liked to say, but a dialogue about how to live.

Is the student a scion of high-minded liberals who think that religion is the Oxycontin—the redneck heroin—of Redneck Nation? Then on might come William James and *The Varieties of Religious Experience* or Schopenhauer's essays on faith. It's this kind of dialogue, deliberate, gradual, thoughtful, that students immersed in the manic culture of Internet and Adderall are conditioned not to have. The first step for the professor now is to slow his classroom down. The common phrase for what he wants to do is telling: We "stop and think." Stop. Our students rarely get a chance to stop: They're always in motion, always spitting out what comes first to mind, never challenging, checking, revising.

Not long ago a young man came to my office, plopped down, and looked at me with tired urgency. "Give me ten minutes on Freud," he said. "Convince me that he really has something important to tell me." Despite appearances, this was a good moment. It was a chance to try to persuade him to slow it down. Get one of Freud's books—*Civilization and Its Discontents* is usually the best place to start—read it once and again, then come back for a talk.

When you have that kind of conversation, one on one, you begin, however modestly, to create a university. Why does the encounter need to take place face-to-face, rather than online? Because the student and teacher need to create a bond of good feeling, where they are free to speak openly with each other. They need to connect not just through cold print but through gestures, intonations, jokes. The student needs to discover what the teacher knows and what she exemplifies about how to live; the teacher needs contact with the student's energy and hopes. That kind of connection happens best in person; perhaps it can only happen that way.

This Socratic education, the goal of which is self-knowledge, is not a luxury. Over years of teaching I have seen that those students who, through whatever form of struggle, really have come to an independent sense of who they are and what they want are the ones who genuinely thrive in the world. Thoreau says that if you advance in the direction of your dreams, you'll find uncommon success, and teaching a few generations of students has persuaded me that he is right. The ones who do what they love without a lot of regard for conventional success tend to turn out happy and strong.

We teachers need to remind ourselves from time to time that our primary job is not to help our students to acquire skills, marketable skills, bankables. And we don't preeminently teach communication and computation and instill habits of punctuality and thoroughness. We're not here to help our students make their minds resemble their laptops, fast and feverish. We didn't get into teaching to make trains of thought run on time.

As for our students, all honor to them: They may have something to teach the five-drafter. By their hunger for more life, they convey hope that the world is still a splendid place, worth seeing and appreciating. Into spontaneity they can liberate us. But life is more than spontaneity and whim. To live well, we must sometimes stop and think and then try to remake the work in progress that we currently are. There's no better place for that than a college classroom where, together, we can slow it down and live deliberately.

And to that end (Edmundosaurus, take the microphone): No more laptops in my classroom. You can leave them at home. You can check 'em at the door.

FELLOW STUDENTS

Who Are You and What Are You Doing Here?

A Word to the Incoming Class

Welcome and congratulations: Getting to the first day of college is a major achievement. You're to be commended, and not just you, but the parents, grandparents, uncles, and aunts who helped get you here.

It's been said that raising a child effectively takes a village: Well, as you may have noticed, our American village is not in very good shape. We've got guns, drugs, wars, fanatical religions, a slime-based popular culture, and some politicians who—a little restraint here—aren't what they might be. Merely to survive in this American village and to win a place in the entering class has taken a lot of grit on your part. So, yes, congratulations to all.

You now may think that you've about got it made. Amid the impressive college buildings, in company with a high-powered faculty, surrounded by the best of your generation, all you need is to keep doing what you've done before: Work hard, get good grades, listen to your teachers, get along with the people around you, and you'll emerge in four years as an educated young man or woman. Ready for life.

Do not believe it. It is not true. If you want to get a real education in America, you're going to have to fight—and I don't mean just fight against the drugs and the violence and against the slime-based culture that is still going to surround you. I mean something a little more disturbing. To get an education, you're probably going to have to fight against the institution that you find yourself in—no matter how prestigious it may be. (In fact, the more prestigious the school, the more you'll probably have to push.) You can get a terrific education in America now—there are astonishing opportunities at almost every college—but the education will not be presented to you wrapped and bowed. To get it, you'll need to struggle and strive, to be strong, and occasionally even to piss off some admirable people.

I came to college with few resources, but one of them was an understanding, however crude, of how I might use my opportunities there. This I began to develop because of my father, who had never been to college—in fact, he'd barely gotten out of high school. One night after dinner, he and I were sitting in our kitchen at 58 Clewley Road in Medford, Massachusetts, hatching plans about the rest of my life. I was about to go off to college, a feat no one in my family had accomplished in living memory. "I think I might want to be prelaw," I told my father. I had no idea what being prelaw was. My father compressed his brow and blew twin streams of smoke, dragonlike, from his magnificent nose. "Do you want to be a lawyer?" he asked. My father had some experience with lawyers, and with policemen, too; he was not well disposed toward either. "I'm not really sure," I told him, "but lawyers make pretty good money, right?"

My father detonated. (That was not uncommon. He detonated a lot.) He told me that I was going to go to college only once, and that while I was there I had better study what I wanted. He said that when rich kids went to school, they majored in the subjects that interested them, and that my younger brother Philip and I were as good as any rich kids. (We were rich kids minus the money.) Wasn't I interested in literature? I confessed that I was. Then I had better study literature, unless I had inside information to the effect that reincarnation wasn't just hype, and I'd be able to attend college thirty or forty times. If I had such info, prelaw would be fine, and maybe even a tour through invertebrate biology could also be tossed in. But until I had the reincarnation stuff from a solid source, I better get to work and pick out some English classes from the course catalog.

"How about the science requirements?" I asked.

"Take 'em later," he said. "You never know."

My father, Wright Aukenhead Edmundson, Malden High School class of 1948 (by a hair), knew the score. What he told me that evening at the Clewley Road kitchen table was true in itself, and it also contains the germ of an idea about what a university education should be. But apparently almost everyone else—students, teachers, trustees, and parents—see the matter much differently. They have it wrong.

Education has one salient enemy in present-day America, and that enemy is education—university education in particular. To almost everyone, university education is a means to an end. For students, that end is a good job. Students want the credentials that will help them get ahead. They want the certificate that will grant them access to Wall Street, or entrance into law or medical or business school. And how can we blame them? America values power and money, big players with big bucks. When we raise our children, we tell them in multiple ways that what we want most for them is success—material success. To be poor in America is to be a failure. It's to be without decent health care, without basic necessities, often without dignity. Then there are those backbreaking student loans: People leave school as servants, indentured to pay massive bills, so that first job better be a good one. Students come to college with the goal of a diploma in mind—what happens to them in between, especially in class-rooms, is often of no deep and determining interest to them.

In college, life is elsewhere. Life is at parties, at clubs, in music, with friends, in sports. Life is what celebrities have. The idea that the courses you take should be the primary objective of going to college is tacitly considered absurd. In terms of their work, students live in the future and not the present; they live with their prospects for success. If universities stopped issuing credentials, half of the clients would be gone by tomorrow morning, with the remainder following fast behind.

The faculty, too, is often absent: Their real lives are also elsewhere. Like most of their students, they aim to get on. The work they are compelled to do to advance—get tenure, promotion, raises, outside offers—is, broadly speaking, scholarly work. No matter what anyone says, this work has precious little to do with the fundamentals of teaching. The proof is that virtually no undergraduate students can read and understand their professors' scholarly publications. The public senses this disparity and so thinks of the professors' work as being silly or beside the point. Some of it is. But the public also senses that because professors don't pay full-bore attention to teaching, they don't have to work very hard—they've created a massive feather bed for themselves and called it a university.

This is radically false. Ambitious professors, the ones who, like their students, want to get ahead in America, work furiously. Scholarship, even if pretentious and almost unreadable, is nonetheless labor-intensive. One can slave for a year or two on a single article for publication in this or that refereed journal. These essays are honest: Their footnotes reflect real reading, real assimilation, and real dedication. Shoddy work—in which the author cheats, cuts corners, copies from others—is quickly detected. The people who do the work have highly developed intellectual powers, and they push themselves hard to reach a certain standard. That the results have almost no practical relevance for students, the public, or even, frequently, other scholars is a central element in the tragicomedy that is often academia.

The students and the professors have made a deal: Neither of them has to throw himself heart and soul into what happens in the classroom. The students write their abstract, overintellectualized essays; the professors grade the students for their capacity to be abstract and overintellectual— and often genuinely smart. For their essays can be brilliant, in a chilly way; they can also be clipped from the Internet, and often are. Whatever the case, no one wants to invest too much in them—for life is elsewhere. The professor saves his energies for the profession, while the student saves his for friends, social life, volunteer work, making connections, and getting in position to clasp hands on the true grail, the first job.

No one in this picture is evil; no one is criminally irresponsible. It's just that smart people are prone to look into matters to see how they might go about buttering their toast. Then they butter their toast.

As for the administrators, their relation to the students often seems based not on love but fear. Administrators fear bad publicity, scandal, and dissatisfaction on the part of their customers. More than anything else, though, they fear lawsuits. Throwing a student out of college for this or that piece of bad behavior is very difficult, almost impossible. The student will sue your eyes out. One kid I knew (and rather liked) threatened on his blog to mince his dear and esteemed professor (me) with a samurai sword for the crime of having taught a boring class. (The class *was* a little boring—I had a damn cold—but the punishment seemed a bit severe.) The dean of students laughed lightly when I suggested that this behavior might be grounds for sending the student on a brief vacation. I was, you might say, discomfited, and showed up to class for a while with my cell phone jiggered to dial 911 with one touch.

Still, this was small potatoes. Colleges are even leery of disciplining guys who have committed sexual assault, or assault plain and simple. Instead of being punished, these guys frequently stay around, strolling the quad and swilling the libations, an affront (and sometimes a terror) to their victims.

You'll find that cheating is common as well. As far as I can discern, the student ethos goes like this: If the professor is so lazy that he gives the same test every year, it's okay to go ahead and take advantage—you've got better things to do. The Internet is amok with services selling term papers, and those services exist, capitalism being what it is, because people purchase the papers—lots of them. Fraternity files bulge with old tests from a variety of courses. Periodically, the public gets exercised about this situation and there are articles in the national news. But then interest dwindles and matters go back to normal.

One of the reasons professors sometimes look the other way when they sense cheating is that it sends them into a world of sorrow. A friend of mine had the temerity to detect cheating on the part of a kid who was the nephew of a well-placed official in an Arab government complexly aligned with the U.S. Black limousines pulled up in front of his office and disgorged decorously suited negotiators. Did my pal fold? No, he's not the type. But he did not enjoy the process.

What colleges generally want are well-rounded students, civic leaders, people who know what the system demands, how to keep matters light and not push too hard for an education or anything else; people who get their credentials and leave professors alone to do their brilliant work so they may rise and enhance the rankings of the university. Such students leave and become donors and so, in their own turn, contribute immeasurably to the university's standing. They've done a fine job skating on surfaces in high school—the best way to get an across-the-board outstanding record—and now they're on campus to cut a few more figure eights.

In a culture where the major and determining values are monetary, what else could you do? How else would you live if not by getting all you can, succeeding all you can, making all you can?

The idea that a university education really should have no substantial content, should not be about what John Keats was disposed to call "Soul-making," is one that you might think professors and university presidents would be discreet about. Not so. This view informed an address that Richard Brodhead gave to the senior class at Yale before he departed to become president of Duke. Brodhead, an impressive, articulate man, seems to take as his educational touchstone the Duke of Wellington's precept that the Battle of Waterloo was won on the playing fields of Eton. Brodhead suggests that the content of the course isn't really what matters. In five years (or five months, or minutes), the student is likely to have forgotten how to do the problem sets and will only hazily recollect what happens in the ninth book of *Paradise Lost*. The legacy of their college years will be a legacy of difficulties overcome. When they face equally arduous tasks later in life, students will tap their old resources of determination, and they'll win.

All right, there's nothing wrong with this as far as it goes—after all, the student who writes a brilliant forty-page thesis in a hard week has learned more than a little about her inner resources. Maybe it will give her needed confidence in the future. But doesn't the content of the courses matter at all?

On the evidence of this talk, no. Trying to figure out whether the stuff you're reading is true or false and being open to having your life changed is a fraught, controversial activity. Doing so requires energy from the professor—which is better spent on other matters. This kind of perspective-altering teaching and learning can cause the things that administrators fear above all else: trouble, arguments, bad press, et cetera. After the kid-samurai episode, the chair of my department not unsympathetically suggested that this was the sort of incident that could happen when you brought a certain intensity to teaching. At the time I found this remark a tad detached, but maybe he was right.

So if you want an education, the odds aren't with you: The professors are off doing what they call their own work; the other students, who've doped out the way the place runs, are busy leaving their professors alone and getting themselves in position for bright and shining futures; the student-services people are trying to keep everyone content, offering plenty of entertainment and building another state-of-the-art workout facility every few months. The development office is already scanning you for future donations.

So why make trouble? Why not just go along? Let the profs roam free in the realms of pure thought, let yourselves party in the realms of impure pleasure, and let the student-services gang assert fewer prohibitions and newer delights for you. You'll get a good job, you'll have plenty of friends, you'll have a driveway of your own.

You'll also, if my father and I are right, be truly and righteously screwed. The reason for this is simple. The quest at the center of a liberal arts education is not a luxury quest; it's a necessity quest. If you do not undertake it, you risk leading a life of desperation—maybe quiet; maybe, in time, very loud—and I am not exaggerating. For you risk trying to be someone other than who you are, which, in the long run, is killing.

By the time you come to college, you will have been told who you are numberless times. Your parents and friends, your teachers, your counselors, your priests and rabbis and ministers and imams have all had their say. They've let you know how they size you up, and they've let you know what they think you should value. They've given you a sharp and protracted taste of what they feel is good and bad, right and wrong. Much is on their side. They have confronted you with scriptures—holy books that, whatever their actual provenance, have given people what they feel to be wisdom for thousands of years. They've given you family traditions— you've learned the ways of your tribe and community. And, too, you've been tested, probed, looked at up and down and through. The coach knows what your athletic prospects are, the guidance office has a sheaf of test scores that relegate you to this or that ability quadrant, and your teachers have got you pegged. You are, as Foucault might say, the intersection of many evaluative and potentially determining discourses: You, boy, you, girl, have been made.

And—contra Foucault—that's not so bad. Embedded in all of the major religions are profound truths. Schopenhauer, who despised belief in transcendent things, nonetheless taught Christianity to be of inexpressible worth. He couldn't believe in the divinity of Jesus or in the afterlife, but to Schopenhauer, a deep pessimist, a religion that had as its central emblem the figure of a man being tortured on a cross couldn't be entirely misleading. To the Christian, Schopenhauer said, pain was at the center of the understanding of life, and that was just as it should be.

One does not need to be as harsh as Schopenhauer to understand the use of religion, even if one does not believe in an otherworldly God. And all those teachers and counselors and friends—and the prognosticating uncles, the dithering aunts, the fathers and mothers with their hopes for your fulfillment, or their fulfillment in you—should not necessarily be cast aside or ignored. Families have their wisdom. The question "Who do they think you are at home?" is never an idle one.

The major conservative thinkers have always been very serious about what goes by the name of common sense. Edmund Burke saw common sense as a loosely made but often profound collective work in which humanity deposited its hard-earned wisdom—the precipitate of joy and tears—over time. You have been raised in proximity to common sense, if you've been raised at all, and common sense is something to respect, though not quite—peace unto the formidable Burke—to revere.

You may be all that the good people who raised you say you are; you may want all they have shown you is worth wanting; you may be someone who is truly your father's son or your mother's daughter. But then again, you may not be.

For the power that is in you, as Emerson suggested, may be new in nature. You may not be the person that your parents take you to be. And—this thought is both more exciting and more dangerous—you may not be the person that you take yourself to be, either. You may not have read yourself aright, and college is the place where you can find out whether you have or not. The reason to read Blake and Dickinson and Freud and Dickens is not to become more cultivated or more articulate or to be someone who, at a cocktail party, is never embarrassed (or can embarrass others). The best reason to read them is to see if they know you better than you know yourself. You may find your own suppressed and rejected thoughts following back to you with an "alienated majesty." Reading the great writers, you may have the experience Longinus associated with the sublime: You feel that you have actually created the text yourself. For somehow your predecessors are more yourself than you are.

This was my own experience reading the two writers who have influenced me the most, Sigmund Freud and Ralph Waldo Emerson. They gave words to thoughts and feelings that I had never been able to render myself. They shone a light onto the world, and what they saw, suddenly I saw, too. From Emerson I learned to trust my own thoughts, to trust them even when every voice seems to be on the other side. I need the wherewithal, as Emerson did, to say what's on my mind and to take the inevitable hits. Much more I learned from the sage—about character, about loss, about joy, about writing and its secret sources, but Emerson most centrally preaches the gospel of self-reliance, and that is what I have tried most to take from him. I continue to hold in mind one of Emerson's most memorable passages: "Society is a joint-stock company, in which the members agree, for the better securing of his bread to each shareholder, to surrender the liberty and culture of the eater. The virtue in most request is conformity. Self-reliance is its aversion. It loves not realities and creators, but names and customs."

Emerson's greatness lies not only in showing you how powerful names and customs can be, but also in demonstrating how exhilarating it is to buck them. When he came to Harvard to talk about religion, he shocked the professors and students by challenging the divinity of Jesus and the truth of his miracles. He wasn't invited back for decades.

From Freud I found a great deal to ponder as well. I don't mean Freud the aspiring scientist, but the Freud who was a speculative essayist and interpreter of the human condition like Emerson. Freud challenges nearly every significant human ideal. He goes after religion. He says that it comes down to the longing for the father. He goes after love. He calls it "the overestimation of the erotic object." He attacks our desire for charismatic popular leaders. We're drawn to them because we hunger for absolute authority. He declares that dreams don't predict the future and that there's nothing benevolent about them. They're disguised fulfillments of repressed wishes.

Freud has something challenging and provoking to say about virtually every human aspiration. I learned that if I wanted to affirm any consequential ideal, I had to talk my way past Freud. He was—and is—a perpetual challenge and goad.

Never has there been a more shrewd and imaginative cartographer of the psyche. His separation of the self into three parts, and his sense of the fraught, anxious, but often negotiable relations among them (negotiable when you come to the game with a Freudian knowledge), does a great deal to help one navigate experience. (Though sometimes—and I owe this to Emerson—it seems right to let the psyche fall into civil war, accepting barrages of anxiety and grief for this or that good reason.)

The battle is to make such writers one's own, to winnow them out and to find their essential truths. We need to see where they fall short and where they exceed the mark, and then to develop them a little, as the ideas themselves, one comes to see, actually developed others. (Both Emerson and Freud live out of Shakespeare—but only a giant can be truly influenced by Shakespeare.) In reading, I continue to look for one thing—to be influenced, to learn something new, to be thrown off my course and onto another, better way.

My father knew that he was dissatisfied with life. He knew that none of the descriptions people had for him quite fit. He understood that he was always out of joint with life as it was. He had talent: My brother and I each got about half the raw ability he possessed, and that's taken us through life well enough. But what to do with that talent—there was the rub for my father. He used to stroll through the house intoning his favorite line from Groucho Marx's ditty "Whatever It Is, I'm Against It." (I recently asked my son, now twenty-one, if he thought I was mistaken in teaching him this particular song when he was six years old. "No!" he said, filling the air with an invisible forest of exclamation points.) But what my father never managed to get was a sense of who he might become. He never had a world of possibilities spread before him, never made sustained contact with the best that has been thought and said. He didn't get to revise his understanding of himself, figure out what he'd do best that might give the world some profit.

My father was a gruff man but also a generous one, so that night at the kitchen table at 58 Clewley Road he made an effort to let me have the chance that had been denied to him by both fate and character. He gave me the chance to see what I was all about, and if it proved to be different from him, proved even to be something he didn't like or entirely comprehend, then he'd deal with it.

Right now, if you're going to get a real education, you may have to be aggressive and assertive.

Your professors will give you some fine books to read, and they'll probably help you understand them. What they won't do, for reasons that perplex me, is ask you if the books contain truths you could live your life by. When you read Plato, you'll probably learn about his metaphysics and his politics and his way of conceiving the soul. But no one will ask you if his ideas are good enough to believe in. No one will ask you, in the words of Emerson's disciple William James, what their "cash value" might be. No one will suggest that you might use Plato as your bible for a week or a year or longer. No one, in short, will ask you to use Plato to help you change your life.

That will be up to you. You must put the question of Plato to yourself. You must ask whether reason should always rule the passions, philosophers should always rule the state, and poets should inevitably be banished from a just commonwealth. You have to ask yourself if wildly expressive music (rock and rap and the rest) deranges the soul in ways that are destructive to its health. You must inquire of yourself if balanced calm is the most desirable human state.

Occasionally—for you will need some help in fleshing out the answers—you may have to prod your professors to see if they will take the text at hand—in this case the divine and disturbing Plato—to be true. And you will have to be tough if the professor mocks you for uttering a sincere question instead of keeping matters easy for all concerned by staying detached and analytical. (Detached analysis has a place, but in the end you've got to speak from the heart and pose the question of truth.) You'll be the one who pesters your teachers. You'll ask your history teacher about whether there is a design to our history, whether we're progressing or declining, or whether, in the words of a fine recent play, *The History Boys*, history's "just one fuckin' thing after another." You'll be the one who challenges your biology teacher about the intellectual conflict between evolutionist and creationist thinking. You'll not only question the statistics teacher about what numbers *can* explain but what they can't.

Because every subject you study is a language, and since you may adopt one of these languages as your own, you'll want to know how to speak it expertly and also how it fails to deal with those concerns for which it has no adequate words. You'll be looking into the reach of every metaphor that every discipline offers, and you'll be trying to see around their corners.

The whole business is scary, of course. What if you arrive at college devoted to premed, sure that nothing will make you and your family happier than life as a physician, only to discover that elementary school-teaching is where your heart is?

You might learn that you're not meant to be a doctor at all. Of course, given your intellect and discipline, you can still probably be one. You can pound your round peg through the very square hole of medical school, then go off into the profession. And society will help you. Society has a cornucopia of resources to encourage you in doing what society needs done but that you don't much like doing and are not cut out to do. To ease your grief, society offers alcohol, television, drugs, divorce, and buying, buying, buying what you don't need. But all those, too, have their costs.

Education is about finding out what form of work for you is close to being play—work you do so easily that it restores you as you go. Randall Jarrell once said that if he were a rich man, he would pay money to teach poetry to students. (I would, too, for what it's worth.) In saying that, he (like my father) hinted in the direction of a profound and true theory of learning.

Having found what's best for you to do, you may be surprised by how far you rise, how prosperous, even against your own projections, you become. The student who eschews medical school to follow his gift for teaching small children spends his twenties in low-paying but pleasurable and soul-rewarding toil. He's always behind on his student-loan payments; he still lives in a house with four other guys, not all of whom got proper instructions on how to clean a bathroom. He buys shirts from the Salvation Army, has intermittent Internet, and vacations where he can. But lo—he has a gift for teaching. He writes an essay about how to teach, then a book—which no one buys. But he writes another—in part out of a feeling of injured merit, perhaps—and that one they do buy.

Money is still a problem, but in a new sense. The world wants him to write more, lecture, travel more, and will pay him for his efforts, and he likes this a good deal. But he also likes staying around and showing up at school and figuring out how to get this or that little runny-nosed specimen to begin learning how to read. These are the kinds of problems that are worth having, and if you advance, as Thoreau asked us to do, in the general direction of your dreams, you may have them. If you advance in the direction of someone else's dreams—if you want to live someone else's dreams rather than yours—then get a TV for every room, buy yourself a lifetime supply of your favorite quaff, crank up the porn channel, and groove away. But when we expend our energies in rightful ways, Robert Frost observed, we stay whole and vigorous and we don't get weary. "Strongly spent," the poet says, "is synonymous with kept."

Do Sports Build Character?

The first year I played high school football, the coaches were united in their belief that drinking water on the practice field was dangerous. It made you cramp up, they told us. It made you sick to your stomach, they said. So during practice, which went on for two and a half hours, twice a day, during a roaring New England summer, we got no water. Players cramped up anyway; players got sick to their stomachs regardless. Players fell on their knees and began making soft plaintive noises; they were helped to their feet, escorted to the locker room, and seen no more. On the first day of double sessions, there were about 120 players—tough Irish and Italian kids and a few blacks—and by the end of the twelve-day ordeal there were sixty left. Some of us began without proper equipment. I started without cleats. But this was not a problem: Soon someone who wore your size shoes or shoulder pads would quit, and then you could have theirs.

The coaches didn't cut anyone from my high school squad that year. Kids cut themselves. Guys with what appeared to me to be spectacular athletic talent would, after four days of double-session drills, walk hangdog into the coaches' locker room and hand over their pads. The coaches rarely tried to encourage them to stay. If a kid couldn't take it, he couldn't take it. There was no water and there were no compassionate paternal talks. There were the two-and-a-half-hour practices twice a day;

each of which ended with grass drills. We formed ranks and ran in place; when the coach blew the whistle, we jumped up, spread-eagled ourselves in the air, and went bang onto the hard ground. Then we got up and started running in place again. Some guys went bang and stayed down on the deck panting, which meant that they needed to quit. They brought their dirty practice gear home, got it washed by their mothers, and presented it in a white, fresh-smelling bundle, like a fluffy loaf of home-baked bread, to the coaches the next morning. When I asked one of them why he quit, he said simply, "I couldn't take it."

Could I? There was no reason going in to think that I would be able to. I was buttery soft around the waist, nearsighted, not especially fast, and not quick at all. It turned out that underneath the soft exterior I had some muscle and that my lung capacity was well developed, probably from vicious bouts of asthma I'd had as a boy, when I'd fought for air as hard as any marathon runner, perhaps harder. (The marathon runner has the luxury of stepping out of the race; not the asthmatic.) But compared to my fellow ballplayers, my physical gifts were meager. What I had was a will that was anything but weak. It was a surprise to me, and to everyone who knew me, how ferociously I wanted to stay with the game.

Still, things did not look promising. Sometimes after morning practice I was so dazed that it took me an hour to shower and get dressed. By the time I was in my street clothes, the locker room was usually empty. Sometimes I wasn't sure that I would be able to find my way to the bus stop and get home, so I went below the bleachers and fell asleep, woke up two hours later, hiked to a convenience store to buy what passed for a lunch, and then went to sleep under the stands again. By four o'clock, when the other players were returning, I was in front of my locker and dressing in slow motion. In an hour I was on the field, ready to go. I cried in my sleep once at the thought that the next day I would have to go back to practice. But I went. I didn't miss a day, didn't fake an injury, didn't duck a drill, and at the end of double sessions—a shock to myself—I was a ballplayer.

Did I love the game? I surely liked it. I liked how when I was deep in fatigue, I became a tougher, more daring person, even a reckless one. One night, scrimmaging, I went head-on with the star running back, a guy who outweighed me by twenty pounds and was far faster and stronger. I did what the coaches said: I squared up, got low (in football, the answer to every difficulty is to get low, or get lower), and planted him. I did that? I asked myself. Me? I liked being the guy who could do that—sometimes, though alas, not often enough. The intensity of the game was an inebriate. It conquered my grinding self-consciousness, brought me out of myself.

I liked the transforming aspect of the game: I came to the field one thing, a diffident guy with a slack body, and I worked like a dog and so became something else, a guy with some physical prowess and a touch more faith in himself. Mostly I suppose I liked the whole process because it was so damn hard. I didn't think I could make it and no one I knew did either. I knew that my parents were ready to console me if I came home bruised and dead weary and said that I was quitting. In time, one of the coaches confessed to me that he was sure I'd be gone in a few days. I had not succeeded in anything for a long time: I was a crappy student; socially I was close to a wash; my part-time job was scrubbing pans in a hospital kitchen; the first girl I liked in high school didn't like me; the second and the third jumped in behind and followed her lead. But football was something I could do, or at least do halfway. (I was never going to be anything like a star.) It was hard and it took some strength of will and—clumsily, passionately—I could do it.

"Long live what I badly did at Clemson," James Dickey says in "The Bee," the poem about his football days at college. Dickey wasn't much of a player, either, it seems. He remembers his inept lunges into the line and recalls the coaches badgering him, not unlike the way they badgered me: " 'God damn you Dickey, *dig*!' " The old coaches have come back to Dickey years later, when he's afflicted by the malaise of middle age. They holler at him to get the lead out and to sprint for all he's worth into the midst of ferocious California freeway traffic, where his son, stung by a bee and terrified, has blindly run. Dickey digs. He leaves his feet—the ballplayer's most desperate maneuver. He makes it. "I have him where / He lives," the poet says, "and down we go singing with screams into / The dirt." And the screams of the coaches turn, finally, into whispers of approval. Dead coaches, like Shag Norton, Dickey's backfield coach, live in the air, the poet tells his son; they live in the ear. They want you better than you are. They scream at you when something must be saved.

I understand, I think. Though I never had much overt affection for the coaches (or they for me), I knew that the objective of the game on the deepest level wasn't to score touchdowns or make tackles or to block kicks. The game was much more about practice than about the Saturday-afternoon contests themselves. And practice was about trying to do something over and over again and failing and failing and then finally succeeding partway. Practice was about showing up and doing the same

drills day after day and getting stronger and faster by tiny, tiny incre-
ments and then discovering that by the end of the season you were effectively another person. But mostly football was about those first days of
double sessions when everyone who stuck with it did something he imagined was impossible and so learned to recalibrate his instruments. In the
future what immediately looked impossible to us—what said Back Off,
Not for You—had to be looked at again and maybe attempted anyway.
We'd already done something we thought we couldn't: Maybe this next
citadel would fall, this next granite block would give way to shape and
proportion, with a dose, maybe a double dose, of the effort we'd applied
on that miserable unyielding field under the sun that turned your helmet
into a boiling cauldron and your brain—truly, it sometimes felt this
way—into simmering mush.

When we seemed to get hurt on the field, when we went down and
didn't immediately get up, the coaches had a common reaction: "Get up
and walk it off." Sometimes, granted, the stretcher had to come out, but
not often. It was surprising how many times it was possible to rise like
Lazarus after a collision that felt like a couple of bowling balls rolling
together. I once tried to tackle a tight end who was six inches taller and
fifty pounds heavier than I was. I bounced off and hit the so-called turf
so hard that I felt the fillings in the back of my mouth jump; I passed out
for an instant and woke up thinking my back was broken. "Get up. Walk
it off. You're all right." I did and I was.

Tim Green, the onetime star defensive end for the Atlanta Falcons,
makes a point about playing ball, a point that carries over into other areas
of experience. There's one factor at the heart of the game, he says. And
that is you have to get up. You get smacked around and knocked to the
ground on at least half the plays, but then you have to get up. You have
to rise and go on to the next play. "I am defeated all the time," says
Emerson, "yet to victory I am born." Football demonstrates that one is
defeated, knocked down, time after time, and it also shows that victory
is an uncertain thing, whether you think you're born to it or not.

Speaking for myself, I've never had to call on the spirit of grass drills
or double sessions or channel an old coach in order to save myself or a
child—there's never been that drastic a moment. (Lord defend me from
such.) But I do recall what it felt like when, having thrown all I thought I
had into writing a chunk of my dissertation, I came back from the job
market a complete flop. I had come in with hopes that pointed to the
heights: I didn't want merely any academic job, though at the time that

would have been hard enough. I wanted one of the dozen or so best ones that every year had about four hundred applicants apiece. If I couldn't get one, I decided, I'd quit and do something else. After the grand belly flop—like a grass drill drop, with no control—I knew that I'd have to work on a level higher by far than I had on anything I'd ever approached. I'd coasted at my ease through grad school, or so it now seemed. So I began living in the library, much in the way that I lived at the football stadium my first summer on the team, arriving in the stacks early, leaving only to go to the gym in the late afternoon and to eat dinner, then returning until past dark. I built a wall of books on my table as though to cloister myself in like a medieval monk. Did I call on the old spirit of double sessions? Quietly, pretty quietly, I did. I kept it largely to myself, since most scholars don't see much symmetry between what they do and what runners and jumpers and (especially) blockers and tacklers attempt. I read every book in the library on John Keats, the subject of my first chapter, and most of the articles. I wrote and rewrote my first paragraph about thirty times—like those grass drills, over and over and over again. When the summer was through I had a chapter I could be proud of and that I knew would take me where I wanted to go.

Doctoral dissertations are tougher than one might imagine: It's lonely work and no one (sometimes least of all your dissertation adviser, who has other things to do) cares much if you flourish or pucker on the vine. But compared to what others are compelled to endure—severe illness, divorce, the mortal sickness of a child—sitting in an air-conditioned library trying to make sense out of the way other people have tried to make sense of the world isn't all that daunting. But others, I know, have called on their experience in sports to summon larger doses of courage. They've used their old sports experience as a map to take them back to their reserves of strength they had forgotten they possessed. "Diversity of strength will attend us," the poet says, "if but once we have been strong." For many of us, the time of being strong was the time we played a sport. Do sports build character? Of course they do. Who could doubt it?

Sports are many things, but one of the things they are is an imitation of heroic culture. They mimic the martial world; they fabricate the condition of war. (Boxing doesn't fabricate war; it *is* war and, to my mind, not a sport. As Joyce Carol Oates says, you play football and baseball and basketball. No one "plays" boxing.) This fabrication is in many ways a good thing—necessary to the health of a society. For it seems to me that Plato is right and that the desire for glory is part of everyone's spirit. Plato called this desire *thymos*, and he associated its ascendancy and celebration with Homer. The objective of his great work, *The Republic*, is to show how for a civilization to truly thrive, it must find a way to make the drive for glory subordinate to reason. Plato believes that war is sometimes necessary, but that going to war should be up to the rulers, the philosopher kings, who have developed their minds fully. Some of us, Plato says, have a hunger for martial renown that surpasses others', and those people are very valuable and very dangerous. They need praise when they fight well (for material rewards don't mean much to them), and they need something to keep them occupied when no war is at hand. Sport is a way to do this. Plato would probably approve of the way athletics function in our culture—they let the most thymotic of us express the hunger for conquest, and they allow the rest of us to get our hit of glory through identification.

But there are warriors and there are *warriors*; there are athletes and there are *athletes*. In the Western heroic tradition, the paragon of the humane warrior is Homer's Hector, prince of the Trojans. He is a fierce fighter: On one particular day, no Greek can stand up to him; his valor puts the whole Greek army to route. Even on an unexceptional day, Hector can stand against Ajax, the Greek giant, and trade blow for blow with him. Yet as fierce as Hector can be, he is also humane. He is a loving son to his aged parents, a husband who talks on equal terms with his wife, Andromache, and he is a tenderhearted father. He and King Priam, his own father, are the only ones in Troy who treat Helen, the ostensible cause of the war, with kindness. One of the most memorable scenes in *The Iliad* comes when Hector strides toward his boy, Astyanax, coming fresh from the battlefield. The child screams with fright at the ferocious form, encased in armor, covered with dust and gore. Hector understands his child in an instant and takes off his helmet, with its giant horsehair plume, then bends over, picks his boy up, and dandles him while Andromache looks on happily. Astyanax—who will soon be pitched from off the battlements of Troy when the Greeks conquer the city—stares up at his father and laughs.

The scene concentrates what is most appealing about Hector—and about a certain kind of athlete and warrior. Hector can turn it off. He can stop being the manslayer that he needs to be out there on the windy plains of Troy and become a humane husband and father. The scene shows him in his dual nature—warrior and man of thought and feeling. In a sense, he is the figure that every fighter and everyone who takes the athletic field should aspire to emulate. He is the Navy Seal or the Green Beret who would never kill a prisoner; the fearless fighter who could never harm a woman or a child. In the symbolic world of sports, where the horrors and the triumphs of combat are only mimicked, he is the one who comports himself with extreme gentleness off the field, who never speaks ill of an opponent, who never complains, never whines. The dual nature of the noble athlete finds a concentrated image in football: When the play starts, the player goes all out, takes chances, is reckless; when the whistle blows, he becomes his civilized self again, doesn't argue or complain, but walks with dignity back to his huddle. Plato greatly admired people who, though possessed with strong will, could still use their reason and their fellow feeling to temper themselves.

But *The Iliad* is not primarily about Hector. It is the poem of Achilles and his wrath. After Hector kills Achilles' dear friend Patroclus, Achilles goes on a rampage, killing every Trojan he can. All humanity leaves him; all mercy is gone. At one point, a Trojan fighter grasps his knees and begs for mercy. Achilles taunts him. Look at me, he says, so strong and beautiful, and someday I too shall have to die. But not today. Today is your day. At one point a river close to the city, the River Scamander, becomes incensed over Achilles' murdering spree. The hero has glutted Scamander's waters with blood and its bed with bodies. The river is so enraged that it tries to drown the hero. When Achilles finally gets to Hector, he slaughters him before the eyes of his parents, Hecuba and Priam, and drags his body across the plains of Troy. Achilles is drunk on rage, the poem tells us. His rational mind has left him, and he is mad with the joy of slaughter. The ability to modulate character that Hector shows—the fierce warrior becoming the loving father—is something Achilles does not possess. He is as mad now as a wild beast. Achilles, one feels, could not stop himself if he wished to: A fellow Greek who somehow insulted him when he was on his rampage would be in nearly as much danger as a Trojan enemy. Plato would recognize Achilles as a man who has lost all reason and who has allowed *thymos* to dominate his soul.

This ability to go mad—to become berserk—is inseparable from Achilles' greatness as a warrior. It is part of what sets him above the more circumspect Hector on the battlefield. When Hector encounters Achilles for the last time, Hector feels fear. Achilles in his wrath has no idea what fear is, and that is part of what makes him unstoppable.

Achilles' fate is too often the fate of warriors and, in a lower key, of athletes. They unleash power in themselves that they cannot discipline. They leave the field of combat or the field of play and they are still ferocious, or they can be stirred to ferocity by almost nothing. They can let no insult pass. A misplaced word sends them into a rage. A mild frustration turns them violent. *Thymos*, as Plato would have said, has taken over their souls, and reason no longer has a primary place—in some cases it has no place at all.

The kind of intensity that sports—and especially kinetic sports like football—can provoke is extremely necessary for any society: *Thymos* must have its moment. But that intensity is mortally dangerous for society and for individuals, too. Sports can lead people to brutal behavior—I see no way to avoid the conclusion. To any dispassionate observer it is clear that athletes find themselves in more brawls, more car wrecks, more spousal assaults, more drunken-driving episodes than the average run of the population. Sports can teach people to modulate their passions—they can help them be closer to Hector. But they can foment cruelty as well. Athletes, as everyone who went to an American high school will tell you, can be courtly, dignified individuals. But they're often bullies as well; they often seek violence for its own sake. They take crude pleasure in dominating others; they like to humiliate their foes off the field as well as on.

All too often, the players who go all out on the field and can't readily turn it off when they're outside their games are the best players. They're the most headlong, the most fearless, the most dedicated. And when they encounter a modulated, more controlled antagonist in a game, often the more brutal player wins.

The great athlete runs on instinct—everyone knows that. But a by-product of running on instinct is that you lose the habit of thought. Thought is what slows you down, makes you overly self-conscious, and gives the other guy time to beat you to the ball. Listening to most sports figures talk is like listening to the paint dry, and this is not necessarily because they don't have any mental endowments. It seems rather that to develop that kind of spontaneity that sports require, you have to stifle the mental endowments that you do have: The habit of thought will only take you so far as an athlete or as a hand-to-hand warrior. It does happen that great athletes can show an inclination for thinking: Muhammad Ali had the inclination, but not much ability; Bill Russell seems to have had some of both. But this is not common, and for good reason.

Lawrence Taylor was one of the best players ever to play in the National Football League. With his speed and ferocity and his ability to run down the opposing quarterback, he made football into a different, more violent game. But he was often as much in a fury off the field as on. By his own account, Taylor led the life of a beast: Drunk, brawling, high on coke, speeding in his car, he was a peril to anyone who came near him. His coach, Bill Parcells, helped him to cultivate this off-field character, knowing that it contributed to his prowess when he played. If the best players are—or often are—the ones who are the least controlled, the ones in whom at all times passion for preeminence trumps reason, then it is not entirely clear that one can readily say what American coaches and boosters of all sorts love to say, that sports always build character. If having a good character means having a coherent, flexible internal structure where the best part rules over the most dangerous, then sports may not always be something conducive to true virtue.

My own experience in high school confirms this view. Playing football made me more confident; it gave me powers of resolve that I'd draw on later in life, and I'm grateful for those things. But it also made me more brutal. I came to crave the physical stimulation of the game—I came to like hitting and even being hit. When the season ended, I found myself re-creating the feeling of football in a string of fistfights and mass brawls. I didn't become a thug—far from it. But I did let the part of me that sought power and standing—over others—go way too far. Having been down that road, the chances of my taking it again are greater, I suspect, than they are for other men. Once the path has been cut, it stays open. I once shocked a colleague, and myself, by admitting that if someone ran a light and smashed up my car (which I loved more than I should), the chances of my popping him in the jaw were probably much greater than the chances of the average professional guy doing so. Once the punch in the mouth is part of your repertoire—once you've done it a few times as an adult—it never really goes away.

There's another major difficulty with sports, especially with sports played by males. When males get together in groups, they often act badly. They appoint by quiet consensus an alpha male and they follow his lead; they become more literal, more obvious; they jostle and compete. And they're also disposed to scapegoating. Homosexuality—or any indication of homosexuality—has tended to send heterosexual male athletes into a horrible spin when they're together in groups. The male sports world has been a dramatically antigay world. Those players who are homosexual have known that they must hide it on pain of humiliation or even physical harm.

In the world of sports, hostility to homosexuals and to anything perceived as unmanly has been heightened to an extreme degree. The player enters a world of brutal distinctions—of rejection and scapegoating—and, not surprisingly, he risks becoming more brutal himself.

Sports are also—it almost goes without saying—an intensely hierarchical world. In sports your identity and prowess are one and the same. When one teammate looks at another, what he sees first is how good the other is. He makes a quick calculation: Am I more or less able than he is? Or are we, perhaps, the same? Sports are about standings, and not just of the team against other teams but within the team itself. Everyone has a place in the hierarchy, and that hierarchy is constantly shifting. This sense of relative human importance is almost completely unsentimental—there's an accuracy of evaluation in sports that presides nowhere else in the world; there's no affirmative action on a football field. Everyone on a team knows who he is better than and who is better than he, and he acts his part. On NBA teams, the alpha dog, the best player on the team, determines what tunes they'll listen to in the locker room and sets the tone for how the players will connect with the coach and how they'll comport themselves on the court with the referees and off it with the public. A world that is so intensely hierarchical is a clear, energizing world where meaning is available all the time. Who are you? I'm the best center in the league, or the second best, or whatever. And I'm working to rise, or to stay on top—or whatever. One of the joys of sports lies in knowing who you are and where you are and what you have to do to ascend. Such knowledge is not available to most people in the world and they often envy it, or they tap into it vicariously by becoming fans.

Yet a world of omnipresent hierarchy is also, by definition, a world that is low on compassion and kindness. The great spiritual teachers—Jesus, Confucius, the Buddha—taught, perhaps above every other tenet, that we are all the same and that we are all part of one great life. They taught compassion, which is the feeling that you and I and all of us live in a world of suffering and grief and that our first duty is to treat each other with loving-kindness. The world of sport is a pagan world—the agonistic world that came before the great spiritual teachers—in which compassion is not a prominent value. True, professional athletes often take part in the culture of compassion: They show up at children's hospitals and attend worthy fund-raisers. These gestures serve to salve the conscience of a public that cannot rest fully content with a world of unsentimental strife. The public has an allegiance both to such strife and to the tenets of kindness and compassion. Many Americans attend church on Sunday and listen to the loving Gospel of the Savior and then repair home to their television sets, turn on the game, and watch young men try to bust each other's spleens. We must create a variety of fictions to live comfortably with this state of affairs.

From the perspective of the great teachers, it's demeaning and foolish to reduce people to their prowess at one thing or another. When I was at my best playing football, I was counted as one of the pack, a genuine player, and it put some bounce in my step. Now a late-career pickup basketball player, I'm the guy who misses too many jump shots in a row and gets the ball taken away from him by quicker guys—and while I'm on the court, that's all I am. The rest of my identity is eclipsed by it. The great teachers tell us that the only road to happiness is having a sense of common being with all others we see and acting out of that sense at all times. When you do so, you lose your meager and vain individuality in something larger and you can stop striving, stop desiring to ascend. You can rest. The more ambitious you are, the more competitive you are, the less often the feeling of serene being—in which, as Wordsworth says, "with an eye made quiet by the power of harmony and the deep power of joy, we see into the life of things"—will come your way. The individual who lives in such a spirit, Schopenhauer tells us, is the one who, when he passes another on the street, says to himself, "That too is me." Those who whisper, however subliminally, "That is another," live in the purgatory of individual pride and individual desire. Do sports encourage you to be part of a group, the team? The team, to this way of thinking, is simply an extension of "me," since it is defined by the desire for supremacy over others.

Do sports build character? Sports are what Derrida, in an essay on Plato, associates with something called the *pharmakon*, a substance that is both a poison and a remedy. Sports can do great good: build the body, create a stronger, more resilient will, impart confidence, stimulate bravery, and even foment daring. But at the same time, sports can and often do brutalize the player—they make him more violent, more aggressive. They make him intolerant of gentleness; they help turn him into a member of the pack, which defines itself by maltreating others: the weak, the differently made. One might say that the use of intelligence is needful here. One must think hard and think well and, in Plato's spirit, one must use the mind to give the thymotic drives of the soul full recognition and reasonable play, but at the same time to keep them in check. This is an ideal—Hector's ideal, we might call it—and it is not an impossible one. But there is something in the drive for glory that despises all reflection. A certain sort of glory seeking must in fact overcome reflection, as Achilles shows. So sports will always be a world of danger, as well as one rich with human possibility.

Glorious Failure

2005 Convocation Address, University of Virginia

Thank you. I'm very pleased and very honored to be here, and without false modesty, I really feel a certain amount of doubt that I have anything new to say to so distinguished and successful a group of people, but thank you anyway for asking me.

I'm addressing, I know, some of the most accomplished students at the university and also their parents, people who've had great success in one of the most difficult of all arts, the art of raising children. I myself have children and I think I can begin to understand what this day means to the parents and the grandparents and sisters and brothers and uncles who've made the trip to Charlottesville, and from my heart, warmest congratulations for what you've achieved and what is likely to be achieved in the future.

This is, as I say, a remarkably successful group of people, and what I'm going to be talking about is not success at all. What I'm going to be talking about is failure and the necessary role that failure plays in anything that would qualify as authentic success. I'm going to come out in favor of failure. I'm going to say some good things in behalf of it. I'm going to enjoin you before you leave this university, and maybe sometime afterward, to fail a little bit more.

But before I do that, I want to tell you something. Let me put it this way—it's a narrative, and if you laugh, it's a joke; if you nod your head wisely, it's a story; and if you get up and leave, it's really bad. Here it is. Once upon a time there was a man named Joseph. He was a good husband, a good father, a good provider. He lived well in the world. He was also a religious man. He prayed regularly, gave money to his church; he was upright, good, and strong. He had everything he wanted in the world except for one thing. He wanted more than anything else to win the lottery, so he would pray regularly and he would say, "Oh, Lord, I've been a good man. I've sacrificed, I've prayed. I've held up my end of the bargain. Please, I would like to win the lottery." Years went by. Still no lottery win. Joseph became a little more insistent—"Lord, I've sacrificed, I've prayed, I've done your good works, I've done your bidding in every way. Now, what about that lottery?"

This goes on for years until Joseph begins to get a little bit irritated with the Lord. "Lord, when am I going to win the lottery?" Still nothing. Finally, one day Joseph begins to entreat the Lord again and a voice comes to him as from above. It says, "Joseph."

"Hmmm, yes."

"This is the Lord."

"Finally. Lord, I've sacrificed, I've prayed, I've been an upright and good man. I've done all of your bidding. When am I going to win the lottery?"

"Joseph, be calm."

"Lord, please, when?"

"Joseph, I have one piece of advice for you."

"Lord, what is it? I'll do anything."

"Joseph, buy a ticket."

Buy a ticket. That's the subject of my talk. Well, you laughed, so it turned out to be a joke. I'm very glad about that.

The last time I was here in U Hall, I have to admit the joke was on me. I took my son, whom I'm very proud to have here today, to a concert by a guy named Ludacris, who's a rapper. I like Ludacris a lot. It turned out that none of the other parents were available to take their children to that show. I don't really know why. And I sat up in section 32, right there, and I was enjoying the show, and then suddenly the person who was standing roughly where I am now—that was Ludacris—looked up and said something like this: "I want to send one out to the elderly dude jamming in the back."

And it was strange because I was up there by myself and I looked around for the elderly dude and I didn't see him and then 'Cris—I call him 'Cris because we're kind of friendly—helped me out by having somebody shine a big spotlight up there, so I could look for the elderly dude. But the problem was the light was really in my eyes and I couldn't see him for anything.

You know Oscar Wilde's great line? The tragedy of getting older is not that one is old, it's that one is young. I know what you thought I was going to say—I like Ludacris. I know you thought I was going to say something bad about your music, rap and all that. I know you did. But you know, from a baby boomer perspective, the way we sometimes look at it is this: You gave us Britney Spears and we gave you the Rolling Stones. It's hardly fair.

Well, that was a bittersweet moment that Ludacris provided for me here. I'm pleased to revisit the scene of that semitrauma and fundamentally to have it healed by President Casteen's very generous introduction of me.

But as he was talking about the list of my accomplishments—of which I'm duly proud, I suppose—I flashed on something else that I often have occasion to think about. Those are things that come off my résumé and, as I say, it's a good and fine résumé and many of you who are out there today are compiling résumés that will be better and finer by far. But one of the things I think about when I hear that résumé is another résumé that I have, and that résumé I call my ghost résumé. And what's on my ghost résumé are all the things that went awry, the essays that didn't work, the book projects that fell apart, the writing that seemed like it was coming from the pen of Samuel Johnson on Tuesday and turned out on Friday not to make much sense at all.

I think about my first book, *Towards Reading Freud*, Princeton University Press. The struggle to get that book published, the war to get that book published, is something that I dare say Napoleon would've admired. It was a two-year push, maybe three. But it doesn't say that on the résumé. It simply says, "Princeton University Press." It just says all of the good stuff. There's a whole litany of failures there back behind the accomplishments, and they continue to happen. I continue to try things that don't work, try things that half work, try things that need to be revised five times before they're ever going to work.

When I was a young man I had a myth of my own. It's the myth of arrival, and what that myth said was that at a certain point you get to a place in your career and everything goes well. Everything you do works, because you're a success and that's that. I'm here to tell you that that point does not exist. But I'm proud of those failures because they made possible what successes I was able to achieve. I surprised myself occasionally, and that felt pretty good. Yeats said, "That which fascinates is the most difficult among things not impossible." And I've always wanted to be fascinated by what I'm doing, and that means I've done difficult things. Or at least things that have been difficult for me. If you do difficult things, take on truly challenging ventures, you will at least occasionally fail. But you'll be fascinated, too. You'll be awake.

I was a student of failure for a long time. I've watched people who are remarkable successes, the people I admired most, going through their lives compiling failure after failure. The first person I encountered in that regard and the one whose work really changed my life was Malcolm X. I remember reading Malcolm X's book. It was the first book that I ever bought with my own money, a book that I read all the way through without stopping, as I recall it. It just fascinated me. I remember Malcolm X as a street thug going to jail in Boston. He lived close to me. I remember him going to jail and getting into arguments in the prison yard and feeling that he couldn't keep up with the arguers. Though he was smart, he had a good mind, he didn't know much. And he knew that the way to learn something was to read, and he went to the prison library and he got out as many books as he could. He said: I went down those pages and fifteen, twenty words were words I didn't know. So I went and I got the dictionary and I started reading the dictionary but I didn't remember the words, so I copied down the words and I copied down their definitions. I copied the whole dictionary. You can't believe what a world opened up to me at that point, Malcolm X said.

He had led a miserable failure of a life, and suddenly he was an intellectual and a dynamic man. He went on from there to be a preacher among the black Muslims for the Reverend Elijah Muhammad— dramatic, not always right in my view, but surely provocative all the time. He provoked thought—that's what Malcolm did. Everywhere he went, he provoked thinking. He went on to embrace a different kind of Islam in which he held out hope for the brotherhood of all regardless of color. Malcolm X was somebody who looked back repeatedly, looked back on failures as well as successes, and used those failures as an opportunity to do something else. He didn't have one life or two. He had three or four because of the resiliency that he possessed.

Another one of my heroes in the art of failure is Walt Whitman. Walt Whitman at the age of thirty-two was absolutely nothing, absolutely nothing. He was not good at anything. He taught school for a while and he was bad at that and for this reason: He refused to whip his students. He wrote temperance novels of an unreadable badness. He wrote newspaper pieces that really don't hold up anymore. But then suddenly reading

Emerson and going to the opera and walking the streets of New York City and writing in his notebook, strange and wonderful thoughts started to come to pass. Suddenly Whitman was writing ecstatically—outside himself—and the result of that amazing faith in his own possibilities amidst failure was the best book of American poetry, from my point of view, ever written, *Leaves of Grass*. He sent it off to the most formidable literary figure in America at the time, Ralph Waldo Emerson, Emerson, somebody who combined all the prestige of every American Nobel Prize winner alive today. Emerson took the volume, read it, and said, "I find it the finest piece of wit and wisdom that America has yet contributed." And he told Whitman as much, and Whitman printed it on the spine of the book and sent it out. Good for him.

Whitman went on to live the life that he imagined in *Song of Myself* and in *Leaves of Grass*. In the 1860s, he became a male nurse in the hospitals in Washington. He tended the men, the wounded, Union troops and Confederate both. He took their letters down. He gave them small presents. He made their last moments at least something like bearable. He'd walk in the street in the morning and exchange glances with Abraham Lincoln and I like to think that the two of them recognized each other as having something quite unusual, because if you're going to look for failure in American literature and American history: How many elections did Abraham Lincoln win? Not many. Not many, but he came back every time.

Failure is a big part of education, it seems to me, and we're lucky at the University of Virginia because our most exemplary figures are figures who were not successful all the time, not even close to it. I'm pleased and proud to be wearing my doctoral robes from Yale University, but Yale was a school where I often felt you had it or you didn't, you knew it or you didn't, whereas at Virginia I feel there are many, many chances.

The life of Edgar Allan Poe, Virginia's most famous graduate, was a disaster, right? Alcohol problems, health problems, gambling problems, every deficiency under the sun. For a while, one of the great scholarly debates in Poe studies was whether in fact he had died drunk and in the gutter or not. Whether he died that way or not, it was not unhabitual for Poe to be loaded and half out of his head. Yet he turned out a spectacular amount of writing, not just the short stories but a novel, essays, and critical studies. He was a reviewer like nobody else. He worked ferociously and he opened up a whole nightmare world in his art, the world of the House of Usher, the world of all those horrible tales. Introduced us to nightmares; in some ways he pioneered the art of psychoanalysis and developed gothic art, which has its resonances in some of the best writing going on today—as well as in *Saw II* through *XXXX*.

I think of Thomas Jefferson, a true cultural and political hero, author of the Declaration of Independence, Statutes of Religious Freedom, founder of the University of Virginia, and yet in many ways a deeply flawed man in his relations to his slaves. The way he treated Sally Hemings and the children he bore with her doesn't bear easy consideration. But I like to think of Jefferson as somebody who on some level, acknowledging his flaws, helped in his way to make people in posterity free in ways that he himself couldn't make the people around him free. When the revelations finally came out about Jefferson and Sally Hemings, the response that I heard from a number of black people, charitable in their response to failure, went like this—it's good finally to be able to welcome Thomas Jefferson into the family.

One problem with success is that people ask you to do the successful things over and over and over again. We all know people who've written the same book, painted the same picture, sung the same song time and time and time again. There's a wonderful moment on a Joni Mitchell album when she says, after somebody asked her to do "Circle Game" one more time, "You know, nobody ever said to Van Gogh, 'Paint *A Starry Night* again, man.'" But the wonderful thing about Joni Mitchell is that she has tried everything in music. She's worked with jazz musicians, she's done folk rock, she's composed on her own. Her originality is simply stunning. Her breadth is stunning. Most of us now know her as the voice of the sixties. She's more than that. She's a good painter, too. One time I saw Joni Mitchell, it was in New York City and she had a big band with her. That was the experiment of the day. It was simply awful, but I was pleased to pay my enormous sum. I felt like I'd given each member of the band about five dollars in order to continue a career of tremendous failure and tremendous success.

Is it F. Scott Fitzgerald who said there are no second acts in American life? It's possible that in an American life there's nothing but second acts. Hillary Rodham Clinton was in many ways in disgrace for eight years; the remark about cookies was just the beginning of it; the failure of the health care plan with Ira Magaziner; thoughtless remarks; the embarrassment of living with Bill. As they say in Arkansas, he's a dog who won't always stay on the porch. But now she's reinvented herself and become one of the most respected, tough-minded, intelligent, and hardworking—however you think about her politics—people in the United States Senate. A second act in American life. And there surely must be second acts in American life when you can turn on the TV and see Donald Trump standing there in front of you.

One way to think about education and what we're trying to do here is that we want to give a dramatic second chance to people. People come to us having been lovingly socialized by their mothers and fathers, by their ministers and priests, and by their families, and as beautiful as that process of socialization is, sometimes it fails, sometimes it doesn't work. People need to find a new way to talk about themselves and their worlds. People need to find a new thing to be. People need, as it were, a rebirth, often of a secular sort. In my classes, they sometimes learn from Wordsworth how much nature truly means to them and how much guarding the natural world can do. They learn from Blake what it means to be an energized prophet for social change, or they learn from Jane Austen what it can mean to be somebody who loves the world as it is and lives happily within it.

This need for a second chance, this need for change, is no insult to the parents who've socialized our students the first time through. Parental love is like the sun—it's bright and endless and free and is often never thanked, but provides people with the confidence to take another chance, to do another thing, to start again.

I've talked about a lot of people here in my pantheon—Hillary Clinton and Donald Trump and, more seriously, Thomas Jefferson and Edgar Allan Poe, but I want to end with one particular hero of mine, Saul Bellow, who died this year. Bellow was a simply amazing writer with a huge achievement, but what was the best moment of his life, he tells us, came in the midst of failure. He was in Paris in his thirties on a Guggenheim Fellowship. He had just finished publishing two novels, a little bit sterile, a little bit staid. "I wrote them," he said, "to satisfy the English professors," at which my heart quails a little bit. He was halfway through another novel about two brothers living in a mental institution, as I remember—dismal stuff. "At a certain point," he said, "in the middle of Paris not hearing English anymore, away from my own everyday language, the language became precious and rare and more intimate and immediate to me and I began to write something entirely new, something that was entirely a surprise to myself."

That surprise became a book called *The Adventures of Augie March*, and in it Bellow is successful in creating a new voice. I'll read you a couple of lines from it and you'll see. Here's the beginning: "I am an American," says Augie, "Chicago born—Chicago, that somber city—and go at things as I have taught myself, free-style, and will make the record in my own way: first to knock, first admitted; sometimes an innocent knock, sometimes a not so innocent." It's beautiful stuff. Then, fifteen hundred manuscript pages later, Bellow, looking back through Augie's eyes, trying to figure out if he's made anything at all or if he's failed again and maybe half-satisfied if he has, says, "I may well be a flop in this line of endeavor. Columbus too thought he was a flop, probably, when they sent him back in chains. Which didn't prove there was no America."

Let me close by asking you to succeed as much as you can, but in the process of succeeding, I hope that you'll generate a really remarkable ghost résumé made of the failures that come from trying to do things that you need to do, that are hard to do, and that are demanding to do. Whether it seems in character or not, it's often the time to start the band, to write the poem, to begin the business, to initiate anything that's new and challenging and difficult.

I told you that story which turned out to be a joke about buying a ticket. But there's one thing I didn't tell you. Tickets are expensive. It's hard to draft that novel, hard to get the band together, hard to learn how to shoot a movie. Tickets are expensive, especially the risky ones, but they're infinitely worth buying. So buy a ticket, buy a ticket, buy one.

Thanks.

The Globalists

Members of the Chinese Red Army are boarding our ship. I'm a hundred yards from the gangway, but still I recognize them. They're wearing dome-shaped hats with snap earmuffs. The red stars pinned to the center of the khaki domes, like the Buddhist third eye, the eye of wisdom, are sparkling. We—seven hundred students and forty or so faculty members sailing with an outfit called Semester at Sea—docked here in Shanghai, China, yesterday. The city is polluted as a cesspool and it's booming. We're told that on a good day you can't see the sun until two o'clock in the afternoon and that it's gone by three o'clock, four tops. Today there's been no sun, period, only smoke and fog so dense that you feel like you could reach out and grab a handful and roll it up like a dirty snowball. It's surprising I can see those stars twinkling Maoist red on the heads of the cadres, but I can.

Hold on, though. Those aren't Red Army troops: They're our students. Obviously they've picked up the hats in the souvenir kiosks in town. Some are wearing T-shirts featuring Chairman Mao; others are wearing straw harvest-the-rice domes, also bedecked with red stars. Have the kids gone communist? Are they turning pink?

What they're supposed to be doing is getting a global education. They're supposed to be in the process of becoming citizens of the world. That's the objective of our trip, which has taken us to Brazil and South Africa, Mauritius and Malaysia and India, and will hit Vietnam and Japan before we're done. We're off to acquire a "global education." That seems to be the hot term now in higher-ed circles. But when I ask around among my colleagues—well-traveled, dedicated types—they don't seem to have much more idea what global education is than I do. (And I haven't got any idea at all.) I've taken to watching the students to see if they might offer a hint. It'll have to be a visual cue, I'm afraid: Like my colleagues, they don't seem disposed to ready definitions. They're on the ship, most of them say, to see the world and to have a good time.

Pretty quickly I learn that the Red Army togs don't have anything to do with a new Marxist consciousness and commitment to the Little Red Book. The students think the hats and T-shirts look cool, period. They like the screaming red of the stars; they like the dour, doughy face of the chairman as much as Andy Warhol did—and they're too young to have heard Lennon tell them what doesn't happen to people who go around carrying his image.

But what do the Chinese on the streets of Shanghai think when they see Americans decked out in Marxwear? Probably something like what we would think if we saw Chinese tourists marching down Fifth Avenue wagging American flags. We'd figure they were crazy about the U.S.A. We'd think we were the shining apple of their eye. Presumably the Chinese who see the regalia think that our kids are in love with China. They must feel that the American visitors somehow support—or at least accept—the regime, with its commitment to one-party rule: no freedom of speech, no press freedom, limited freedom of religion, no significant freedom to assemble. The preeminent freedom in China now is the freedom to make money.

Our young globalists needed to think twice about their wardrobes. When classes started again on the ship, there were more than a few sessions about political life in current China and what it meant to appear to endorse it. It was time to talk about the price of political naïveté, and many of us teachers did.

But our students—our budding globalists—brought something besides their naïveté to China and to the other countries we visited. They brought something that, from what I can tell, America excels in exporting. They brought friendliness. Everywhere we went we saw the kids on the street, palling around with local people, trying to speak their language, making jokes, hacking around. They'd talk to anyone they met—rich or poor, old or young. If the people they met knew English, well and good. If not, our kids went to sign language or strained to pick up a few words of the local tongue. The students told their life stories and heard their new pals' tales in exchange. One of my students said he spent three hours talking with the eighty-year-old owner of a dinky restaurant he ate at in Shanghai. "I never laugh so much," she said to him at the end of the evening. "You my crazy American son." Another student told me about meeting everyone on hand in a bar in Malaysia. "We loved them," he said. "And I think they were jazzed we were there."

To my eye, the people the kids encountered in China and Vietnam and India and Brazil and all the other places we went *were* jazzed. Our gang stormed onto the scene, and whatever was fixed and set in the local social configuration quickly became unglued. The students stumbled around in other languages; they ate anything they were served; they almost never slept. And they were persistently, almost insanely open.

Did they get taken? Constantly. At our pre-port meeting before Shanghai, we learned about how young Chinese students would come on in a friendly way and then take foreign visitors off to a "traditional" tea ceremony. Two hours later, their friendly hosts would hit them with bills for seventy-five dollars for a couple of cups of tea and a few grains of rice. Did our students heed the warnings? Of course they didn't. "I felt bad getting ripped off like that," one of them, who didn't have money to spare, told me, "but to tell you the truth, I really liked the girls who did it, and they taught me a lot about China. Anyway. I had fun." People who are morbidly afraid of being taken are among the worst kinds of travelers—suspicious and locked down like clams. They'll get into a half-hour verbal brawl with a taxi driver over two dollars. They'll be so steamed about it all day that they can't enjoy the bronzes in the Shanghai Museum or the street life in Hong Kong. Our kids were never afraid of being taken. When they got mad—everyone who travels gets mad—they were over it in five minutes.

"Sometimes," one of my colleagues said, "our students think that they can replace politeness with friendliness." Well, they did seem to feel that way—if you didn't move fast on that ship, they could run you down. And it was not always a good idea to get between them and the dessert trays, especially when the ship was pitching. Politeness wasn't their long suit.

But having seen them in action on shore and listened to their stories, I'm persuaded that friendliness does trump politeness, and with ease. American friendliness was surely behind a pronouncement we heard a thousand times: "We're not so happy with American government, but Americans? We like them a lot." The kids provided commercial opportunity to almost all who encountered them (they generally seemed to have more money than was good for them; more money, say, than their worthy professors), but that wasn't the whole story. Living in America, it's easy to forget how stratified many cultures are. The caste system isn't strictly legal in India anymore, but there's no doubt that it's still in play. (Indians I met claimed they could recognize another person's caste at a glance.) In South Africa, even after apartheid, the old racial categories still abide. The first conversation I had there was with a cab driver, a Xhosa, who told a nasty joke about the foreskin of the Zulu running for president. Among the Chinese, your education level seems to determine who you are and how you are treated.

This isn't to say that America's a country without class distinctions. But America is a country where nearly the worst thing you can be is a snob. A rich guy isn't worth much, by our account, if he can't yak a little about baseball or the movies with the guy who mows his lawn or the woman who bags the groceries. (Granted, this is in part because the rich guy may be bagging groceries or mowing lawns a year from now.) The unpardonable American social crime is looking down your nose at someone. The great public virtue is being open and easygoing—the great public virtue is friendliness. Our students brought friendliness abroad in barrels, our equivalent of export oil.

The laureate of this sort of thing is Walt Whitman, who began his own anonymous review of his first volume with the words, "An American bard at last!" Almost every American who looks into Whitman understands his egalitarian side immediately. It's rare, at least in my experience, that non-Americans do. (D. H. Lawrence, for example, seemed to think that Whitman was out of his mind.) "Walt Whitman, an American," the hobo bard chants in "Song of Myself":

> *one of the roughs, a kosmos,*
> *Disorderly fleshy and sensual. . . . eating and drinking and breeding,*
> *No sentimentalist. . . . no stander above men and women or apart*
> *   from them. . . . no more modest than immodest.*

"No stander above men and women or apart from them": That's the key phrase. "By God!" he says later in the same section, "I will accept nothing that all cannot have their counterpart of on the same terms." My students read these passages—with the waves slapping away on the side of the classroom—and by and large they bought them. Maybe on some level they already knew what Whitman had to tell them.

But, you may say, the reason that the kids are so open and appealing is that they're innocents. Their naïveté is what's beguiling. And part of what creates that innocence is ignorance. They don't go from place to place pressed to the ground with the burden of the past—in part because they don't know much about that past. They go around grinning, wearing Red Army regalia, with no real clue about the horrors of the Cultural Revolution.

Maybe there's some truth in this indictment. But if so, it makes clear what one objective of a genuine college education now might be—for students and teachers both. Do the students need historical instruction? Sure, so do we all. If we're going to be global citizens, we'd better know something about the biography of the globe. But I wonder if it would be possible for our students to learn as much and still keep alive the quality that really does make them stand out in the best possible way. They broke a lot of ice on our trip, even if they did drive me half crazy with the stuff they didn't know and didn't always want to know. And truly, I couldn't say I was half as open as they were. I didn't meet as many people, didn't show all of those I did meet what was best about America. Is it possible to combine knowledge and friendliness? Could we educate our students (and ourselves) in the ways of both global innocence and global experience? If we could, maybe we'd be creating citizens of the world, American style.

The Corporate City and the Scholarly Enclave

Where should you go to college—assuming you're a high school student and getting ready for this new phase of your life? Where should you encourage your son or daughter to go—assuming that you're a parent?

As a college professor, I get asked the where-to-go question frequently, and I know that all of us teaching in colleges and universities do too. How should one answer? What is the right thing to say to someone deciding on his or her future? For myself, I'm inclined to respond by posing another question.

Are you looking for a corporate city, or are you looking for a scholarly enclave?

Neither of these kinds of schools exists in its pure form. To the scholarly enclave, even the most ideal, there will always be a practical, businessy dimension. Somebody's got to keep the books and pay the bills. And even in the most corporate of colleges, there will be islands of relative scholarly idealism.

Many, if not most, American high school students have already had a taste of the corporate city. These are students and parents who are emerging from the mouth of that great American dragon called the "good high school." I won't hide my prejudices: I have a lot of qualms about the good American high school. Most good high schools now look to me like credential factories. They are production centers that kids check in to every day. The motivated, success-oriented students set to work from the moment of arrival, producing something, manufacturing something. And what they produce are credentials. High schools now are credential factories in overdrive.

It doesn't mean that students don't have to work to get those credentials: Of course they do. It takes lots of effort, planning, and organization—and it takes some smarts—to get what students, the workers in the high school factory, are out to get. Students feel that they need to get A's—they need to excel in their courses. They also feel they need to stimulate the goodwill of their teachers and their guidance counselors: Those recommendations are crucial. Students in high school now also need to rack up lots of extracurriculars: They need to do some community service; they need to be president (or, maybe better, treasurer) of a club or two; it's good as well if they can play at least one varsity sport, or, if they are prone to stumbling over their own feet (as I was in high school), they can at least manage a team or keep the uniforms clean.

High school now is about being an all-arounder. You've got to be good at your classes, but you've also got to shine as a citizen and a general hand-waving, high-enthusiasm participant. To do this, you've often got to make yourself into a superb time manager. You give each activity the amount of time and effort required so that you can reach the so-called standard of excellence. You give it that much, but you give it no more. Do I really need to read the whole book to get an A in English, the student asks herself? Probably she doesn't. Do I need a tutor and extra time to score a top grade in math? Perhaps yes. If so, the money is well spent and so is the time. Will it look better to put in two hours a week volunteering at the hospital or four at the soup kitchen? Does the guidance counselor say that both will look about the same to the college admissions board? Then better to do the hospital: You'll need those extra two hours for prom committee.

High school students need to produce A's. High school students need to produce credentials. No A's, no first-tier college (probably). No credentials, no grandly embossed letters of acceptance—or at least no chirpy e-mail notifications of entrance into the class of 2017.

You'll discern here that I'm not entirely approving of the good American high school and its MO—but on some level I think that I understand what's up. Even if the current mode of high school education—for the good student at the good high school—doesn't especially appeal to a student, what is she supposed to do about it? A fifteen-year-old standing up at a school meeting and saying that she's mad as heck about being slapped on an assembly line, or that she's mad at her parents for slapping here there, or that she's mad at herself—that's not going to do very much. She's going to feel alone and lonely and sad, and anyway she may not even be able to find the words to express her feelings. She probably hasn't read about or even heard the name Mario Savio, who made a speech at the University of California, Berkeley, in 1964. I understand that quite often high school history courses now don't take you all the way up through the period of the Vietnam War, but stop at the end of World War II because "we've run out of time."

Mario Savio stood up at Sproul Plaza at Berkeley and said that as a college student, as a Berkeley student, he too often felt like a piece of raw material that was getting processed by his university and by his society. He believed that many of his contemporaries felt the same way. And then he talked back to that condition. He said, "But we're a bunch of raw materials that don't mean to be—have any process upon us. Don't mean to be made into any product! Don't mean—Don't mean to end up being bought by some clients of the university, be they the government, be they industry, be they organized labor, be they anyone! We're human beings!" We're not products, Mario Savio says: We're human beings. He says it in a broken-up Bob Dylan and Woody Guthrie sort of way, but he says it. Probably a young guy or girl going to high school now hasn't heard of Mario Savio or listened to his famous lines from Sproul Plaza.

They are lines to which young people will respond differently. Some may say: I love high school. I love the hustle and bustle and the classes and the clubs and the staying up late and the social life and the prom and the messing with Facebook. I love striving for success. I like the game and I like the rewards of the game, and so—give me some more.

Some rising high school seniors may be ready for more of the same— assuming what I've said about American high schools now is right or half right. And if so, they need to apply to and eventually install themselves in the kind of college I call the corporate city.

What do you get there in the corporate city? You get more of the same. Everyone is on the make; everyone is trying to succeed. A tremendous amount of networking goes on because people have come to realize that as the old saying runs, It's often not what you know but who you know. Students still study. But in the old high school tradition, you study only as much as you need to study to get your A's. If expedient but slightly shady means of A-getting arise, you may even evaluate them using a risk-reward equation. That is, you balance what can be gained against the pains of getting caught. And even if you don't cheat per se, you're always ready to cut academic corners. Do I really have to read all of *King Lear* to ace the test? Probably you don't. At a certain point—tragic inevitability being what it is—you probably know what's going to happen to the king and to Cordelia, too. When in doubt, turn to the Spark Notes or the cyber equivalent thereof.

You'll have to get by on only a little sleep—but there are ways to make that possible, some quite legal, the others semilegal (legal, that is, for the person for whom the Adderall prescription was originally written, but perhaps not legal for you). You'll be awake and alert for as much as twenty hours of the twenty-four doing a hypercharged version of what you did in high school. You'll be meeting people, connecting with future allies for the wars of life, succeeding in your courses, engaging in lots of activities. In short, you'll be doing more than building your résumé. You'll be putting your résumé on steroids.

Universities that have made themselves into corporate cities are not hard to spot. Most of the students—and many members of the faculty—are buzzing from place to place, always feeling a bit self-important, always feeling a bit behind, like that poor rabbit in *Alice in Wonderland*. The people who represent corporate universities to you—the tour guides and the rest—will talk a lot about new computer initiatives, about partnering with business, and about the creation of young leaders. They'll talk about recent grads who have hit the Silicon Valley jackpot. These are near kids who have made pots of money and—one feels this by implication—are soon going to spread some around their former school, to which they are extremely grateful. You'll hear the word *excellence* about a billion times.

Now, even in the middle of corporate universities, you will find people who are not playing the game. These are not necessarily people who don't show up at a boring class, who smoke a lot of weed, who read books that aren't assigned, who play in bands with bizarre names, and who wear T-shirts that are distressingly original. Though sometimes they are. But what truly characterizes people who are living in, or who want to live in, a scholarly enclave?

It's pretty simple, really. They are at school seeking knowledge so as to make the lives of other human beings better. They will not tell you this when you ask them about it in casual conversation. But it is true. They want to be teachers and scientists and soldiers and doctors and legal advocates for the poor. They want to contribute something to curing cancer; they want to make sure the classics of Roman literature don't die; they want to get people excited about the art of Picasso and maybe inspire people to make some (Picasso-inspired) art of their own; they want to be sure that when a foreign nation is inclined to threaten (I mean really threaten) the peace of the United States of America, that nation has to think twice and twice again.

Do these people want some recognition? Do they want to get paid? Yes, in varying degrees they do. There are very few people who are entirely unselfish in this world, and sometimes they don't live too long. But the people I'm talking about often put others first. They have a love for humanity in them, and it is this love that chiefly motivates what they do, even if they don't tell you so every five minutes. They want to make the world better and they are honest with themselves about doing this: They know that any quest that involves status and enrichment is dangerous and that it can take them away from what really matters. They know that the human capacity for self-deception is boundless and they are always on the lookout for the moment when their pride eclipses their love for the world.

How do you find these people, and how do you find the schools where they are plentiful—what I've called the scholarly enclaves? That is, how do you find them if they are what you are looking for? You visit, you look, and you listen. When people start talking about leadership and incentives (and especially something called "incentivizing") and becoming an academic entrepreneur, you are probably in the wrong place. (Whenever people make fritters of English, I daresay that you're in the wrong place.) When people talk about innovation and "partnering" with big-money institutions, I would advise you to run. If you hear the word *excellence* more than twice in a sentence, you are hereby empowered to pop the speaker twice (but very gently) in the nose.

Why is *excellence* a bad word? It's not, in and of itself. But people around universities who use it are people who want to talk about worldly distinction without talking about ethics. *Excellence* means we're smart, we're accomplished, we're successful—and we can be these things without any obligation to help our fellow human beings. When colleges start talking about "humane excellence" or "generous excellence," then I'll want to listen.

You also have my permission—in fact my encouragement—to gently snout-pop people who talk about "leadership." Why is leadership so bad? In itself, it's not. But what people usually mean by a leader now is someone who, in a very energetic, upbeat way, shares all of the values of the people who are in charge. Leaders tend to be little adults, little grown-ups who don't challenge the big grown-ups who run the place. Grown-ups—people like me—need to be challenged, and we rely on young people to do it. When people say "leaders" now, what they mean is gung ho "followers." As an English professor, I don't really care for Mario Savio's grammar and diction. But was he an authentic leader? Was he someone who offered students a new and controversial way to think of their lives and then to live their lives? Yes, I think that he was. But no college dean or president, now or ever, would use the word *leader* to describe Mario: Most of them reserve the word for followers, for people who follow them.

The residents of scholarly enclaves are harder to spot than the denizens of the corporate university, and I can't give you a definitive field guide to finding them. But I'll say first that they don't talk about being a leader and being an entrepreneur. They talk about working in a lab or developing a questionnaire for psychological research or writing a novel, or getting people who don't belong in jail out of jail, or defending their country against its enemies. And they are not smiling all the time. They are aware of the enormous gap between what humans aspire to and what remains to be done. They tend to take joy in their work, but they never feel that they have quite gotten it right. The people in the corporate university are forever pleased with themselves. They are always succeeding, getting A's that will soon be converted into dollars.

Their view is often that everyone wants the same things that they do. They think that people who claim to work for humanity want wealth and fame too—the achievers are just more honest about the matter. The people who serve the poor themselves want to be rich: They are just too chicken to be candid about their desire and then, in the current vernacular, to go for it. And who knows, maybe this is true. This view has some important upholders: Freud and Nietzsche and (in his way) Adam Smith feed it, and they are anything but fools. But geniuses are not always right.

The people who dedicate themselves to helping humanity are not, let me say, sacrificing themselves to a life of pain and sorrow. In fact, it is only through unselfish effort on behalf of something larger than yourself that anything like happiness arises. The happiness-through-material-goods-and-success industry has to throw ads at you twenty-four hours a day to persuade you that its way of life is the best one. The happiness industry protests too much. Would it need to be as clamorous as it is about consumer bliss if there really was such a thing as consumer bliss?

Where should a young person now go to college? It depends. Does she want more of the good American high school with its hustle and bustle, its strivings for excellence, its fixation on leadership, its partnering and incentivizing and getting proactive, and succeeding, succeeding, succeeding? Or does she want something else?

The English Major

Lately, when the time of year comes for college sophomores to trundle off to the offices of their faculty advisers to declare their majors, it's not hard to predict what's going to happen. There will be more economics majors surely and more business majors too. What there almost certainly won't be are more English majors. The English major has been declining drastically over the past decades. In 1970, about 8 percent of students were English majors; by 2004 (the last date for which figures are available), it was 4 percent. By now it may be down to 2 or 3. It's distressing to me, and not just because I happen to be an English prof. I think that a lot of students are making a mistake—losing one of the greatest chances life offers. If I could, I'd yell over the transoms of my colleagues' offices in economics and business and all the other purportedly success-ensuring disciplines.

I'd tell the kids to drop what they were doing and get themselves over to the English department. I'd tell them to sign on before it was too late.

An English major, you see, is much more than thirty-two or thirty-six credits including a course in Shakespeare, a course on writing before 1800, and a three-part survey of English and American lit. That's the outer form of the endeavor. It's what's inside that matters. It's the character forming—or (dare I say?) Soul-making—dimension of the pursuit that counts. And what is that precisely? Who is the English major in his ideal form? What does the English major have and what does he want and what does he in the long run hope to become?

The English major is, first of all, a reader. She's got a book pup-tented in front of her nose many hours a day; her Kindle glows softly late into the night. But there are readers and there are *readers*. There are people who read to anesthetize themselves—they read to induce a vivid, continuous, and risk-free daydream. They read for the same reason that people grab a glass of chardonnay—to put a light buzz on. The English major reads because as rich as the one life he has may be, one life is not enough. He reads not to see the world through the eyes of other people but effectively to *become* other people. What is it like to be John Milton, to be Jane Austen, to be Chinua Achebe? What is it like to be them at their best, at the top of their games? The English major wants the joy of seeing the world through the eyes of people who—let us admit it—are more sensitive, more articulate, shrewder, sharper, more alive than they themselves are. The experience of changing minds and hearts with Proust or James or Austen is one that is incomparably enriching. It makes you see that there is more to the world than you had ever imagined was possible. You see that life is bigger, sweeter, more tragic and intense—more alive with meaning than you had thought.

Real reading is *reincarnation*. There is no other way to put it. It is being born again into a higher form of consciousness than we ourselves possess. When we walk the streets of Manhattan with Walt Whitman or contemplate our hopes for eternity with Emily Dickinson, we are reborn into more ample and generous minds. "Life piled on life / Were all too little," says Tennyson's Ulysses, and he is right. Given the ragged magnificence

of the world, who would wish to live only once? The English major lives
many times through the astounding transportive magic of words and the
welcoming power of his receptive imagination. The economics major? In
all probability he lives but once. If the English major has the wherewithal
for it, the energy and the openness of heart, he lives not once but hundreds
of times. Not all books are worth being reincarnated into, to be sure—
but those that are win Keats's sweet phrase: "a joy forever."

The economics major lives in facts and graphs and diagrams and
projections. Fair enough. Without these things, we are told (and perhaps
in part believe) there would be no civilized world. But the English major
lives elsewhere. Remember the tale of that hoary patriarchal fish that
David Foster Wallace made famous? The ancient swimmer swishes his
slow bulk by a group of young carp suspended in the shallows. "How's
the water?" the ancient asks. The carp keep their poise, like figures in a
child's mobile, but say not a word. The old fish gone, one carp turns to
another and speaks the signal line, "What's water?"

The English major knows that the water we humans swim in is not any
material entity. Our native habitat is language, words, and the English
major swims through them with the old fin's enlivening awareness. But
all of us, as the carp's remark suggests, live in a different relation to
language. I'll put it a little tendentiously: Some of us speak, others are
spoken. "Language speaks man," Heidegger famously said. To which I
want to reply, Not all men, not all women: not by a long shot. Did language
speak Shakespeare? Did language speak Spenser? Not by a long shot.
Milton, Chaucer, Woolf, Emerson? No, not even close.

What does it mean to be spoken by language? It means to be a vehicle
for expression and not a shaper of words. It means to rely on clichés and
preformulated expressions. It means to be a channeler, and what you
channel is ad-speak and sports jargon and the latest in psychological
babble. You sound not like a living man or a woman but like something
much closer to a machine, trying to pass for human. You never know how
you feel or what you want in life because the words at your disposal are
someone else's words and don't represent who *you* are and what *you* want.
You don't and can't know yourself. You don't and can't know the world.

The businessman rattles about excellence and leadership and partnering and productivity. The athlete clones away about the game plan
and the coach and one play at a time and the inestimable blessing of
having teammates who make it all possible. The politician proses about
unity and opportunity and national greatness and what's in it for the

middle class. When such people talk, they are not so much human beings as they are tape loops.

The essayist John Jeremiah Sullivan catches this sort of sensibility in its extreme form in an essay about reality TV shows. There, verbal channeling reaches an almost unimaginable degree of intensity: "big mouths spewing fantastic catchphrase fountains of impenetrable self-justification; spewing dark prayers calling on God to strike down those who would fuck with their money, their cash, and always knowing, always preaching. Using weird phrases that nobody uses except that everybody uses them now. Constantly talking about 'goals.' " "Fantastic catchphrase fountains of impenetrable self-justification": Yeah, that's about it.

The English major at her best isn't used by language; she uses it. She bends it and tropes it and inflects it with irony and lets hyperbole bloom like a firework flower when the time's right. She knows that language isn't there merely to represent the world as it is, was, and shall be. Language is there to *interpret* the world—language lets her say how she feels and lets others know.

The English major believes in talk and writing and knows that any worthwhile event in life requires commentary and analysis in giant proportion. She believes that the uncommented-upon life is not worth living. Then, of course, there is the commentary upon the comments. There must be, as Eliot says, a thousand visions and revisions before the taking of the toast and tea—and a few after as well to accompany the capons and the sack.

But I sometimes think that the English major's most habitual feeling about the linguistic solution in which she swims isn't practical at all. What she feels about language most of the time is wonder and gratitude. For language is a stupendous gift. It's been bequeathed to us by all of the foregoing generations. And it is the creation of great souls like Shakespeare and Chaucer to be sure. But language is also the creation of salesmen and jive talkers, jocks and mountebanks, hookers and heroic warriors. We spend our lives, knowingly or not, trying to say something impeccably. We long to put the right words in the right order. (That, Coleridge said, is all that poetry really comes down to.) And when we do, we are on the lip of adding something to the language. We've perhaps made a contribution, however small, to what the critic R. P. Blackmur called the stock of available reality. And when we do, we've lived for a moment with the immortals. Richard Poirier once called poetry the Olympics of Language—precisely so.

I love Wordsworth and Shakespeare and Donne. But I like it when a fellow pickup b-ball player points to a nervous guy skittering off to the bathroom just as the game's about to start: "He's taking a chicken pee." Yup—hit it on the head. I like it when in the incomparable "Juicy," Biggie Smalls describes coming up in life by letting us know that once "Birthdays was the worst days / Now we sip champagne when we thirs-tay." (And to advertise his new erotic ascent: "Honeys play me close like butter play toast.") Language, a great poem in and of itself, is all around us. We live in the lap of enormous wonder, but how rarely do most of us look up and smile in gratitude and pleasure? The English major does that all the time.

The English major: in love with language and in love with life—or at least hungry for as much life as he can hold. But there's something else, too. The English major immerses himself in books and revels in language for a purpose. You might even call it a high purpose, if you're disposed to such talk. (I sometimes am.) The English major wants to use what he knows about language and what he's learning from books as a way to confront the hardest of questions. He uses these things to try to figure out how to live. His life is an open-ended work in progress and it's never quite done, at least until he is. For to the English major the questions of life are never closed. There's always another book to read; there's always another perspective to add. He might think that he knows what's what as to love and marriage and the raising of children. But he's never quite sure. He takes tips from the wise and the almost wise that he confronts in books and sometimes (if he's stupendously lucky) in life. He measures them and sifts them and brings them to the court of his own experience. (There is a creative reading as well as a creative writing, Emerson said.) He's always ready to change his mind. Darwin on nature—or Wordsworth? Freud on love, or Percy Bysshe Shelley? Blake on sex, or Arthur Schopenhauer? Or perhaps none of the above. He doesn't give up his view easily, but it's nonetheless always up for debate and open for change. He's an unfinished guy, she's an unfinished woman. Which can be embarrassing and discomfiting from time to time, when he's with the knowing ones, the certain ones: those who are, often in all too many ways, finished.

Love for language, hunger for life, openness and a quest for truth or truths: Those are the qualities of my English major in the ideal form. But of course now we're talking about more than a mere academic major. We're talking about a way of life. We're talking about a way of living that places inquiry into how to live in the world—what to be, how to act, how to move through time—at its center. What we're talking about is a path to becoming a human being, or at least a better sort of human being than one was at the start. An English major? To me an English major is someone who has decided, against all kinds of pious, prudent advice and all kinds of fears and resistances, to major, quite simply, in becoming a person. Once you've passed that particular course of study—or at least made some significant progress on your way—then maybe you're ready to take up something else.

My First Intellectual

Doug Meyers came to Medford High School with big plans for teaching his philosophy course. Together with a group of self-selected seniors, he was going to ponder the eternal questions: beauty, truth, free will, fate, that sort of thing. The class would start out reading *The Story of Philosophy*, by Will Durant, then go on to Plato's dialogues, some Aristotle, Leibniz (a particular favorite of Meyers's), maybe just a little bit of Kant, then into a discussion of Bertrand Russell's effort to clear the whole thing up with an injection of clean scientific logic. Meyers had just graduated from Harvard. All of his intellectual aspirations were intact.

On the first day of class, we saw a short, slight man with olive skin—we thought he might be Mexican—wearing a skinny tie and a moth-eaten legacy suit with a paper clip fastened to the left lapel. On his feet were Ivy League gunboat shoes, lace-ups designed in homage to the *Monitor* and the *Merrimack*. He had hunched shoulders, a droopy black mustache, and Valentino-type eyes, deep brown, sensuous, and penitential. Even when he strove for some dynamism, as he did that first day, explaining his plans for the course, he still had a melancholy Castilian presence, the air of an instinctively comprehending reader of *Don Quixote*.

Having outlined the course, he turned away from us and began writing on the blackboard, in a script neater than any we would see from him again. It was a quotation from Nietzsche. He told us to get out our papers and pens and spend a couple of pages interpreting the quote "as a limbering-up exercise." I had never heard of Nietzsche. I had never read all the way through a book that was written for adults and that was not concerned exclusively with football.

The day before, I'd sat in the office of Mrs. Olmstead, the senior guidance counselor, whose perfume conjured up the sound of Mantovani's string section, sentimental, lush, and all-enfolding. We talked about

Massachusetts Bay Community College, Salem State Teachers College; we discussed my working for the city of Medford—perhaps I'd start by collecting barrels, then graduate in time to a desk job (my father had some modest connections). I mentioned joining the marines. (I might have made it in time for the Cambodia invasion.) Nothing was resolved.

As I was mumbling my way out the door, Mrs. Olmstead began talking about a new teacher who was coming to the school, "someone we're especially proud to have." He was scheduled to teach philosophy. I didn't know what philosophy was, but I associated it with airy speculation, empty nothing; it seemed an agreeable enough way of wasting time.

So there I was in a well-lit top-floor room, wearing, no doubt, some sharp back-to-school ensemble, pegged pants and sporty dice-in-the-back-alley shoes, mildly aching from two or three football-inflected injuries, and pondering the Nietzsche quotation, which I could barely understand. I felt dumb as a rock, a sentiment with which I, at seventeen, had some prior experience. But by putting the quotation on the board, Meyers showed me that in at least one department his powers of comprehension were a few notches lower than mine. He had misunderstood Medford High School entirely. The appearances had taken him in. No doubt he'd strolled through the building on the day before students arrived; he'd seen desks, chalkboards, large windows that slid up and open with a cheering metallic gurgle, supply closets stocked full of paper and books, all the paraphernalia of education. He had seen those things and he'd believed that he was in a school, a place where people quested, by their lights and by fits and starts, for the truth, its elaborations and its antitheses.

But I had acquired a few facts that Meyers would not have been primed to receive at Harvard, or at prep school, or at any of the other places where he had filled his hours. Medford High School, whatever its appearances, was not a school. It was a place where you learned to do—or were punished for failing in—a variety of exercises. The content of these exercises didn't matter at all. What mattered was form—repetition and form. You filled in the blanks, conjugated, declined, diagrammed, defined, outlined, summarized, recapitulated, positioned, graphed. It did not matter what: English, geometry, biology, history, all were the same. The process treated your mind as though it was a body part capable of learning a number of protocols, simple choreographies, then repeating, repeating.

Our bodies themselves were well monitored. When the bell rang, we rose and filed into the corridor, stayed in line, spoke quietly if at all, entered the next class, were ordered to sit down, sit quietly, feet beneath the desk, all day long presided over by teachers, a significant fraction of whom were going—at greater or lesser velocities, ending sometimes with a bang, sometimes with subdued, heart-emptying sobs—out of their minds. At least two that I can remember had been mastered by a peculiar form of speech: You couldn't say they were talking to themselves, but they were not clearly addressing anyone on the outside, either. Poetry, Mill said, is not heard but overheard. This was overheard, but no way close to poetry. This was the way souls in purgatory mutter and carry on. When these teachers were overwhelmed—it wasn't hard to do: We stole Miss McDougle's rank book; we locked her once, briefly, in the supply closet—they called for a submaster, Sal Todaro, or, more feared, Dan O'Mara, Dandy Dan, to restore order. The place was a shabby Gothic cathedral consecrated to Order, and maybe it was not without its mercies. If you'd done what you should have at Medford High, the transition into a factory, into an office, into the marines would be something you'd barely notice; it would be painless, sheer grease.

Before Meyers arrived, I never rebelled against the place, at least not openly. I didn't in part because I believed that Medford High was the only game there was. The factories where my father and uncles worked were extensions of the high school; the TV shows we watched were manufactured to fit the tastes for escape that such places form; the books we were assigned to read in class, *Ivanhoe*, *Silas Marner*, *The Good Earth*, of which I ingested about fifty pages each, could, as I saw it then (I've never had the wherewithal to check back into them), have been written by the English teachers, with their bland, babbling goodness and suppressed hysterias. Small bursts of light came through in the Beethoven symphonies my father occasionally played at volume on our ancient stereo (the music sounded like it was coming in over a walkie-talkie) and the Motown tunes I heard on Boston's black radio station, WILD, but these sounds were not connected to any place or human possibility I knew about. So I checked out. I went low to the ground, despondent, suspicious, asleep in the outer self, barely conscious within.

This condition Doug Meyers changed. That now, however imperfectly, I can say what's on my mind, and that I know what kind of life I hope for, I owe not to him alone, of course, but to many. Doug Meyers pushed open the door to those others, though, other worlds, other minds. And pretty much on his own, Meyers taught me how to teach. I'm not sure if I've ever heard his sort of approach described before, but I think it's as good now as it was when I first encountered him almost thirty years ago.

For three months, Meyers did his best with Will Durant and *The Story of Philosophy*. We barely gave him an inch. Gubby Shea (Kevin Shea on his report cards and disciplinary citations) made enormous daisy chains out of the elastics he used to bind the advertising circulars he delivered in Jamaica Plain and Mattapan on Saturday mornings or sat, his body tight with concentrated energy, inking in all of the *o*'s in the textbook, a brilliant, futile parody of life at Medford High. Jeff Stanwick pried tufts of grass off the soles of his soccer cleats; Michael de Leo and John Aquino, wide receiver and quarterback for the Medford Mustangs (I blocked for them, sporadically), contemplated pass plays and the oncoming game with Newton, or Somerville, or Everett. Debbie Lauria was high school beautiful. Susan Rosenberg, the school's only hippie—she wore wire-rimmed glasses and work boots—conversed with Meyers on subjects no one else cared about. She and Joseph Jones were about the only ones with anything to say.

Joseph was a hater. He hated communism, hated drugs, hated women's lib (as it was then called), hated Susan, hated Meyers. He was stumpy and strong with acne on his face so livid it looked like someone had sprayed it on that morning. He wore Sears Roebuck short-sleeved, stain-holding shirts that reeked of the night shift. Joseph called himself conservative, but he was only that because he hadn't yet encountered a recruiter from a brownshirt operation.

Meyers wrote him off from the start. He didn't try to convert Joseph or to understand his painful home life or to contact his suppressed inner self. By indulging Joseph a little, putting his blather into cogent form for him and us, Meyers might have "gotten a good discussion going"—every teacher's dream. Instead Meyers talked with serene intelligence to Susan and anyone else who cared to volunteer and treated Joseph with subtle, and occasionally not so subtle, derision.

For Meyers thought well of himself. He wouldn't pander. And we all wondered, if unspokenly, where this guy might have gotten his considerable lode of self-esteem. Teachers, as we could have told him, were losers, out-and-out. And this one in particular wasn't strong or tough or worldly. He wore ridiculous clothes, old formal suits and that weird paper clip in his lapel; he talked like a dictionary; his accent was overcultivated, queer, absurd. He was a compendium of odd mannerisms, starting with the way he swung his right hand from the wrist laterally as he spoke. Yet he thought highly of himself. And not much at all, it wasn't difficult to see, of us. Except for Susan, whom he addressed in affectionate tones, Meyers spoke to the class with perpetual irony. He mocked us, and not always so genially, for never doing the reading, never knowing the answer, never having a thought in our heads. We were minor-league fools, his tone implied, for ignoring this chance to learn a little something before being fed live and whole to what was waiting. For our part, we sat back, let him wrangle with Joseph, and waited to see what would turn up.

One day in mid-December or so, Meyers walked in and told us to pass back our copies of *The Story of Philosophy.* Then he told us that he had some other books for us to read but that we'd have to pay for them ourselves. (Gubby Shea piped up immediately to say that this was fine with him, since he'd finished inking in the *o*'s of the Durant.) Meyers, it turned out, had asked no one's permission to do this; it just struck him as a good idea to try to get people who never picked up a book to do some reading by giving them work that might speak to their experience. At Medford High, this qualified as major educational innovation, real breakthrough thinking. And of course there were plenty of rules against using books that hadn't been approved by the school board, weren't purchased through public funding, and so on.

The books that Meyers picked were on a theme, though I had no idea of that at the time. *The Stranger, One Flew Over the Cuckoo's Nest, Group Psychology and the Analysis of the Ego, Siddhartha:* The first three were about the oppressions of conformity (among other things), the last about the Buddha's serene, fierce rebellion against it. We were all weighed down by conformity, Meyers knew. And he also knew that we, his self-selected seniors, were oppressors in our own right, passing on the ways of the system to the weaker, homelier, duller kids. These were revelations that emerged slowly for us as we talked not just about the high school and its day-to-day machinations but also about sports, sororities, circles of friends and families and what they closed out. We learned to use some unfamiliar language to talk about ourselves and so became, for a few moments at a time, strangers in our own lives, the subjects of new kinds of understanding and judgment.

I don't want to idealize this process. For the first few weeks, since virtually no one but Susan would read a book at home, we simply sat in a circle and read the pages aloud in turn. Periodically Meyers would ask a question, and usually, in the beginning, it was he who would answer it or decide finally to let it drop. One day, when we were reading *The Stranger*, Meyers asked us about solitude. What does it mean to be alone? Is it possible? What would it mean to be genuinely by oneself? Susan Rosenberg raised her hand, no doubt ready to treat us to a description of Zen meditation and its capacity to melt the ego beyond solitude into pure nothingness. But Meyers must have seen something ripple across Debbie Lauria's beautiful face. He gestured in her direction, though she hadn't volunteered.

Debbie was a high school princess, a sorority girl whose autobiography, I'd have guessed, would have translated into a graph peaking from prom to prom, with soft valleys of preparation in between. What Debbie did was run through a litany of defenses against being alone. She mentioned listening to the radio and talking on the phone, then playing the songs and conversations over in her mind, and myriad other strategies, ending, perceptively enough, with expectation, our habit of blocking out the present by waiting for things to happen in the future. But Debbie did not express herself with detachment. She said "I": "This is how I keep from being alone."

"And why," asked Meyers, "is it hard to be alone?"

"Because," Debbie answered, "I might start to think about things."

Debbie had been, up until that point, one of the Elect, predestined for all happiness; suddenly she had gone over to the terminally Lost. One of the great sources of grief for those who suffer inwardly is their belief that others exist who are perpetually and truly happy. From the ranks of the local happy few, Debbie had just checked out, leaving some effective hints about those she'd left behind.

The book that mattered to me wasn't *The Stranger*, which had gotten Debbie going, or Freud's book on the herd instinct (when I was writing my dissertation, a literary critical reading of Freud, my working text of *Group Psychology* was, somehow, the one that had belonged to Gubby Shea, with the o's colored in to about page 20), but Kesey's *One Flew Over the Cuckoo's Nest*. It's a hard book for me to read now, with its pumped-up cartoon hero, Randall Patrick McMurphy. But at the time it was everything. I read it in a lather, running through it in about ten hours straight, then starting in again almost immediately.

But that didn't happen right off. It was probably on the fifth day of reading the book out loud in class that a chance remark Meyers made caught my attention, or what there was of it then to catch. He said that prisons, hospitals, and schools were on a continuum, controlling institutions with many of the same protocols and objectives, and that Kesey, with his bitter portrait of the mental hospital, might be seen as commenting on all these places.

This idea, elementary as it was, smacked me with the force of revelation. Here was a writer who was not on the side of the teachers, who in fact detested them and their whole virtuous apparatus. That the book was in part crude and ugly I knew even at the time: Blacks in it are twisted sadists, the women castrators or sweet whores. But it was the antiauthoritarian part that swept me in; here was someone who found words, gorgeous, graffiti-size, and apocalyptic, for what in me had been mere inchoate impulses, dumb groans of the spirit laboring away in its own darkness.

"You can't like that book anymore," said a well-meaning, department-broken professor of English I ran into after giving a lecture in California. "You used to be able to like it, but not anymore," he said, not smugly, not knowingly, but a little wistfully. I understood what he meant, but I couldn't share the genteel sentiment. That book pulled me out of where I was. So it wasn't angelic: If you'll consent only to being saved by an angel, you may have some time to wait.

During the period when we were reading Kesey aloud and discussing him, Doug Meyers started bringing things into class. Every Friday we got some music: I remember hearing Billie Holiday, Mozart, the Incredible String Band, the Velvet Underground. The selection standard was simple—things he liked that we probably would not have heard. He also showed us art books, read a poem from time to time, and brought in friends of his to explain themselves. Meyers loved the things he offered us, but he loved them in a quirky way: He seemed to look affectionately askance at everything he cared about. What love you could find in Medford culture, where you could find it, wasn't always so easy to distinguish from the mechanism of hunger and satiety.

A panel of Students for a Democratic Society members appeared one day to debate the Vietnam War with us. (Most of us were in favor.) One February day, a group of black students burst into the room during class and announced that this was the anniversary of Malcolm X's death. Meyers looked up mildly from his place in the circle and asked the foremost of them, "And when was he born, Malcolm Little?" The young man, knew, or said he did, and gave a date. Meyers nodded and invited them to sit down and talk about politics. It was the first time I'd had an extended conversation about these things with black students, and more than a few followed. These discussions didn't stop the ongoing racial guerrilla war at Medford High, but they were something.

As time went on, word spread around the school that odd things were happening in Meyers's classroom. It was known that once, on a torpid winter day, he brought us all outside for a snowball fight. Joseph—no surprise—got it going by heaving a jagged ice chunk, caveman style, at Meyers. Meyers, who looked that day like a Mexican padre, with his long black coat and broad-brimmed black hat, responded by trying to pitch Joseph into a snowbank. Meyers was ill coordinated but determined. From where I stood, it looked as if Joseph was being attacked by a giant crow. When Joseph shook the snow off his parka and stepped up for retaliation, a bunch of us pelted him with snowballs.

As the weather warmed up, the class occasionally went outside to sit on the grass and hold discussions. This sometimes resulted in one or two of us nodding off, but Meyers didn't much care; he had most of us most of the time now. He sat cross-legged, wise-medicine-man-style, and swung his wrist and laughed, and we answered the questions he asked, because what he thought mattered probably did. It was a first, this outdoors business; no one at Medford High would have imagined doing it.

One Thursday afternoon, just as we were wrapping up a discussion of Thoreau, Meyers gave us a solemn, mischievous look, the sort of expression shrewd old rabbis are supposed to be expert in delivering, and said, "There's been some doubt expressed about our going outside." Then he told a story. In the faculty cafeteria, with plenty of the other teachers milling around, Meyers had been approached by Dandy Dan O'Mara, the submaster, the disciplinarian. O'Mara had the sly bullying style of a hard Irish cop. He had a barroom face, red nose, watery eyes, the hands of someone who worked for a living. He was stepping up to put Meyers in his place.

O'Mara got rapidly to the point. What would happen, he'd asked Meyers, if everyone held class outside? Now, this was familiar stuff to us all. O'Mara's question came out of that grand conceptual bag that also contained lines like "Did you bring gum for everyone?" and "Would you like to share that note with the whole class?" O'Mara was trying to treat Meyers like a student, like one of us, and in front of his colleagues. At Medford High, there were two tribes, us and them. Meyers had defied the authorities; clearly he had become one of *them*, a student, of no use or interest whatever. But in fact Meyers was of no particular clan but his own, the tribe of rootless, free-speculating readers and talkers and writers who owe allegiance first to a pile of books that they've loved, and then, only secondly, to other things.

O'Mara did not know this. Nor did he know that Meyers, however diminutive, mild, and Mandarinly self-effacing, thought himself something of a big deal. So O'Mara would not have been prepared when Meyers drew an easy breath and did what every high school kid would like to do when confronted with this sort of bullying. He didn't fight it, didn't stand on his dignity. He simply ran with it. What if everyone held class outside on sunny days? Suppose that happened? And from there, Meyers went on to draw a picture of life at Medford High School—a picture that had people outside on the vast lawn talking away about books and ideas and one thing and another, hanging out, being lazy and being absorbed, thinking hard from time to time, and reveling in the spring. It was Woodstock and Socrates' agora fused, and Meyers spun it out for us, just as he had for O'Mara. What if that happened, he asked us (and the submaster)? How tragic would it be?

This vision of the renovated school took a long time to unfold, and it had something like a musical form, ebbing and rising, threading back through major themes and secondary motifs. And in my mind's eye, I could see O'Mara wilting, growing too small for his wrinkled, sad clothes. He would soon know, as we did, that Meyers could produce plenty more of this (he was the most eloquent man I'd met) and that it was time to cut and run. What struck me about the performance (and I believed Meyers's rendition of it, word for word—he was unfailingly, often unflatteringly honest) was that it was done with words alone, nothing equivalent to the body blows Kesey's R. P. McMurphy specializes in.

We went outside whenever we chose to after that. It was very odd: I had been at Medford High for three years, and I had never seen

O'Mara's side lose a round. I'd seen a kid from the city's preeminent street gang, the South Medford Bears, spit in a teacher's face, but soon enough the police wagon was there and the big boy was trussed and bawling and on the way to jail. After class was over on the day that Meyers told us the O'Mara story, John Aquino, the quarterback of the football team and very little in line with the stereotype, said to me, "You know, Meyers can really be an asshole when he wants to be." In Medford, there were fifty intonations you could apply to the word *asshole*. Spun right, the word constituted high praise.

O'Mara was a broad target. America was in crisis then; people were assuming intense allegorical identities—pig, peacenik, hawk, dove. O'Mara had turned into an ugly monolith, at least in our eyes. In Asia, the Vietcong were making fools of his spiritual brethren, Johnson, Westmoreland, McNamara, and the rest. His sort was on the run. In the next few years it would get even worse for them. But Meyers, for his part, hadn't treated O'Mara as among the lost, even though he probably had it coming. Instead he'd invited him to a party, an outdoor extravaganza. At the time, O'Mara surely couldn't discern the invitation in Meyers's extended aria, but who knows what he might have seen later on as he turned it all over in his mind.

That year of teaching was the last for Doug Meyers. He got married, went to law school, and, I heard, eventually moved to Maine, where he could pursue a life a little akin to the one Thoreau, his longtime idol, managed to lead during his stay at Walden. I haven't seen Meyers in about twenty-five years. But I do carry around with me the strong sense that the party he invited us to, me and Carla and Gubby and Michael de Leo and Dandy Dan O'Mara (but not Joseph, no, not everyone, quite), is still a live possibility. Sometimes I even stumble on an installment of it, or help make one.

I had great teachers after Doug Meyers, some of the world's most famous in fact, but I never met his equal. What I liked most about him, I suppose, was that for all the minor miracle of what he accomplished with us, he was no missionary: He served us but also himself. He got what he wanted out of Medford High, which was a chance to affront his spiritual enemies, though with some generosity, and to make younger people care about the sorts of things he cared about, to pull them out of their parents' orbit and into his. All good teaching entails some kidnapping; there's a touch of malice involved.

As well as some sorrow. Good teachers have many motivations, but I suspect that loneliness is often one of them. You need a small group, a coterie, to talk to; unable to find it in the larger world, you try to create it in the smaller sphere of a classroom. Meyers, who seemed at times a little lost in his life, a brilliant orphan, did something like that with us. (When he saw the material he had to work with on that first day, he must have been on the verge of stepping out the window.) Whatever his motives, part of what I admired about him was his streak of arrogance. His goodness had some edge to it.

It would be a mistake to believe that what Meyers taught about teaching was that always and until the end of time you should draw the chairs into a circle, read pop-cult marvels like *Cuckoo's Nest*, and apply them directly to the situation at hand. No, Meyers taught something else entirely. When I call him to mind in that long black padre coat, he reminds me of Groucho Marx in *Horse Feathers*, duck-walking at top throttle back and forth in front of a whole congress of professors, singing out his Marxian ditty with the gorgeous refrain, "Whatever it is, I'm against it!"

What Meyers taught—or at least what I gleaned from him—is that anything that's been successfully institutionalized, however rebellious it may seem or however virtuous, is stifling. What's called subversion only lasts for an instant in a school or a hospital or a home; it's quickly swept up to become part of the protocol, an element in "the way we do things around here." At the time, Kesey and Camus collided well enough with the dead protocols of Medford High, but now, for all I know, they fit in fine—maybe alienation has become standard issue. What to do then? When Bacchus is ascendant, when all the world is a pop-cult blast, then maybe you become a high priest of Apollo, with his hard graces. Teachers, freelance spirit healers that they are or ought to be, make a diagnosis, pour out a cure or two, then see what happens. Or so Meyers did with us.

Such teaching incites friction. Many students, the successes in particular, resent it and respond with civil venom. And teachers, undercompensated as they usually are, often yearn for some adulation to balance the books. It's tough to be both broke and unloved.

"Whenever others agree with me," the sublime Oscar Wilde said, "I know that I must be wrong." When students love you from day one, when you succeed too fast, chances are that Wilde's dictum applies. And when the world does eventually come around to your way of thinking, maybe then it's time to deliver your premises a salutary whack: "Whatever it is," chants Groucho from the wings, "I'm against it."

This approach isn't without its costs. One pays for the kind of mental exhilaration that Meyers initiated. One pays in self-doubt and isolation, in the suspicion that what seems to be true resistance is merely a perverse substitute for genuine talent, a cheap way of having something to say. Meyers's path, so appealing in its first steps, separated me from my family and cut me loose from religion. It sent me adrift beyond the world bordered by TV and piety and common sense. One step down that road followed another, and now I probably could not turn around if I wished to.

Still, the image I most often hit on when I think about Meyers glows brightly enough. It's late spring, a gloomy dead day. He's brought in a record by the Incredible String Band. He's at the back of the room standing beside the beat-up phonograph. I dislike the record and open my book, *The Autobiography of Malcolm X*, which has not been assigned in any class, and disappear into it. Meyers cranks the music a little louder. I keep reading. But then, curious, I raise my head. The racket of the String Band floods in. And there in the back of the room, Meyers is dancing away. He's a so-so dancer at best, stiff and arrhythmic. Not until I saw Bob Dylan in concert did I ever see anyone dance as self-consciously. Yet it struck me that this was probably the first time anyone had ever danced in this building. The air was so heavy with gray institutional weight: I can't imagine that anyone but Meyers could have pulled it off.

But here he was, dancing away. It was like a few good new words coming into the language, some strokes of light rendered by a painter for the first time, though with an unsteady enough hand. Meyers had scored a benevolent victory over the place. (You could say he'd beaten Medford High at its own game, but really he'd shown it a new one.) He had a right to a little celebration.

The Pink Floyd Night School

"So, what are you doing after graduation?"

In the spring of my last year in college I posed that question to at least a dozen fellow graduates-to-be at my little out-of-the-way school in Vermont. The answers they gave me were satisfying in the extreme: not very much, just kick back, hang out, look things over, take it slow. It was 1974. That's what you were supposed to say.

My classmates weren't, strictly speaking, telling the truth. They were, one might even say, lying outrageously. By graduation day, it was clear that most of my contemporaries would be trotting off to law school and graduate school and to cool and unusual internships in New York and San Francisco.

But I did take it slow. After graduation, I spent five years wandering around doing nothing—or getting as close to it as I could manage. I was a cab driver, an obsessed moviegoer, a wanderer in the mountains of Colorado, a teacher at a crazy grand hippie school in Vermont, the manager of a movie house (who didn't do much managing), a crewman on a ship, and a doorman at a disco.

The most memorable job of all, though, was a gig on the stage crew for a rock production company that worked Jersey City. We did our shows at Roosevelt Stadium, a grungy behemoth that could hold sixty thousand, counting seats on the grass. I humped amps out of the trucks and onto the stage; six or so hours later I humped them back. I did it for the Grateful Dead and Alice Cooper and the Allman Brothers and Crosby, Stills & Nash on the night that Richard Nixon resigned. But the most memorable night of that most memorable job was the night of Pink Floyd.

Pink Floyd demanded a certain quality of sound. They wanted their amps stacked high, not just onstage, where they were so broad and tall and forbidding that they looked like a barricade in the Paris Commune. They also wanted amp clusters at three highly elevated points around the stadium, and I spent the morning lugging huge blocks of wood and circuitry up and up and up the stairs of the decayed old bowl.

There was one other assignment: installing and inflating a parachute-like white silken canopy roof that Pink Floyd required over the stage. It took about six hours to get the thing up and in position. We were told that this was the first use of the canopy. Pink's guys had some blueprints, but those turned out not to be of much use. Eventually the roof did rise and inflate by means of a lot of spontaneous knot tying and strategic rope tangling.

Pink Floyd went on at about ten that night, but the amp clusters that we'd expended all that servile sweat to build didn't work—Jersey City being Jersey City, people had sat on them, kicked them, or cut the cords. So Pink made its noise, the towers stayed mute, the mob flicked on lighters at the end, and then we spent three hours breaking the amps down and loading the truck. We felt we'd wasted our time on the speakers up high on the stadium steps, so we refused to go after them. After some sharp words, Pink's guys had to scramble up and retrieve them.

There was, for the record, almost always tension between the roadies and the stage crew. One time, at a show by (if memory serves) Queen, their five roadies got into a brawl with a dozen of our stage-crew guys; then the house security, mostly Jersey bikers and black-belt karate devotees, heard the noise and jumped in. The roadies held on for a while, but finally they saw it was a lost cause. One of them grabbed a case of champagne from the truck cab and opened a bottle and passed it around—all became drunk and happy.

Pink's road manager wanted the inflatable canopy brought down gently, then folded and packed securely in its wooden boxes. The problem was that the thing was full of helium and no one knew where the release valve was; we'd also secured it to the stage with so many knots of such foolish intricacy that their disentanglement would have given a gang of sailors pause. Everyone was tired. Those once intoxicated were no longer. It was four A.M. and time to go home.

An hour went into concocting strategies to get the floating pillowy roof down. It became a regular seminar. Then came Timmy our crew chief, who looked like a good-natured Viking captain and who defended the integrity of his stage crew at every turn, even going so far as to have screamed at Stevie Nicks, who was yelling at me for having dropped a guitar case, that he was the only one who had the right to holler at Edmundson. Faced with the Pink Floyd roof crisis, Timmy did what he always could be counted on to do in critical circumstances, which is to say, he did something.

Timmy walked softly to a corner of the stage, reached into his pocket, removed a buck knife, and with it began to saw one of the ropes attaching the holy celestial roof to the earth. Three or four of us, his minions, did the same. "Hey, what are you doing?" wailed Pink's head roadie. "I'll smash your—" Only then did he realize that Timmy had a knife in his hand, and that most of the rest of us did, too. In the space of a few minutes, we sawed through the ropes.

There came a great sighing noise as the last thick cord broke apart. For a moment there was nothing; for another moment, more of the same.

Then the canopy rose into the air and began to float away, like a gorgeous cloud, white and soft. The sun at that moment burst above the horizon and the silk bloomed into a soft crimson tinge. Timmy started to laugh a big beer-bellied laugh. We all joined. Even Pink's guys did. We were like little kids on the last day of school. We stood on the naked stage, watching the silk roof go up and out, wafting over the Atlantic. Some of us waved.

"So, what are you doing after graduation?" Thirty-five years later, a college teacher, I ask my students the old question. They aren't inclined to dissimulate now. The culture is on their side when they tell me about law school and med school and higher degrees in journalism and business, or when they talk about a research grant in China or a well-paying gig teaching English in Japan.

I'm impressed, sure, but I'm worried about them too. Aren't they deciding too soon? Shouldn't they hang out a little, learn to take it slow? I can't help it. I flash on that canopy of white silk floating out into the void. I can see it as though it were still there. I want to point up to it. I'd like for all my students to see it, too.

FELLOW TEACHERS

A Word to the New
Humanities Professor

Welcome to the university—marvelous to have you here. Congratulations on your appointment to assistant professor! A position like yours is hard to get—but you know that. But perhaps what you don't know is this: Such a position is even harder to keep. You've already achieved a great deal and maybe you've done that by accepting no one's counsel but your own. If so, fine. But maybe a word of assistance and a word or two of warning might be helpful. So—if you like—listen.

If success is what you crave, if prosperity and esteem, tenure, preferment, and promotion are what you desire—and who does not?—then you might begin by studying your admissions-office brochure, the pictorial ad for your school. Whatever its overt designs, this book is also a manual for pedagogical success, a discreet academic version of *The Book of the Courtier.*

In these brochures, these ads, two photographic genres predominate. One genre is a version of romance; its subject is easy pleasure, the world as the readers wish it to be. Students are arrayed in a conversational garland, lounging on well-tended grass. The sun smiles down. They are talking freely, savoring one another's company. If there are books on hand, they've been tossed carelessly aside. This is not about dialogue or dialectic, not about effort. These students are in the Bower of Bliss, intoxicated by each other's presences, relaxed, happy, stress-free.

The other sort of photograph is quite different. In this genre, which is a version of Futuristic Utopian, a group of students presses tightly in on a large, forbidding piece of electronic equipment. It is high-tech, high-powered, and, to you probably, completely mysterious. This picture is not about good times. Serious business is unfolding. A thrill of purposeful engagement rises from the page.

Generally missing from both sorts of pictures are intrusive adults, professorial types, who might inhibit the fun in the first kind of picture or undermine the students' pure self-motivation in the second. What is missing from both these sorts of photographs, to put it bluntly, is you, the professor. And in this there is a valuable lesson. Don't let it be lost.

Pleasure and high-powered training: The sweetly meandering discussion and the high-tech initiation, these are the things a student can now expect, in fact demand, from an American college. You, invisible, self-abnegating, ever agreeable, will provide these commodities. You will provide them or—more than likely—you will find yourself another line of work.

How does a contemporary humanities professor abet the pursuit of enjoyment?

First of all, he must contrive to present all course material in an agreeable manner. Reading assignments should be slight: For one semester, three or four "long" books, that is, books of more than 250 pages, will more than do. The instructor must understand that those students who actually read the books will for the most part do so glancingly. In high school they have learned to budget their time, which means they have learned to skim, extracting "the main points." The teacher should not be surprised to see that those books that *have been* opened are streaked occasionally with highlighter. Those who have "read" an assigned novel will, in general, know who the main characters are and what, in broad terms, has come to pass.

But they will not at all object to being reminded of these things, and those who have decided not to crack the book will believe it to be the professor's responsibility—what else is she being paid for?—to tell them in amusing detail what went on inside. Some students believe it is up to the teacher to describe the book so appealingly (to advertise it, in short) that later in life, given leisure, they might have a look.

The summary and description should be carried on in a diverting way. There ought to be copious reference to analogous themes and plots in recent popular culture. Jokes ought to be offered at the expense of at least some of the characters, preferably all. The author, no matter how distinguished, should be referred to with no more veneration than attachés to the creator of a reasonably successful TV sitcom. In no event should the instructor hint that the author or the characters in the book are in any way superior to the students who have condescended to encounter them.

Students should be assured continually that by virtue of living later in time than the author, they naturally know a great deal more than he possibly could. Sometimes authors will anticipate, or dimly guess at, a piece of contemporary wisdom, in which case they are to be gently congratulated. Generally, authors whose works appeared more than two decades ago are caught up in errors endemic to their times and need to be brought up short. The teacher should give the students every chance to do so. If this process can be effected with the aid of an up-to-date theoretical vocabulary, then all the better.

The proper atmosphere for an enjoyable classroom is relaxed and cool. The teacher should never get exercised about anything, under pain of being written off as a buffoon. Nor should she create an atmosphere of vital contention where students lose their composure, speak out, become passionate, express their deeper thoughts and fears, or do anything else that will, later on, cause them embarrassment. Embarrassment is the worst thing that can befall one; it must be avoided at whatever cost.

It is important here to distinguish being cool from being ironic. Cool is a state of superiority maintained at a consistent level. It is an attitude. Cool does not fluctuate. It is democratic and egalitarian in that it meets all phenomena with the same measure of blank detachment. It is programmatic and readily assumed.

Irony is something different. To be ironic is to express skepticism about this or that outside phenomenon, and also—at times—about one's own powers of apprehension and judgment. Cool never undermines the self; it is directed outward. Irony can be self-subverting. It can demonstrate lack of self-esteem, and is therefore to be avoided.

Irony is also inconsistent, in that it relies on judgment. The ironist is more skeptical about some things than others and communicates as much. Irony, by virtue of being selective, is elitist. Irony can also hurt people's feelings. One must never be ironic in front of students because some of them will not understand the application of the irony. They will become confused and possibly offended. Irony can also make things unclear. One is bound as a professor to be as clear as possible at all times.

Satire—that is to say, protracted irony—is pure poison; no customer-respecting professor should ever conceive of indulging in it.

Cool, on the other hand, is okay. Being cool is a sign of confidence. Being cool indicates that one has made all of the judgments that matter in life and made them correctly. Cool is consistent, steady, and reliable, where irony is uncertain, fluctuating, and insecure. Cool is irony that has become frozen over time.

The teacher should be friendly, though not overly intimate; she should be concerned but not intrusive. She should be in her office as many hours per week as possible. Office availability shows dedication and indicates that the student is getting a good value for his dollars. But the student almost never visits the office. One-on-one conversation can sometimes drift toward disturbing topics—why I'm desperate to transfer to the commerce school, although all of my favorite classes are in the arts; why my sorority has never had a black member; why I have to take these pills so as not to become disablingly depressed. Such topics can make the student uncomfortable. Comfort is all.

E-mail is the preferred form of communication. With e-mail, there is more control. The conversation is in no danger of jumping the rails. One can ask one's own businesslike questions; one can set the tone. The professor should answer e-mail communications within three hours' time. She should not refer the student to this or that book but answer personally, from her own knowledge, with the fewest necessary number of words.

The professor should continually make self-mocking references to her authority and her stock of learning. She should indicate that all the time she has spent acquiring her knowledge may have been wasted, given new developments, such as the Internet, which have changed everything, making much of the past irrelevant. The professor should refer with a respect that stops tastefully short of sycophancy to the large stock of pop-culture knowledge that all of her students possess simply by virtue of having grown up with unparalleled access to TV, movies, and recorded music. She should compliment their remarkable "visual literacy" from time to time. She should use this term—which generally refers to such feats as identifying the TV shows parodied in a given *Simpsons* episode—in rebutting Philistines from outside the academy who claim that many students are now willfully nonliterate, don't read and don't want to.

In choosing what to teach, the professor should meet students halfway. He should realize that he has his culture, which may feature, let us say, the novels of Jane Austen and Charles Dickens; the poetry of Emily Dickinson and Walt Whitman; the historical works of Frances Parkman and Edward Gibbon; the psychoanalysis of Freud; the social thought of Plato, Jefferson, Marx, and Arendt; and the jazz of Coltrane. But students have their culture, too. Insofar as he is in a position to do so, he should offer— it would be presumptuous to say "teach"—courses in the more demotic, vital, and diverse popular culture that the students endorse.

In doing so, it is important that he not be chauvinistic. He must take seriously the possibility that another's experience with Anne Rice might be as vitally nourishing as his own experience with Emily Dickinson. He must consider the possibility that Dickinson, with her difficulty, helps sustain an elitist high culture and that reading and teaching her reaffirms class divisions, while Rice, whose accounts of sadomasochistic and pedophilic bliss are available to all, moves us toward equality. He must, in short, learn as much as possible from his students.

He must take very seriously (but never quite so far as to articulate) the central lesson that his students have to instill: that he is a service provider, not entirely unlike the dentist, the stockbroker (before online trading), and the man who comes to clean the pool. He must remember that he works for them, and that they, all things considered, are very indulgent bosses, but that he ought not to forget how the rolls are buttered and by whom.

As to grades, he should understand that students care nothing about them. They say this repeatedly, in e-mails, and in his office, when they come, so it must be so. But this established truth needs elaboration. Students do not care about grades as long as certain protocols are observed. The first of these protocols is what one might call the default standard. The default standard dictates that if a student comes periodically to class, does some self-determined quotient of the reading, and hands in a semblance of every assignment, the grade will be a B-plus. All other grades are A's.

This sort of grading, which may appear unjustifiably high to outsiders, is pedagogically useful in that it keeps the students happily engaged and does not discourage them (students now are easily discouraged). It also induces them to write positive course evaluations. Negative course evaluations can have an unfortunate effect on a professor's career. Negative course evaluations that include charges of, say, racism or sexism, no matter how imaginary, can have disastrous effects. It is best to follow the grading policies that have been laid down, informally, by the students.

Pay lip service to administrators' calls for tightening grades, but understand who, in this instance, the real policy makers are.

If you follow this advice, elaborating and extending it as you see the
need, you will be likely to produce the right quotient of enjoyment to
succeed as a current professor of humanities. But enjoyment production
is only half of your job. For students are aware that college is also serious
business. There is a time for relaxation, but there is also a time to set to
work.

Besides creating pleasure, you must also help the student to acquire
skills that he or she can turn to profit in the future. You are a facilitator—
not a "sage on the stage" but a "guide on the side." You must teach—no,
rather, you must help the students to acquire—skills in communication,
critical thinking, technology, and teamwork. Without these skills, it is
unlikely that anyone can be truly successful in tomorrow's high-stress,
high-competition world. Without these skills, a person cannot call him-
or herself truly educated.

As a communications facilitator, you will be compelled to work very
hard. Your comments on all written products submitted by students must
be copious. The students and their families are paying good money, and
it is here that they want to see you earn it. It is important that your
comments be clear, precise, and practical. Students need to know what
they have to do in order to improve as communicators. Note every error;
correct every mistake in grammar, spelling, and punctuation. When an
argument is not well structured or when a sentence is ambiguous, show
the student how to remedy the problem. Rewrite the relevant passages if
need be.

You must understand that writing is a form of technology the function of which is to transfer information from one person to another, or
one site to another. Nothing must be lost in the transfer. It is not your
function to comment on the ideas per se. Students' ideas are their own
and they have a personal validity. You have no right to judge them. What
you can judge is skill at expression and presentation. A paper arguing
that Hamlet and Iago are actually brothers separated at birth may seem
to you misguided. This fact is irrelevant. The issue for you to ponder is
whether the essay is well written, presents its points lucidly, and is organized along coherent lines. To succeed in life, a person needs to know
how to get his ideas across. You are instrumental in helping students to
develop this capacity.

Lack of clarity that comes from technical inability is something that you must remedy. But there are other kinds of occlusion that you also need to help students avoid. Though a metaphor can sometimes make things more understandable, the general tendency of metaphor is to produce multiple meanings, and those meanings lead to imprecision, and accordingly to confusion. It is a good idea to help students purge their writing of metaphors, similes, and other potentially mystifying figures of speech. Poetic writing, which was once thought to enrich experience by unfolding more and more layers of meaning and possibility, is now understood to be counterproductive.

Like irony, metaphor can make matters confusing and cause people to feel uncomfortable. Metaphor and irony can make students feel stupid and, at a good college, where students have high SAT scores, no one can accurately be described as stupid. Metaphor, like irony, can contribute to self-esteem problems. But once one has realized that the purpose of writing is to convey information and not to unfold or discover the life of the inner self, or to create original visions of the world (we now know that there is no such thing as originality), then problems associated with metaphor and other mannered forms of writing tend to disappear.

As everyone now realizes, the computer is the most significant invention in the history of humankind. Students who do not master its intricacies are destined for a life of shame, poverty, and neglect. Every course you teach should be computer oriented. Computers are excellent research tools, and so your students should do a lot of research. If you are studying a poem by Blake like "The Chimney Sweeper," which depicts the debasement and exploitation of young boys whose lot, it's been said, is not altogether unlike the lot of many children now living in American inner cities, you should charge your students with using the computer to compile as much interesting information about the poem as they can. They can find articles about chimney sweepers from 1790s newspapers; contemporary pictures and engravings that depict these unfortunate little creatures; critical articles that interpret the poem in a seemingly endless variety of equally valid and interesting ways; biographical information about Blake, with hints about events in his own boyhood that would have made chimney sweepers a special interest; portraits of the author at various stages of his life; maps of Blake's London. Together the class can create a Blake–Chimney Sweeper website: www .blakesweeper.edu.

Instead of spending class time wondering what the poem might mean, and what application it might have to present-day experience—activities that can produce only disagreement and are probably futile anyway since there is no truth about literary works, just interpretations—students can compile information about the poem. They can set the poem in its historical and critical context, showing first how the poem is the product of the past and implicitly how it really has nothing to do with the enlightened present except as an artful curiosity; and second how, given the number of ideas about it already available, adding more thoughts would be superfluous.

Computers have made everything much easier in life, chiefly because you can buy anything you want using them and get it delivered almost immediately. But the Internet is also good because it erases the old puzzlement about the differences among wisdom, knowledge, and information. Everything that can be accessed online is equal to everything else. No piece of data is intrinsically more important or more profound than any other. Therefore, there really is no more wisdom; there is no more knowledge; there is only information. Nothing has to be taken as a challenge or an affront to what one currently knows and values. And that fact can be very freeing.

At one time, ill-natured people used to say that excessive use of certain kinds of technology, and uncritical celebration of it, could be bad for you. These people—many of whom belonged to something called the Frankfurt School, had to flee Hitler's Germany, and thus had developed a resentful attitude toward life—said that technology could make you someone who felt possessed with godlike powers. If you spent too much time manipulating objects, these people suggested, you could begin treating people as though they were objects, too.

They felt that technology gave you an abstract and utilitarian relation to life, and that instead of seeing rocks and flowers and trees, you began seeing foundation material, interior decor, and timber. They thought that technology could make you cold and unsympathetic to the living world. Another man, a philosopher who wrote earlier in this century and was taken to be very gifted but who discredited his work by becoming a Nazi, talked about how technology could make one forget the strangeness of Being. Technology, as he saw it, tended to separate us from wonder and from questions like "Why is there something instead of nothing at all?" But things have changed. With the coming of the computer, most of us have stopped worrying about these issues and nothing really bad has happened. It seems clear that we did not need to be concerned about them and that the resentful men and women, probably because of their traumatic life experiences, had it wrong.

Another thing that students need to acquire are skills in group interaction. It is important that you break your students into groups as much as possible and let them engage in the uninhibited exchange of ideas, their ideas. As everyone now knows, the students have within them the answers to all questions that matter; they merely need a supportive and nonjudgmental environment for their thoughts to emerge. (Plato, it turns out, was right when he endorsed anamnesis, the view that we all knew the truth in a prior life but that, on being born, forget it, so that we need not so much to be informed as to be reminded. Or at least Plato was right about American students of the present.) It is important that you do not intrude on these discussions with your sophisticated terms and your experienced perspective. Keep in mind: Your views may be flawed. And the students, given time, will do productive work on their own.

But of course answers are not really the point. The point is learning to work together and to get along. High grades should go to the people who cooperate best, no matter what you, with your biases, might think about the eventual product. In the future, it may be very important to be able to please and even placate the group. Learning how to submit your so-called individuality to a collective may be a good professional skill and could be a good survival skill as well.

Pleasure and training: These are the things that you offer, and the more modestly and unobtrusively you do so, the better. If you do your job well, you will get the appreciation you deserve. Students in coming years will write you letters about their prosperity and happiness and about how much you did to facilitate them. They will thank you for your patience and your ability to convey important skills. They will praise your powers of communication. They will say that they never could have done it without you, and you will feel both grateful and exalted.

But the road will not always be smooth. Sometimes you will encounter a student who offers a particular challenge, and you must be ready for it. This is the sort of student who comes to college with mistaken expectations. Perhaps he has spent some time reading about Socrates, who asked annoying, self-important questions about everything; or perhaps in high school he had a teacher who encouraged her students to ask about what bearing the things they were reading might have on their lives.

This student comes to college expecting more of the Socrates business. He doesn't care all that much about skills and wants to know whether you think his ideas are true or not. He doesn't write all that badly, but often he sinks into needless ambiguity and confusion. He talks a lot in class. One time, a colleague of yours sees him in the library with a book open. He is laughing his head off. Another time he is seen reading the newspaper and crying. Why, your colleague asks, would anyone read the front page of a newspaper and weep?

This student works hard; in fact he works too hard. He's in your office all the time asking bothersome questions wanting to know the names of fresh books to read, as though the syllabus isn't enough. He writes stories and other things that are not assigned. He plays in a band.

He is also cynical. He laughs at you and others when you talk about cultivating skills that will land good jobs. He mocks the whole idea of training. He says that most of the Internet looks like an electronic shopping mall to him. He says that he has no idea what he wants to do in life; he's uncertain what way of living is the best. He's confused about what goodness really is, who possesses it, and how it might be acquired. He'll be happy to talk about job skills, he says, but only after he's got these questions answered, or at least is on the way to answering them. Though he often says abrupt and potentially embarrassing things to them, many of the other students seem to like him.

It's important to use patience when dealing with such students. They are a challenge, certainly, but they can also be very rewarding. Guiding them from their current confusions onto a better path can provide one of the strongest professional satisfactions there is.

One of the difficulties in doing so, one must confess, is the kind of feelings these students can provoke in you, the teacher. They often bring on a very powerful nostalgia. They take you back to a time before graduate school when you too perhaps thought that certain great works of art and reflection could guide you to a new sort of self. They make you recall when you thought that it might be worthwhile to try to become more like this or that hero or thinker you encountered in a book. These students take you back to a very impassioned time, to be sure. But it was also a turbulent and unproductive time. You know better now, and with your guidance so will this wayward, gifted student. This student needs you. He needs your wisdom and experience. He needs you to put him on one of the straighter, more satisfying roads.

Despite his apparent confidence, and even occasional bursts of what appears to be joy, this is really a troubled individual. Deep in his heart he does not want to be as he is. On some level he wants to change. For to be someone who sits in the library, in public, reading a common everyday newspaper with tears flowing down his cheeks, what kind of life is that? What kind of future could such behavior, uncorrected, ever prepare him for?

Against Readings

If I could make one wish for the members of my profession—college and university professors of literature—I would wish that for one year, two, three, or five, we give up readings. By a reading, I mean the application of an analytical vocabulary—Marx's, Freud's, Foucault's, Derrida's, or whoever's—to describe and (usually) judge a work of literary art. I wish that we'd declare a moratorium on readings. I wish that we'd give readings a rest.

This wish will strike most academic literary critics and perhaps others as well as—let me put it politely—counterintuitive. Readings, many think, are what we do. Readings are what literary criticism is all about. They are the bread and butter of the profession. Through readings we write our books; through readings we teach our students. And if there were no more readings, what would we have left to do? Wouldn't we have to close our classroom doors, shut down our office computers, and go home? The end of readings, presumably, would mean the end of our profession.

So let me try to explain what I have in mind. For it seems to me that if we kicked our addiction to readings, our profession would actually be stronger and more influential, our teaching would improve, and there would be more good books of literary criticism to be written and accordingly more to be read.

In my view—a view informed by, among others, William Blake, Ralph Waldo Emerson, and Matthew Arnold—the best way to think of a literary education is as a great second chance. We all get socialized once. We spend the first years of our lives learning the usages of our families, our neighborhoods, our religions, our schools, and our nations. We come to an understanding of what's expected: We come to see what the world takes to be good and bad, right and wrong. We figure out ways to square the ethics of our church with the ethics of our neighborhood—they aren't always the same, but one reason that religions survive and thrive is that they can enter into productive commerce with the values present in other spheres of life. Kids go to primary school so that they can learn their ABCs and math facts, certainly. But they also go to be socialized: They go to acquire a set of more or less public values. Then it's up to them (and their parents) to square those values with the home truths they've acquired in their families. Socialization isn't a simple process, but when it works well, it can produce individuals who thrive in themselves and either do no harm to others or make a genuine contribution to society at large.

But primary socialization doesn't work for everyone. There are always people—how many it's tough to know, but surely a minority—who don't see their own natures fully reflected in the values that they're supposed to inherit or assume. They feel out of joint with their times. The gay kid who grows up in a family that thinks homosexuality is a sin. The young guy with a potent individualist streak who can't bear the drippy collectivism foisted on him by his ex-hippie parents and his purportedly progressive school. The girl who is supposed to be a chip off the old legal block and sit someday on the Supreme Court but only wants to draw and paint; the guy destined (in his mom's heart) for Princeton who's born to be a carpenter and has no real worldly ambitions, no matter how often he's upbraided.

To be young is often to know—or to sense—what others have in mind for you and not to like it. But what is harder for a person who has gone unhappily through the first rites of passage into the tribe is to know how to replace the values she's had imposed on her with something better. She's learned a lot of socially sanctioned languages, and still none of them are hers. But are there any that truly might be? Is there something she might be or do in the world that's truly in keeping with the insistent but often speechless self that presses forward internally?

This, I think, is where literature can come in—as can all of the other arts and in some measure the sciences, too. By venturing into what Arnold called "the best that has been known and thought," a young person has the chance to discover new vital possibilities. Such a person sees that there are other ways of looking at the world and other ways of being in the world than the ones that she's inherited from her family and culture. She sees, with Emily Dickinson, that a complex, often frayed, often humorous dialogue with God *must* be at the center of her life; she sees with Charles Dickens that humane decency is the highest of human

values and understands that her happiness will come from shrewdly serving others; she likes the sound of Blake and—I don't know—forms a better rock band than the ones we've been hearing for the last decade and more; he seconds Johnson and Burke and becomes a conservative, in his way twice wiser than NPR-addicted, Prius-proselytizing Mom and Dad.

In short, the student reads and feels that sensation that Emerson describes so well at the beginning of "Self-Reliance": "In every work of genius we recognize our own rejected thoughts: they come back to us with a certain alienated majesty." The truth of what we're best fit to do is latent in all of us, Emerson suggests, and I think this to be right. But it's also true that we, and society, too, have plenty of tricks for keeping that most important kind of knowledge out of reach. Society seems to have a vested interest in telling us what we should do and be. But often its interpretation of us—fed through teachers and guidance officers and priests and ministers and even through our loving parents—is simply wrong When we feel—as Longinus said we will in the presence of the sublime—that we have created what in fact we've only heard, then it's time to hearke with particular attention and see how this startling utterance might b beckoning us to think, or speak, or even to live differently.

Everyone who teaches literature has probably had at least one su golden moment. I mean the moment where, reading casually or readi intently, being lazy or being responsive, one is shocked into recogniti "Yes," one says, "that's the way it really is." Then, often, a rather antir mian utterance comes: "They say it's not so, but I know it is. I alw have."

One of my own such moments occurred reading *The Autobiogra of Malcolm X*—something I've mentioned before, but that seems to well worth elaborating on. It didn't really figure: That shouldn't have I *the* book (as it was at least for a little while) for a white, Irish Catholi growing up outside of Boston. What Malcolm had to say about race nated with me: There was a low-grade race war in my school at the and he changed my thoughts about it pretty directly. In sum, I beg see how scary it must be to be black in America, to be in real danger of the time from white officials and white cops and white kids (ki altogether unlike me and my pals).

But what really struck me in that book, oddly enough, was Mal hunger for learning. By now nearly everyone knows the story Malcolm, in prison, found himself unfit for the arguments that p ated in the prison yard (or at least one quadrant of it) and too

subjects under the moon and sun: race, sex, politics, history. He had opinions, but he couldn't back them up. He had almost no facts in his mental files. The answer was simple: He needed to start reading. So he loaded his cell with meaty works from the prison library. But of course smart as the then Malcolm Little was, he hadn't much formal education and the books were loaded with words he didn't understand, placed like land mines in every paragraph. He looked them up in the dictionary, but there were simply too many of them. In the process of running around in the dictionary, he'd forget what the paragraph at hand was supposed to be about.

But this didn't induce him to give up. Instead, Malcolm sat down with a dictionary and a notebook and began copying down the dictionary—starting maybe with *aardvark*—and moving on down the line. It took a while and it wasn't the most scintillating of pastimes, but when it was over, Malcolm Little could read.

And he read ferociously. The whole world of thought came into being for him: history, philosophy, literature, science. He vowed then that he would be a reader for the rest of his life, a learner; and in time he would vow to use his book-won knowledge, along with a considerable quotient of street smarts, to help himself through life and to do what he could for his people. In the beginning, doing what he could for black people meant bedeviling the white man; in time, it meant doing his part to serve all of humanity.

I was thrilled to read this. It turned out that I—despite being about as impatient with formal schooling as Malcolm was—had some intellectual aspirations, too. I was curious about things, after my fashion. Malcolm was black, I was white: Still, my seventeen-year-old self saw him as someone I could, in certain regards, try to emulate. I could read to satisfy my thirst for knowledge; I could use what I learned to make my life a little better, and maybe help some other people along the way. It was an unlikely conversion experience, maybe, but ultimately that's what it was.

I suspect that virtually everyone who teaches literature has had such an experience, and maybe more than one. They've read Emerson or Orwell or Derrida or Woolf and have been moved to change the way they do what they do—or they've chosen another way of life altogether. And even if they don't change, they've had the chance to have their fundamental values challenged. Sometimes a true literary education appears to leave a student where he was at the beginning. But that state is only apparent. Confronted by the best that's been thought and said, he's come

to reconsider his values and views. What was once flat dogma turns into lively commitment and conviction.

But I think that the experience of change is at the heart of literary education. How does it come about? For me, it had a long foreground to be sure, but most immediately I was guided by a teacher. He told me that I—I in particular—might get something worth keeping out of *The Autobiography of Malcolm X*. And I suspect that's how many of us teachers found the books that have made us who we are. Teachers who've been inspired by great works have been moved to pass the gift on. "What we have loved, others will love," says Wordsworth, addressing his friend Coleridge in *The Prelude*—"and we will teach them how."

I think that the highest objective for someone trying to provide a literary education to students is to make such moments of transformation possible. Teachers set the scene for secular conversion. These conversions may be large scale—like the one that Whitman seems to have undergone when he read Emerson's "The Poet" and realized that though Emerson could not himself become the American poet prophesied in the essay, he, Walt Whitman, actually could. But the changes that literary art rings can be relatively minor, too. Reading a book may make a person more receptive to beauty than he otherwise would have been; might make him more sensitive to injustice; more prone to be self-reliant. Granted, books can have negative effects, too. One has read *Don Quixote*; one has read *Madame Bovary*. The Don is led astray by reading airy books about chivalry—he becomes a knight (and all too often an absurd one) in a post-chivalric time. Everyone who takes off to become a hero in a trash TV show, a cheap movie, or a shoddy book is a sad descendant of Don Quixote. Emma Bovary's fictive life concentrates the lives of all too many people, men and women both, who have drawn their view of love from wish-fulfilling novels. They expect more out of erotic life than erotic life can generally deliver: They turn their erotic lives into their spiritual lives—and that too often ends in failure and disillusionment.

But a prerequisite for sharing literary art with young people should be the belief that overall, its influence can be salutary; it can aid in growth. No one would teach history, after all, if he believed that all, or most, forms of historical knowledge were destructive deceptions; one would not teach music if one felt, as Plato did, that most of it disrupts the harmony of the soul.

I said that transformation was the highest goal of literary education. The best purpose of all art is to inspire, said Emerson, and that seems right to me. But that does not mean that literary study can't have other beneficial effects. It can help people learn to read more sensitively; help them learn to express themselves; it can teach them more about the world at large. But the proper business of teaching is change—for the teacher (who is herself a work in progress) and (preeminently) for the student.

Nor do I think that everyone who picks up a book must seek the sublime moment of unexpected but inevitable connection. People read for diversion, for relaxation, to inform themselves, to stave off anxiety in airplanes when the flight attendant is out of wine and beer. A book can make a good doorstop and a fine paperweight—there's no end of uses for a book. But if you're going to take a book into a room where the objective is to educate people—education being from the Latin *educere*, meaning "lead out of," and then presumably toward something—then you should consider using the book to help lead those who want to go out from their own lives into another, if only a few steps.

If this is what you want to do, then readings will only get in your way. When you launch, say, a Marxist reading of William Blake, you effectively use Marx as a tool of analysis and judgment. To the degree that Blake anticipates Marx, Blake is prescient and to be praised. Thus the Marxist reading approves of Blake for his hatred of injustice, his polemic against imperialism, his suspicion of the gentry, his critique of bourgeois art as practiced by the likes of Sir Joshua Reynolds. But Blake, being Blake, also diverges from Marx. He is, presumably, too committed to something akin to liberal individualism; he doesn't understand the revolutionary potential latent in the proletariat; he is, perhaps, an idealist who believes that liberation of consciousness matters more than—or at least must precede—material liberation; he has no clear theory of class conflict. Thus Blake, admirable as he may be, needs to be read with skepticism; he requires a corrective, and the name of that corrective is Karl Marx. Just so, the corrective could also be called Jacques Derrida (who would illuminate Blake the logocentrist); Foucault (who would demonstrate Blake's immersion in and implicit endorsement of an imprisoning society); Kristeva (who would be attuned to Blake's imperfections on the score of gender politics); and so on down the line. The current sophisticated critic would be unlikely to pick one master to illuminate the work at hand—he would mix and match as the occasion required. But to enact a reading means to submit one text to the terms of another; to allow one text to interrogate another—then often to try, sentence, and summarily execute it.

The problem with the Marxist reading of Blake is that it robs us of some splendid opportunities. We never take the time to arrive at a Blakean reading of Blake, and we never get to ask whether Blake's vision might be true—by which I mean, following William James, whether it's good in the way of belief. The moment when the student in the classroom or the reader perusing the work can pause and say: "Yes, that's how it is; Blake's got it exactly right," disappears. There's no chance for the instant that Emerson and Longinus evoke, when one feels that he's written what he's only read, uttered what he's only heard.

Nor—it's worth pointing out—does Marx get much real opportunity here either. He's assumed to be a superior figure: There are in fact any number of Marxist readings of Blake out there; I know of no Blakean readings of Marx. But the student who has heard the teacher unfold a Marxist reading of a work probably doesn't get to study Marx per se. He never gets to have a potential moment of revelation reading *The Manifesto* or *The Grundrisse*. Marx too disappears from the scene, becoming part of a technological apparatus for processing other works. No one asks: Is what Marx is saying true? Is Foucault on to something? Is what Derrida believes actually the case? They're simply applied like paint to the side of a barn; the paint can go on roughly or it can go on adroitly, with subtle variations of mood and texture. But paint is what it is.

It should be clear here that my objection isn't to theoretical texts per se. If a fellow professor thinks that Marx or Foucault or Kristeva provides a contribution to the best that has been thought and said, then by all means read and study the text. (I've studied these writers with students and not without profit.) But the teacher who studies, say, Foucault probably needs to ask what kind of life Foucault commends. Is it one outside of all institutions? Is it one that rebels against all authority? Can that life be in any way compatible with life as a professor or a student? These are questions that are rarely asked about what are conceived of as the more radical thinkers of the era. It is not difficult to guess why this is so.

I've said that the teacher's job is to offer a Blakean reading of Blake, or an Eliotic reading of Eliot, and that's a remark that can't help but raise questions. The standard for the kind of interpretation I have in mind is actually rather straightforward. When a teacher admires an author enough to teach his work, then it stands to reason that the teacher's initial objective ought to be framing a reading that the author would approve. The teacher, to begin with, represents the author: He analyzes the text sympathetically, he treats the words with care and caution and with due respect. He works hard with the students to develop a vision of what the world is and how to live that rises from the author's work and that, ultimately, the author, were he present in the room, would endorse. Northrop Frye does something very much like this in his book on Blake, *Fearful Symmetry*; George Orwell achieves something similar in his famous essay on Dickens. In both cases, the critic's objective is to read the author with humane sensitivity, then synthesize a view of life that's based on that reading. Schopenhauer tells us that all major artists ask and in their fashion answer a single commanding question: "What is life?" The critic works to show how the author frames that query and how he answers it. Critics are necessary for this work because the answers that most artists give to major questions are indirect. Artists move forward through intuition and inference: They feel their way to their sense of things. The critic, at his best, makes explicit what is implicit in the work.

This kind of criticism is itself something of an art, not a science. You cannot tell that you have compounded a valid reading of Dickens any more than that you have compounded a valid novel or a valid play. When others find your Dickensian endorsement of Dickens to be of use to them, humanly, intellectually, spiritually, then your endorsement is a success. The desire to turn the art of reading into a science is part of what draws the profession to the application of sterile concepts.

Perhaps an analogy will be helpful. Let us say that a friend of ours has been seriously ill, or gone through a bad divorce, or has fallen wildly, unexpectedly in love. The friend tells us all about it, from beginning to end, with all the sensitivity she can muster. The story is long and complex and laced with nuance. We listen patiently and take it in. Later on we're faced with explaining this situation to a third person, a mutual friend of us both. Our confiding friend, our first one, wants this to happen: She wants her friends to know the story. How do we proceed? Surely we proceed as sensitively and humanely as possible. We honor our first friend's way of understanding the illness or the love affair. If we are a good friend, we tell the story such that, were the first friend there in the room, she would nod with gratitude.

We may not believe the first friend's entire sense of the story. We may have a different idea of what happened and why. But we honor our first friend by keeping true to her insofar as we can. We do not, say, begin with a Freudian or Marxist reinterpretation of what it is she has told us. If we do, we are no friend at all. We have not given someone we care about due consideration.

Just so, we need to befriend the texts that we choose to teach. They too are the testaments of human beings who have lived and suffered in the world. They too deserve honor and respect. If you have a friend whose every significant utterance you need to translate into another idiom—whose two is not the real two, as Emerson says—then that is a friend you need to jettison. That is simply to say that you do not need to keep company with someone you take to be a liar. If there are texts that you cannot befriend, then leave them to the worms of time—or to the kinder ministrations of others.

In a once famous essay, "Against Interpretation," Susan Sontag denounced interpretation and called for an "erotics of art." She wanted immersion in the text, pleasure, the drowning of self-consciousness. She sought ecstatic immediacy. To be against readings, as I am, is not to be against interpretation. Interpretation entails the work, often difficult, often pleasurable, of parsing the complexities of meaning a given text offers. It means being alert to connotation; it means reading for tone; it means being able to make what is implicit in a piece of writing clearly explicit. Interpretation is necessary if we are to decide what vision of the world the text endorses.

To be against readings is also not to be against criticism. Once the author's vision of what Wallace Stevens calls "how to live, what to do" is made manifest, it's necessary to question it. In time, I learned to ask whether Malcolm X's views about Jews and women were conducive to a good life for anyone. His sense of race relations, early and late in the book, also needed some examination and some skeptical questioning. But this sort of questioning needs to occur once the author's vision is set forth in a comprehensive, clear, sympathetic manner. Criticism is getting into skeptical dialogue with the text. Mounting a conventional academic reading—applying an alternative set of terms—means closing off the dialogue before it has a chance to begin.

You may find that after you've listened to your friend's story about her love affair or divorce that you can't buy everything she says. Her vision is self-idealizing or skewed. Then, as a friend, you need to bring your reservations forward and discuss them with her. So it is with the text: The teacher and students inquire into it, and often too they answer on its behalf. But it all begins with a simple gesture. It all begins by befriending the text.

That gesture of befriending should have a public as well as a classroom dimension. The books that we professors of literature tend now to write are admirable in many ways. They are full of learning, hard work, honesty, and intelligence that sometimes in its way touches on brilliance. But they are also, at least in my judgment, usually unreadable. They are composed as performances. They are meant to show, and often to show off, the prowess of the author. They could not conceivably be meant to provide spiritual or intellectual nourishment. No one could read a representative instance of such writing and decide, based on it, to change her life. Our books are not written from love but from need.

I think that it is possible to write books and essays on behalf of literature that will demonstrate its powers of renovation and inquire into the limits of those powers. Such books can and should be inspiring not only to members of the profession but to educated (or self-educated) and curious members of the general public who are willing to do some hard intellectual work. As a profession, our standing in and impact upon society beyond our classrooms now is minuscule. Yet we are copiously stocked with superb talent: Some of the best young minds in America continue to be drawn to the graduate study of literature. But unless we professors change our ways and stop seeking respectability and institutional standing at the expense of genuine human impact, we are destined, as Tennyson has it, to rust unburnished, never to shine in use.

One must admit that it's possible to develop too exalted a sense of the transforming powers of literature and the other arts. What worked for me and you may not have a universal application. It's probable that most people will be relatively content to live within the ethical and conceptual world that their parents and their society pass on to them. Edmund Burke and Samuel Johnson thought of common-sense opinion as a great repository of wisdom stored through the ages, augmented and revised through experience, trial and error, until it became in time the treasure of humanity. Perhaps the conservative sages were right. But there will always be individuals who cannot live entirely by the standard dispensation and who require something better—or at least something else. This group may be small (though I think it larger than most imagine), but its members need what great writing can bring them very badly indeed. We professors of literature hold the key to the warehouse where the loaves lie fresh and steaming while outside people hunger for them, sometimes dangerously. We ought to do all we can to open the doors and dispense the bread: We should see how far it'll go.

Narcissus Regards His Book/The Common Reader Now

Who is the common reader now? I do not think that there is any way to evade a simple answer to this question. Common readers—which is to say the great majority of people who continue to read—read for one purpose and one purpose only. They read for pleasure. They read to be entertained. They read to be diverted, assuaged, comforted, and tickled.

The evidence for this phenomenon is not far to seek. Check out the bestseller lists, even in the exalted *New York Times*. See what Oprah's reading. Glance at the Amazon top one hundred. Look around on the airplane. The common reader—by which I don't mean the figure evoked by Doctor Johnson and Virginia Woolf, but the person toting a book on the train or loading one into his iPod or Kindle or whatever—the contemporary common reader reads for pleasure, and easy pleasure at that. Reading, where it exists at all, has largely become a relatively unprofitable wing of the diversion industry.

Life in America now is all too often one of two things. Often it is work. People work very hard indeed—often it takes two incomes to support a family, and few are the full-time professional jobs that currently require only forty hours a week. And when life is not work, what is it? When life isn't work, it is play. That's not hard to understand. People are tired, stressed, drained: They want to kick back a little. That something done in the rare off-hours should be strenuous seems rather unfair. Frost talked about making his vocation and his avocation one, and about his work being play for mortal stakes: For that sort of thing, assuming it was ever possible, there is no longer the time.

But it's not only the division of experience between hard labor and empty leisure that now makes reading for something like mortal stakes a very remote possibility. Not all that long ago—fifteen years, not much more—students paraded through the campuses and through the quads, chanting variations on a theme: Hey-hey, ho-ho, they jingled, Western culture's got to go. The marches and the chants and the general skepticism about something called the canon seemed to some an affront to all civilized values.

But maybe not. Maybe this was a moment of real inquiry on the kids' part. What was this thing called Western culture? Who created it? Who sanctioned it? Most important—what was so valuable about it? Why did it matter to study a poem by Blake, or to ponder a Picasso or comprehend the poetry latent in the religions of the world?

I'm not sure that the teachers and scholars ever offered a very good answer to those implied queries. The conservatives, protected by tenure, immersed in the minutiae of their fields, slammed the windows closed and cranked the radiators when the parade passed by. They went on with what they were doing. Those who concurred with the students brought mikes and drums themselves and joined the march. They were much in demand in the media—figures of great interest. The *Post* was calling; the *Times* was on the other line. Was it true? Were the professors actually repudiating the works that they had purportedly been retained to preserve?

It was true—and there was more, the rebels yelled. They thought they would have the microphones in their hands all day and all of the night. They imagined that teaching Milton with an earring in one ear would never cease to fascinate the world.

But it did. The media—most inconstant of lovers—came and the media went, and the academy was left with its cultural authority in tatters. How could it be otherwise? The news outlets sell one thing above all others, and that is not so much the news as it is newness. What one buys when one buys a daily paper, what one purchases when one purchases a magazine, is the hypothesis that what is going on right now is amazing, unprecedented, stunning. Or at least worthy of intense concentration. What has happened in the past is of correspondingly less interest. In fact, it may barely be of any interest at all. Those who represented the claims of the past should never have imagined that the apostles of newness would give them a fair hearing or a fair rendering, either.

Now the people who were kids when the Western canon went on trial and received summary justice are working the levers of culture. They are the editors and the reviewers and the arts feature writers and the ones who interview the novelists and the poets—to the degree that anyone interviews the poets. Though the arts interest them, though they read this and they read that—there is one thing that makes them very nervous indeed about what they do. They are not comfortable with—errrr—judgments of quality. They are not at ease with "the whole evaluation thing." They may sense that Blake's *Songs* are in some manner more valuable, more worth pondering, more worth preserving than *The Simpsons*. They may *sense* as much. But they do not have the terminology to explain why. They never heard the arguments. The professors who should have been providing them when the No More Western Culture marches were going on never made a significant peep. They never quoted Matthew Arnold on the best that's been thought and said—that would have been embarrassing. They never quoted Emerson on the right use of reading—that might have been silly. (It's to inspire.) They never told their students how Wordsworth saved Mill's life by restoring to him his ability to feel. They never showed why difficult pleasure might be superior to easy ones. They never even cited Wilde on the value of pure and simple literary pleasure.

The academy failed and continues to fail to answer the question of value, or to echo the best of the existing answers. But entertainment culture suffers no such difficulty. Its rationale is simple, clear, and potent. The products of the culture industry are good because they make you feel good. They produce immediate and readily perceptible pleasure. Beat that, Alfred, Lord Tennyson. Touch it if you can, Emily Dickinson.

So the arbiters of culture—the academy's former students—went the logical way. They said: If it makes you feel good, it must be. If Stephen King and John Grisham bring pleasure, why, then let us applaud them. Let's give them awards, let's break down the walls of the old clubs and colleges and give them entry forthwith. The only really important question to pose about a novel by Stephen King, we now know, is whether it offers a vintage draught of the Stephen King experience. Does it deliver the spine-shaking chills of great King efforts past? Is the mayhem cranked to the desirable degree? Do homebody sadists and ordinary everyday masochists get what they want and need from the product?

What's not asked in the review and the interview and the profile is whether a King book is worth writing or worth the reading. It seems that no one anymore has the wherewithal to say that reading a King novel is a major waste of human time. No chance. If people want to read it, if they get pleasure from it, then it must be good. What other standard is there?

Media now do not seek to shape taste. They do not try to educate the public. And this is so in part because no one seems to know what literary and cultural education would consist of. What does make a book great anyway? And public media do not try to shape taste for another reason: It annoys the readers. They feel insulted, condescended to—they feel dumb. And no one, now, will pay you for making him feel dumb. Public entertainment generally works in just the opposite way—by making the consumer feel like a genius. No, even the most august publications and broadcasts no longer attempt to shape taste. They merely seek to reflect it. They hold the cultural mirror up to the reader—what the reader likes, the writer and the editor like. They hold the mirror up to the reader and—what else can he do?—the reader falls in love. The common reader today is someone who has fallen in love—with himself.

Freud tells us that people tend to love after two patterns—we are narcissistic lovers or we are anaclitic lovers. We either love versions of ourselves or we love others based on idealized imagoes from childhood. What Freud does not say, but may be true nonetheless, is that a culture can draw people away from anaclitic or idealizing love in the direction of love of self. Our culture, which revolves around the imperial prerogatives and consumer pleasures of self, seems to have done precisely that.

Narcissus in his current post-Freudian guise looks into the book review and finds it good. Narcissus peers into Amazon's top one hundred, and lo, he feels the love. Nothing insults him; nothing pulls him away from that gorgeous smooth watery image below. The editor sells it to him cheap; the professor who might want to intervene—coming on like that Miltonic voice does to Eve gazing lovingly on herself in the pool: "What thou seest / What there thou seest . . . is thyself," it says—the professor has other things to do.

The intervening voice in Milton (and in Ovid, Milton's original in this) is a source of influence. Is it possible that in the world now there are people who might suffer not from an anxiety that they might be influenced but rather from an anxiety that they might never be? Perhaps not everyone loves himself with complete conviction and full abandon. Maybe there remain those who look into the shimmering flattering glass of current culture and do not quite like what they see. Maybe life isn't working for them as well as it is supposed to for all in this immeasurably rich and unprecedentedly free country.

Reading in pursuit of influence—that I think is the desired thing. It takes a strange mixture of humility and confidence to do as much. For suppose one reads anxious about *not being influenced*. To do so is to admit that one is imperfect, searching, unfinished. It's difficult to do when one is young, at least at present: Some of the oldest individuals I meet lately are under the age of twenty-one. It is difficult to do when one is in middle age: for that is the time of commitments. One has a husband or a wife, a family and job, and—who knows?—a career. Having second thoughts then looks like a form of weakness: It makes everyone around you insecure. One must stand steady and sometimes one must pretend. And in old age—early or late—how can one still be a work in progress? That's the time, surely, to have assumed one's permanent form.

That's the time to have balanced accounts, gained traction, become the proper statue to commemorate one's proper life.

Of his attempts at works of art, one writer observed: Finished? They are never finished. At a certain point someone comes and takes them away. (At a certain point, something comes and takes us away—where, we do not know.) We too are never truly finished. What Narcissus wanted was completion, wholeness: He wanted to *be* that image in the water and have done with it. There would be no more time, no more change, no more revision. To be willing to be influenced, even up to the last, is tantamount to declaring that we'll never be perfect, never see as gods see— even that we don't know who and what we are, why (if for any reason) we are here, and where we'll go.

The desire to be influenced is always bound up with some measure of self-dislike, or at least with a dose of discontent. While the current culture tells us to love ourselves as we are—or as we will be after we've acquired the proper products and services—the true common reader does not find himself adequate at all. He looks in the mirror of his own consciousness and he is anything but pleased. *That* is not what he had in mind at all. That is not what *she* was dreaming of.

But where is this common reader—this impossible, possible man or woman who is both confident and humble, both ready to change and skeptical of all easy remedies? *That* common reader is in our classrooms, in our offices, before the pages of our prose and poems, watching and wondering and hoping to be brought, by our best ministrations and our love, into being.

The Uncoolness of Good Teachers

There's a scene in the movie *Almost Famous* that, at least for my money, can tell you as much about good teaching as a term's worth of courses at any currently flourishing graduate school of education. William Miller, aspiring rock journalist, is talking on the phone to the old pro, Lester Bangs. William's working on a profile of a group called Stillwater (whose music doesn't run terribly deep), and some of the band members have been softening him up—making friends with him. Don't buy it, says Bangs. "They make you feel cool. And hey. I met you. You are not cool." William has to confess as much: "Even when I thought I was," he says, "I knew I wasn't." But then Lester Bangs opens up, too: "*We're* uncool," he proclaims. And though uncool people don't tend to get the girl, being uncool can help you develop a little spine. It's too easy out there for the handsome and the hip—their work almost never lasts. Then Bangs throws out his rock-Bogart clincher: "The only true currency in this bankrupt world is what we share with someone else when we're uncool."

Bangs is filling the role of teacher here, and he's a pretty good one in large part because he's willing to be uncool and admit it. Why are good teachers strange, uncool, offbeat?

Because really good teaching is about not seeing the world the way that everyone else does. Teaching is about being what people are now prone to call counterintuitive, but to the teacher means simply being honest. The historian sees the election not through the latest news blast but in the context of presidential politics from Washington to the present. The biologist sees a natural world that's not calmly picturesque but a jostling, striving, evolving contest of creatures in quest of reproduction and survival. The literature professor won't accept the current run of standard, hip clichés but demands bursting metaphors and ironies of an insinuatingly serpentine sort. The philosopher wants an argument as escape-proof as an iron box: What currently passes for logic makes him want to grasp himself by the hair and yank himself out of his seat.

Good teachers perceive the world in alternative ways and they strive to get their students to test out these new, potentially enriching perspectives. Sometimes they do so in ways that are, to say the least, peculiar. The philosophy prof steps in through the window the first day of class and asks her students to write down the definition of the world *door*. The elementary school teacher sees that his kids can't figure out how the solar system works by looking at the astronomy book. So he takes them outside and designates each one as a planet or a major moon and gets them rotating *and* revolving around each other in the grassy field. (For his own safety—and perhaps for other reasons—he plays the part of the sun.) The high school teacher, struck by his kids' conformity, performs an experiment. He sends the hippest guy in the class off on an errand, and while he's gone draws pairs of lines on the board, some equal, some unequal. When the hip kid comes back, he asks the class, who're in on the game, which lines are the same length, which are different, and, as they've been instructed, they answer the wrong way. They're surprised at how often the cool kid disobeys the evidence of his own eyes and goes along with the pack; a few hours later, at home, they're surprised at how good they were at fooling their friend, and how much pleasure they took in making him the butt of the experiment.

From the standard vantage point, these gambits can look like pointlessly offbeat things to do. But the good teacher knows that they can crack the shell of convention and help people look freshly at life. The good teacher is sometimes willing to be a little ridiculous: He wears red or green socks so a kid will always have an excuse to start a conversation with him; she bumbles with her purse to make her more maladroit kids feel at ease.

Good teachers know that now, in what's called the civilized world, the great enemy of knowledge isn't ignorance, though ignorance will do in a pinch. The great enemy of knowledge is knowingness. It's the feeling encouraged by TV and movies and the Internet that you're on top of things and in charge. You're hip and always know what's up. Good teachers are constantly fighting against knowingness by asking questions, creating difficulties, raising perplexities. And they're constantly dramatizing their own aversion to knowingness in the way they walk and talk and dress—in their willingness to go the Lester Bangs route.

Needless to say, teachers can get a lot out of unorthodox teaching, too. The person who turned the bunch of elementary school kids into a spinning solar system wasn't a freshly minted Master of Arts in Teaching. It was Ludwig Wittgenstein, the most influential Western philosopher of the twentieth century. Wittgenstein spent time at Cambridge, arguing with Bertrand Russell and terrorizing undergraduates, but he also did stints as an elementary school teacher. He seems to have loved these gigs and to have been good at them, though he was prone to pull the ears of students slow to master their math facts. Wittgenstein probably found that by getting out of the conventional high-powered university he could let his thoughts loose, ponder things in a freer and less constrained way. After the elementary school teaching run, Wittgenstein went to work on what would become *Philosophical Investigations*, as original a piece of philosophy as the twentieth century produced. In it, he was not unwilling to get down to basics. The former grade school teacher wasn't afraid to pose elementary questions.

But a lot of teachers want to be with it. Unlike Lester (and Ludwig), many of them, maybe even most, want to be cool. How do you become a hip teacher? It's pretty easy, actually. You emulate your students. You do what they do, but with a little bit of adult élan. You like what they like: listen to their tunes, immerse in their technology. In this way, you can get popular fast, but you're also letting the students become *your* teachers.

The most common way to become a hip teacher now—there have been other ways; there will be more—is to go wild for computers. Students love computers; you get points for loving them more. At my school a prof whose energy and ingenuity I have to admire provides his students with handheld wireless input gizmos that have a dozen buttons on them. (I understand they look like TV remotes—not a good sign.) Every five or ten minutes, the prof stops teaching and checks with the kids to see if they're following along. Cool. Many other teachers have turned their classes into light and laser shows. Around the corner, we can expect 3-D glasses.

In order to stay current and be hip, teachers have let students bring their computers into the classroom. There, behind the screens, they do many things, which may include taking class notes or looking up references the teacher makes. But then, too, they may not. Many current teachers are afraid to ban computers from their classrooms. It'll make them unpopular, unhip.

Anyone tempted by this mode of going about things, where the teacher and the student switch roles, should consider the philosophy of education put forward by a chaired senior colleague of Lester Bangs, someone who achieved yet greater distinction as an on-screen pedagogue and who provides one of the constant refrains of this book. "Whatever it is," Groucho Marx merrily sang in *Horse Feathers*, "I'm against it." If it's TV and cultural studies, I'm against it; if it's computers and the hype that surrounds the wireless classroom, I'm against it.

A good teacher is often a Groucho Marxist because the job is to provide alternatives to *whatever* is out there. It's to provide an alternative to convention and conformity. Convention fits some people, but not all. (Maybe not even most.) In fact, even the most conventionally minded people often relish putting aside their conformity for a while and exposing their hidden sides. And here the genius of Lester Bangs–style pedagogy really shines through. "The only true currency in this bankrupt world," he says, "is what we share with someone else *when* we're uncool." When. Uncoolness can be a state that anyone slides into, a state where we're more open, vulnerable, and susceptible to being surprised than at other times when we've got the cold deflective armor on. Teachers live for the moments when their students—and they themselves—cast off the breastplates and iron masks and open up. And good teachers are always ready for those moments to happen.

"I'm glad you were home," William tells Bangs after they've had their rock heart-to-heart on the telephone.

"I'm always home," Bangs assures him. "I'm uncool."

Teaching the Truths

Standing in front of me is the World Spirit, the zeitgeist, the Rude Beast Slouching Towards Bethlehem, or at least he's a significant contender for the role. But the odd thing is that the Spirit, who is decked in thick glasses, weary heel-worn shoes, and an affectionately tended goatee, is refusing to act the part. Before *him* is a lot of the sort of detritus that ought to be swept into the dustbin of history—me, that is, and a handful of other humanities professors—and he has a right, it would seem, to scoff at us human irrelevancies once or twice, then flourish the broom. But that's not what he's doing. The Spirit of the Age talks a lot, almost uncontrollably, about his great love, computers, and he flies off occasionally into hyperlinked digressions, mentally double clicking on phrases from off-the-point sentences past, but by and large the Spirit seems a pretty nice guy.

We're here, we half a dozen or so professors, to learn how to "integrate computing into humanities instruction." In return for sitting through a few training sessions and promising to use technology in a course sometime, we each get temporary use of a jazzy laptop computer. Integrating computing into humanities instruction: This is code, really, for transferring as much as possible of what we know and can do over to the computer. I'm learning how to set up websites full of information about the courses I'm teaching. At the website for my class on dystopias and utopias, Beyond *1984*, you should be able to access all the reading, the relevant articles, my notes for lectures and presentations, your classmates' essays. In the chat room I could set up, you'd talk on with your fellow dys- and utopic students. If I arrange things right, another university computer advocate has informed me, my workload will sink "exponentially."

"Exponentially." Hmmm. In fact, as I figure it, the workload will near the vanishing point. I'll only be needed to grade the papers. I won't be gone, per se; tenure will probably protect me, no matter how flagrantly irrelevant I become. No, I'm heading to the metaphorical dustbin, but my graduate students may be going there literally. We humanities professors are, it would seem, over, played out. The World Spirit doesn't need to gloat; he can just pass serenely through, like the whirlwind angel in Exodus, blowing the husks and shells into the desert and away.

The Exodus angel may be on to something. We humanities professors *have* been working to put ourselves beside the point. (Though maybe it's not too late . . .) So there's no reason why, if things continue in their current course, the cheerful logorrheic in front of me won't have his way.

One example: The teaching of writing has been all but transformed over the past decade. Many teachers once regarded writing as a way to unfold and even to discover an inner self. Writing was, to take a phrase from Keats, a form of "Soul-making." A flexible, potent individual style signified supple, developing character. Now we know better. Writing, it turns out, is a technology. It's a way of transferring information from one site to another. Thus it needs to be clean, clear, fluent, but also rather anonymous, unclouded by excess metaphor or perplexing irony. One learns "communication," not self-excavation, self-making.

Now that the computer is at the center of every course, every area of inquiry is more and more defined by the resources of the computer. Computers are splendid research tools. Good: More and more the curriculum turns in the direction of research. We don't attempt to write as Dickens would, to experiment with thinking as he might, were he alive today. Rather, we research Dickens. We delve into his historical context, learn what the newspapers were gossiping about on the day installment one of *Bleak House* hit the stands. We shape our tools, as Marshall McLuhan famously said, and thereafter our tools shape us.

One can be fully grateful for the best blessings of technology. One can be receptive to many of the pleasures that come out of American popular culture. Yet one can still feel, as I do, that education needs to be about more than training and entertaining, about learning how to do a lucrative job and how to disperse the money that job creates. William Carlos Williams said that people die every day for want of what's to be found in "despised poems." Hyperbolical as the line may be, I think there's something to it. We need the study of history and literature and art, and as more than modes of diversion and more than testing grounds for practical skills.

But what is it precisely that the humanities offer? Pragmatically, what can they do?

The answers I'll offer are both old and new, both conservative and radical, geared to bring full comfort to neither left nor right. And the answers begin where good taste demands that, as of now, one shouldn't tread.

I teach at the University of Virginia, and not far from me down Route 29, in Lynchburg, Virginia, is the church of Jerry Falwell. Falwell, it's well-known, taught the word of God, the literal, unarguable truth as it was revealed to him in the Bible, and as it must be understood by all heaven-bound Christians.

For some time, I thought that we at the University of Virginia had nothing consequential to do with the Reverend Falwell. Occasionally, I get a book through interlibrary loan from Falwell's Liberty University; sometimes the inside cover contains a warning to the pious suggesting that though this volume may be the property of the Liberty University library, its contents, insofar as they contradict the Bible (which means the Bible according to Falwell), are of no particular value.

It's said that when a certain caliph was on the verge of burning the great library at Alexandria, scholars fell on their knees in front of him and begged him to reconsider. "There are two kinds of books here," the caliph reputedly said. "There are those that contradict the Koran—they are blasphemous. And there are those that corroborate the Koran—they are superfluous." And then: "Burn the library." Given the possibilities that the caliph's behavior opened up, it's a good thing that Liberty has a library at all.

Thomas Jefferson, our founder, was a deist (maybe worse than that, the orthodox of Virginia used to whisper). The architecture of the university's central grounds, designed by Jefferson, is emphatically pre-Christian, based on Greek and Roman models. In fact the Rotunda, once the university's library, is designed in homage to the Roman Pantheon, a temple to the twelve chief pagan gods. As soon as they saw the university, local divines became apoplectic. Where was the church? Unlike Princeton and Harvard, the university didn't have a Christian house of worship in its midst. From pulpits all over Virginia, ministers threatened the pagan enclave with ruin from above.

Jefferson—deist (maybe worse), scientist, revolutionary, seems to have believed that the best way to deal with religion was to banish it, formally, from the university, then go on to teach the useful arts of medicine, commerce, law, and the rest. The design of my university declares victory over what the radicals of the Enlightenment would have called superstition, and what most Americans currently call faith or spirituality. And we honor Jefferson now by, in effect, rendering unto Falwell that which is Falwell's.

In fact, humanists in general have entered into an implied bargain with Falwell & Company. They do the soul crafting. They administer the spiritual education. They address the hearts of the students—and in some measure of the nation at large. We preside over the minds. We shape intelligences; we train the faculties. In other words, we teachers cut an implicit deal with religion and its promulgators. They do their thing, we do ours. But isn't that the way it should be? Isn't religion private? Spirituality, after all, is everyone's personal affair. It shouldn't be at the core of college education; it should be passed over in silence. What professor would have the bad taste to puncture the walls of his students' privacy by asking them uncomfortable questions about ultimate values?

Well, me. But then, I got into the teaching business for the reason, I suspect, that many people did. I thought it was a high-stakes affair, a place where, for want of a better way to put it, souls are won and lost. I thought Socrates' line about summed it up: "This discussion," he said, referring to an exchange with his students, "is not about any chance question, but about the way that one ought to lead one's life."

"How do you imagine God?" If you're going to indulge in embarrassing behavior, if you're going to make your students "uncomfortable" (still often the worst thing for a student to be now), why not go all the way? This, or some variant, is the question that lately has been inaugurating my classes—not classes in religion but classes in Shakespeare, in Romantic poetry, in major nineteenth-century novels. That is, the embarrassing question begins courses of study with which—according to Jefferson, according to Falwell, according to the great majority of my colleagues in the humanities—such a query has nothing to do.

What kind of answers do I get? Quite marvelous ones, often. After the students who are disposed to walk out have, sometimes leaving an editorial sigh hanging in the air, and there's been time for reflection and some provisional writing, answers come. Here I can provide only a taste of them.

Some of the accounts are on the fluffy side. I've learned, or relearned, the view that God is love and only love; I've heard that God is nature, that God is light, that God is all the goodness in the universe. I hear tales about God's interventions into the lives of my students, interventions that save them from accidents and deliver them from sickness while others fall by the way. There's a whole set of accounts that are on the all-benevolent side—smiling, kindly, but more than a little under-ramified, insufficiently thought-out. If God is all things, or abides in all things, as I've heard it said, what is the source of evil? (By now it's clear to the students that bad taste is my métier—once this is understood, they can be quite indulgent.) A pause, then often an answer, sometimes not a bad one. The most memorable of the exponents of smiling faith was a woman named Susan who called her blend of creamy benevolence—what else?—Susanism.

Some of the responses are anything but under-elaborated. These tend to come from orthodoxly religious students, many of whom are well trained, maybe overtrained, in the finer points of doctrine. I get some hard-core believers. But it would be difficult to call them Falwell's children, because they're often among the most thoughtful students in the class. They, unlike the proponents of the idea that God is light, period, are interested in major questions. They care about knowing the source of evil. They want to know what it means to live a good life. And though they're rammed with doctrine, they're not always creatures of dogma. There's often more than a little room for doubt. And even if their views are sometimes rock-wall solid, these students don't mind being tested. They're willing to put themselves into play because, given their interests, they don't mind that this "is not about any chance question, but about the way that one ought to lead one's life."

Religion is a good place to start a humanities course, even if what we're going on to do is read the novels of Henry James, in part because religion is likely to be the place where you can find what the philosopher (and anti-philosopher) Richard Rorty calls a person's "final vocabulary." A final vocabulary is the ultimate set of terms that we use in order to confer value on experience. It's where our principles lie. When someone talks about the Ten Commandments, or the Buddha's four noble truths, or the innate goodness of human beings in their natural state, or history being the history of class conflict, and does so with a passion, then in all likelihood the person has revealed the core of her being. She's touched on her ultimate terms of commitment, the point beyond which mere analysis cannot go. Rorty puts it this way: "All human beings carry about a set of words which they employ to justify their actions, their beliefs, and their lives. These are the words in which we formulate praise of our friends and contempt of our enemies, our long-term projects, our deepest self-doubts and our highest hopes. They are the words in which we tell, sometimes prospectively and sometimes retrospectively, the story of our lives."

Sometimes there's apparently no "there" there. That is, the students seem to have no ultimate vocabularies. The anti-philosophy of "whatever" is in place. But that can be a merely superficial condition. If you keep asking, values often do emerge. And when they don't, the students sometimes are willing to ask themselves why. Somehow they feel the pain of that void. They feel what Kundera, thinking of Nietzsche, called an unbearable lightness of being. Within that void, or against the solid wall of conviction, humanistic learning can fruitfully take place.

In Rorty's idiom, the word "final" is ironic. That is, a major step in educating oneself comes with the conviction that all of one's most dearly held beliefs should be open to change. One's final vocabulary is final only for now. Certain people, says Rorty, "are always aware that the terms in which they describe themselves are subject to change, always aware of the contingency and fragility of their final vocabularies, and thus of their selves." Rorty believes that such people are the exception, not the rule. I'm not so sure. I think that one can begin by assuming that any student who turns up in a humanities course is open to influence, open to change.

It's time, perhaps, for something like a thesis statement: The function of a liberal arts education, as I see it, is to rejuvenate, reaffirm, replenish, revise, overwhelm, replace, reorder, or maybe just slightly retouch the web of words that Rorty calls the final vocabulary. A language, Wittgenstein thought, is a way of life. A new language, whether we learn it from a historian, a poet, a painter, or a composer of music, is potentially also a new way to live.

While I'm asking my questions about imagining God, what's going on in the classrooms of colleagues down the hall and across the country?

Often some very good things. (It's not all training, not all entertaining.) No matter what humanities teachers may profess in their published papers, in the classrooms matters are often much different. Professors of literature and history and philosophy and religious studies generally have something in common. They attempt to teach one essential power, and they often do so with marked success. That one thing is reading. They cultivate attentiveness to written works, careful consideration, thoughtful balancing, coaxing out of disparate meanings, responsiveness to the complexities of sense. They try—we try, for I'm of this party, too—to help students become more and more like what Henry James said every author should be, someone on whom nothing is lost. Attentiveness to words and, with the habits of concentration developed on words, an attentiveness to life—that is one aim of a humanities education.

But there are limits to close reading. It's said that the Harvard scholar Walter Jackson Bate used to do a Marx Brothers–style routine to dramatize them. "Close reading," he'd mutter, and push the book up near his nose. "Closer reading"—chuckling, digging his face down into the book. Then, finally, "very close reading," where nose and book kissed and not a word of print was legible. The point is that with a certain kind of exclusive attention to the page, life disappears. The connection between word and world goes dark.

This is the fate of reading when we do not move beyond interpretation. It is possible, I fully believe, to read a book in such a way that we can bring forth an interpretation that the author would approve. We can, with careful study, with disciplined effort, concoct a vision of Wordsworth's Nature that the poet would find acceptable; we can imagine what Shelley meant by liberty. We can evoke uncertainties, mysteries, and doubts when those are a poet's Keatsian designs. Critics who do not believe that this is possible may forget how often in day-to-day life we're called upon to relay the story of a protracted illness, a divorce, a long-worked-for triumph as we've heard it recounted by another. Are poems so much more difficult to render?

But then comes the next step, the critical one. I've asked my students what they believe. I've asked them what the word at hand means. Now the final question: Is the work true? That's a question simple to phrase but hard to answer.

Does the work contain live options? Does it offer paths they might wish to take, modes of seeing and saying and doing that they can put into action in the world? How, to phrase the matter in slightly different terms, does the vision at hand, the author's vision, cohere with or combat (or elaborate, or reorder, or simply fail to touch—the possibilities are endless) your own vision of experience, your own final vocabulary?

Do you want to affirm Wordsworth's natural religion? It's not as far-fetched a question as it might sound at a moment when many consider ecological issues to be the ultimate issues on the world's horizon. Is it true what Wordsworth suggests in "Tintern Abbey" about the healing powers of Nature and memory? Can they fight off depression? Not an empty question in an age when antidepressive drugs have become so sadly common. Is Milton's Satan the shape that evil now most often takes—flamboyant, grand, and self-regarding? Or is Blake's Satan—a supreme administrator, mild, bureaucratic, efficient, and congenial, an early exemplar of Hannah Arendt's "banality of evil"—a better emblem? Or, to strike to the center of the tensions that often exist between secular and religious writing, who is the better guide to life, the Jesus of the Gospels or the Prometheus of Percy Bysshe Shelley, who learned so much from Christ but rejected so much as well—in particular Jesus' life of committed celibacy?

Yes, one might say, but those are Romantic writers, polemicists, authors with a program. How about other writers? How about, for instance, the famous poet of negative capability, who seems to affirm nothing, Shakespeare? The most accomplished academic scholars of Shakespeare generally concur: They cannot tell for certain what Shakespeare believed on *any* consequential issue.

But in fact Shakespeare has been the object for what may be the most formidable act of literary criticism yet performed. If Sigmund Freud drew on any author for his vision of human nature—right or wrong as that vision may be—it was Shakespeare. The Oedipal complex, to cite just one of Freud's Shakespearean extractions, ought just as well to be called the Hamlet complex. From Shakespeare, Freud might also have drawn his theories of sibling rivalry; of the tragic antipathy between civilization and the drives; of bisexuality; of patriarchal presumption; of male jealousy; of the intertwinings of love and authority; of humor as an assault on the superego—of a dozen matters more. In larger-scale terms, Freud's tragic sense—his commitment to stoical renunciation as the best response to life's inevitable grief—finds considerable corroboration in the world of Shakespeare's plays. Shakespeare may not have affirmed any ideas directly; he is not, it's true, a polemicist in the way that Blake is. But Freud's contestable truths can be fairly extracted from Shakespeare, put on display, and offered to the judgment of the world. (Rather implicitly and quite brilliantly, Freud succeeds in befriending the spirit of Shakespeare's work in the way that I described in the chapter against readings.) Does Shakespeare/Freud work? Does their collaboration, if it is fair to call it that, illuminate experience, put one in a profitable relation to life? Does it help you live rightly and enjoy your being in the world?

But what does all of this have to do with religion? Why ask, on day one, the grating question about God?

Because in a fundamental sense Matthew Arnold's view on the relations between poetry and faith is, I believe, an accurate one. If religious faith wanes in the world—or in a given individual—then the next likely source of meaning may well be literature. The literature we have come to value, most especially the novel, is by and large anti-transcendental. It does not offer a vision of the world as existing under the guidance of a deity. It suggests, though often it does not assert, that we humans have to make our own way without the strains and the comforts of faith.

The teaching of literature I want to commend does not argue that always and for everyone a secular, imaginative vision must replace faith.

Rather, this sort of teaching says that a most pressing spiritual and intellectual task of the moment is to create a dialogue between religious and secular approaches to life. Many of my students leave class with their religious convictions deepened. They are more ardent and thoughtful believers than when they began. The aim is not conversion. It is the encounter between the transcendental and the worldly. The objective is to help the students place their ultimate narratives in the foreground and render them susceptible to influence.

Most professors of the humanities seem to have little interest in religion as a field of live options. Most of them, from what I can see, have had their crises of faith early in life and have adopted, almost as second nature, a secular view of experience. Others keep their religious commitment separate from their pedagogy and have been doing so for so long that they are hardly aware of it.

But what is old to the teacher is new to the student. The issue of belief matters greatly to the young, or at least it does in my experience. They want to know how to navigate life, what to be, what to do. Matters of faith or worldliness are of great import to our students, and by turning away from them, by continuing our treaty with Falwell where we tutor the mind and he takes the heart and spirit, we do them injustice.

Is it a form of therapy that I am endorsing here? Yes and no. Yes, in that this form of teaching, like Socrates', like Freud's, offers possibilities for change that are not only intellectual but emotional as well. When we're talking about ultimate values, feelings come into play; tensions similar to those met with in a Freudian therapeutic exchange can arise. But there is also a crucial difference. Patients come to psychoanalysis because they suffer from the past—their experience of various events prevents their living with a reasonable fullness in the present. The form of pedagogy I am describing, which is anything but new, assumes a certain ability to live within the present (that is to say, a certain sanity) and so aims itself directly at the future. What *will* you be? What *will* you do?

There is a story about a psychoanalyst who, at the end of the first-day intake interview, asked his patients an unexpected question. "If you were cured, what would you do?" There would come forth a list. "I'd get married." "I'd travel." "I'd come back and study law." To which the therapist sometimes replied, "Well, then, why don't you simply go out and do those things?" At the moment when he posed the possibility, the therapist stopped being a therapist in the Freudian sense and became something rather different.

A scene of instruction can illustrate the kind of teaching I want to commend. One of my recent students, a young woman, professes herself to be an ardent Christian. She believes in doing unto others as you would have them do unto you, in turning the other cheek. She believes Jesus to be the most perfect being. But she reads *The Iliad* and, after a period of languor, she's galvanized by it. What sweeps her in is the vision of a life where triumph matters over everything. The warriors in the poem seek first place all the time. Envy is not a vice to them; it's entirely creditable. The young woman who, it comes out, wants to be a well-to-do corporate lawyer has no trouble seeing something of herself in the unapologetic ambitions of Homer's heroes.

But then, too, she wants to be a Christian. Jesus' originality lies in part in his attempt to supersede the ambition and self-vaunting of Homer's heroes—qualities still very much alive in the Roman empire into which Jesus was born. Which will it be, my student needs to ask herself, Jesus or Achilles? Of course, what she needs is some live synthesis of the two. And it is her task to arrive at it. But without the encounter with Homer, and without our raising the simple and supposedly elementary question of identification—is there anything in you that is Achillean?—she might not have had access to her own divided state. This was an instance not only of reading and interpreting a book—we spent a long time coming to understand the heroic code and considering Homer's highly equivocal attitude toward it—but of allowing the book to interpret and read the reader. It was a moment, I would say, of genuine humanistic education.

The questions I want to ask may seem elementary compared to the sophisticated queries that a theoretically charged Foucauldian may offer in class. But many of us—teachers and students both—do not know what we think about major personal issues. And it is with them that we need to begin. Being a beginner in humanistic inquiry is something to be treasured; sophistication too rapidly attained can be self-defeating. Thus that great violinist on hearing a young, technically brilliant prospective student: "I will never be able to teach him anything. He lacks inexperience." Or Emerson, in a lovely moment from his journals: "Don't let them eat their seed-corn; don't let them anticipate, ante-date, and be young men, before they have finished their boyhood."

What is the teacher's role in this? I think it begins with a realization of what literature and art, at least since the Romantic period, have offered to us. This is the view that there are simply too many sorts of human beings, too many idiosyncratic constitutions, for any simple map of human nature, or any single guide to the good life, to be adaptable for us all. This realization, which coincides with the foundations of widespread democracy as well as with the flourishing of novels, holds that there are multiple ways of apprehending experience and multiple modes of internal organization, or disorder. Accordingly, there are many, many different ways to lead a satisfying, socially constructive life. This, or something like it, is what Milan Kundera is getting at when he calls the characters—and by implication the narrating voices—encountered in fiction "experimental selves." There are multiple ways to go, and confining theories of the self, even those as admirably worked out as, say, Plato's or Kant's, cannot encompass the range of human difference.

The teacher, in other words, begins the secular dialogue with faith by offering the hypothesis that there is no human truth about the good life, but that there are many human truths, many viable paths. To set his students on them, he offers them multiple examples of what Arnold (in what is justifiably the most famous phrase about the objectives of literary education) called the best that has been known and thought. This multiplying of possibilities—a condition enhanced by the rapid diffusion of culture around the globe—makes literature, which is inevitably the effusion of an individual mind, the most likely starting place. I would even say it's the center of humanistic education. As literary works are multiple, so are the number of possibly usable human visions of experience.

Beginning with this hypothesis, the teacher's task is often one of inspired impersonation. Against her students' final vocabularies, against their various faiths, she, with a combination of disinterest and passion, hurls alternatives. Impersonation: The teacher's objective, in the approach I'm describing, is to offer an inspiring version of what is most vital in the author. She merges with the author, becomes the creator, and in doing so makes the past available to the uses of the present. The teacher listens to criticisms, perhaps engenders some herself, but always finally is the author's advocate, his attorney for explication and defense.

Is *The Iliad* a book replete with vital possibilities, or is it a mere historical curiosity? Is it locked in the past, or a potent guide to the present and the future? A number of my students—men and women both—initially thought it was a period piece and nothing more. The way the poem treated women disgusted them. In *The Iliad*, they said, a woman has the status of a few bullocks or a bronze tripod or two. Some, like Helen, are beautiful, and that beauty is a sort of power, but it is a limited and debased one compared to what the men have.

The class was about ready to concur when one of the women students, usually quiet, spoke up. She said that the poem mattered to her because she could see things from Achilles' point of view. The passage that caught her attention first was the one where Achilles' father tells him that he must be the best in every undertaking. He must simply never take second place. "I'm an athlete, I swim," she said, "and that's how I was raised by my parents and my coaches. After a while, though, I had to stop living like that. It's too much."

"Have you ever wanted to go back to it?" someone asked, perhaps me.

"Yes," she said, "all the time. It makes life incredibly intense." And you could see, if you looked hard, that what had once been closed off and left behind began to open again. The life of full unbridled competition is not for everyone, and it will not be approved by all. But if it is your highest aspiration, the thing you most want, then whether you take the path or not, it is worth knowing about your attraction to it. Achilles' life is the life of *thymos*, and if you are, at whatever depths, an individual driven by *thymos*—by the desire for glory and praise, despite the moral censors you've thrown up against that drive—you need to deal with the fact in one way or another. I know no better means to begin to do so than through Homer.

Every essay on education needs a villain. There has to be someone or something preventing the liberal arts from being the world-changing enterprise we all suspect that they can be. And I suppose so far I have supplied a few. There are the spirits of training and of entertaining, and there's the refusal on the part of professors, even the best intentioned, to engage with questions of belief—to hear, in other words, a famous line of Wallace Stevens's: "Say that final belief / Must be in a fiction. It is time to choose." But of course to be a humanist—and the questions that emanate from humanism are ultimately the ones that this essay endorses—one must declare war on what's been called the cultural left, who are supposedly busy condemning all of Western literature for not living up to their own high political standards.

And in one measure, I'm willing to do that. The kind of teaching I part company with, the kind that seems to me most destructive to the freedom of self-making, is the kind that simply applies a standing set of terms to every text that comes to hand. These forms of teaching are a little like bad translation. Every work, alas, is rewritten in the terms of Foucault, of feminism, of Marx, and that is the end of the story.

Surely there are plenty of good questions about gender to pose to *The Iliad*. But if we simply look for a way to apply the theory, apply the denunciation, and do no more, then the free space that helped one student see her own attraction to the athlete's life and helped another to see her divided mind, her pull toward the goodness of the Gospels and the potency that Homer describes—that free space collapses.

And as I have suggested, the theorist almost never turns and interrogates the theoretical terms at hand. He never asks how well Foucault could work as a guide to life. (That is, does he tell a truth?) The theorist generally does not pause to wonder how one would live, if one could live, with the wild hatred of all authority that Foucault endorses. Could you really teach in an institution as authority-based as a university and preach the gospel according to Foucault? It seems to me highly unlikely. But for many theorists, the application of the terms is enough. Rather than sending one nineteenth-century novel after another grinding through the mills of Foucault, why not teach Foucault straight out, and see how much of his purported wisdom can really stand the test of experience? (For myself, I find it hard to think of Foucault without thinking of Emerson's marvelous line: "I hate the builders of dungeons in the air.")

And yet there is a good deal to learn from the cultural left. For, to put it bluntly, they are the ones who believe that books can change people. They don't stop at mere interpretation. They understand that what is at issue in a literary education is belief. In some measure, they've kept the spirit of Socrates alive.

The fall of the liberal arts—which seems to many to be impending—isn't so much about heroes and villains as it is about well-intentioned people forgetting to ask and answer the kinds of questions that got them interested in reading to begin with. Professors, when young, read books as if their lives depended on it; older now, they enjoin their students to read and think as though what chiefly depends on it is their careers.

The spirit of education I want to encourage is better enacted and expressed by Harold Bloom. "We all of us go home each evening and at some moment in time, with whatever degree of overt consciousness, we go over all the signs that the day presented to us. In those signs we seek only what can aid the continuity of our own discourse, the survival of those ongoing qualities that will give what is vital in us even more life.

This seeking is the Vichian and the Emersonian making of significance into meaning, by the single test of aiding our survival." This is what we do, or ought to do, with books: turn their signification into meaning, into possibility. So Emerson himself suggests when, asking what the purpose of books is, he says simply that they should contribute to the thing in life that matters most to him. Books should inspire.

And the test of a book, from this perspective, lies in its power to map or transform a life. The question we would ultimately ask of any work of art is this: Can you live it? It you cannot, it may still command considerable interest. The work may charm, it may divert. It may teach us something about the large world; it may convey or refine a remote point. But if it cannot help some of us to imagine a life, or unfold one already latent in us, then it is not a major work, and probably not worth the time of students who, at their period in life, are looking to respond to very pressing questions. They are on the verge of choosing careers, of marrying, of entering the public world. They are in dire need of maps—or of challenges to their existing sense of the terrain.

Popular culture, which is more and more taught at universities, generally cannot offer this. The objective of a good deal of rock music and film is to convey the pleasing illusion that people can live in the way that the singers and the actors comport themselves when they are on. Occasionally, I suppose, a performer comes through. Keith Richards seems to be, in life, the Keith that he evokes when he's onstage. Most people probably don't have the guts or the constitution for it.

Yet what David Denby says about movie love still strikes me as true: "Movie love puts people in touch with their own instincts and pleasures. Movies can lead to self-reconciliation, and that is one reason why they have inspired an almost unlimited affection." Movies tap into the fantasy life, and insofar as fantasy is being washed over by the gray waves of the reality principle, we need it to be restored. We need a new, larger self-synthesis that pays heed to the more refractory desires, or fantasies. But those fantasies cannot generally be the blueprint for a life, not in the way that the vision of Henry James, say, can conceivably be.

If resistance to popular culture is the teacher's objective, as it often is now, other problems arise. For the simple fact is that analysis will always be in arrears to the production of diverting images. While critique lingers over this or that blockbuster film, it becomes old news, the stuff of yesterday's generation. Brilliant analyses of *Titanic* are still coming out from learned journals and, in class, confronting students who were too young to have seen the film when it came out.

The central question to pose about works of popular culture, it seems to me, is this: Can you live it? Could you build a life around its visions? Given the work at hand, different people will answer differently. Some people will say yes to Bob Dylan (I would), yes to Muddy Waters and the blues tradition he works in, yes to Robert Altman or Stanley Kubrick. But you'll find far fewer people, I think, who'll be able to say yes to the Rolling Stones or Britney Spears. This doesn't mean that the Stones, and, who knows, maybe even Britney, are without their value. Fantasy matters. But I think that teaching such work to people who are looking for answers to primary questions may not be the best way to use their time.

Some humanities teachers, sometimes the best of them, feel that they're fighting in a lost if noble cause. They believe that the proliferation of electronic media will inevitably put them out of date. They see the time their students spend with TV and movies and on the Internet, and they feel that what they have to offer—words—must look shabby and old-fashioned by contrast. But this is not the case.

When human beings attempt to come to terms with who they are and who they wish to be, the most effective medium is verbal. Through words we represent ourselves to ourselves, we expand our awareness of the world, we step back, gain distance, on what it is we've said. And then we are in a position to change. Images, however exhilarating, do not generally function in this way. Words allow for a precision and nuance that images do not seem, for most people, to be able to provide. In a culture that changes at the velocity that ours does, the power of self-revision is centrally important. Self-aware self-revision is very difficult, if not impossible, outside of language.

Overall there is something to be learned from the analysis of popular culture. But we teachers can do better. We can strike to the central issues that confront the young, rather than working on the peripheries.

The other great apparent alternative to the self-creating approach I am describing goes under the name of multiculturalism. Know the other, says the multiculturalist. I could not agree more. A segment of the curriculum *should* be devoted to studying the literature and arts of cultures that are resolutely different from Western traditions. In them we may sometimes find truths that directly serve our present needs for revelation. We may read them and say: "Yes, that's how it is." But books from far-flung cultures can also teach us how many different ways of being there are in the world. In fact, this is probably their likeliest gift.

My fear about the multicultural curriculum is that it may ask students to know others before they know themselves. If we learn only or chiefly of difference without taking the time to find, or make, the inner being, we risk being walking voids, readily taken up by, say, commercial interests, ever ready to use our college-won knowledge of others for the purposes of exploiting them. Asks David Rieff: "Are the multiculturalists truly unaware of how closely their treasured catchphrases—'cultural diversity,' 'difference,' 'the need to do away with boundaries'—resemble the stock phrases of the modern corporation: 'product diversification,' 'the global marketplace,' and the 'boundary-less company'?" Where the inner void was, where the unbearable lightness was, there the corporation may well open its franchise.

Most of our ideas about influence are negative. Freud speaks of the transference, the influx of past memories that distort an existing erotic or power relation. Bloom writes of influence anxiety. And so the thought of being remade by the poets can cause people certain qualms. And yet perhaps the process I am describing is often not so much a matter of remaking or conversion as it is of recognition. T. S. Eliot observed that one of the things that poetry does is to find words for feelings that have abided unnamed in the heart. Maybe, on a larger scale, the process I am describing is simply one in which the self recognizes its own larger yet unarticulated order as it is shadowed forth in the thoughts of another. And then, of course, there is work to do, the work of completing the vision. As Nietzsche said, "No one can extract from things, books included, more than he already knows."

Proust, who is probably our preeminent theorist of a benevolent influence, observes that

> The mediocre usually imagine that to let ourselves be guided by the books we admire robs our faculty of judgment of part of its independence. "What can it matter to you what Ruskin feels: feel for yourself." Such a view rests on a psychological error which will be discounted by all who have accepted a spiritual discipline and feel thereby that their power of understanding and of feeling is infinitely enhanced and their critical sense never

paralyzed . . . There is no better way of coming to be aware of
what one feels oneself than by trying to recreate in oneself what
a master has felt. In this profound effort it is our own thought
itself that we bring out into the light together with his.

But the fact remains, as Proust elsewhere admits, that books can only
put you on the edge of a spirited secular life. You must claim the rest, pass
over the threshold for yourself.

Some will object to this vision of education. They will say that it is
dangerous to talk about crucial matters in a classroom. A student's path
may be radically changed by such discussion. The path may be blocked.
It may become confused. But so may a life be ruined by not thinking. So
may a life be ruined that never leaves the provinces of easy, unexamined
faith in the transcendent. So may a life be wasted that gives to Falwell
what he claims to be his and takes the slim remainder, worshipping
diminutive Apollo with his toy computer, or small-time Dionysus with
his Saturday nights. People can become distressed when they imagine a
world in which all of us, inspired by poets and other artists, create our
own lives, with only community welfare and our privately perceived failures to rein us in. They fear chaos, they say. They fear disorder. But
perhaps what they fear, most truly, is democracy.

Under the Sign of Satan: Blake in the Corporate University

"I in my Selfhood am that Satan. I am that Evil One!"

WILLIAM BLAKE, *MILTON*

Imagine waking up in a world gone wrong. You can feel it: Things are out
of joint. The center's not quite holding and all the rest. Yet imagine that
world as being more agreeable—more secure, more organized, more civilized (in a certain sense)—than any world you had ever imagined inhab-
iting. One has a wealthy sponsor. One is sheltered, valued. There is the
matter of prestige. There is a firm sense of identity, at the very least. One
can do one's work. Distractions are few, privileges many. Yet still there is
little doubt: One lives in a world gone wrong.

William Blake found himself in such a position when he turned
himself over to the protection of his prosperous, kindly friend William
Hayley. Hayley rescued Blake and his wife Catherine from poverty

(maybe from financial ruin) and from the neglect that had plagued the poet-painter's work. Hayley brought Blake out of the blighted, glorious London that he loved and into the countryside. (Blake's attitude toward nature was complex, but overall unfavorable.) Hayley gave Blake time, space, and money. He tried to make the poet into a success.

Blake's grand-sized visionary paintings didn't sell? No one wanted to buy his gorgeous, sometimes rather garishly illuminated books? Very well. Hayley wanted Blake to succeed. And Blake did not wish to be dependent on Hayley's charity forever. So Hayley put Blake to work painting miniatures, tiny portraits for broaches and necklaces. Blake, who loved to be expansive, was going to be compelled to do small things. But Hayley loved Blake—Blake knew it. He truly wanted this man of genius to prosper, gain recognition, stand on his feet and all the rest. In a sense, Blake never had a better friend than William Hayley.

2

No one liked it when Hulk Hogan came to town. At least no one I know did. Hulk came to Charlottesville to perform with his wrestling troupe at the John Paul Jones Arena at the University of Virginia. We had imagined, my faculty friends and I, that the arena would be the site for UVA basketball games and maybe a graduation ceremony or two on rainy days. But not long after the grand opening of the arena, we heard about Hulk and his crew, and we heard of a performance by something called monster trucks. The climax, I understood, came when a particularly monstrous monster truck, with tires taller than two or three men, rode over the tops of a line of parked vehicles, crushing them into metal pulp.

When the subject of Hulk Hogan and the monster trucks arose, my faculty buddies and I *looked* at each other in exasperated ways and blew out exasperated columns of air as if to scatter the wrestlers and the steroidal trucks like so many leaves. But we did not *say* all that much. No, not much at all.

The University of Virginia, like virtually all universities, is a corporation. It requires revenues. It needs to generate funds. There is an operating budget and expenses must be met, among them the expenses of maintaining me in the English department, and my friends in music and architecture and religious studies.

That universities are becoming more corporate in orientation and aim is news to no one at all. We—like every other school that aspires to a certain status, a certain measure of success—have added layer upon layer of administrators. We have brought on no end of fund-raisers. More than that, many of the deans once charged with overseeing academic affairs are now also out seeking money from donors. A story that appeared not terribly long ago in the *New York Times* tells us that over the past two decades, colleges and universities in America have doubled their full-time support staff. Enrollment has increased only 40 percent; full-time instructors rose by only 50 percent, and many of those new instructors are non–tenure track. The article goes on to say that "the growth in support staff included some jobs that did not exist 20 years ago, like environmental sustainability officers and a broad array of information technology workers. The support staff category includes many different jobs, like residential-life staff, admissions and recruitment officers, fund-raisers, loan counselors and all the back-office staff positions responsible for complying with the new regulations and reporting requirements college faces."

With these changes, a new institutional culture is coming into being. Universities now teem with people who must do what people who work in corporations do: be responsive to their superiors, direct their underlings, romance their BlackBerries, subordinate their identities, refrain from making mistakes, keep a gimlet eye always on the bottom line. Organization men and women have come and they are doing what they can—for an administrator must administer something—to influence the shape of the university. Are they having a shaping influence on the students? Often they do not have to, for many of our students—not all, but many—are already organization men and women. Though "organization man" is not the name in favor now; the current term of art is "leader."

How does a young person begin to qualify to become what is now called a leader? The essayist William Deresiewicz talks about the endless series of hoops that students have to jump through now if they hope to get into the right colleges. "Courses, standardized tests, extra-curriculars in school, extra-curriculars outside school. Test prep courses, admissions coaches, private tutors." What you get at the end, he says, are "kids who have been trained to be excellent hoop jumpers." They are, as one member of the generation observes, "excellent sheep."

All colleges and universities want leaders. They want to recruit them from high school. They want to cultivate them once they've arrived. Colleges are determined to graduate leaders and to send them into the world to become prosperous and grateful alumni. But who is a leader? A leader is someone who is drawn to organizations. He learns their usages. He internalizes their rules. He merges his identity with that of the organization. He always says "we." He starts at the bottom, a leader in training. Then he progresses, always by gradual steps, as close to the top as his powers will allow. He begins "mentoring" other leaders. In his assent, he is assiduous to get along with people. He blends in like a white moth on a whitewashed picked fence. Everyone likes him. He gives no offense and where possible he takes none. He questions the presiding powers but in the manner of a minor angel, inquiring into the ways of his more opulently fledged brethren.

3

In "London," perhaps his best-known poem, Blake takes on the role of the biblical prophet—Isaiah, Ezekiel, Jeremiah—and rambles through the great city. What he sees stuns him. He is sick to articulate rage about it. The human aspirations to kindliness, community, and gentleness have been drowned in hypocrisy. The little chimney sweep's cry "every black'ning church appalls." The sweeps, orphaned, sold into something tantamount to slavery, get no succor from the church. Their cries blacken an already black, hulking monolith. The soldier's sigh "runs in blood down palace walls." Wars far away—in America, among other places— have sent soldiers off to risk their lives, not for noble ends but to suppress liberty and open up new markets for British merchants.

But perhaps worst of all in Blake's London is the state of love. (Blake greatly values heterosexual love—is in love with it.) The wandering prophet, edging toward rage, about to go over to Rintrah, as Blake liked to put it, hears "how the youthful harlot's curse / Blasts the newborn infant's tear / And blights with plagues the marriage hearse." Prostitution—sex for money—is to Blake one of the worst human depravities. The man of property, subject to an arranged marriage, flies to the prostitute. She gives him an escape from his loveless marriage; she gives him some measure of intrigue and excitement. She also gives him syphilis, which ruins the marriage and infects his child and wife.

The church should engender a community of loving-kindness. The army should encourage bravery in just wars. Lovers should meet and love regardless of finances and social class. Sexual joy should be the culmination of real attraction of body and mind, whether sanctified by marriage or not. Prophets should not be compelled to rage blindly through the streets of London, witnesses to human despair. "I mark," says Blake, "in every face I meet / Marks of weakness, marks of woe." The prophet should offer wise and genial counsel and not be compelled to tremble with rage.

4

The engineering student sits in the fiction writer's office and asks questions about her craft. This fiction thing, this art thing, what is it about? What is it about *exactly*? He has read some novels. He plans to read many more. His grade-point average is high. His SAT scores are also impressive. A nearly perfect score on the verbals: He makes sure to mention this. He is—he knows—very smart.

But this fiction thing and poetry as well. How does one begin? (The fellow who wrote *Crying of Lot 49*—what was his name?—he was an engineering student, no?) There are, one hears, guide books, which give step-by-step instructions. Does the teacher advise trying one?

The teacher's way of writing fiction is to find an image, something that lodged in her mind for no reason that she can understand. She writes the image down. She describes it as well as she can from a vantage point that is—maybe—not quite her own.

And then what? The student is truly interested.

She waits then to see what will happen from there.

And?

Sometimes something happens. Sometimes nothing.

This is writing? This is what you do?

Other people do it differently. But yes. I wait to see what will happen. She tells the students that if she lets her attention float with just the right amount of freedom, she'll eventually go somewhere she's fascinated by going.

Why don't you just start with what fascinates you?

I don't always know, the writer confesses. I don't always really know.

5

Satan weeps frequently. It is surprising, but it is true. In Blake's epic, *Milton*, Satan is a cultivated, thoughtful, highly sensitive specimen of what the eighteenth century liked to call a Man of Sensibility. He is not overwhelmingly intellectual. He appears to put feelings before thoughts. Nor is he the fiery, rather charismatic figure that Milton conjures up with a massive more-than-Achillean shield and a spear to which the tallest Norwegian pine tree is but a wand. Blake's Satan has no tail, no claws, no fangs, no cloven foot, not even an odor of pitch on arrival and departure. This Satan is urbanely kind. He is Hayley, the man who brought Blake out of London to Felpham, so Blake the genius might be saved. Of course there are the miniatures, which Blake does not wish to paint. "When Hayley finds out what you cannot do / That is the very thing he'll set you to," Blake complains. There are also some tensions in sensibility: Hayley, who is Satan, is rather on the refined side. "Hayley on his toilette seeing the soap / Cries, 'Homer is very much improv'd by Pope.' " Hayley prefers Pope's refined translations of *The Iliad* and *The Odyssey* to Homer's actual unflinching vision. Being on the toilet close to his odorous humanity makes Hayley long for purity, long for Pope.

Hayley—and Satan, too—love poetry. They are drawn to poets; they find them mysterious, alluring, perhaps rather enviable. But then comes the question: Why should they, Satan and Hayley, not be poets as well? Already they have succeeded brilliantly at what they've set their hands to do. Hayley is good at business, better than good. As to Satan—here matters get more complicated. Satan has a cosmic role: He presides over time, clock time, ordering, duration. He is the lord of Chrons. All forms of regulation, consistency, and order fall under his power. He grinds time the way a farmer grinds wheat. No sand grain passes through the glass of time without Satan's awareness and approval. He propels the sun punctually through the houses of the zodiac. He measures the shadows on the moon's white face. He is God as a watchmaker, God as a supreme engineer.

But this is not enough for him. Satan also wants to be a poet. He is infatuated with Palamabron, the giant figure who wields the harrow. Palamabron breaks in order to create again; he engraves the soil; his work is sustenance to those who hunger in spirit as well as body. Palamabron concentrates all that Blake feels to be true about true artists. An idealization? Yes, maybe. But Blake deals in giant forms—grand, emblematic concentrations of force.

Finally Satan prevails upon Los, father of the eternals, to let him take Palamabron's harrow from his hands. What happens then? "Satan labour'd all day—it was a thousand years." Or at least it probably felt that way to Blake—the age of Pope and Dryden and Joshua Reynolds and Locke and Hobbes is a desert of tedium to Blake. It probably feels like a millennium. Engineers, people who wanted to understand art, draw blueprints, then get to work constructing things, were now the lords of light who lived where true thinkers and artists should have resided. A mess!

The mess has a double dimension, though. Palamabron's poetic attendants—Blake calls then gnomes—take over Satan's time-grinding mills. They get drunk as a tribe of monkeys and stumble around singing the songs of Palamabron. Minutes presumably last hours now; sometimes seconds probably expand into days; some days go blink and are gone. Another mess! The gnomes want to get back to the field, start engraving, start creating again—though getting drunk and messing with temporality is probably diverting to them for a little while.

Satan always wants to grasp the harrow—he wants to be lord high commissioner of everything and creator spirit, all at the same time. He wants to dominate time—as the bureaucrat of the minute—and also to live outside of time where real creation takes place. He wants to engineer odes.

Sometimes Blake loses all of his patience with Satan and wants to purge him out and away. Get thee behind me, and all of that. In *Milton* there is a culminating scene in which Blake, possessed by an apocalyptic fury, goes on about being washed clean in the blood of the lamb and purging away all of the nonhuman until "Generation is swallowed up in Regeneration," nature is swallowed up by true human culture. No more Satan then, no more crippling dualisms, just the bliss of ongoing creation, which Blake calls Eden.

6

Yet at other times one feels that Blake rather likes Satan, much as he rather liked Hayley. "Corporeal friends are spiritual enemies," Blake famously said. Yes, perhaps. But perhaps only to the measure that artists, spiritual questers, allow them to be. Palamabron could presumably have told Los—the executive faculty of the mind, the spirit of the age, whatever he might be—to Take Off when he demanded the plough for Satan. Artists need Satan to run the world. There must be surgeons and airline pilots and directors of academic fund-raising. Satan is, after all, "Prince of the Starry Hosts / And of the Wheels of Heaven," and in this there is some honor—as long as Satan retains his place and stays off Palamabron's rightful turf.

Artists need a Satanic side sometimes, too. You've got to know how to butter your parsnips, Frost said. ("Provide! Provide!" He cries out to his old crone who was once a star of the silver screen and is now scouring the front steps "with pail and rag.") Satan often knows where the butter dish is stored.

It can be tempting for the artist to give up and to hand everything over to Satan. Or to be too compliant when Satan asks: Are there books with blueprints for how to write a poem? Of course there are, the weary and neglected writer replies. Good ones, too. She resolves that tonight maybe she'll have a peek.

The contemporary artist can be prone to forget what he stands for in a way that Blake never did. Or he can get weary, as Blake surely did, of endorsing his ideals in a culture that cares little for them. Blake knew what he wanted: love that exalted lover and beloved; he knew that the measure of a society is the care, affection, and wisdom that it expends on children. Blake disliked war. He preferred what he called "mental fight." But he surely preferred just wars, like the American Revolution, which gladdened and amazed him, to unjust ones. He wanted poets to be prophets and call things as they saw them. He told us these things in "London." He seems to have meant them. He left his giant forms to remind us.

Hulk Hogan and those monster trucks are giant forms in their own ways. They are, I suppose, Satan's idea of poetry at its very worst: obvious, noisy, and lucrative. They're such gross caricatures that in time even Satan is probably made weary of them. He would dearly love it, I half believe, if Palamabron in his current form would take the harrow out of his hands and if he would tell Hulk, who seems as amiable as Hayley, that it is time to go home. But the contemporary Palamabron has experienced deconstruction and pragmatism and cultural studies and he knows how to see the world with what Nietzsche called a "perspectival seeing." He doubts his every reflex, Palamabron does. He cannot love what he loves. He cannot believe in eternal truth or everlasting beauty. So now he abides Satan, who in his heart probably does not want to be tolerated half so well.

For why did the administrators who are coming more and more to dominate the academic scene come to academia in the first place? Why didn't they stay in business where the salaries are higher, the perks cushier, and where everyone seems to receive weekly and free of charge a zippy new handheld wireless device? Maybe they came because they wanted to learn things—enduring things, humane things. They wanted to be in a place where people talked about Plato and Blake and Shakespeare and Schopenhauer, rather than exclusively about Hulk Hogan and the bottom line. I sometimes think that there are more *potential* intellectual idealists among the administrators than among the faculty. But as long as we professors can't tell them exactly what's wrong with Hulk Hogan and the monster trucks, what are they supposed to do? As long as we can't say why Shakespeare is better than the next episode of *Jersey Shore*, how will they help us and help universities to be enduring centers of learning and of art?

If you don't cultivate (and discipline) Satan, he'll grow ever more powerful and ever more pragmatic. He'll come to represent worldly values and nothing else and his confidence in these values will grow and grow. So when Satan in his current guise finally tells Palamabron to fall down and worship him, what will—what can?—Palamabron do?

A Note on the Author

Mark Edmundson is University Professor at the University of Virginia and a prizewinning scholar. In addition to *Why Write?*, *Why Teach?*, and *Why Read?*, he is the author of *Self and Soul: A Defense of Ideals, Teacher: The One Who Made the Difference, The Death of Sigmund Freud,* and *The Fine Wisdom and Perfect Teachings of the Kings of Rock and Roll*. His writing has appeared in such publications as *New Republic*, the *New York Times Magazine*, the *Chronicle of Higher Education*, the *Nation*, the *American Scholar, Raritan, London Review of Books*, and *Harper's*. He lives in Batesville, Virginia.